Programming ArcGIS with Python Cookbook

Second Edition

Over 85 hands-on recipes to teach you how to automate your ArcGIS for Desktop geoprocessing tasks using Python

Eric Pimpler

BIRMINGHAM - MUMBAI

Programming ArcGIS with Python Cookbook

Second Edition

First published: February 2013

Second edition: July 2015

Production reference: 1230715

Published by Packt Publishing Ltd.
Livery Place
35 Livery Street
Birmingham B3 2PB, UK.

ISBN 978-1-78528-289-8

www.packtpub.com

Credits

Author
Eric Pimpler

Reviewers
Mohammed Alhessi
Matthew Bernardo
Rahul Bhosle
Kristofer Lasko
Doug McGeehan
Ann Stark, GISP

Commissioning Editor
Akram Hussain

Acquisition Editors
Kevin Colaco
Usha Iyer
Greg Wild
Rebecca Youe

Content Development Editor
Adrian Raposo

Technical Editor
Shivani Kiran Mistry

Copy Editor
Sonia Michelle Cheema

Project Coordinator
Sanchita Mandal

Proofreader
Safis Editing

Indexer
Mariammal Chettiyar

Graphics
Disha Haria

Production Coordinator
Nilesh R. Mohite

Cover Work
Nilesh R. Mohite

About the Author

Eric Pimpler is the founder and owner of GeoSpatial Training Services (`http://geospatialtraining.com/`) and has over 20 years of experience implementing and teaching GIS solutions using Esri, Google Earth/Maps, open source technology. Currently, Eric is focusing on ArcGIS scripting with Python and the development of custom ArcGIS Server web and mobile applications using JavaScript. Eric is the author of *Programming ArcGIS with Python Cookbook and Building Web* and *Mobile ArcGIS Server Applications with JavaScript*, both by *Packt Publishing*.

Eric has a bachelor's degree in geography from Texas A&M University and a master's degree in applied geography with a focus on GIS from Texas State University.

About the Reviewers

Mohammed Alhessi is a GIS professional and instructor who is interested in geospatial theory, algorithms, and applications. He has a good amount of experience in GIS analysis, development, and training. He has conducted quite a few training courses for people from different backgrounds. The courses have been diverse in terms of subjects and have included, but are not limited to, Enterprise Geodatabase Administration in MS SQL Server, spatial data analysis and modeling, and Python scripting for ArcGIS.

He has worked at the University of Stuttgart as a GIS developer, where he programmed Geoprocessing tools using Java and Python. He is involved in many local GIS projects, providing consultancy for the local community. He is currently a lecturer at the Islamic University—Gaza, Palestine. He also holds classes at University College of Applied Sciences, Gaza.

Mohammed has a master's degree in geomatics engineering from the University of Stuttgart. He also has a bachelor's degree in civil engineering from the Islamic University—Gaza.

Matthew Bernardo is the senior GIS analyst at Newport Renewables, a renewable energy firm based in Newport. An avid outdoorsman and technophile, he is drawn to the assimilation of environment and technology that GIS offers. Over the last few years, he has used GIS and Python programming to answer complex questions in many fields, including renewable energy, intelligence analysis, remote sensing, marine science, environmental science, and town planning.

He has a BS in environmental science from the University of Rhode Island and a graduate certificate in geospatial intelligence from Penn State.

Rahul Bhosle earned his bachelor of engineering degree in information technology from Shivaji University, India, and a master of geospatial information science and technology from North Carolina State University. Currently, he is a Geospatial Developer at GIS Data Resources, Inc. By profession, he is a geospatial developer. He has experience in the fields of Python, JavaScript, ArcGIS Suite, GeoServer, PostGIS, PostgreSQL, SQL Server, Leaflet, Openlayers, Machine Learning, and NoSQL.

Kristofer Lasko earned his bachelor's degree in geographical sciences from the University of Maryland. He subsequently earned a master's degree in geospatial information science from the University of Maryland. He teaches a graduate and undergraduate GIS course at the University of Maryland. He began learning about Python several years ago, when he found it necessary to automate mundane tasks as well as process large volumes of geospatial data.

He is currently a PhD student at the University of Maryland, where he's studying geographical sciences. He has previously worked at NASA's Goddard Space Flight Center and NASA's Jet Propulsion Lab. He has also worked as a GIS and remote sensing analyst at the University of Maryland. His current research focuses on the burning of crop residue in Vietnam.

His website can be viewed at `http://terpconnect.umd.edu/~klasko/cv.html`.

Doug McGeehan is a third year PhD student at the Missouri University of Science and Technology in Rolla, Missouri, USA, where he's studying computer science under the supervision of Dr Sanjay Madria and Dr Dan Lin. In 2013, he received his bachelor's degree in computer science from Missouri University of Science and Technology, having already published two papers in computational geometry and working as a computational cartographer for the United States Geological Survey (USGS).

Ann Stark, a GISP since 2005, has been active in the GIS profession for 20 years. She is passionate about GIS and is an active and engaging member of the GIS community in the Pacific Northwest of the United States, coordinating local user groups and serving as the president of the region's GIS professional group. She is an enthusiastic teacher who explains how to effectively use Python with ArcGIS and maintains a blog devoted to the topic at `https://gisstudio.wordpress.com/`. She co-owns a GIS consulting business, Salish Coast Sciences, which provides strategic planning, process automation, and GIS development services.

To unwind from technology, Ann enjoys spending time with her husband and son at their urban farm in the heart of the city, where they seek to live sustainably and as self-sufficiently as an urban farm allows.

Table of Contents

Preface

ArcGIS is an industry-standard geographic information system from Esri.

This book will show you how to use the Python programming language to create geoprocessing scripts, tools, and shortcuts for the ArcGIS for Desktop environment.

It will make you a more effective and efficient GIS professional by showing you how to use the Python programming language with ArcGIS for Desktop to automate geoprocessing tasks, manage map documents and layers, find and fix broken data links, edit data in feature classes and tables, and much more.

Programming ArcGIS with Python Cookbook Second Edition, starts by covering fundamental Python programming concepts in an ArcGIS for Desktop context. Using a how-to instruction style, you'll then learn how to use Python to automate common important ArcGIS geoprocessing tasks.

In this book, you will also cover specific ArcGIS scripting topics that will help save you time and effort when working with ArcGIS. Topics include managing map document files, automating map production and printing, finding and fixing broken data sources, creating custom geoprocessing tools, and working with feature classes and tables, among others.

In *Programming ArcGIS with Python Cookbook Second Edition*, you'll learn how to write geoprocessing scripts using a pragmatic approach designed around accomplishing specific tasks in a cookbook style format.

What this book covers

Chapter 1, Fundamentals of the Python Language for ArcGIS, will cover many of the basic language constructs found in Python. Initially, you'll learn how to create new Python scripts or edit existing scripts. From there, you'll get into language features, such as adding comments to your code, variables, and the built-in typing systems that makes coding with Python easy and compact. Furthermore, we'll look at the various built-in data types that Python offers, such as strings, numbers, lists, and dictionaries. In addition to this, we'll cover statements, including decision support and looping structures for making decisions in your code, and/or looping through a code block multiple times.

Chapter 2, Managing Map Documents and Layers, will use the ArcPy mapping module to manage map document and layer files. You will learn how to add and remove geographic layers from map document files, insert layers into data frames, and move layers around within the map document. You will also learn how to update layer properties and symbology.

Chapter 3, Finding and Fixing Broken Data Links, will teach you how to generate a list of broken data sources in a map document file and apply various ArcPy mapping functions to fix these data sources. You will learn how to automate the process of fixing data sources across many map documents.

Chapter 4, Automating Map Production and Printing, will teach you how to automate the process of creating production-quality maps. These maps can then be printed, exported to image file formats, or exported to PDF files for inclusion in map books.

Chapter 5, Executing Geoprocessing Tools from Scripts, will teach you how to write scripts that access and run geoprocessing tools provided by ArcGIS.

Chapter 6, Creating Custom Geoprocessing Tools, will teach you how to create custom geoprocessing tools that can be added to ArcGIS and shared with other users. Custom geoprocessing tools are attached to a Python script that processes or analyzes geographic data in some way.

Chapter 7, Querying and Selecting Data, will teach you how to execute the Select by Attribute and Select by Location geoprocessing tools from a script to select features and records. You will learn how to construct queries that supply an optional where clause for the Select by Attribute tool. The use of feature layers and table views as temporary datasets will also be covered.

Chapter 8, Using the ArcPy Data Access Module with Feature Classes and Tables, will teach you how to create geoprocessing scripts that select, insert, or update data from geographic data layers and tables. With the new ArcGIS 10.1 Data Access module, geoprocessing scripts can create in-memory tables of data, called cursors, from feature classes and tables. You will learn how to create various types of cursors, including search, insert, and update.

Chapter 9, Listing and Describing GIS Data, will teach you how to obtain descriptive information about geographic datasets through the use of the ArcPy Describe function. As the first step in a multistep process, geoprocessing scripts frequently require that a list of geographic data be generated followed by various geoprocessing operations that can be run against these datasets.

Chapter 10, Customizing the ArcGIS Interface with Add-ins, will teach you how to customize the ArcGIS interface through the creation of Python add-ins. Add-ins provide a way of adding user interface items to ArcGIS for Desktop through a modular code base designed to perform specific actions. Interface components can include buttons, tools, toolbars, menus, combo boxes, tool palettes, and application extensions. Add-ins are created using Python scripts and an XML file that define how the user interface should appear.

Chapter 11, Error Handling and Troubleshooting, will teach you how to gracefully handle errors and exceptions as they occur while a geoprocessing script is executing. ArcPy and Python errors can be trapped with the Python try/except structure and handled accordingly.

Chapter 12, Using Python for Advanced ArcGIS, covers the use of the ArcGIS REST API with Python to access services exposed by ArcGIS Server and ArcGIS Online. You will learn how to make HTTP requests and parse the responses, export maps, query map services, perform geocoding, and more. Also covered in this chapter are some miscellaneous topics related to ArcPy FieldMap and FieldMappings, as well as working with ValueTables.

Chapter 13, Using Python with ArcGIS Pro, covers some distinctions between the new ArcGIS Pro environment and ArcGIS for Desktop related to Python and, in particular, the Python Window for writing and executing code.

Appendix A, Automating Python Scripts, will teach you how to schedule geoprocessing scripts to run at a prescribed time. Many geoprocessing scripts take a long time to fully execute and need to be scheduled to run during nonworking hours on a regular basis. You will learn how to create batch files containing geoprocessing scripts and execute these at a prescribed time.

Appendix B, Five Python Recipes Every GIS Programmer Should Know, will teach you how to write scripts that perform various general purpose tasks with Python. Tasks, such as reading and writing delimited text files, sending e-mails, interacting with FTP servers, creating ZIP files, and reading and writing JSON and XML files, are common. Every GIS programmer should know how to write Python scripts that incorporate these functionalities.

What you need for this book

To complete the exercises in this book, you will need to have installed ArcGIS for Desktop 10.3 at either the Basic, Standard, or Advanced license level. Installing ArcGIS for Desktop 10.3 will also install Python 2.7 along with the IDLE Python code editor. The text is also appropriate for users working with ArcGIS for Desktop 10.2 or 10.1. *Chapter 13, Using Python with ArcGIS Pro,* requires ArcGIS Pro version 1.0.

Who this book is for

Programming ArcGIS with Python Cookbook, Second Edition, is written for GIS professionals who wish to revolutionize their ArcGIS workflow with Python. Whether you are new to ArcGIS or a seasoned professional, you almost certainly spend time each day performing various geoprocessing tasks. This book will teach you how to use the Python programming language to automate these geoprocessing tasks and make you a more efficient and effective GIS professional.

Sections

In this book, you will find several headings that appear frequently (Getting ready, How to do it, How it works, There's more, and See also).

To give clear instructions on how to complete a recipe, we use these sections as follows:

Getting ready

This section tells you what to expect in the recipe, and describes how to set up any software or any preliminary settings required for the recipe.

How to do it…

This section contains the steps required to follow the recipe.

How it works…

This section usually consists of a detailed explanation of what happened in the previous section.

There's more…

This section consists of additional information about the recipe in order to make the reader more knowledgeable about the recipe.

See also

This section provides helpful links to other useful information for the recipe.

Conventions

In this book, you will find a number of text styles that distinguish between different kinds of information. Here are some examples of these styles and an explanation of their meaning.

Code words in text are shown as follows: "we have loaded the `ListFeatureClasses.py` script with IDLE."

A block of code is set as follows:

```
import arcpy
fc = "c:/ArcpyBook/data/TravisCounty/TravisCounty.shp"
# Fetch each feature from the cursor and examine the extent
# properties and spatial reference
for row in arcpy.da.SearchCursor(fc, ["SHAPE@"]):
  # get the extent of the county boundary
  ext = row[0].extent
  # print out the bounding coordinates and spatial reference
  print("XMin: " + ext.XMin)
  print("XMax: " + ext.XMax)
  print("YMin: " + ext.YMin)
  print("YMax: " + ext.YMax)
  print("Spatial Reference: " + ext.spatialReference.name)
```

When we wish to draw your attention to a particular part of a code block, the relevant lines or items are set in bold:

```
import arcpy
fc = "c:/data/city.gdb/streets"
# For each row print the Object ID field, and use the SHAPE@AREA
# token to access geometry properties
with arcpy.da.SearchCursor(fc, ("OID@", "SHAPE@AREA")) as cursor:
  for row in cursor:
    print("Feature {0} has an area of {1}".format(row[0],
    row[1]))
```

Any command-line input or output is written as follows:

```
[<map layer u'City of Austin Bldg Permits'>,
<map layer u'Hospitals'>, <map layer u'Schools'>,
<map layer u'Streams'>, <map layer u'Streets'>,
<map layer u'Streams_Buff'>, <map layer u'Floodplains'>,
<map layeru'2000 Census Tracts'>, <map layer u'City Limits'>,
<map layer u'Travis County'>]
```

New terms and **important words** are shown in bold. Words that you see on the screen, in menus or dialog boxes for example, appear in the text like this: "go to **Start** | **All Programs** | **ArcGIS** | **Python 2.7** | **IDLE**".

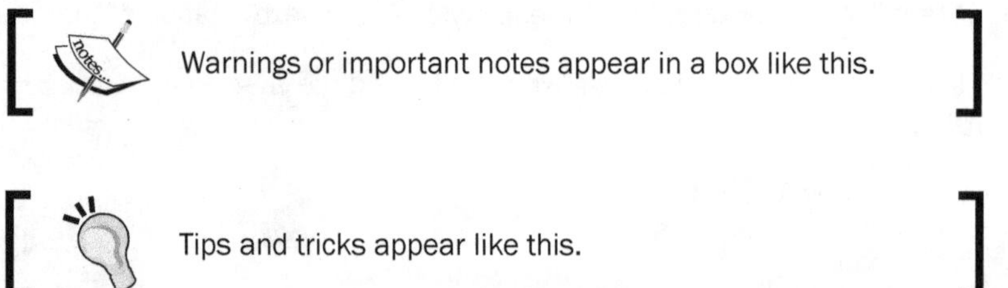

Reader feedback

Feedback from our readers is always welcome. Let us know what you think about this book—what you liked or disliked. Reader feedback is important for us as it helps us develop titles that you will really get the most out of.

To send us general feedback, simply e-mail `feedback@packtpub.com`, and mention the book's title in the subject of your message.

If there is a topic that you have expertise in and you are interested in either writing or contributing to a book, see our author guide at `www.packtpub.com/authors`.

Customer support

Now that you are the proud owner of a Packt book, we have a number of things to help you to get the most from your purchase.

Downloading the example code

You can download the example code files from your account at `http://www.packtpub.com` for all the Packt Publishing books you have purchased. If you purchased this book elsewhere, you can visit `http://www.packtpub.com/support` and register to have the files e-mailed directly to you.

Errata

Although we have taken every care to ensure the accuracy of our content, mistakes do happen. If you find a mistake in one of our books—maybe a mistake in the text or the code—we would be grateful if you could report this to us. By doing so, you can save other readers from frustration and help us improve subsequent versions of this book. If you find any errata, please report them by visiting `http://www.packtpub.com/submit-errata`, selecting your book, clicking on the **Errata Submission Form** link, and entering the details of your errata. Once your errata are verified, your submission will be accepted and the errata will be uploaded to our website or added to any list of existing errata under the Errata section of that title.

To view the previously submitted errata, go to `https://www.packtpub.com/books/content/support` and enter the name of the book in the search field. The required information will appear under the **Errata** section.

Piracy

Piracy of copyrighted material on the Internet is an ongoing problem across all media. At Packt, we take the protection of our copyright and licenses very seriously. If you come across any illegal copies of our works in any form on the Internet, please provide us with the location address or website name immediately so that we can pursue a remedy.

Please contact us at `copyright@packtpub.com` with a link to the suspected pirated material.

We appreciate your help in protecting our authors and our ability to bring you valuable content.

Questions

If you have a problem with any aspect of this book, you can contact us at `questions@packtpub.com`, and we will do our best to address the problem.

1
Fundamentals of the Python Language for ArcGIS

Python supports many of the programming constructs found in other languages. In this chapter, we'll cover many of the basic language constructs found in Python. Initially, we'll cover how to create new Python scripts and edit existing scripts. From there, we'll delve into language features, such as adding comments to your code, creating and assigning data to variables, and built-in variable typing with Python, which makes coding with Python easy and compact.

Next, we'll look at the various built-in data types that Python offers, such as strings, numbers, lists, and dictionaries. Classes and objects are a fundamental concept in object-oriented programming and in the Python language. We'll introduce you to these complex data structures, which you'll use extensively when you write geoprocessing scripts with ArcGIS.

In addition to this, we'll cover statements, including decision support and looping structures to make decisions in your code, and/or looping through a code block multiple times along with the `with` statement, which is used extensively with the `cursor` objects from the ArcPy data access module that are used to insert, search, and update data. Finally, you'll learn how to access modules that provide additional functionality to the Python language. By the end of this chapter, you will have learned the following:

- How to create and edit new Python scripts in IDLE
- How to create and edit scripts in the ArcGIS Python window
- The language features of Python
- Comments and data variables
- Built-in data types (strings, numbers, lists, and dictionaries)

- Complex data structures
- Looping structures
- Additional Python functionalities

Using IDLE for Python script development

As mentioned in the preface, when you install ArcGIS for Desktop, Python is also installed along with a tool called **IDLE** that allows you to write your own code. IDLE stands for **Integrated DeveLopment Environment**. Since it is available with every ArcGIS for Desktop installation, we'll use IDLE for many of the scripts that we write in this book along with the Python window embedded in ArcGIS for Desktop. As you progress as a programmer, you may find other development tools that you prefer over IDLE. There are many other development environments that you may want to consider, including PyScripter, Wingware, Komodo, and others. The development environment you choose is really a matter of preference. You can write your code in any of these tools.

The Python shell window

To start the IDLE development environment for Python, you can navigate to **Start** | **All Programs** | **ArcGIS** | **Python 2.7** | **IDLE**. Please note that the version of Python installed with ArcGIS will differ depending upon the ArcGIS version that you have installed. For example, ArcGIS 10.3 uses Python 2.7, whereas ArcGIS 10.0 uses version 2.6 of Python.

A Python shell window similar to this screenshot will be displayed:

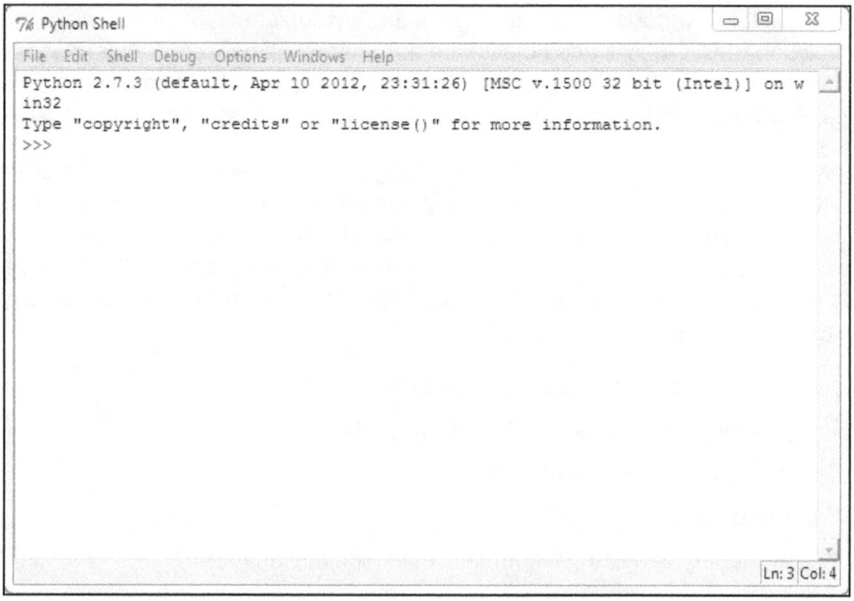

```
Python Shell
File  Edit  Shell  Debug  Options  Windows  Help
Python 2.7.3 (default, Apr 10 2012, 23:31:26) [MSC v.1500 32 bit (Intel)] on w
in32
Type "copyright", "credits" or "license()" for more information.
>>>
Ln: 3 Col: 4
```

The Python shell window is used for output and error messages generated by scripts. A common mistake for beginners is to assume that the geoprocessing scripts will be written in this shell window. This is not the case. You will need to create a separate code window to hold your scripts.

Although the shell window isn't used to write entire scripts, it can be used to interactively write code and get immediate feedback. ArcGIS has a built-in Python shell window that you can use in a similar way. We'll examine the ArcGIS Python window in the next chapter.

The Python script window

Your scripts will be written in IDLE inside a separate window known as the **Python script window**. To create a new code window, navigate to **File** | **New Window** from the IDLE shell window. A window similar to this will be displayed:

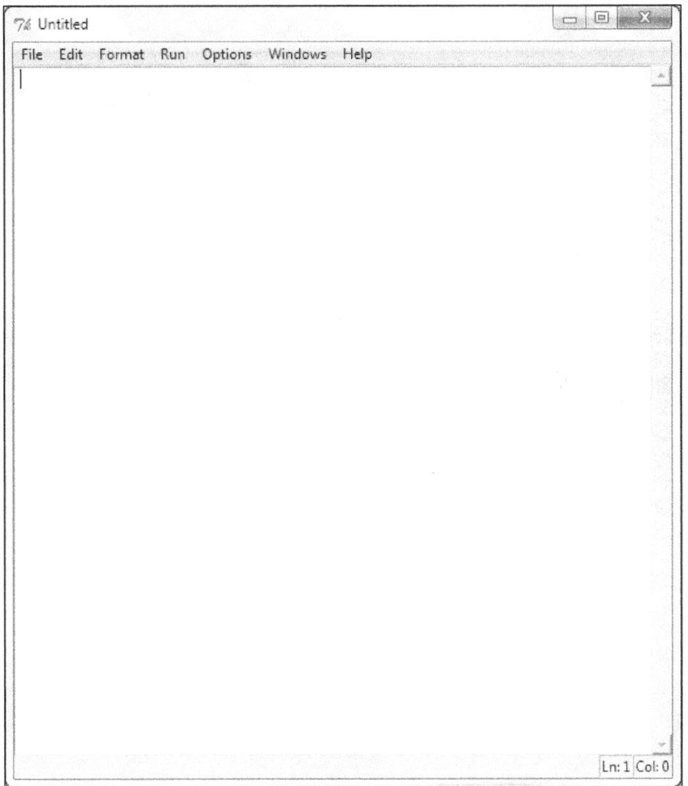

Your Python scripts will be written inside this new code window. Each script will need to be saved to a local or network drive. By default, scripts are saved with a `.py` file extension to signify that it is a Python script.

Editing existing Python scripts

Existing Python script files can be opened by selecting **File** | **Open** from the IDLE shell window. Additionally, a Python script can be opened from Windows Explorer by right-clicking on the file and selecting **Edit with IDLE**, which brings up a new shell window along with the script loaded in the Python script editor. You can see an example of this in the following screenshot:

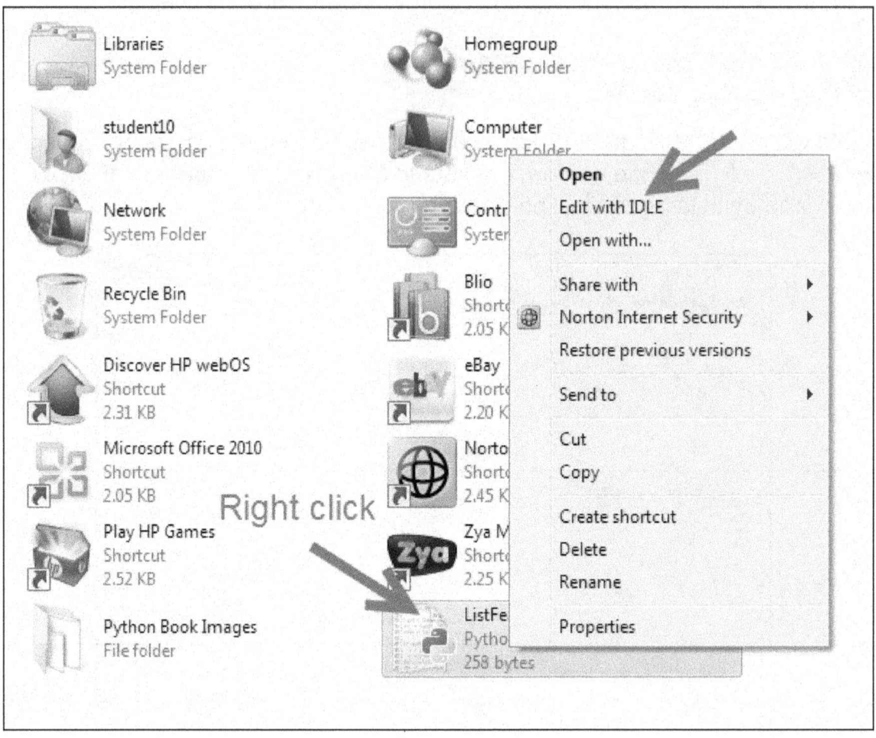

In this instance, we have loaded the `ListFeatureClasses.py` script with IDLE. The code is loaded inside the script window:

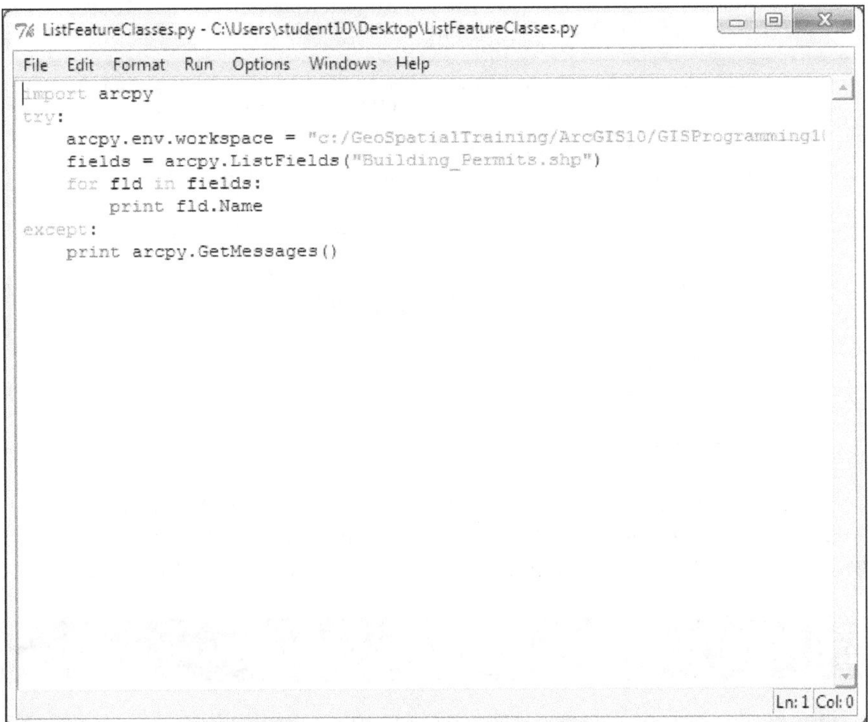

Now that the code window is open, you can begin writing or editing code. You can also perform some basic script debugging with the IDLE interface. Debugging is the process of identifying and fixing errors in your code.

Executing scripts from IDLE

Once you've written a geoprocessing script in the IDLE code window or opened an existing script, you can execute the code from the interface. IDLE does provide functionality that allows you to check the syntax of your code before running the script. In the code window, navigate to **Run** | **Check Module** to perform a syntax check of your code.

Any syntax errors will be displayed in the shell window. If there aren't any syntax errors, you should just see the prompt in the shell window. While the IDLE interface can be used to check for syntax errors, it doesn't provide a way to check for logical errors in your code nor does it provide more advanced debugging tools found in other development environments, such as PyScripter or Wingware.

Once you're satisfied that no syntax errors exist in your code, you can run the script. Navigate to **Run** | **Run Module** to execute the script:

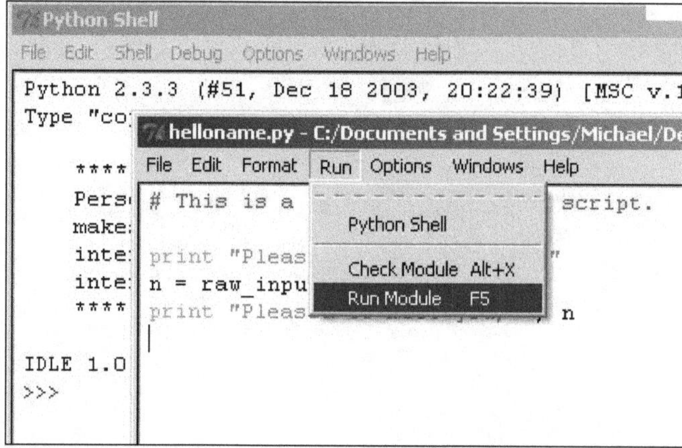

Any error messages will be written to the shell window along with the output from the `print` statements and system-generated messages. The `print` statement simply outputs text to the shell window. It is often used to update the status of a running script or to debug the code.

Using the ArcGIS Python window

In this recipe, you'll learn how to use the ArcGIS Python window. In the last section, you learned how to use the IDLE development environment for Python, so this section will give you an alternative to write your geoprocessing scripts. Either development environment can be used, but it is common for people to start writing scripts with the ArcGIS for Desktop Python window and then move on to IDLE or another development environment when scripts become more complex.

The ArcGIS Python window

The ArcGIS Python window is an embedded, interactive Python window in ArcGIS for Desktop 10.x. It is newer and ideal for testing small blocks of code, learning Python basics, building quick and easy workflows, and executing geoprocessing tools. For new programmers, the ArcGIS Python window is a great place to start!

The ArcGIS Python window has a number of capabilities in addition to being the location to write your code. You can save the content of the window to a Python script file on a disk or load an existing Python script into the window. The window can be either pinned or floating. While floating, the window can be expanded or contracted as you wish. The window can also be pinned to various parts of the ArcGIS display. You can also format the font and text colors displayed in the window by right-clicking on the window and selecting **Format**.

Displaying the ArcGIS Python window

The Python window can be opened by clicking on the Python window button on the Standard ArcGIS for Desktop toolbar, as seen in the screenshot. This is a floating window, so you can resize as needed and also dock it at various places on the **ArcMap** interface:

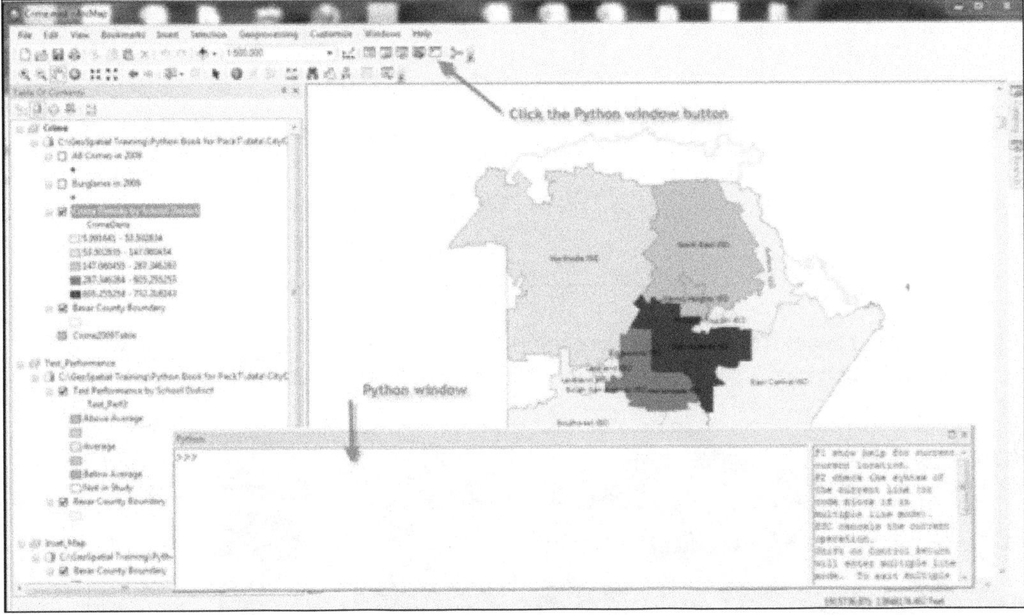

The Python window is essentially a shell window that allows you to type in statements one line at a time, just after the >>> line input characters. On the right-hand side of the divider, you will find a help window.

You can load an existing script by right-clicking inside the Python window and selecting **Load...** from the menu. You can also format the font and text colors displayed in the window by right-clicking on the window and selecting **Format**. You will be provided with White and Black themes; you can select fonts and colors individually:

Click on the **Set Black Theme** button to see an example. If you spend a lot of time writing code, you may find that darker themes are easier on your eyes:

```
Python
>>> import arcpy
...
... try:
...     arcpy.env.workspace = "c:/ArcpyBook/data/"
...     fields = arcpy.ListFields("Building_Permits.shp")
...     for fld in fields:
...         print fld.name
... except:
...     print arcpy.GetMessages()
...
...
```

```
F1 show help for current
cursor location.
F2 check the syntax of
the current line (or
code block if in
multiple line mode).
ESC cancels the current
operation.
Shift or Control Return
will enter multiple line
mode.  To exit multiple
line mode (execute the
code block) enter Return
```

The ArcGIS Python window also provides code-completion functionalities that make your life as a programmer much easier. You can try this functionality by opening the ArcGIS Python Window and typing `arcpy` followed by a dot on the first line. ArcPy is a module-oriented package, which means that you access the properties and methods of an object using a dot notation. Notice that a drop-down list of available items is provided. These are the tools, functions, classes, and extensions that are available for this particular object. All objects have their own associated items, so the list of items presented will differ depending on the object that you have currently selected:

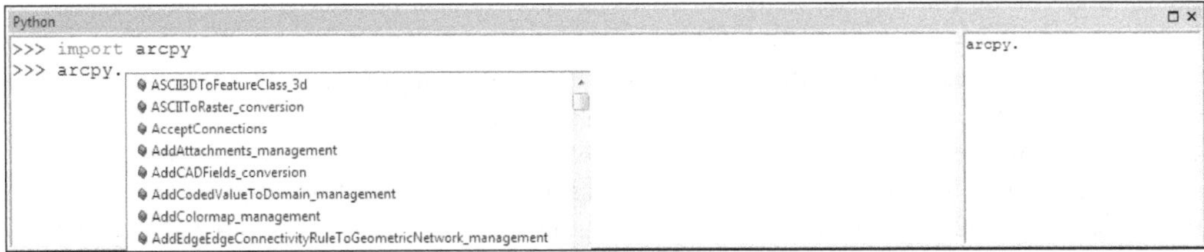

This is an auto-filtering list, so as you begin typing the name of the tool, function, class, or extension, the list will be filtered according to what you have typed:

You can choose to have the Python window auto-complete the text for you by selecting an item from the list using your mouse or by using the arrow keys to highlight your choice, and then using the *Tab* key to enter the command. This autocompletion feature makes you a faster, more efficient programmer. Not only is it easy to use, but it also dramatically cuts down the number of typos in your code.

Python language fundamentals

To effectively write geoprocessing scripts for ArcGIS, you are going to need to understand at least the basic constructs of the Python language. Python is easier to learn than most other programming languages, but it does take some time to learn and effectively use it. This section will teach you how to create variables, assign various data types to variables, understand the different types of data that can be assigned to variables, use different types of statements, use objects, read and write files, and import third-party Python modules.

Commenting code

Python scripts should follow a common structure. It is a commonly accepted practice that the beginning of each script should serve as documentation, detailing the script name, author, and a general description of the processing provided by the script. This introductory documentation will help you and other programmers in the future to quickly scan the details and purpose of a script. This documentation is accomplished in Python through the use of comments. Comments are lines of code that you add to your script that serve as a documentation of what functionality the script provides. These lines of code begin with a single pound sign (#) or a double pound sign (##), and are followed by whatever text you need to document the code. The Python interpreter does not execute these lines of code. They are simply used to document your code. In the next screenshot, the commented lines of code are displayed with a single pound sign that prefixes the line of code. You should also strive to include comments throughout your script to describe important sections of your script. This will be useful to you (or another programmer) when the time comes to update your scripts:

ListFields.py - C:/Users/student10/Desktop/ListFields.py

File Edit Format Run Options Windows Help

```
# Programmer: Eric Pimpler
# Script Title: ListFields.py
# Description: Generates a list of fields for a shapefile
# Last Updated: 7/10/2012

import arcpy
try:
    arcpy.env.workspace = "c:/GeoSpatialTraining/ArcGIS10/GISProgramming
    fcs = arcpy.ListFields("Building_Permits.shp")
    for fld in fields:
        print fld.Name
except:
    print arcpy.GetMessages()
```

Ln: 15 Col: 0

Downloading the example code

You can download the example code files for all Packt books you have purchased from your account at `http://www.PacktPub.com`. If you have purchased this book elsewhere, you can visit `http://www.PacktPub.com/support` and register to have the files e-mailed directly to you.

Importing modules

Although Python includes many built-in functions, you will frequently need to access specific bundles of functionality, which are stored in external modules. For instance, the `Math` module stores specific functions related to processing numeric values and the `R` module provides statistical analysis functions. We haven't discussed the topic of functions yet, but basically functions are a named block of code that execute when called. Modules are imported through the use of the `import` statement. When writing geoprocessing scripts with ArcGIS, you will always need to import the `arcpy` module, which is the Python package that is used to access GIS tools and functions provided by ArcGIS. The `import` statements will be the first lines of code (not including comments) in your scripts. The following line of code imports the `arcpy` and `os` modules. The Python `os` module provides a way of interfacing with the underlying operating system:

```
import arcpy
import os
```

Variables

At a high level, you can think of a variable as an area in your computer's memory that is reserved to store values while the script is running. Variables that you define in Python are given a name and a value. The values assigned to variables can then be accessed by different areas of your script as needed, simply by referring to the variable name. For example, you might create a variable that contains a feature class name, which is then used by the **Buffer** tool to create a new output dataset. To create a variable, simply give it a name followed by the assignment operator, which is just an equals sign (=), and then a value:

```
fcParcels = "Parcels"
fcStreets = "Streets"
```

The following table illustrates the variable name and value assigned to the variable using the preceding code example:

Variable name	Variable value
`fcParcels`	`Parcels`
`fcStreets`	`Streets`

There are certain naming rules that you must follow when creating variables, including the following:

- It can contain letters, numbers, and underscores
- The first character must be a letter
- No special characters can be used in a variable name other an underscore
- Python keywords and spaces are not permitted

There are a few dozen Python keywords that must be avoided, including `class`, `if`, `for`, `while`, and others. These keywords are typically highlighted in a different font color from other Python statements.

Here are some examples of legal variable names in Python:

- `featureClassParcel`
- `fieldPopulation`
- `field2`
- `ssn`
- `my_name`

These are some examples of illegal variable names in Python:

- `class` (Python keyword)
- `return` (Python keyword)
- `$featureClass` (illegal character, must start with a letter)
- `2fields` (must start with a letter)
- `parcels&Streets` (illegal character)

Python is a case-sensitive language, so pay particular attention to the capitalization and naming of variables in your scripts. Case-sensitivity issues are probably the most common source of errors for new Python programmers, so always consider this as a possibility when you encounter errors in your code. Let's look at an example. The following is a list of three variables; note that although each variable name is the same, the casing is different, resulting in three distinct variables:

- `mapsize = "22x34"`
- `MapSize = "8x11"`
- `Mapsize = "36x48"`

If you print these variables, you will get the following output:

```
print(mapsize)
>>> 22x34

print(MapSize)
>>> 8x11  #output from print statement

print(Mapsize)
>>>36x48  #output from print statement
```

Python variable names need to be consistent throughout the script. The best practice is to use camel casing, wherein the first word of a variable name is all lowercase and then each successive word begins with an uppercase letter. This concept is illustrated in the following example with the `fieldOwnerName` variable name. The first word (`field`) is all lowercase followed by an uppercase letter for the second word (`Owner`) and third word (`Name`):

```
fieldOwnerName
```

In Python, variables are dynamically typed. **Dynamic typing** means that you can define a variable and assign data to it without specifically defining that a variable name will contain a specific type of data. Commonly used data types that can be assigned to variables include the following:

Data type	Example value	Code example
String	`"Streets"`	`fcName = "Streets"`
Number	`3.14`	`percChange = 3.14`
Boolean	`True`	`ftrChanged = True`
List	`"Streets", "Parcels", "Streams"`	`lstFC = ["Streets", "Parcels", "Streams"]`
Dictionary	`'0':Streets,'1':Parcels`	`dictFC = {'0':Streets,'1':Parcels]`
Object	`Extent`	`spatialExt = map.extent`

We will discuss each of these data types in greater detail in the coming sections.

For instance, in C#, you would need to define a variable's name and type before using it. This is not necessary in Python. To use a variable, simply give it a name and value, and you can begin using it right away. Python does the work behind the scenes to figure out what type of data is being held in the variable.

In the following C# code example, we've created a new variable called `aTouchdown`, which is defined as an integer variable, meaning that it can contain only integer data. We then assign the `6` value to the variable:

```
int aTouchdown;
aTouchdown = 6;
```

In Python, this variable can be created and assigned data through dynamic typing. The Python interpreter is tasked with dynamically figuring out what type of data is assigned to the variable:

```
aTouchdown = 6
```

There may be times when you know that your script will need a variable, but don't necessarily know ahead of time what data will be assigned to the variable. In these cases, you could simply define a variable without assigning data to it. Here, you will find a code example that depicts creating a variable without assigning data:

```
aVariable = ''
aVariable = NULL
```

Data that is assigned to the variable can also be changed while the script is running.

Variables can hold many different kinds of data, including primitive data types, such as strings and numbers, along with more complex data, such as lists, dictionaries, and even objects. We're going to examine the different types of data that can be assigned to a variable along with various functions that are provided by Python to manipulate the data.

Built-in data types

Python has a number of built-in data types. The first built-in type that we will discuss is the `string` data type. We've already seen several examples of `string` variables, but these types of variables can be manipulated in a lot of ways, so let's take a closer look at this data type.

Strings

Strings are ordered collections of characters that store and represent text-based information. This is a rather dry way of saying that string variables hold text. String variables are surrounded by single or double quotes when being assigned to a variable. Examples could include a name, feature class name, a `Where` clause, or anything else that can be encoded as text.

String manipulation

Strings can be manipulated in a number of ways in Python. String concatenation is one of the more commonly used functions and is simple to accomplish. The + operator is used with `string` variables on either side of the operator to produce a new `string` variable that ties the two string variables together:

```
shpStreets = "c:\\GISData\\Streets" + ".shp"
print(shpStreets)
```

Running this code example produces the following result:

```
>>>c:\GISData\Streets.shp
```

String equality can be tested using Python's == operator, which is simply two equals signs placed together. Don't confuse the equality operator with the assignment operator, which is a single equals sign. The equality operator tests two variables for equality, while the assignment operator assigns a value to a variable:

```
firstName = "Eric"
lastName = "Pimpler"
firstName == lastName
```

Running this code example produces the following result because the `firstName` and `lastName` variables are not equal:

```
>>>False
```

Strings can be tested for containment using the `in` operator, which returns `True` if the first operand is contained in the second:

```
fcName = "Floodplain.shp"
print(".shp" in fcName)
>>>True
```

I have briefly mentioned that strings are an ordered collection of characters. What does this mean? It simply means that we can access individual characters or a series of characters from the string and that the order of the characters will remain the same until we change them. Some collections, such as a dictionary, do not maintain a set order. In Python, this is referred to as **indexing** in the case of accessing an individual character, and **slicing** in the case of accessing a series of characters.

Characters in a string are obtained by providing the numeric offset contained within square brackets after a string. For example, you could obtain the first string character in the `fc` variable by using the `fc[0]` syntax. Python is a zero-based language, meaning the first item in a list is `0`. Negative offsets can be used to search backwards from the end of a string. In this case, the last character in a string is stored at the `-1` index. Indexing always creates a new variable to hold the character:

```
fc = "Floodplain.shp"
print(fc[0])
>>>'F'
print(fc[10])
>>>'.'
print(fc[13])
>>>'p'
```

The following image illustrates how strings are an ordered collection of characters with the first character occupying the **0** position, the second character occupying the **1** position, and each successive character occupying the next index number:

While string indexing allows you to obtain a single character from a `string` variable, string slicing enables you to extract a contiguous sequence of strings. The format and syntax is similar to indexing, but with the addition of a second offset, which is used to tell Python which characters to return.

The following code example provides an example of string slicing. The `theString` variable has been assigned a value of `Floodplain.shp`. To obtain a sliced variable with the contents of Flood, you would use the `theString[0:5]` syntax:

```
theString = "Floodplain.shp"
print(theString[0:5])
>>>Flood
```

> Python slicing returns the characters beginning with the first offset up to, but not including, the second offset. This can be particularly confusing for new Python programmers and is a common source of errors. In our example, the returned variable will contain the `Flood` characters. The first character, which occupies the `0` position, is `F`. The last character returned is the `4` index, which corresponds to the `d` character. Notice the `5` index number is not included since Python slicing only returns characters up to, but not including, the second offset

Either of the offsets can be left off. This, in effect, creates a wild card. In the case of `theString[1:]`, you are telling Python to return all characters starting from the second character to the end of the string. In the second case, `theString[:-1]`, you are telling Python to start at character zero and return all characters except the last.

Python is an excellent language to manipulate strings and there are many additional functions that you can use to process this type of data. Most of these are beyond the scope of this text, but in general, all the following string manipulation functions are available:

- String length
- Casing functions for conversion to upper and lowercase
- The removal of leading and trailing whitespace
- Finding a character within a string
- The replacement of text
- Splitting into a list of words based on a delimiter
- Formatting

Your Python geoprocessing scripts for ArcGIS will often need to reference the location of a dataset on your computer or, perhaps, a shared server. References to these datasets will often consist of paths stored in a variable. In Python, pathnames are a special case that deserve some extra mention. The backslash character in Python is a reserved escape character and a line continuation character, thus there is a need to define paths using two back slashes, a single forward slash, or a regular single backslash prefixed with `r`. These pathnames are always stored as strings in Python. You'll see an example of this in the following section.

The example for an illegal path reference is as follows:

```
fcParcels = "c:\Data\Parcels.shp"
```

The example for legal path references are as follows:

```
fcParcels = "c:/Data/Parcels.shp"
fcParcels = "c:\\Data\\Parcels.shp"
fcParcels = r"c:\Data\Parcels.shp"
```

Numbers

Python also has built-in support for numeric data, including `int`, `long`, `float`, and `complex` values. Numbers are assigned to variables in much the same way as strings, with the exception that you do not enclose the value in quotes and obviously, it must be a numeric value.

Python supports all the commonly used numeric operators, including addition, subtraction, multiplication, division, and modulus or remainder. In addition to this, functions used to return the absolute value, conversion of strings to numeric data types, and rounding are also available.

Although Python provides a few built-in mathematical functions, the math module can be used to access a wide variety of more advanced `math` functions. To use these functions, you must specifically import the `math` module as follows:

```
import math
```

Functions provided by the `math` module include those that return the ceiling and floor of a number, the absolute value, trigonometric functions, logarithmic functions, angular conversion, and hyperbolic functions. It is worth noting that there is no simple function to calculate mean or average and these will have to be coded to be calculated. More details about the `math` module can be found by navigating to **All Programs** | **ArcGIS** | **Python 2.7** | **Python Manuals**. After opening the python manual, navigate to **Python Standard Library** | **Numeric and Mathematical Modules**. You can also reference this for any data types, syntax, built-in functions, and other things that you wish to understand in more detail, of which there are too many to be covered here.

Lists

A third built-in data type provided by Python is lists. A list is an ordered collection of elements that can hold any type of data supported by Python as well as being able to hold multiple data types at the same time. This could be numbers, strings, other lists, dictionaries, or objects. So, for instance, a list variable could hold numeric and string data at the same time. Lists are zero-based, with the first element in the list occupying the **0** position. This is illustrated here:

Each successive object in the list is incremented by one. Additionally, lists have the special capability of dynamically growing and shrinking.

Lists are created by assigning a series of values enclosed by brackets. To pull a value from a list, simply use an integer value in brackets along with the variable name. The following code example provides an illustration of this:

```
fcList = ["Hydrants", "Water Mains", "Valves", "Wells"]
fc = fcList[0] ##first item in the list - Hydrants
print(fc)
>>>Hydrants
fc = fcList[3]  ##fourth item in the list - Wells
print(fc)
>>>Wells
```

You can add a new item to an existing list by using the `append()` method, as seen in this code example:

```
fcList.append("Sewer Pipes")
print(fcList)
>> Hydrants, Water Mains, Valves, Wells, Sewer Pipes
```

You can also use slicing with lists to return multiple values. To slice a list, you can provide two offset values separated by a colon, as seen in the following code example. The first offset indicates the starting index number and the second indicates the stopping point. The second index number will not be returned. **Slicing** a list always returns a new list:

```
fcList = ["Hydrants", "Water Mains", "Valves", "Wells"]
fc = fcList[0:2] ##get the first two items - Hydrants, Water Mains
```

Lists are dynamic in nature, meaning that you can add and remove items from an existing list as well as change the existing contents. This is all done without the need to create a new copy of the list. Changing values in a list can be accomplished either through indexing or slicing. Indexing allows you to change a single value, while slicing allows you to change multiple list items.

Lists have a number of methods that allow you to manipulate the values that are part of the list. You can sort the contents of the list in either an ascending or descending order through the use of the `sort()` method. Items can be added to a list with the `append()` method, which adds an object to the end of the list, and with the `insert()` method, which inserts an object at a position within the list. Items can be removed from a list with the `remove()` method, which removes the first occurrence of a value from the list, or the `pop()` method, which removes and returns the object at the end of the list. The contents of the list can also be reversed with the `reverse()` method.

Tuples

Tuples are similar to lists but with some important differences. Just like lists, tuples contain a sequence of values. The contents of a tuple can include any type of data just like lists. However, unlike lists, the contents of a tuple are static. After a tuple has been created, you can't make any changes to the sequence of the values nor can you add or remove values. This can be a good thing for situations where you want data to always occupy a specific position. Creating a tuple is as simple as placing a number of comma-separated values inside parentheses, as shown in the following code example:

```
fcTuples = ("Hydrants", "Water Mains", "Valves", "Wells")
```

You've probably noticed that creating a tuple is very similar to creating a list. The only difference is the use of parentheses instead of square braces around the values.

Similar to lists, tuple indices start with an index value of `0`. Access to values stored in a tuple occurs in the same way as lists. This is illustrated in the following code example:

```
fcTuples = ("Hydrants", "Water Mains", "Valves", "Wells")
print(fcTuples[1])
>>>Water Mains
```

Tuples are typically used in place of a list when it is important for the contents of the structure to be static. You can't ensure this with a list, but you can with a tuple.

Dictionaries

Dictionaries are a second type of collection object in Python. They are similar to lists, except that dictionaries are an unordered collection of objects. Instead of fetching objects from the collection through the use of an offset, items in a dictionary are stored and fetched by a key. Each key in a dictionary has an associated value, as seen here:

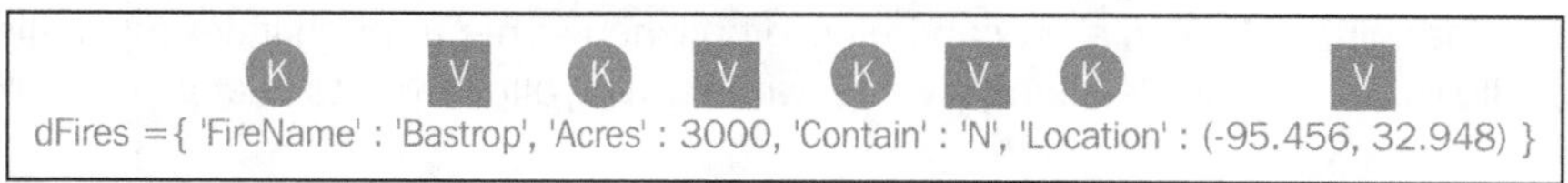

Similar to lists, dictionaries can grow and shrink in place through the use of methods on `dictionary`. In the following code example, you will learn to create and populate a dictionary and see how values can be accessed through the use of a key. Dictionaries are created with the use of curly braces. Inside these braces, each key is followed by a colon and then a value is associated with the key. These key/value pairs are separated by commas:

```
##create the dictionary
dictLayers = {'Roads': 0, 'Airports': 1, 'Rail': 2}

##access the dictionary by key
print(dictLayers['Airports'])
>>>1
print(dictLayers['Rail'])
>>>2
```

Basic `dictionary` operations include getting the number of items in a dictionary, acquiring a value using a key, determining if the key exists, converting the keys to a list, and getting a list of values. The `dictionary` objects can be changed, expanded, and shrunk in place. What this means is that Python does not have to create a new `dictionary` object to hold the altered version of the dictionary. Assigning values to a `dictionary` key can be accomplished by stating the key value in brackets and setting it equal to some value.

Unlike lists, dictionaries can't be sliced due to the fact that their contents are unordered. Should you have the need to iterate over all the values in a dictionary, simply use the `keys()` method, which returns a collection of all the keys in the dictionary and can then be used individually to set or get their value.

Classes and objects

Classes and objects are a fundamental concept in object-oriented programming. While Python is more of a procedural language, it also supports object-oriented programming. In object-oriented programming, classes are used to create object instances. You can think of classes as blueprints for the creation of one or more objects. Each object instance has the same properties and methods, but the data contained in an object can and usually will differ. Objects are complex data types in Python composed of properties and methods, and can be assigned to variables just like any other data type. Properties contain data associated with an object, while methods are actions that an object can perform.

These concepts are best illustrated with an example. In ArcPy, the `extent` class is a rectangle specified by providing the coordinate of the lower-left corner and the coordinate of the upper-right corner in map units. The `extent` class contains a number of properties and methods. Properties include `XMin`, `XMax`, `YMin`, `YMax`, `spatialReference`, and others. The minimum and maximum of `x` and `y` properties provide the coordinates for the extent rectangle. The `spatialReference` property holds a reference to a `spatialReference` object for `extent`. Object instances of the `extent` class can be used both to set and get the values of these properties through dot notation. An example of this is seen in the following code example:

```
# get the extent of the county boundary
ext = row[0].extent
# print out the bounding coordinates and spatial reference
print("XMin: " + str(ext.XMin))
print("XMax: " + str(ext.XMax))
print("YMin: " + str(ext.YMin))
print("YMax: " + str(ext.YMax))
print("Spatial Reference: " + ext.spatialReference.name)
```

Running this script yields the following output:

```
XMin: 2977896.74002
XMax: 3230651.20622
YMin: 9981999.27708
YMax:10200100.7854
Spatial Reference:
NAD_1983_StatePlane_Texas_Central_FIPS_4203_Feet
```

The `extent` class also has a number of methods, which are actions that an object can perform. In the case of this particular object, most of the methods are related to performing some sort of geometric test between the `extent` object and another geometry. Examples include `contains()`, `crosses()`, `disjoint()`, `equals()`, `overlaps()`, `touches()`, and `within()`.

One additional object-oriented concept that you need to understand is **dot notation**. Dot notation provides a way of accessing the properties and methods of an object. It is used to indicate that a property or method belongs to a particular class.

The syntax for using dot notation includes an object instance followed by a dot and then the property or method. The syntax is the same regardless of whether you're accessing a property or a method. A parenthesis and zero or more parameters at the end of the word following the dot indicates that a method is being accessed. Here are a couple of examples to better illustrate this concept:

```
Property: extent.XMin
Method: extent.touches()
```

Statements

Each line of code that you write with Python is known as a **statement**. There are many different kinds of statements, including those that create and assign data to variables, decision support statements that branch your code based on a test, looping statements that execute a code block multiple times, and others. There are various rules that your code will need to follow as you create the statements that are part of your script. You've already encountered one type of statement: variable creation and assignment.

Decision support statements

The `if/elif/else` statement is the primary decision-making statement in Python and tests for a `True/False` condition. Decision statements enable you to control the flow of your programs. Here are some example decisions that you can make in your code: if the variable holds a point feature class, get the `X`, `Y` coordinates; if the feature class name equals `Roads`, then get the `Name` field.

Decision statements, such as `if/elif/else`, test for a `True/False` condition. In Python, a `True` value means any nonzero number or nonempty object. A `False` value indicates *not true* and is represented in Python with a zero number or empty object. Comparison tests return values of one or zero (true or false). Boolean and/or operators return a true or false operand value:

```
if fcName == 'Roads':
  arcpy.Buffer_analysis(fc, "c:\\temp\\roads.shp", 100)
elif fcName == 'Rail':
```

```
    arcpy.Buffer_analysis(fc, "c:\\temp\\rail.shp", 50)
  else:
    print("Can't buffer this layer")
```

The Python code must follow certain syntax rules. Statements execute one after another until your code branches. Branching typically occurs through the use of `if/elif/else`. In addition to this, the use of looping structures, such as `for` and `while`, can alter the statement flow. Python automatically detects statement and block boundaries, so there is no need for braces or delimiters around your blocks of code. Instead, indentation is used to group statements in a block. Many languages terminate statements with the use of a semicolon, but Python simply uses the end of line character to mark the end of a statement. Compound statements include a ":" character. Compound statements follow this pattern, that is, header terminated by a colon. Blocks of code are then written as individual statements and are indented underneath the header.

Looping statements

Looping statements allow your program to repeat lines of code over and over as necessary. `The while` loops repeatedly execute a block of statements as long as the test at the top of the loop evaluates to `True`. When the condition test evaluates to `False`, Python begins interpreting code immediately after the `while` loop. In the next code example, a value of `10` has been assigned to the `x` variable. The test for the `while` loop then checks to see if `x` is less than `100`. If `x` is less than `100`, the current value of `x` is printed to the screen and the value of x is incremented by `10`. Processing then continues with the `while` loop test. The second time, the value of `x` will be `20`; so the test evaluates to `True` once again. This process continues until `x` is equal to or greater than `100`. At this time, the test will evaluate to `False` and processing will stop. It is very important that `the while` statements have some way of breaking out of the loop. Otherwise, you will wind up in an infinite loop. An infinite loop is a sequence of instructions in a computer program that loops endlessly, either due to the loop having no terminating condition, having one that can never be met, or one that causes the loop to start over:

```
x = 10
while x < 100:
      print(x)
      x = x + 10
```

The `for` loops execute a block of statements a predetermined number of times. They come in two varieties—a counted loop to run a block of code a set number of times, and a list loop that enables you to loop through all the objects in a list. The list loop in the following example executes once for each value in the dictionary and then stops looping:

```
dictLayers = {"Roads":"Line","Rail":"Line","Parks":"Polygon"}
for key in dictLayers:
  print(dictLayers[key])
```

There are times when it will be necessary for you to break out of the execution of a loop. The `break` and `continue` statements can be used to do this. The `break` jumps out of the closest enclosing loop, while `continue` jumps back to the top of the closest enclosing loop. These statements can appear anywhere inside the block of code.

Try statements

A `try` statement is a complete, compound statement that is used to handle exceptions. Exceptions are a high-level control device used primarily for error interception or triggering. Exceptions in Python can either be intercepted or triggered. When an error condition occurs in your code, Python automatically triggers an exception, which may or may not be handled by your code. It is up to you as a programmer to catch an automatically triggered exception. Exceptions can also be triggered manually by your code. In this case, you would also need to provide an exception handling routine to catch these manually triggered exceptions.

There are two basic types of `try` statements: `try/except/else` and `try/finally`. The basic `try` statement starts with a `try` header line followed by a block of indented statements. Then, this is followed by one or more optional `except` clauses that name the exceptions that are to be caught. After this, you will find an optional `else` clause at the end:

```
import arcpy
import sys

inFeatureClass = arcpy.GetParameterAsText(0)
outFeatureClass = arcpy.GetParameterAsText(1)

try:
  # If the output feature class exists, raise an error

  if arcpy.Exists(inFeatureClass):
    raise overwriteError(outFeatureClass)
  else:
    # Additional processing steps
    print("Additional processing steps")

except overwriteError as e:
  # Use message ID 12, and provide the output feature class
```

```
    # to complete the message.

    arcpy.AddIDMessage("Error", 12, str(e))
```

The `try/except/else` statement works as follows. Once inside a `try` statement, Python marks the fact that you are in a `try` block and knows that any exception condition that occurs at this point will be sent to the various `except` statements for handling. If a matching exception is found, the code block inside the `except` block is executed. The code then picks up the full `try` statement, which will be mentioned shortly. The `else` statements are not executed in this case. Each statement inside the `try` block is executed. Assuming that no exception conditions occur, the code pointer will then jump to the `else` statement and execute the code block contained by the `else` statement before moving to the next line of code that follows the try block.

The other type of `try` statement is the `try/finally` statement, which allows for finalization actions. When a `finally` clause is used in a `try` statement, its block of statements always run at the very end, whether an error condition occurs or not.

Here is how the `try/finally` statement works: if an exception occurs, Python runs the `try` block, then the `except` block, followed by the `finally` block, and then execution continues past the entire `try` statement. If an exception does not occur during execution, Python runs the `try` block, then the `finally` block. This is useful when you want to make sure an action happens after a code block runs, regardless of whether an error condition occurs. Cleanup operations, such as closing a file or a connection to a database, are commonly placed inside a `finally` block to ensure that they are executed regardless of whether an exception occurs in your code:

```
import arcpy

try:
  if arcpy.CheckExtension("3D") == "Available":
    arcpy.CheckOutExtension("3D")
  else:
    # Raise a custom exception
    raise LicenseError

  arcpy.env.workspace = "D:/GrosMorne"
  arcpy.HillShade_3d("WesternBrook", "westbrook_hill", 300)
  arcpy.Aspect_3d("WesternBrook", "westbrook_aspect")

except LicenseError:
  print("3D Analyst license is unavailable")
except:
  print(arcpy.GetMessages(2))
finally:
  # Check in the 3D Analyst extension
  arcpy.CheckInExtension("3D")
```

With statements

The with statement is handy when you have two related operations that need to be executed as a pair with a block of code in between. A common scenario to use the with statements is opening, reading, and closing a file. Opening and closing a file are the related operations, and reading a file and doing something with the contents is the block of code in between. When writing geoprocessing scripts with ArcGIS, the new cursor objects introduced with version 10.1 of ArcGIS are ideal when using the with statements. We'll discuss the cursor objects in great detail in a later chapter, but I'll briefly describe these objects now. Cursors are an in-memory copy of records from the attribute table of a feature class or table. There are various types of cursors. Insert cursors allow you to insert new records, search cursors are a read-only copy of records, and update cursors allow you to edit or delete records. Cursor objects are opened, processed in some way, and closed automatically using a with statement.

The closure of a file or cursor object is handled automatically by the with statement, resulting in cleaner, more efficient coding. It's basically like using a try/finally block, but with fewer lines of code. In the following code example, the with block is used to create a new search cursor, read information from the cursor, and implicitly close the cursor:

```
import arcpy

fc = "c:/data/city.gdb/streets"

# For each row print the Object ID field, and use the SHAPE@AREA
# token to access geometry properties

with arcpy.da.SearchCursor(fc, ("OID@", "SHAPE@AREA")) as cursor:
  for row in cursor:
    print("Feature {0} has an area of {1}".format(row[0], row[1]))
```

Statement indentation

Statement indentation deserves a special mention as it is critical to the way Python interprets code. Compound statements in Python use indentation to create a group of statements. This includes the if/then, for, while, try, and with statements. The Python interpreter uses indentation to detect these code blocks. The beginning of a compound statement is defined through the use of a colon. All lines following the beginning of the compound statement should be indented the same distance. You can use any number of spaces to define the indentation, but you should use the same indentation level for each statement. A common practice is to define indentation through the use of a tab. When the Python interpreter encounters a line that is less indented, it will assume that the code block has ended. The following code illustrates this concept through the use of a try statement. Notice that there is a colon after the try statement. This indicates that the statements that follow are part of a compound statement and should be indented. These statements will form a code block.

Also, an `if` statement is inside the `try` statement. This too is a compound statement as defined by the colon at the end of the statement. Therefore, any statements that are part of the `if` statement should be further indented. You should also notice that there is a statement that is not indented inside the `if` statement, but is rather at the same level. This `statement4` is part of the `try` code block but not part of the `if` code block:

```
try:
  if <statement1>:
    <statement2>
    <statement3>
  <statement4> <.........>
except:
  <statement>
  <.........>
except:
  <statement>
  <...........>
```

Many languages, including JavaScript, Java, and .NET, use curly braces to indicate a group of statements. Python uses indentation instead of curly braces in an attempt to cut down on the amount of code you have to write and to make code more readable. Anyone who has ever used these other languages can attest to the difficulty in reading code that contains many curly braces. However, indentation does take some getting used to and is critical to the way that Python executes lines of code.

File I/O

You will often find it necessary to retrieve or write information to files on your computer. Python has a built-in object type that provides a way to access files for many tasks. We're only going to cover a small subset of the file manipulation functionality provided, but we'll touch on the most commonly used functions, including opening and closing files, and reading and writing data to a file.

Python's `open()` function creates a file object, which serves as a link to a file residing on your computer. You must call the `open()` function on a file before reading and/or writing data to a file. The first parameter for the `open()` function is a path to the file you'd like to open. The second parameter corresponds to a mode, which is typically read (`r`), write (`w`), or append (`a`). A value of `r` indicates that you'd like to open the file for read-only operations, while a value of `w` indicates you'd like to open the file for write operations. In the event that you open a file that already exists for write operations, this will overwrite any data currently in the file, so you must be careful with the write mode. The append mode (`a`) will open a file for write operations, but instead of overwriting any existing data, it will append the new data to the end of the file. The following code example shows the use of the `open()` function to open a text file in a read-only mode:

```
with open('Wildfires.txt','r') as f:
```

Notice that we have also used the `with` keyword to open the file, ensuring that the file resource will be *cleaned up* after the code that uses it has finished executing.

After a file has been opened, data can be read from it in a number of ways and using various methods. The most typical scenario would be to read data one line at a time from a file through the `readline()` method. The `readline()` function can be used to read the file one line at a time into a string variable. You would need to create a looping mechanism in your Python code to read the entire file line by line. If you would prefer to read the entire file into a variable, you can use the `read()` method, which will read the file up to the **End Of File** (**EOF**) marker. You can also use the `readlines()` method to read the entire contents of a file, separating each line into individual strings, until the EOF is found.

In the following code example, we have opened a text file called `Wildfires.txt` in the read-only mode and used the `readlines()` method on the file to read its entire contents into a variable called `lstFires`, which is a Python list containing each line of the file as a separate string value in the list. In this case, the `Wildfire.txt` file is a comma-delimited text file containing the latitude and longitude of the fire along with the confidence values for each fire. We then loop through each line of text in `lstFires` and use the `split()` function to extract the values based on a comma as the delimiter, including the latitude, longitude, and confidence values. The latitude and longitude values are used to create a new `Point` object, which is then inserted into the feature class using an insert cursor:

```
import arcpy, os
try:

  arcpy.env.workspace = "C:/data/WildlandFires.mdb"
  # open the file to read
  with open('Wildfires.txt','r') as f:   #open the file

    lstFires = f.readlines() #read the file into a list
    cur = arcpy.InsertCursor("FireIncidents")

    for fire in lstFires: #loop through each line
      if 'Latitude' in fire: #skip the header
        continue
      vals = fire.split(",") #split the values based on comma
      latitude = float(vals[0]) #get latitude
      longitude = float(vals[1]) #get longitude
      confid = int(vals[2]) #get confidence value
      #create new Point and set values
      pnt = arcpy.Point(longitude,latitude)
      feat = cur.newRow()
      feat.shape = pnt
      feat.setValue("CONFIDENCEVALUE", confid)
      cur.insertRow(feat) #insert the row into featureclass
```

```
except:
    print(arcpy.GetMessages()) #print out any errors
finally:
  del cur
  f.close()
```

Just as is the case with reading files, there are a number of methods that you can use to write data to a file. The `write()` function is probably the easiest to use and takes a single string argument and writes it to a file. The `writelines()` function can be used to write the contents of a list structure to a file. In the following code example, we have created a list structure called `fcList`, which contains a list of feature classes. We can write this list to a file using the `writelines()` method:

```
outfile = open('c:\\temp\\data.txt','w')
fcList = ["Streams", "Roads", "Counties"]
outfile.writelines(fcList)
```

Summary

In this chapter, we covered some of the fundamental Python programming concepts that you'll need to understand before you can write effective geoprocessing scripts. We began the chapter with an overview of the IDLE development environment to write and debug Python scripts. You learned how to create a new script, edit existing scripts, check for syntax errors, and execute scripts. We also covered the basic language constructs, including importing modules, creating and assigning variables, if/else statements, looping statements, and the various data-types including strings, numbers, Booleans, lists, dictionaries, and objects. You also learned how to read and write text files.

2
Managing Map Documents and Layers

In this chapter, we will cover the following recipes:

- Referencing the current map document
- Referencing map documents on a disk
- Getting a list of layers in a map document
- Restricting the list of layers
- Zooming in to selected features
- Changing the map extent
- Adding layers to a map document
- Inserting layers into a map document
- Updating layer symbology
- Updating layer properties
- Working with time-enabled layers in a data frame

Introduction

The ArcPy mapping module provides some really exciting features for mapping automation, including the ability to manage map documents and layer files, as well as the data within these files. Support is provided to automate map export and print, to create PDF map books, and publish map documents to ArcGIS Server map services. This is an incredibly useful module for accomplishing many of the day-to-day tasks performed by GIS analysts.

In this chapter, you will learn how to use the ArcPy mapping module to manage map documents and layer files. You will also learn how to add and remove geographic layers and tables from map document files, insert layers into data frames, and move layers around within the map document. Finally, you will learn how to update layer properties and symbology.

Referencing the current map document

When running a geoprocessing script from the ArcGIS Python window or a custom script tool, you will often need to make a reference to the map document which is currently loaded in ArcMap. This is typically the first step in your script before you perform geoprocessing operations against layers and tables in a map document. In this recipe, you will learn how to reference the current map document from your Python geoprocessing script.

Getting ready

Before you can actually perform any operations on a map document file, you need to make a reference to it in your Python script. This is done by calling the `MapDocument()` method on the `arcpy.mapping` module. You can reference either the currently running document or a document at a specific location on disk. To reference the currently active document, you simply supply the keyword `CURRENT` as a parameter to the `MapDocument()` function. This loads the currently active document in ArcMap. The following code example shows how a reference to the current active document is obtained:

```
mxd = mapping.MapDocument("CURRENT")
```

You can only use the `CURRENT` keyword when running a script from the ArcGIS Python window or a custom script tool in ArcToolbox. If you attempt to use this keyword when running a script from IDLE or any other development environment, it won't have access to the map document file that is currently loaded in ArcGIS. I should also point out that the `CURRENT` keyword is not case sensitive. You could just as easily use `"current"`.

To reference a map document on a local or remote drive, simply supply the path to the map document as well as the map document name as a parameter to `MapDocument()`. For example, you would reference the `crime.mxd` file in the `c:\data` folder with the following reference: `arcpy.mapping.MapDocument("C:/data/crime.mxd")`.

How to do it...

Follow these steps to learn how to access the currently active map document in ArcMap:

1. Open `c:\ArcpyBook\Ch2\Crime_Ch2.mxd` with ArcMap.
2. Click on the Python window button located on the main ArcMap toolbar.
3. Import the `arcpy.mapping` module by typing the following into the Python window. Here, and in future recipes, we'll assign the `arcpy.mapping` module to a variable called `mapping`. This will make your code easier to read and cut down on the amount of code you have to write. Instead of having to prefix all your code with `arcpy.mapping`, you can just refer to it as mapping. It is not required that you follow this form, but it does make your code cleaner and faster to write. Furthermore, you can name the variable as you wish. For example, instead of calling it `mapping` you may call it `MAP` or `mp` or whatever makes sense.

   ```
   import arcpy.mapping as mapping
   ```

4. Reference the currently active document (`Crime_Ch2.mxd`) and assign the reference to a variable by typing the following into the Python Window below the first line of code that you added in the last step:

   ```
   mxd = mapping.MapDocument("CURRENT")
   ```

5. Set a title for map document:

   ```
   mxd.title = "Crime Project"
   ```

6. Save a copy of the map document file with the `saveACopy()` method:

   ```
   mxd.saveACopy("c:/ArcpyBook/Ch2/crime_copy.mxd")
   ```

7. Navigate to **File** | **Map Document Properties**, in order to view the new title you gave to the map document.
8. You can check your work by examining the `c:\ArcpyBook\code\Ch2\ReferenceCurrentMapDocument.py` solution file.

How it works...

The `MapDocument` class has a constructor that creates an instance of this class. In object-oriented programming, an **instance** is also known as an **object**. The constructor for `MapDocument` can accept either the `CURRENT` keyword or a path to a map document file on a local or remote drive. The constructor creates an object and assigns it to the variable `mxd`. You can then access the properties and methods available on this object using dot notation. In this particular case, we printed out the title of the map document file using the `MapDocument.title` property and we also used the `MapDocument.saveACopy()` method to save a copy of the map document file.

Referencing map documents on a disk

In addition to being able to reference the currently active map document file in ArcMap, you can also access map document files that are stored on a local or remote drive by using the `MapDocument()` constructor. In this recipe, you'll learn how to access these map documents.

Getting ready

As I mentioned earlier, you can also reference a map document file that resides somewhere on your computer or a shared server. This is done simply by providing a path to the file. This is a more versatile way of obtaining a reference to a map document because it can be run outside the ArcGIS Python window. Later, when we will discuss parameters in a script, you'll understand that you can make this path a parameter so that the script is even more versatile, with the ability to input a new path each time it is needed.

How to do it...

Follow these steps to learn how to access a map document stored on a local or remote drive:

1. Open the IDLE development environment from **Start** | **All Programs** | **ArcGIS** | **Python 2.7** | **IDLE**.
2. Create a new IDLE script window by navigating to **File** | **New Window** from the IDLE shell window.
3. Import `arcpy.mapping`:

   ```
   import arcpy.mapping as mapping
   ```

4. Reference the copy of the `crime` map document that you created in the last recipe:

   ```
   mxd =
   mapping.MapDocument("c:/ArcpyBook/Ch2/crime_copy.mxd")
   ```

5. Print the title of the map document:

   ```
   print(mxd.title)
   ```

6. Run the script, and you will see the following output:

   ```
   Crime Project
   ```

7. You can check your work by examining the `c:\ArcpyBook\code\Ch2\ReferenceMapDocumentOnDisk.py` solution file.

How it works...

The only difference between this recipe and the last one is that we provided a reference to a map document file on a local or remote drive rather than using the `CURRENT` keyword. This is the recommended way of referencing a map document file unless you know for sure that your geoprocessing script will be run inside ArcGIS, either in the Python window or as a custom script tool.

Getting a list of layers in a map document

Frequently, one of the first steps in a geoprocessing script is to obtain a list of layers in the map document. Once obtained, your script may then cycle through each of the layers and perform some type of processing. The mapping module contains a `ListLayers()` function, which provides the capability of obtaining this list of layers. In this recipe, you will learn how to get a list of layers contained within a map document.

Getting ready

The `arcpy.mapping` module contains various list functions to return lists of layers, data frames, broken data sources, table views, and layout elements. These list functions normally function as the first step in a multistep process, in which the script needs to get one or more items from a list for further processing. Each of these list functions returns a Python list, which, as you know from earlier in the book, is a highly functional data structure for storing information.

Normally, the list functions are used as a part of a multistep process, in which creating a list is only the first step. Subsequent processing in the script will iterate over one or more of the items in this list. For example, you might obtain a list of layers in a map document and then iterate through each layer looking for a specific layer name, which will then be subjected to further geoprocessing.

In this recipe, you will learn how to obtain a list of layers from a map document file.

How to do it...

Follow these steps to learn how to get a list of layers from a map document:

1. Open `c:\ArcpyBook\Ch2\Crime_Ch2.mxd` with ArcMap.
2. Click on the Python window button from the main ArcMap toolbar.
3. Import the `arcpy.mapping` module:

   ```
   import arcpy.mapping as mapping
   ```

4. Reference the currently active document (`Crime_Ch2.mxd`) and assign the reference to a variable:

```
mxd = mapping.MapDocument("CURRENT")
```

5. Call the `ListLayers()` function and pass a reference to the map document:

```
layers = mapping.ListLayers(mxd)
```

6. Start a `for` loop and print out the name of each layer in the map document:

```
for lyr in layers:
    print(lyr.name)
```

7. Run the script to see the following output (you can check your work by examining the `c:\ArcpyBook\code\Ch2\GetListLayers.py` solution file):

```
Burglaries in 2009
Crime Density by School District
Bexar County Boundary
Test Performance by School District
Bexar County Boundary
Bexar County Boundary
Texas Counties
School_Districts
Crime Surface
Bexar County Boundary
```

How it works...

The `ListLayers()` function retrieves a list of layers in a map document, specific data frame, or layer file. In this case, we passed a reference to the current map document to the `ListLayers()` function, which should retrieve a list of all the layers in the map document. The results are stored in a variable called `layers`, which is a Python list that can be iterated with a `for` loop. This Python list contains one or more `Layer` objects.

There's more...

The `ListLayers()` function is only one of the many list functions provided by the `arcpy.mapping` module. Each of these functions returns a Python list containing data of some type. Some of the other list functions include `ListTableViews()`, which returns a list of `Table` objects; `ListDataFrames()`, which returns a list of `DataFrame` objects; and `ListBoomarks()`, which returns a list of bookmarks in a map document. There are additional list functions, many of which we'll cover later in this book.

Restricting the list of layers

In the previous recipe, you learned how to get a list of layers by using the `ListLayers()` function. There will be times when you will not want a list of all the layers in a map document, but rather only a subset of the layers. The `ListLayers()` function allows you to restrict the list of layers that is generated. In this recipe, you will learn how to restrict the layers returned using a wildcard and a specific data frame from the ArcMap table of contents.

Getting ready

By default, if you only pass a reference to the map document or layer file, the `ListLayers()` function will return a list of all the layers in these files. However, you can restrict the list of layers returned by this function by using an optional wildcard parameter or by passing in a reference to a specific data frame. A wildcard is a character that will match any character or sequence of characters in a search. This will be demonstrated in this recipe.

If you're working with a layer file (`.lyr`), you can't restrict layers with a data frame. Layer files don't support data frames.

In this recipe, you will learn how to restrict the list of layers returned by `ListLayers()` through the use of a wildcard and data frame.

How to do it...

Follow these steps to learn how to restrict a list of layers from a map document:

1. Open `c:\ArcpyBook\Ch2\Crime_Ch2.mxd` with ArcMap.
2. Click on the Python window button from the main ArcMap toolbar.
3. Import the `arcpy.mapping` module:

   ```
   import arcpy.mapping as mapping
   ```

4. Reference the currently active document (`Crime_Ch2.mxd`) and assign the reference to a variable:

   ```
   mxd = mapping.MapDocument("CURRENT")
   ```

5. Get a list of data frames in the map document and search for a specific data frame named `Crime` (please note that text strings can be surrounded by either single or double quotation marks):

   ```
   for df in mapping.ListDataFrames(mxd):
     if df.name == 'Crime':
   ```

6. Call the `ListLayers()` function and pass a reference to the map document, a wildcard to restrict the search, and the data frame found in the last step to further restrict the search. The `ListLayers()` function should be indented inside the `if` statement you just created:

   ```
   layers = mapping.ListLayers(mxd,'Burg*',df)
   ```

7. Start a for loop and print out the name of each layer in the map document:

   ```
   for layer in layers:
       print(layer.name)
   ```

8. The complete script should appear as follows or you can consult the solution file at `c:\ArcpyBook\code\Ch2\RestrictLayers.py`:

   ```
   import arcpy.mapping as mapping
   mxd = mapping.MapDocument("CURRENT")
   for df in mapping.ListDataFrames(mxd):
       if df.name == 'Crime':
           layers = mapping.ListLayers(mxd, 'Burg*', df)
           for layer in layers:
               print(layer.name)
   ```

9. Run the script to see the following output:

   `Burglaries in 2009`

How it works...

The `ListDataFrames()` function is another list function that is provided by `arcpy.mapping`. This function returns a list of all the data frames in a map document. We then loop through each of the data frames returned by this function, looking for a data frame that has the name `Crime`. If we do find a data frame that has this name, we call the `ListLayers()` function, passing in the optional wildcard value of `Burg*` as the second parameter, and a reference to the `Crime` data frame. The wildcard value passed in as the second parameter accepts any number of characters and an optional wildcard character (`*`).

In this particular recipe, we searched for all the layers that begin with the characters `Burg` and have a data frame named `Crime`. Any layers found matching these restrictions were then printed. Keep in mind that all we did in this case was print the layer names, but in most cases, you would be performing additional geoprocessing with the use of tools or other functions, and having a shorter list will speed up your script and will keep things neat and tidy.

Zooming in to selected features

Creating selection sets in ArcMap is a common task. Selection sets are often created as the result of an attribute or spatial query, but they can also occur when a user manually selects features and sometimes, under some additional circumstances. To better visualize selection sets, users often zoom to the extent of the selected feature. This can be accomplished programmatically with Python in several ways. In this recipe, you will learn how to zoom to all the selected features in a data frame as well as an individual layer.

Getting ready

The `DataFrame.zoomToSelectedFeatures` property zooms to the extent of all the selected features from all the layers in the data frame. Essentially, it performs the same operation as the **Selection** | **Zoom to Selected Features** operation. One difference is that it will zoom to the full extent of all the layers if no features are selected.

Zooming to the extent of selected features in an individual layer requires you to use the `Layer` object. The `Layer` object includes a `getSelectedExtent()` method that you can call to zoom to the extent of the selected records. This returns an `Extent` object, which you can then use as a parameter that is passed into the `DataFrame.panToExtent()` method.

How to do it...

Follow these steps to learn how to get and set the active data frame and active view ArcMap:

1. Open `c:\ArcpyBook\Ch2\Crime_Ch2.mxd` with ArcMap.
2. In the ArcMap **Table Of Contents** pane, make sure that `Crime` is the active data frame.
3. In the **Table Of Contents** pane, click on the **List By Selection** button.
4. Make the **Bexar County Boundaries** layer unselectable by clicking on the toggle button just to the right of the layer name:

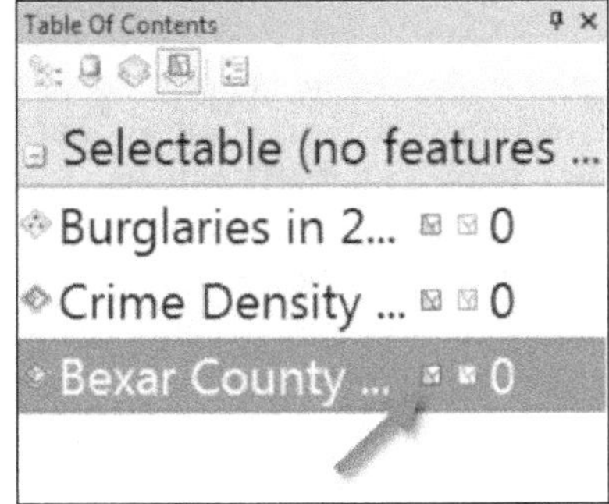

5. Click on the **List By Source** button in the **Table Of Contents** pane. Using the **Select Features** tool, drag a box around the cluster of burglaries inside the **Northside ISD** boundary. This should select the boundaries of a specific school district along with some burglaries as shown in the following diagram:

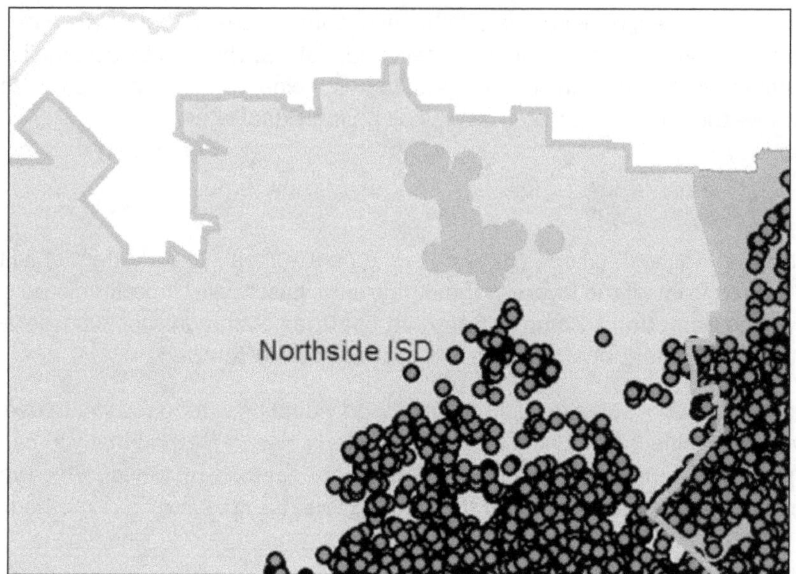

6. Click on the Python window button from the main ArcMap toolbar.
7. Import the `arcpy.mapping` module:
```
import arcpy.mapping as mapping
```
8. Reference the currently active document (`Crime_Ch2.mxd`) and assign the reference to a variable:
```
mxd = mapping.MapDocument("CURRENT")
```
9. Get the active data frame (`Crime`) and zoom to the selected features:
```
mxd.activeDataFrame.zoomToSelectedFeatures()
```
10. If no records have been selected, a call to `zoomToSelectedFeatures()` will zoom to the extent of all the records in the data frame. Clear the selected features by navigating to **Selection** | **Clear Selected Features**. This will clear the selection set. Now, execute the same line of code again to see how this affects the operation of the `zoomToSelectedFeatures()` method:
```
mxd.activeDataFrame.zoomToSelectedFeatures()
```
11. Now, we'll zoom to the extent of the selected features in a specific layer. Using the **Select Features** tool, drag a box around the cluster of burglaries inside the **Northside ISD** boundary.

12. First, get a reference to the `Crime` data frame. Calling the `ListDataFrames()` function and passing in a wildcard of `Crime` will return a Python list containing a single item. We pull this item out using `[0]`, which returns the first and only item in the list:

    ```
    df = mapping.ListDataFrames(mxd, "Crime")[0]
    ```

13. Now, we'll get a reference to the `Burglaries` layer, which contains some selected features. The following code uses a wildcard `*` to search for the **Burglaries in 2009** layer within the data frame that we referenced in the last line of code. The `ListLayers()` function returns a Python list and we use `[0]` to pull out the first and only layer containing the word `Burglaries`:

    ```
    layer = mapping.ListLayers(mxd,"Burglaries*",df)[0]
    ```

14. Finally, we'll set the extent of the data frame by getting the extent of the selected features in the layer:

    ```
    df.extent = layer.getSelectedExtent
    ```

15. The complete script for zooming to the selected features of a layer should appear as follows or you can consult the solution file at `c:\ArcpyBook\code\Ch2\ZoomSelectedExtent.py`:

    ```
    import arcpy.mapping as mapping
    mxd = mapping.MapDocument("CURRENT")
    df = mapping.ListDataFrames(mxd, "Crime")[0]
    layer = mapping.ListLayers(mxd,"Burglaries*",df)[0]
    df.extent = layer.getSelectedExtent
    ```

How it works...

In this recipe, you learned how to zoom to the extent of all the selected records from all the layers in a data frame as well as how to zoom to the extent of all the selected records from a specific layer in a data frame. Zooming to the extent of all the selected records from all the layers in a data frame simply requires that you get a reference to the active data frame and then call `zoomToSelectedFeatures()`.

Zooming to the extent of the selected records within a specific layer requires a little more coding. After importing the `arcpy.mapping` module and getting a reference to the map document, we then got a reference to the `Crime` data frame. Using the `ListLayers()` function we passed in a reference to the data frame as well as a wildcard that searched for the layers that begin with the text `Burglaries`. The `ListLayers()` function returned a Python list and since we knew that we only had one layer that matched the wildcard search, we pulled out the first layer and assigned it to a variable called `layer`. Finally, we set the extent of the data frame using `layer.getSelectedExtent`.

Changing the map extent

There will be many occasions when you will need to change the map extent. This is frequently the case when you are automating the map production process and need to create many maps of different areas or features. There are a number of ways that the map extent can be changed with `arcpy`. However, for this recipe, we'll concentrate on using a definition expression to change the extent.

Getting ready

The `DataFrame` class has an `extent` property that you can use to set the geographic extent. This is often used in conjunction with the `Layer.definitionQuery` property that is used to define a definition query for a layer. In this recipe, you will learn how to use these objects and properties to change the map extent.

How to do it...

Follow these steps to learn how to get a list of layers from a map document:

1. Open `c:\ArcpyBook\Ch2\Crime_Ch2.mxd` with ArcMap.
2. Click on the Python window button from the main ArcMap toolbar.
3. Import the `arcpy.mapping` module:

   ```
   import arcpy.mapping as mapping
   ```

4. Reference the currently active document (`Crime_Ch2.mxd`) and assign the reference to a variable:

   ```
   mxd = mapping.MapDocument("CURRENT")
   ```

5. Create a `for` loop that will loop through all the data frames in the map document:

   ```
   for df in mapping.ListDataFrames(mxd):
   ```

6. Find the data frame called `Crime` and a specific layer that we'll apply the definition query against:

   ```
   if df.name == 'Crime':
     layers = mapping.ListLayers(mxd,'Crime Density by
     School District',df)
   ```

7. Create a `for` loop that will loop through the layers. There will only be one, but we'll create the loop anyway. In the `for` loop, create a definition query and set the new extent of the data frame:

   ```
   for layer in layers:
     query = '"NAME" = \'Lackland ISD\''
     layer.definitionQuery = query
     df.extent = layer.getExtent()
   ```

8. The entire script should appear as follows or you can consult the solution file at `c:\ArcpyBook\code\Ch2\ChangeMapExtent.py`:

```
import arcpy.mapping as mapping
mxd = mapping.MapDocument("CURRENT")
for df in mapping.ListDataFrames(mxd):
    if df.name == 'Crime':
        layers = mapping.ListLayers(mxd,'Crime Density by School District',df)
        for layer in layers:
            query = '"NAME" = \'Lackland ISD\''
            layer.definitionQuery = query
            df.extent = layer.getExtent()
```

9. Save and run the script. The extent of the data view should update so that it visualizes only the features matching the definition expression, as shown in the following screenshot:

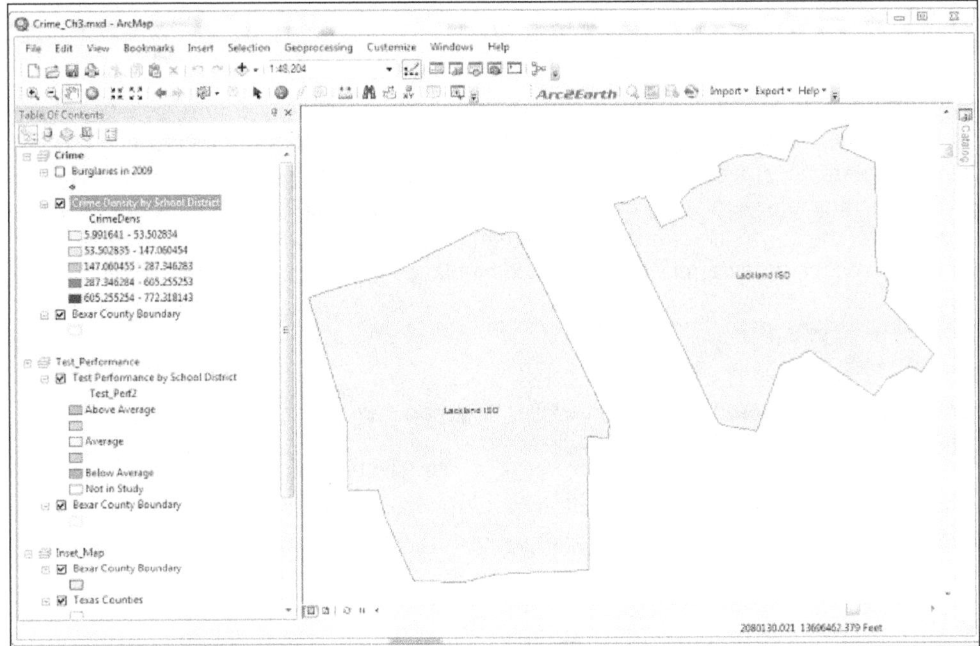

How it works...

This recipe used a definition query on a layer to update the map extent. Near the end of the script, you created a new variable called `query` that held the definition expression. The definition expression was set up to find school districts with a name of **Lackland ISD**. This query string was then applied to the `definitionQuery` property. Finally, the `df.extent` property was set to the returned value of `layer.getExtent()`.

Adding layers to a map document

There will be many situations where you will need to add a layer to a map document. The mapping module provides this functionality through the `AddLayer()` function. In this recipe, you will learn how to add a layer to a map document using this function.

Getting ready

The `arcpy.mapping` module provides the ability to add layers or group layers into an existing map document file. You can take advantage of the ArcMap *auto-arrange* functionality, which automatically places a layer in the data frame for visibility. This is essentially the same functionality as is provided by the **Add Data** button in ArcMap, which positions a layer in the data frame based on geometry type and layer weight rules.

Layers can't be added to a layer file (`.lyr`).

When adding a layer to a map document, the layer must reference an existing layer found in a layer file on disk, the same map document and data frame, the same map document with a different data frame, or a completely separate map document. A layer can be either a layer in a map document or a layer in a `.lyr` file. To add a layer to a map document, you must first create an instance of the `Layer` class and then call the `AddLayer()` function, passing in the new layer along with the data frame where it should be placed and rules for how it is positioned.

How to do it...

Follow these steps to learn how to add a layer to a map document:

1. Open `c:\ArcpyBook\Ch2\Crime_Ch2.mxd` with ArcMap.
2. Click on the Python window button from the main ArcMap toolbar.
3. Import the `arcpy.mapping` module:

   ```
   import arcpy.mapping as mapping
   ```

4. Reference the currently active document (`Crime_Ch2.mxd`) and assign the reference to a variable:

   ```
   mxd = mapping.MapDocument("CURRENT")
   ```

5. Get a reference to the `Crime` data frame, which is the first data frame in the list returned by `ListDataFrames()`. The `[0]` value, specified at the end of the code, gets the first data frame returned from the `ListDataFrames()` method, which returns a list of data frames. Lists are 0-based, so in order to retrieve the first data frame, we provide an index of `0`:

   ```
   df = mapping.ListDataFrames(mxd)[0]
   ```

6. Create a `Layer` object that references a `.lyr` file:

```
layer =
mapping.Layer(r"C:\ArcpyBook\data\School_Districts.lyr")
```

7. Add the layer to the data frame:

```
mapping.AddLayer(df,layer,"AUTO_ARRANGE")
```

8. You can consult the solution file at `c:\ArcpyBook\code\Ch2\AddLayersMapDocument.py`. Run the script. The `School_Districts.lyr` file will be added to the data frame, as shown in the following screenshot:

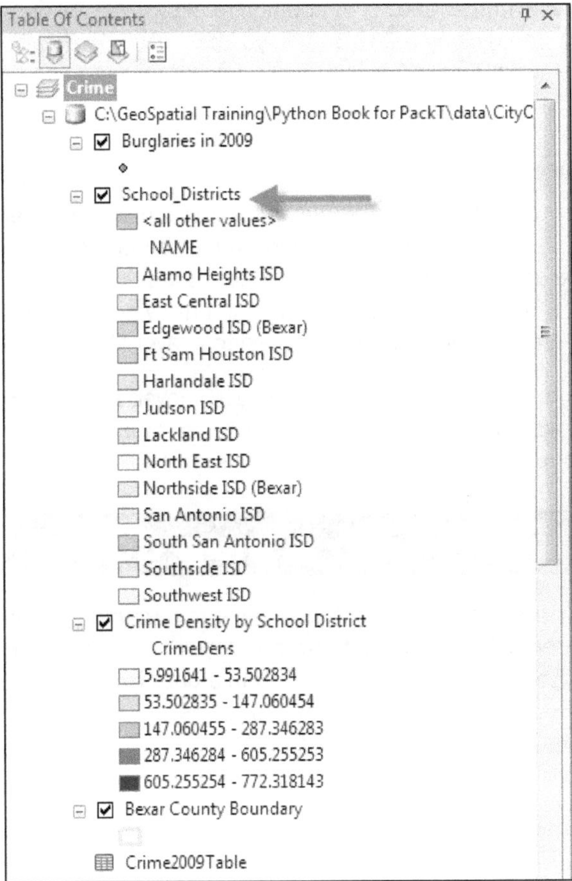

How it works...

In the first two lines, we simply referenced the `arcpy.mapping` module and got a reference to the currently active map document. Next, we created a new variable called `df`, which held a reference to the `Crime` data frame. This was obtained through the `ListDataFrames()` function that returned a list of data frame objects. We then used list access to return the first item in the list, which is the `Crime` data frame. A new `Layer` instance, called `layer`, was then created from a `layer` file stored on disk. This `layer` file was called `School_Districts.lyr`. Finally, we called the `AddLayer()` function, passing in the data frame where the layer should ideally reside along with a reference to the layer, and a parameter indicating that we wanted to use the **auto-arrange** feature. In addition to allowing ArcMap to automatically place the layer into the data frame using auto-arrange, you can also specifically place the layer at either the top or bottom of the data frame or a group layer using the `BOTTOM` or `TOP` position.

There's more...

In addition to providing the capability of adding a layer to a map document, `arcpy.mapping` also provides an `AddLayerToGroup()` function, which can be used to add a layer to a group layer. The layer can be added to the top or bottom of the group layer or you can use auto-arrange for placement. You may also add layers to an empty group layer. However, just as with regular layer objects, group layers cannot be added to a layer file.

Layers can also be removed from a data frame or group layer. `RemoveLayer()` is the function used to remove a layer or group layer. In the event that two layers have the same name, only the first is removed, unless your script is set up to iterate.

Inserting layers into a map document

The `AddLayer()` function can be used to add a layer to a map document either through auto-arrange or as the first or last layer in a data frame. However, it doesn't provide the control you need for inserting a layer in a specific position within a data frame. For this added control, you can use the `InsertLayer()` function. In this recipe, you will learn how to control the placement of layers that are added to a data frame.

Getting ready

The `AddLayer()` function simply adds a layer into a data frame or a group layer and places the layer automatically using auto-arrange. You can choose to have the layer placed at the top or bottom of either. The `InsertLayer()` method allows you to have more precise positioning of a new layer into a data frame or a group layer. It uses a reference layer to specify a location and the layer is added either before or after the reference layer, as specified in your code. Since `InsertLayer()` requires the use of a reference layer, you can't use this method on an empty data frame. This is illustrated in the following screenshot, where **District_Crime_Join** is the reference layer and **School_Districts** is the layer to be added. The **School_Districts** layer can be placed either before or after the reference layer using `InsertLayer()`:

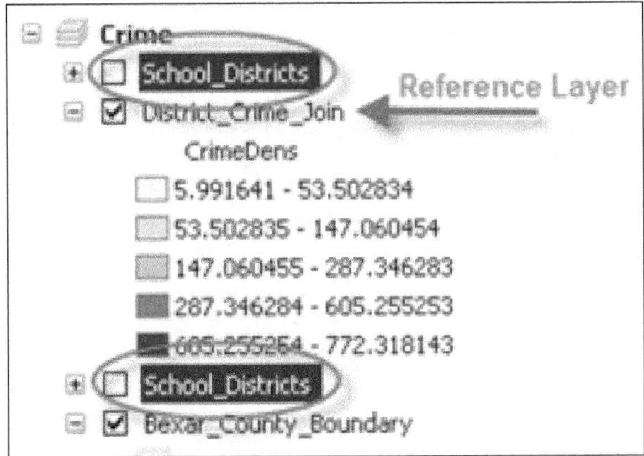

How to do it...

Follow these steps to learn how to use `InsertLayer()` to insert a layer into a data frame:

1. Open `c:\ArcpyBook\Ch2\Crime_Ch2.mxd` with ArcMap.
2. Click on the Python window button from the main ArcMap toolbar.
3. Import the `arcpy.mapping` module:

   ```
   import arcpy.mapping as mapping
   ```

4. Reference the currently active document (`Crime_Ch2.mxd`) and assign the reference to a variable:

   ```
   mxd = mapping.MapDocument("CURRENT")
   ```

5. Get a reference to the `Crime` data frame:

   ```
   df = mapping.ListDataFrames(mxd, "Crime")[0]
   ```

6. Define the reference layer:

```
refLayer = mapping.ListLayers(mxd, "Burglaries*", df)[0]
```

7. Define the layer to be inserted relative to the reference layer:

```
insertLayer =
mapping.Layer(r"C:\ArcpyBook\data\CityOfSanAntonio.gdb\
Crimes2009")
```

8. Insert the layer into the data frame:

```
mapping.InsertLayer(df,refLayer,insertLayer,"BEFORE")
```

9. You can consult the solution file at `c:\ArcpyBook\code\Ch2\InsertLayerMapDocument.py` to verify the accuracy of your code.

10. Run the script. The **Crimes2009** feature class will be added as a layer to the data frame, as seen in the following screenshot:

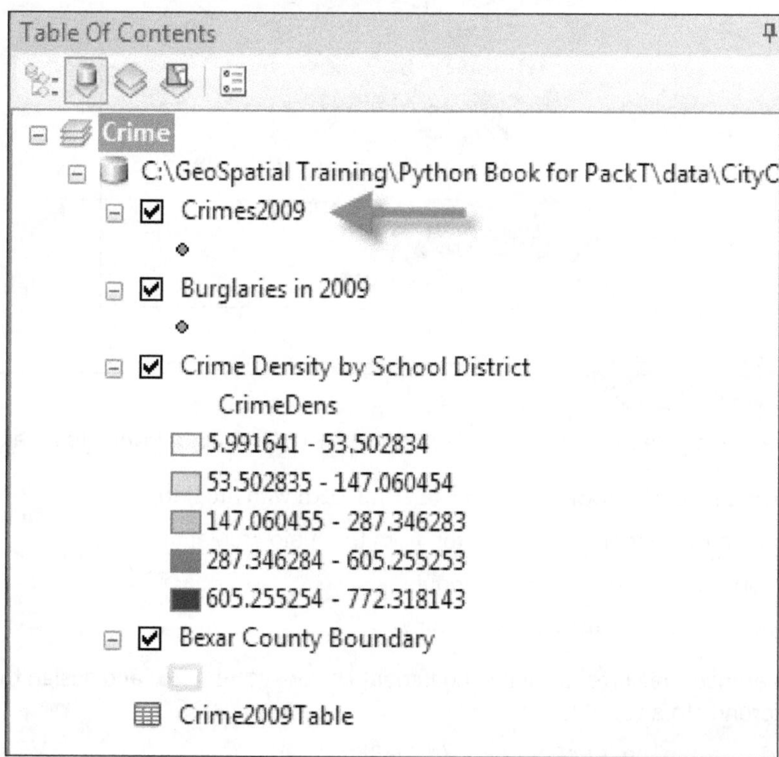

How it works...

After obtaining references to the `arcpy.mapping` module, current map document file, and the **Crime** data frame, our script then defines a reference layer. In this case, we used the `ListLayers()` function with a wildcard of `Burglaries*`, and the **Crime** data frame to restrict the list of layers returned to only one item. This item should be the **Burglaries in 2009** layer. We used Python list access with a value of `0` to retrieve this layer from the list and assigned it to a Layer object. Next, we defined the `insert` layer, a new `Layer` object that references the **Crimes2009** feature class from the `CityOfSanAntonio` geodatabase. Finally, we called the `InsertLayer()` function passing in the data frame, reference layer, layer to be inserted, and keyword indicating that the layer to be inserted should be placed before the reference layer. This is illustrated in the following screenshot:

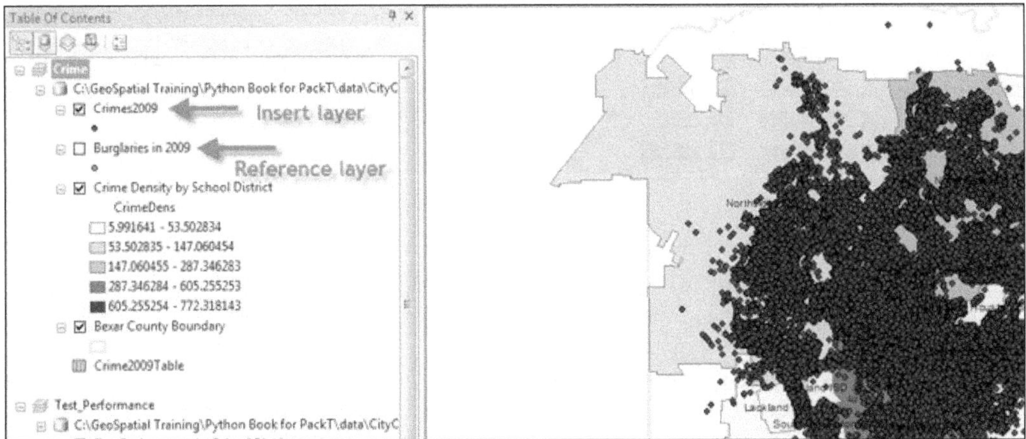

There's more...

You can also reposition a layer that is already in a data frame or a group layer. The `MoveLayer()` function provides the ability to reposition the layer within a data frame or a group layer. Movement of a layer must be within the same data frame. You can't move a layer from one data frame to another. Just as with `InsertLayer()`, `MoveLayer()` uses a reference layer to reposition the layer.

Updating layer symbology

There may be times when you will want to change the symbology of a layer in a map document. This can be accomplished through the use of the `UpdateLayer()` function, which can be used to change the symbology of a layer as well as various properties of a layer. In this recipe, you will use the `UpdateLayer()` function to update the symbology of a layer.

Getting ready

The `arcpy.mapping` module also gives you the capability of updating layer symbology from your scripts by using the `UpdateLayer()` function. For example, you might want your script to update a layer's symbology from a graduated color to a graduated symbol, as illustrated in the following screenshot. `UpdateLayer()` can also be used to update various layer properties, but the default functionality is to update the symbology. Since `UpdateLayer()` is a robust function that is capable of altering both symbology and properties, you do need to understand the various parameters that can be supplied as an input:

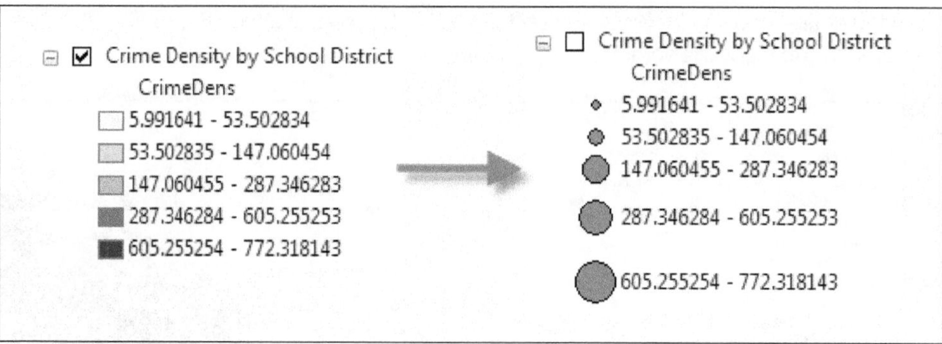

How to do it...

Follow these steps to learn how to update the symbology of a layer using `UpdateLayer()`:

1. Open `c:\ArcpyBook\Ch2\Crime_Ch2.mxd` with ArcMap.
2. Click on the Python window button from the main ArcMap toolbar.
3. Import the `arcpy.mapping` module:

```
import arcpy.mapping as mapping
```

4. Reference the currently active document (`Crime_Ch2.mxd`) and assign the reference to a variable:

```
mxd = mapping.MapDocument("CURRENT")
```

5. Get a reference to the `Crime` data frame:

```
df = mapping.ListDataFrames(mxd, "Crime")[0]
```

6. Define the layer that will be updated:

```
updateLayer = mapping.ListLayers(mxd,"Crime Density by
School District",df)[0]
```

7. Define the layer that will be used to update the symbology:

```
sourceLayer =
mapping.Layer(r"C:\ArcpyBook\data\CrimeDensityGradSym.lyr")
```

8. Call the `UpdateLayer()` function to update the symbology:

```
mapping.UpdateLayer(df,updateLayer,sourceLayer,True)
```

9. You can consult the solution file at `c:\ArcpyBook\code\Ch2\UpdateLayerSymbology.py` to verify the accuracy of your code.
10. Run the script. The **Crime Density by School District** layer will now be symbolized with graduated symbols instead of graduated colors, as shown in the following screenshot:

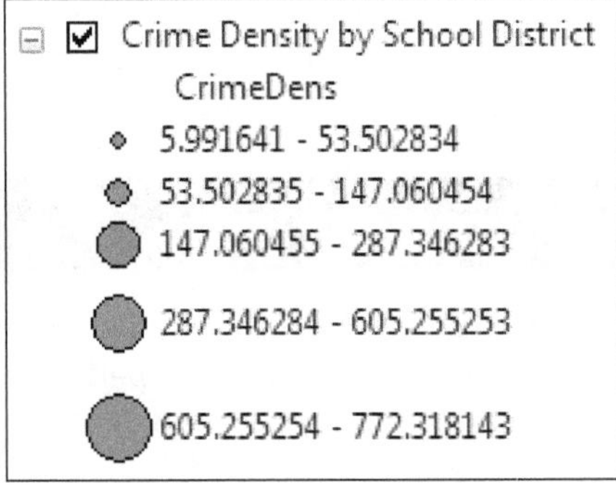

How it works...

In this recipe, we used the `UpdateLayer()` function to update the symbology of a layer. We didn't update any properties, but we'll do so in the next recipe. The `UpdateLayer()` function requires that you pass several parameters including a data frame, layer to be updated, and a reference layer from which the symbology will be pulled and applied to update the layer. In our code, the `updateLayer` variable holds a reference to the **Crime Density by School District** layer, which will have its symbology updated. The source layer from which the symbology will be pulled and applied to the updated layer is a layer file (`CrimeDensityGradSym.lyr`), containing graduated symbols.

To update the symbology for a layer, you must first ensure that the update layer and the source layer have the same geometry (point, line, or polygon). You also need to check that the attribute definitions are the same in some cases, depending upon the renderer. For example, graduated color symbology and graduated symbols are based on a particular attribute. In this case, both the layers had polygon geometry and a `CrimeDens` field containing crime density information.

Once we had references to both the layers, we called the `UpdateLayer()` function, passing in the data frame and layers along with a fourth parameter that indicated that we're updating symbology only. We supplied a `True` value as this fourth parameter, indicating that we were only updating the symbology and not properties:

```
mapping.UpdateLayer(df,updateLayer,sourceLayer,True)
```

There's more...

The `UpdateLayer()` function also provides the ability to remove one layer and add another layer in its place. The layers can be completely unrelated, so there is no need to ensure that the geometry type and attribute field are the same as you would when redefining the symbology of a layer. This switching of layers essentially executes a call to `RemoveLayer()` and then a call to `AddLayer()` as one operation. To take advantage of this functionality, you must set the `symbology_only` parameter to `False`.

Updating layer properties

In the previous recipe, you learned how to update the symbology of a layer. As I mentioned, `UpdateLayer()` can also be used to update various properties of a layer, such as field aliases, query definitions, and others. In this recipe, you will use `UpdateLayer()` to alter various properties of a layer.

Getting ready

You can also use the `UpdateLayer()` function to update a limited number of layer properties. Specific layer properties, such as field aliases, selection symbology, query definitions, label fields, and others, can be updated using `UpdateLayer()`. A common scenario is to have a layer in many map documents that needs to have a specific property changed across all the instances of the layer in all map documents. To accomplish this, you will have to use ArcMap to modify the layer with the appropriate properties and save it to a layer file. This layer file then becomes the source layer, which will be used to update the properties of another layer called `update_layer`. In this recipe, you'll use ArcMap to alter the properties of a layer, save to a layer file (`.lyr`) and then use Python to write a script that uses `UpdateLayer()` to apply the properties to another layer.

How to do it...

Follow these steps to learn how to update layer properties with `UpdateLayer()`:

1. Open `c:\ArcpyBook\Ch2\Crime_Ch2.mxd` with ArcMap. For this recipe, you will be working with the **Burglaries in 2009** feature class, as shown in the following screenshot:

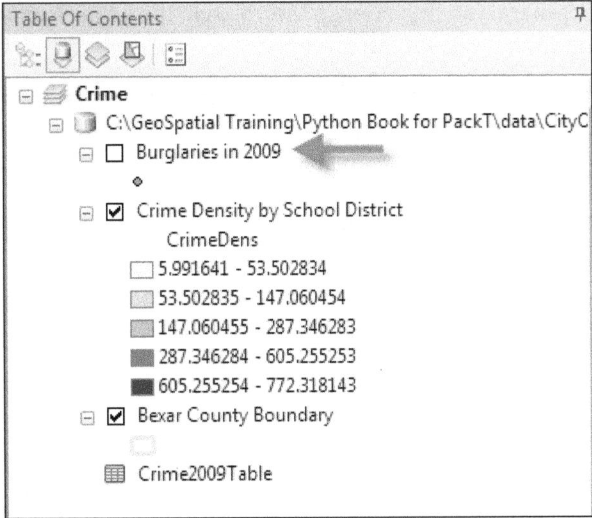

2. Double-click on the **Burglaries in 2009** feature class in the **Crime** data frame to display the **Layer Properties** window, as shown in the following screenshot. Each of the tabs represents properties that can be set for this layer:

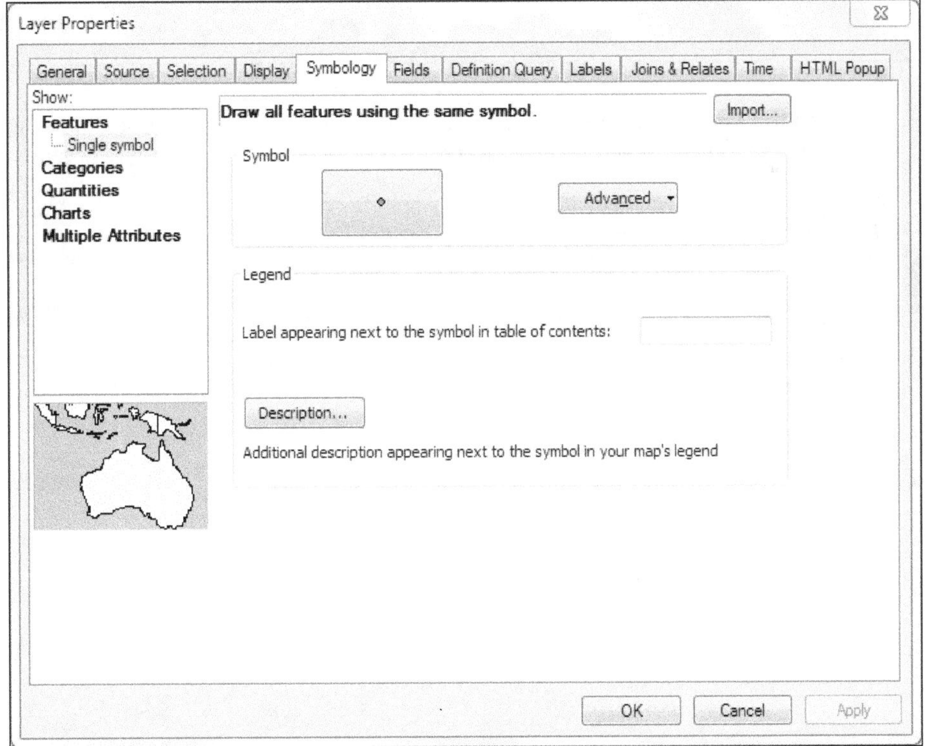

3. Click on the **General** tab and change the value in the **Layer Name:** textbox to the name, as shown in the following screenshot:

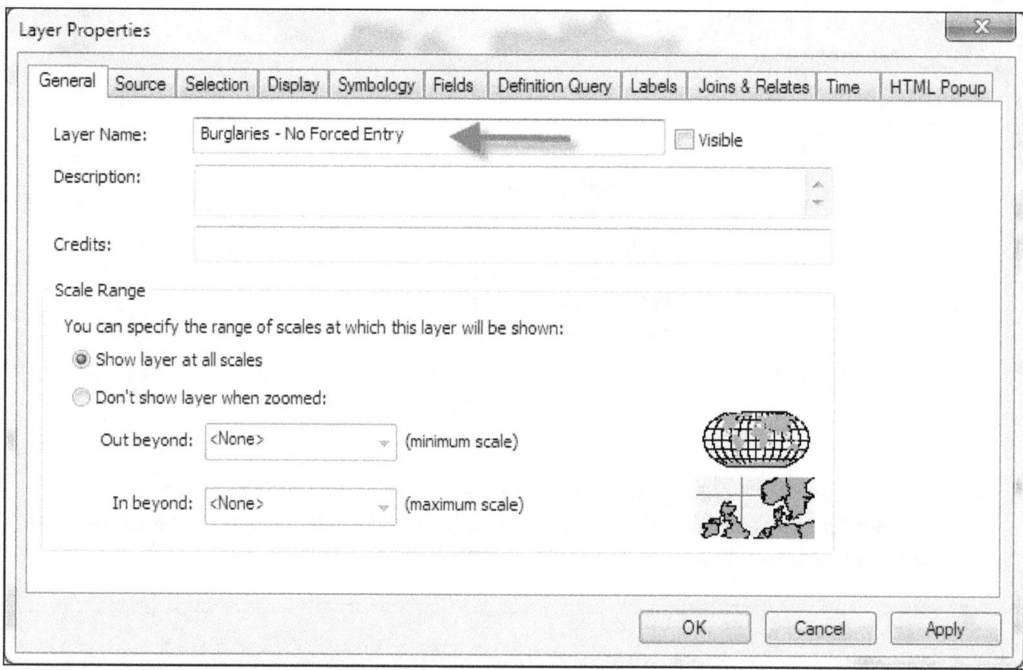

4. Click on the **Definition Query** tab and define the query, as shown in the following screenshot. You can use the **Query Builder...** button to define the query or simply type in the query:

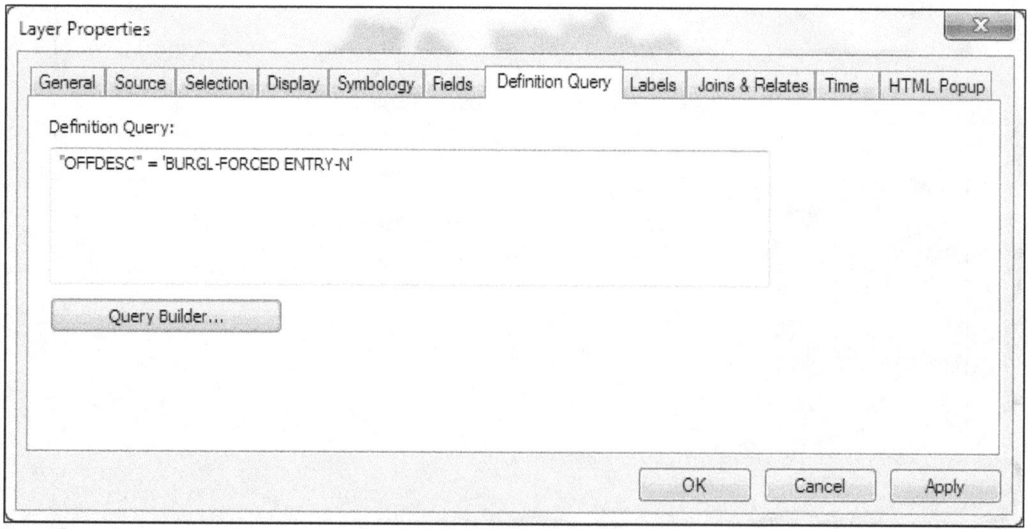

5. Change the alias of the `OFFDESC` field to `Offense Description`, as shown in the next screenshot.
6. Click on the **Fields** tab in **Layer Properties** and make visible only those fields that are selected with a checkmark in the following screenshot. This is done by unchecking the fields that you see in the following screenshot:

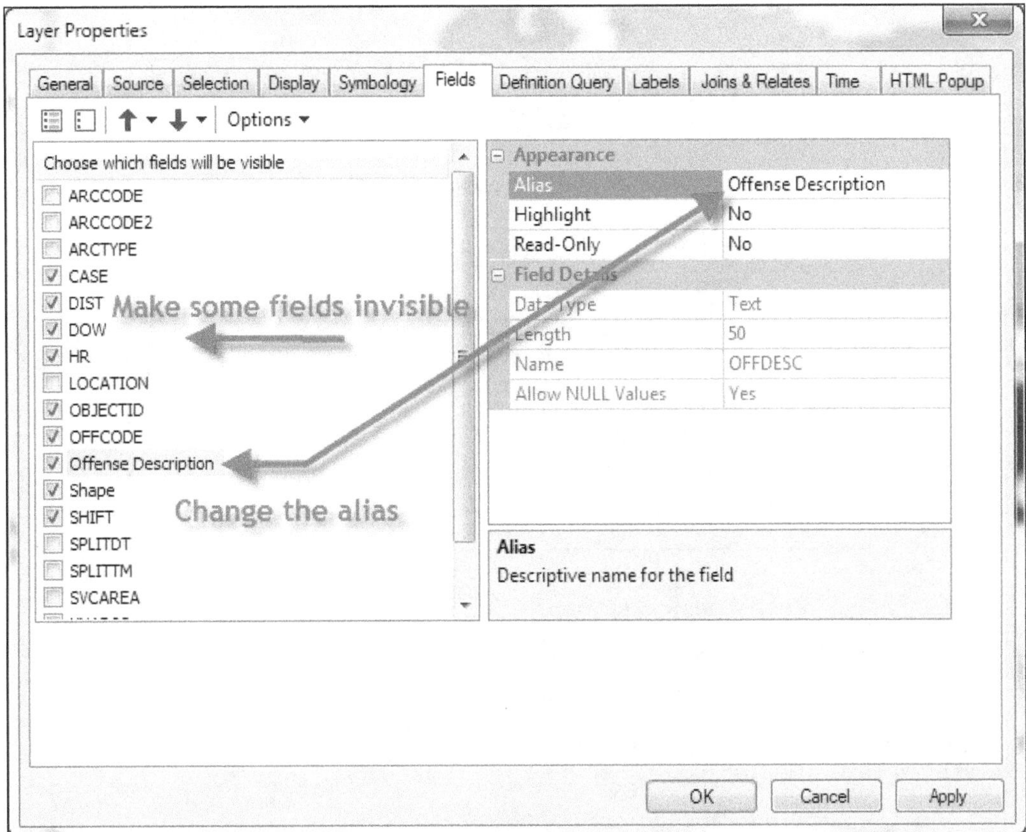

7. Click on **OK** to dismiss the **Layer Properties** dialog.
8. In the data frame, right-click on **Burglaries – No Forced Entry** and select **Save as Layer File**.
9. Save the file as `c:\ArcpyBook\data\BurglariesNoForcedEntry.lyr`.
10. Right-click on the **Burglaries – No Forced Entry** layer and select **Remove**.

11. Using the **Add Data** button in ArcMap, add the `Crimes2009` feature class from the `CityOfSanAntonio` geodatabase. The feature class will be added to the data frame, as shown in the following screenshot:

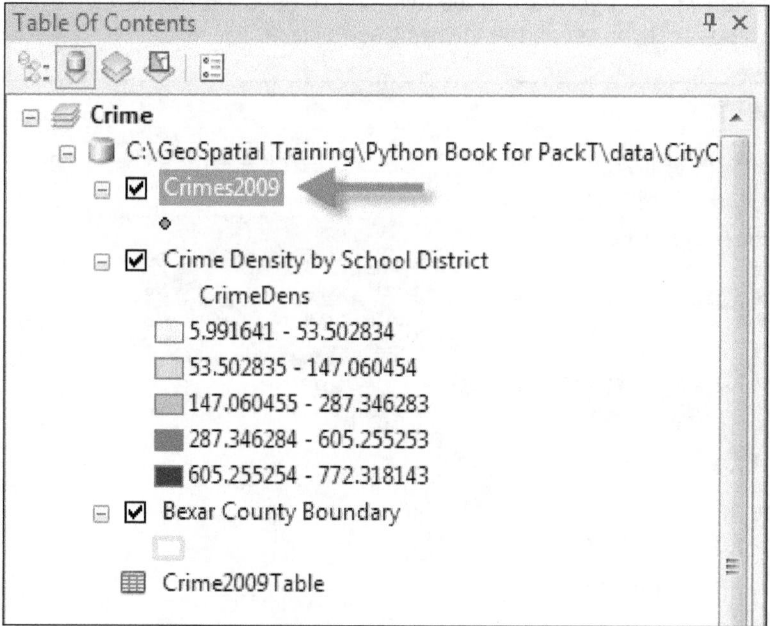

12. Open the Python window in ArcMap.
13. Import the `arcpy.mapping` module:

```
import arcpy.mapping as mapping
```

14. Reference the currently active document (`Crime_Ch2.mxd`) and assign the reference to a variable:

```
mxd = mapping.MapDocument("CURRENT")
```

15. Get a reference to the `Crime` data frame:

```
df = mapping.ListDataFrames(mxd, "Crime")[0]
```

16. Define the layer that will be updated:

```
updateLayer = mapping.ListLayers(mxd,"Crimes2009",df)[0]
```

17. Define the layer that will be used to update the properties:

```
sourceLayer =
mapping.Layer(r"C:\ArcpyBook\data\
BurglariesNoForcedEntry.lyr")
```

18. Call the `UpdateLayer()` function to update the symbology:

```
mapping.UpdateLayer(df,updateLayer,sourceLayer,False)
```

19. You can consult the solution file at `c:\ArcpyBook\code\Ch2\UpdateLayerProperties.py` to verify the accuracy of your code.
20. Run the script.
21. The **Crimes2009** layer will be updated with the properties associated with the `BurglariesNoForcedEntry.lyr` file. This is illustrated in the following screenshot. Turn on the layer to view the definition query that has been applied. You can also open the **Layer Properties** dialog to view the property changes that have been applied to the **Crimes2009** feature class:

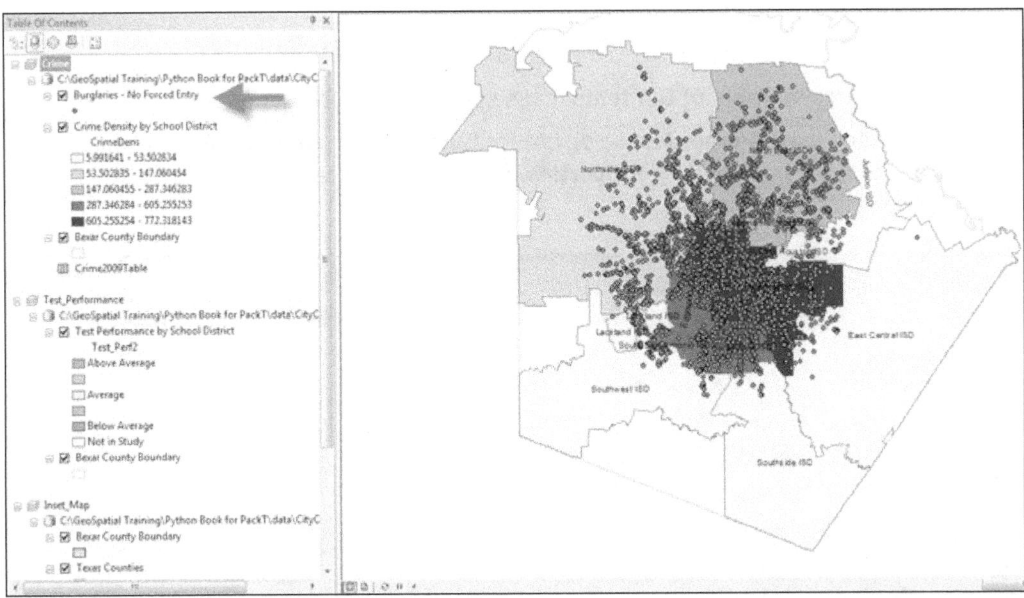

Working with time-enabled layers in a data frame

In this recipe, you will learn how to time-enable a layer and data frame. You will then write a script that cycles through the time range for the layer and exports a PDF map showing crimes through time in seven-day intervals.

Getting ready

The `DataFrameTime` object provides access to time management operations for time-enabled layers in a data frame. This object is returned when you reference the `DataFrame.time` property, and includes properties for retrieving the current time, end time, start time, time step interval, and others that are established by using the **Time Slider Options** dialog box and then saved with the map document. One or more layers in a data frame must be time-enabled for this functionality to be operational.

How to do it...

Follow these steps to learn how to work with time-enabled layers:

1. Open `c:\ArcpyBook\Ch2\Crime_Ch2.mxd` with ArcMap.
2. In the ArcMap **Table Of Contents** make sure `Crime` is the active data frame.
3. Open the **Layer Properties** dialog box for **Burglaries in 2009** by right-clicking on the layer and selecting **Properties**. Select the **Time** tab, as shown in the following screenshot:

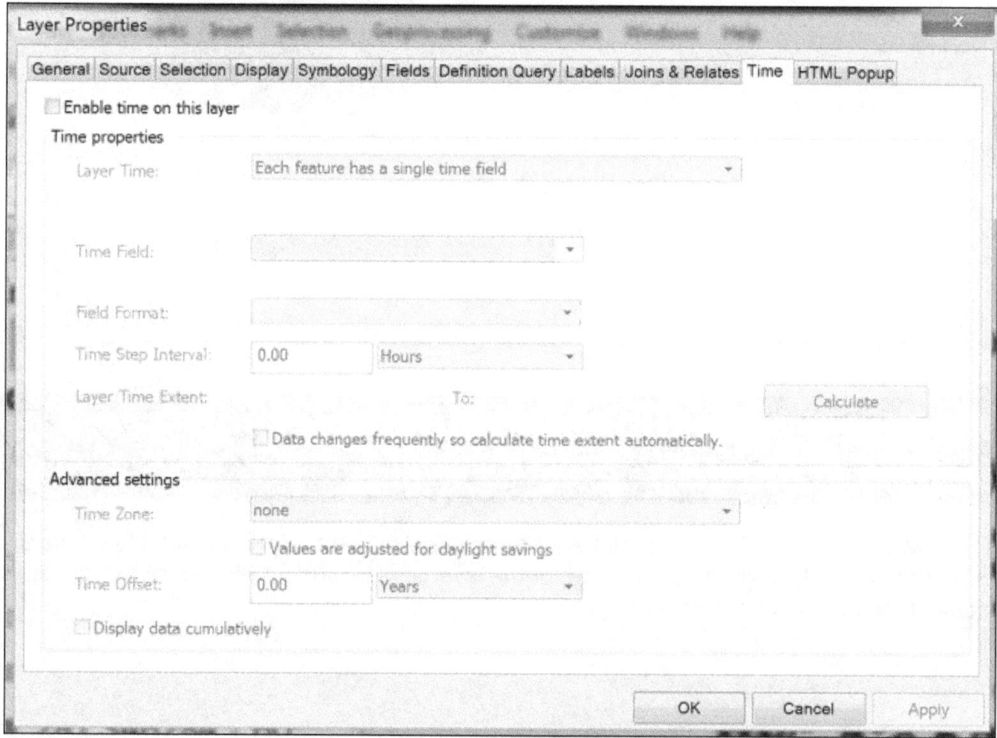

Enable time for the layer by clicking on the **Enable time on this layer** checkbox.

4. Under **Time properties**, select **Each feature has a single time field** for **Layer Time:**. Select the **SPLITDT** field for the **Time Field:**. Define a **Time Step Interval:** of **7.00 Days**, as shown in the following screenshot:

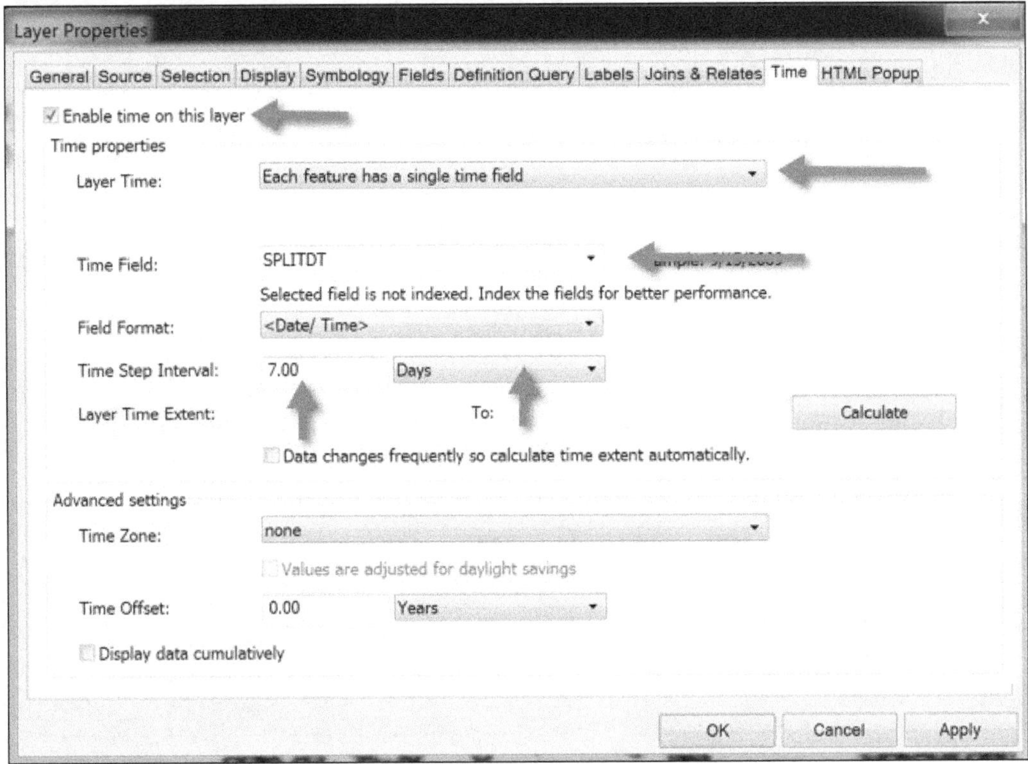

Define the **Layer Time Extent:** by clicking the **Calculate** button, circled in the following screenshot:

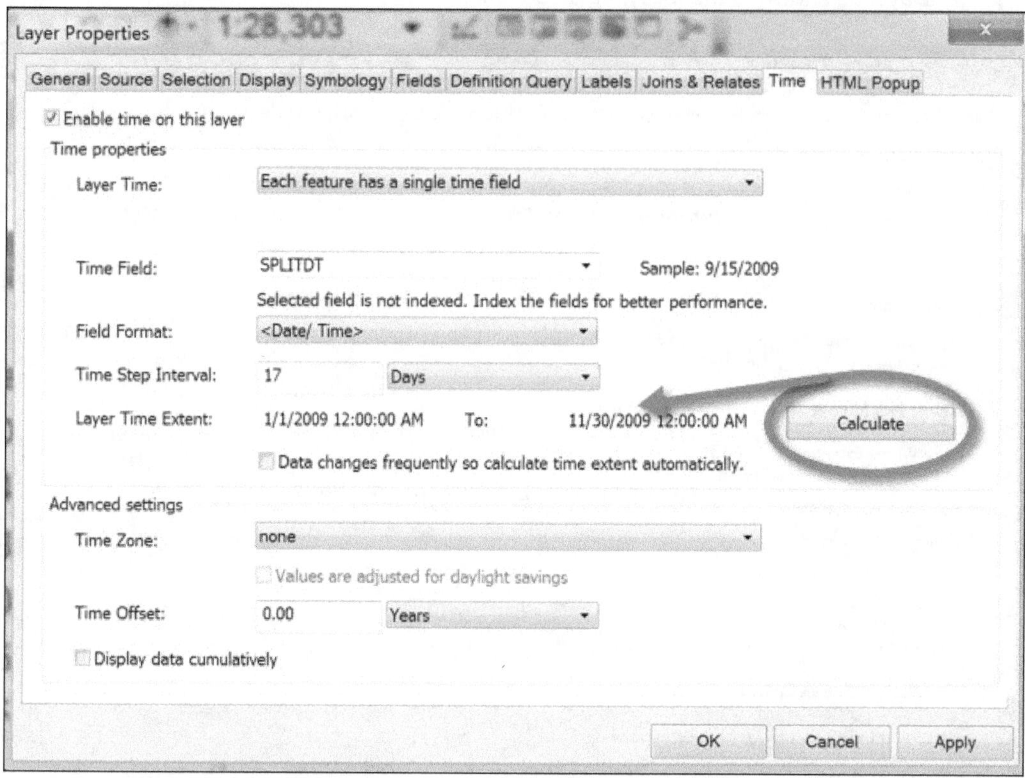

5. Check the **Time Step Interval:** field. You may need to reset that to **7 Days**.
6. Click on **Apply** and then **OK**.
7. In the ArcMap **Tools** toolbar, select the time slider options button to display the **Time Slider Options** dialog as shown in the following screenshot:

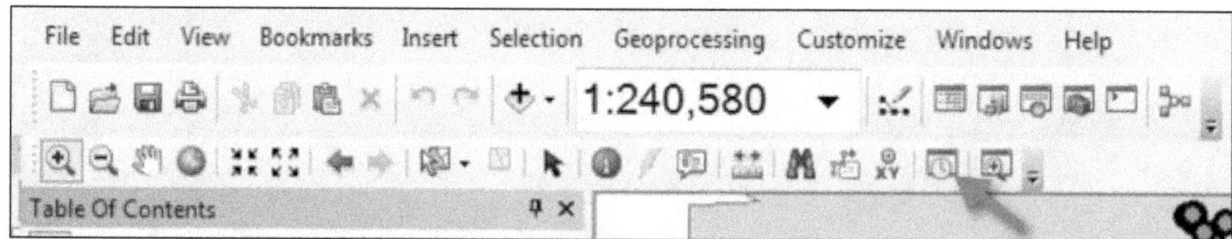

8. On the **Time Display** tab of the **Time Slider Options** dialog, make sure **Time step interval:** is set to **7.0 days.** If not, set it to **7.0 days**. Do the same for the **Time window:** option.

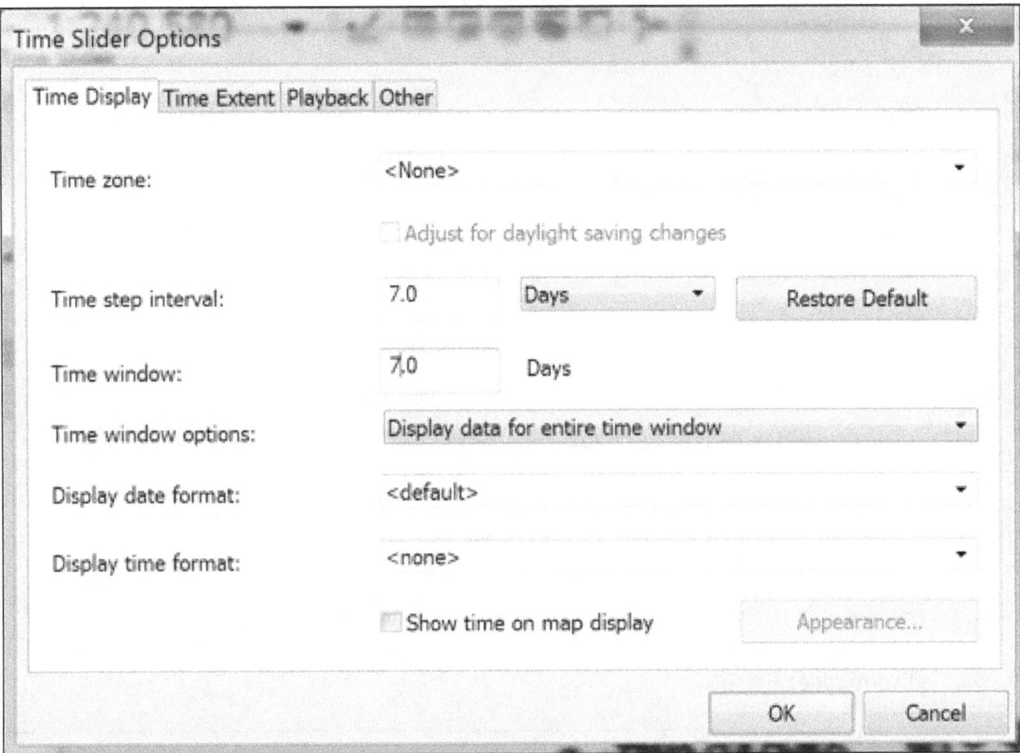

9. Click on **OK**.
10. Save your map document. It's very important that you save the time-enabled data with your map document. The code you write next won't work unless you do so.
11. Open the Python Window.
12. Import the `arcpy.mapping` module:

    ```
    import arcpy.mapping as mapping
    ```

13. Reference the currently active document (`Crime_Ch2.mxd`), and assign the reference to a variable:

    ```
    mxd = mapping.MapDocument("CURRENT")
    ```

14. Retrieve the `Crime` data frame:

    ```
    df = mapping.ListDataFrames(mxd, "Crime")[0]
    ```

15. Generate the `DataFrameTime` object:

    ```
    dft = df.time
    ```

16. Set the `DataFrameTime.currentTime` property to the `DataFrameTime.startTime` property:

    ```
    dft.currentTime = dft.startTime
    ```

17. Start a `while` loop that will loop through the time while the `currentTime` is less than or equal to the `endTime`:

    ```
    while dft.currentTime <= dft.endTime:
    ```

18. Inside the while loop, create a file for each PDF that will be created, export the PDF, and reset the `currentTime` property. The entire `while` loop should appear as follows:

    ```
    while dft.currentTime <= dft.endTime:
            fileName = str(dft.currentTime).split(" ")[0] +
            ".pdf"

            mapping.ExportToPDF(mxd,os.path.join(r"C:\ArcpyBook\Ch2",
            fileName), df)
            print("Exported " + fileName)
            dft.currentTime = dft.currentTime +
    dft.timeStepInterval
    ```

19. The entire script should appear as follows. You can consult the solution file at `c:\ArcpyBook\code\Ch2\TimeEnabledLayers.py` to verify the accuracy of your code:

```
import arcpy.mapping as mapping, os
mxd = mapping.MapDocument("CURRENT")
df = mapping.ListDataFrames(mxd, "Crime")[0]
dft = df.time
dft.currentTime = dft.startTime

while dft.currentTime <= dft.endTime:
    fileName = str(dft.currentTime).split(" ")[0] + ".pdf"
    mapping.ExportToPDF(mxd,os.path.join(r"C:\ArcpyBook\Ch2", fileName))
    print("Exported " + fileName)
    dft.currentTime = dft.currentTime + dft.timeStepInterval
```

How it works...

The `DataFrameTime` object provides access to time management operations in a data frame. Several properties of `DataFrameTime`, including `currentTime`, `startTime`, `endTime`, and `timeStepInterval`, are used in this recipe. Initially, we set the `currentTime` property equal to the `startTime` property. The initial `startTime` was calculated when you set the **Time Step Interval:** properties in ArcMap. The `while` loop was set up to loop as long as the `currentTime` property is greater than the `endTime` property. Inside the loop, we created a `fileName` variable that is set to the `currentTime` property, plus an extension of `.pdf`. We then called the `ExportToPDF()` function, passing in a path and the filename. This should ideally export the page layout view to the PDF file. Finally, we updated the `currentTime` property by the `timeStepInterval` property that was set to **7.0 days** in in the **Time Step Interval:** properties dialog.

3

Finding and Fixing Broken Data Links

In this chapter, we will cover the following recipes:

- Finding broken data sources in your map document and layer files
- Fixing broken data sources with MapDocument.findAndReplaceWorkspacePaths()
- Fixing broken data sources with MapDocument.replaceWorkspaces()
- Fixing individual layer and table objects with replaceDataSource()
- Finding broken data sources in all map documents in a folder

Introduction

It is not uncommon for your GIS data sources to move, migrate to a new data format, or be deleted. The result can be broken data sources in many map documents or layer files. These broken data sources can't be used until they're fixed, which can be an overwhelming process if the same changes need to be made across numerous map documents. You can automate the process of finding and fixing these data sources using `arcpy.mapping`, without ever having to open the affected map documents. Finding broken data sources is a simple process requiring the use of the `ListBrokenDataSources()` function, which returns a Python list of all broken data sources in a map document or layer file. Typically, this function is used as the first step in a script that iterates through the list and fixes the data source. Fixing broken data sources can be made in an individual data layer or across all layers in a common workspace.

Finding broken data sources in your map document and layer files

Broken data sources are a very common problem with map document files. You can use `arcpy.mapping` to identify data sources that have moved, been deleted, or changed in their format.

Getting ready

In ArcMap, a broken data connection is signified by a red exclamation point just before the layer name. This is illustrated in the following screenshot. The `ListBrokenDataSources()` function in `arcpy.mapping` returns a list of layer objects from a map document or layer file that have a broken data connection:

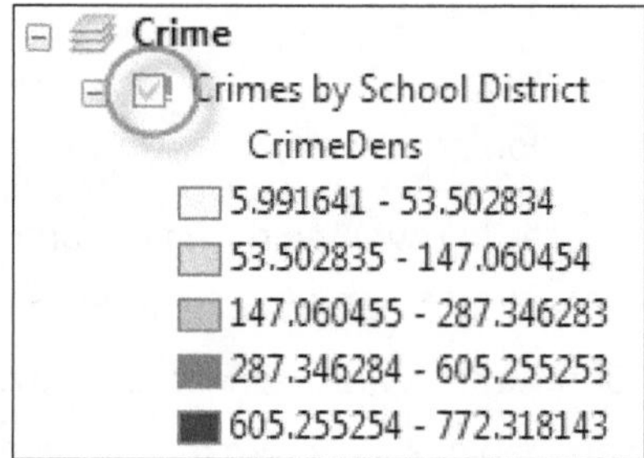

How to do it...

Follow these steps to learn how to find broken data sources in a map document file.

1. Open `C:\ArcpyBook\Ch3\Crime_BrokenDataLinks.mxd` in ArcMap.

   You will see that each of the data sources have been broken. In this case, the data has been moved to another folder, but you'd see the same indicator if the data had been deleted or migrated to a different format. For example, it is not uncommon to convert data from a personal geodatabase to a file geodatabase:

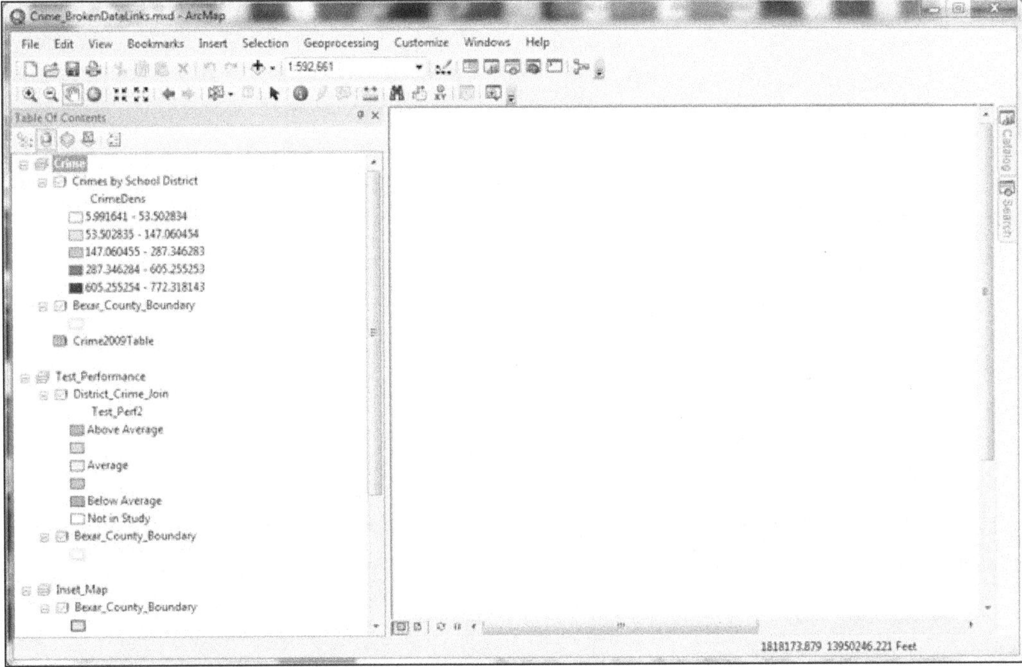

2. Close ArcMap.
3. Open **IDLE** and create a new script window.
4. Import the `arcpy.mapping` module:

```
import arcpy.mapping as mapping
```

5. Reference the `Crime_BrokenDataLinks.mxd` map document file:

```
mxd =
mapping.MapDocument(
r"c:\ArcpyBook\Ch3\Crime_BrokenDataLinks.mxd")
```

6. Get a list of the broken data sources:

```
listBrokenDS = mapping.ListBrokenDataSources(mxd)
```

7. Iterate the list and print out the layer names:

```
for layer in listBrokenDS:
    print(layer.name)
```

The output will be printed as follows:

```
District_Crime_Join
Bexar_County_Boundary
District_Crime_Join
Bexar_County_Boundary
Bexar_County_Boundary
Texas_Counties_LowRes
School_Districts
Crime_surf
Bexar_County_Boundary
Crime2009Table
```

8. Save your script as `FindFixBrokenData.py` in the `c:\ArcpyBook\Ch3` folder.
9. You can check your work by examining the `c:\ArcpyBook\code\Ch3\FindFixBrokenData.py` solution file.

How it works...

The `ListBrokenDataSources()` function returns a Python list of `Layer` objects that have a broken data source. We then use a `for` loop to iterate this list and perform some sort of action for each layer. In this case, we printed out the layer names simply to illustrate the data returned by this function. In a later recipe, we'll build on this code by fixing these broken data sources.

There's more...

In addition to returning a list of broken data sources from a map document file, the `ListBrokenDataSources()` function can also find broken data sources in a (`.lyr`) layer file. Simply pass the path to the layer file to have the function examine the file for broken data sources. Keep in mind that these functions are not needed with `Map` or `Layer` packages, since the data is bundled with these files unlike a layer file.

Fixing broken data sources with MapDocument. findAndReplaceWorkspacePaths()

The `MapDocument.findAndReplaceWorkspacePaths()` method is used to perform global find and replace workspace paths for all the layers and tables in a map document. You can also replace the paths to multiple workspace types at once. For example, you might pass personal and file geodatabase workspace types at the same time.

Getting ready

We need to cover some definitions before examining the methods used to fix datasets. You'll see these terms used frequently when discussing the methods used to fix broken data sources, so you'll need to understand what they mean in this context. A **workspace** is simply a container for data. This can be a folder (in the case of shapefiles), personal geodatabase, file geodatabase, or an ArcSDE connection. A workspace provides the system path to the workspace. In the case of file geodatabases, this would include the name of the geodatabase. A **dataset** is simply a feature class or table within a workspace, and finally, a **data source** is the combination of the workspace and dataset names. Don't confuse a dataset with a feature dataset. The former is just a generic term for data, while the latter is an object within a geodatabase that serves as a container for feature classes and other datasets.

There are three `arcpy.mapping` classes involved in fixing broken data sources. They are `MapDocument`, `Layer`, and `TableView`. Each class contains methods that can be used to fix data sources. In this recipe, we'll examine how you can use the `findAndReplaceWorkspacePaths()` method in the `MapDocument` class to perform global find and replace operations in the layers and tables of a map document.

How to do it...

Follow these steps to learn how to fix layers and tables in a map document using `findAndReplaceWorkspacePaths()`:

1. Open `c:\ArcpyBook\Ch3\Crime_BrokenDataLinks.mxd` in ArcMap.
2. Right-click on any of the layers and select **Properties**.
3. Go to the **Source** tab and you will notice that the location for the layer is `ArcpyBook\Ch3\Data\OldData\CityOfSanAntonio.gdb`. This is a file geodatabase but the location no longer exists. It has moved to the `C:\ArcpyBook\data` folder.
4. Open **IDLE** and create a new script window.
5. Import the `arcpy.mapping` module:

```
import arcpy.mapping as mapping
```

6. Reference the `Crime_BrokenDataLinks.mxd` map document file:

```
mxd =
mapping.MapDocument(
r"c:\ArcpyBook\Ch3\Crime_BrokenDataLinks.mxd")
```

7. Use `MapDocument.findAndReplaceWorkspacePaths()` to fix the source path for each data source in the map document. The `findAndReplaceWorksapcePaths()` method accepts the old path as the first parameter and the new path as the second parameter:

```
mxd.findAndReplaceWorkspacePaths(r"
C:\ArcpyBook\Ch3\Data\OldData\CityOfSanAntonio.gdb", r"
C:\ArcpyBook\Data\CityOfSanAntonio.gdb")
```

8. Save the results to a new `.mxd` file:

```
mxd.saveACopy(r"C:\ArcpyBook\Ch3\Crime_DataLinksFixed.mxd")
```

9. Save the script as `C:\ArcpyBook\Ch3\MapDocumentFindReplaceWorkspacePath.py`.
10. You can check your work by examining the `c:\ArcpyBook\code\Ch3\MapDocumentFindReplaceWorkspacePath.py` solution file.
11. Run the script.
12. In ArcMap, open the `C:\ArcpyBook\Ch3\Crime_DataLinksFixed.mxd` file. You will notice that all the data sources get fixed, as shown in the following screenshot:

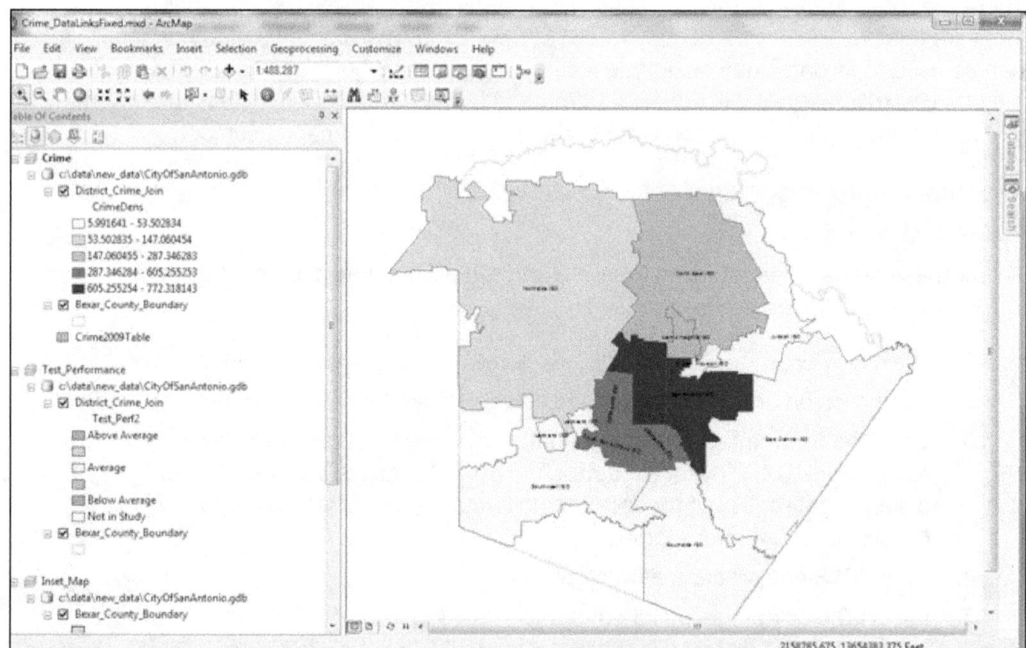

How it works...

The `MapDocument.findAndReplaceWorkspacePaths()` method performs global find and replace workspace paths for all layers and tables in a map document. You can replace the paths for multiple workspace types at once.

There's more...

The `Layer` and `TableView` objects also have a `findAndReplaceWorkspacePaths()` method that performs the same type of operation. The difference is that this method, in the `Layer` and `TableView` objects, is used to fix an individual broken data source rather than a global find, along with the replacement of all broken data sources in a map document.

Fixing broken data sources with MapDocument.replaceWorkspaces()

During the course of normal GIS operations, it is a fairly common practice to migrate data from one file type to another. For example, many organizations migrate data from older personal geodatabase formats to the new file geodatabase types, or perhaps even enterprise ArcSDE geodatabases. You can automate the process of updating your datasets to a different format with `MapDocument.replaceWorkspaces()`.

Getting ready

`MapDocument.replaceWorkspaces()` is similar to `MapDocument.findAndReplaceWorkspacePaths()`, but it also allows you to switch from one workspace type to another. For example, you can switch from a file geodatabase to a personal geodatabase. However, it only works in one workspace at a time. In this recipe, we'll use `MapDocument.replaceWorkspaces()` to switch our data source from a file geodatabase to a personal geodatabase.

How to do it...

Follow these steps to learn how to fix broken data sources using `MapDocument.replaceWorkspaces()`:

1. Open `c:\ArcpyBook\Ch3\Crime_DataLinksFixed.mxd` in ArcMap.

2. Notice that all of the layers and tables are loaded from a file geodatabase called `CityOfSanAntonio.gdb`, as shown in the following screenshot:

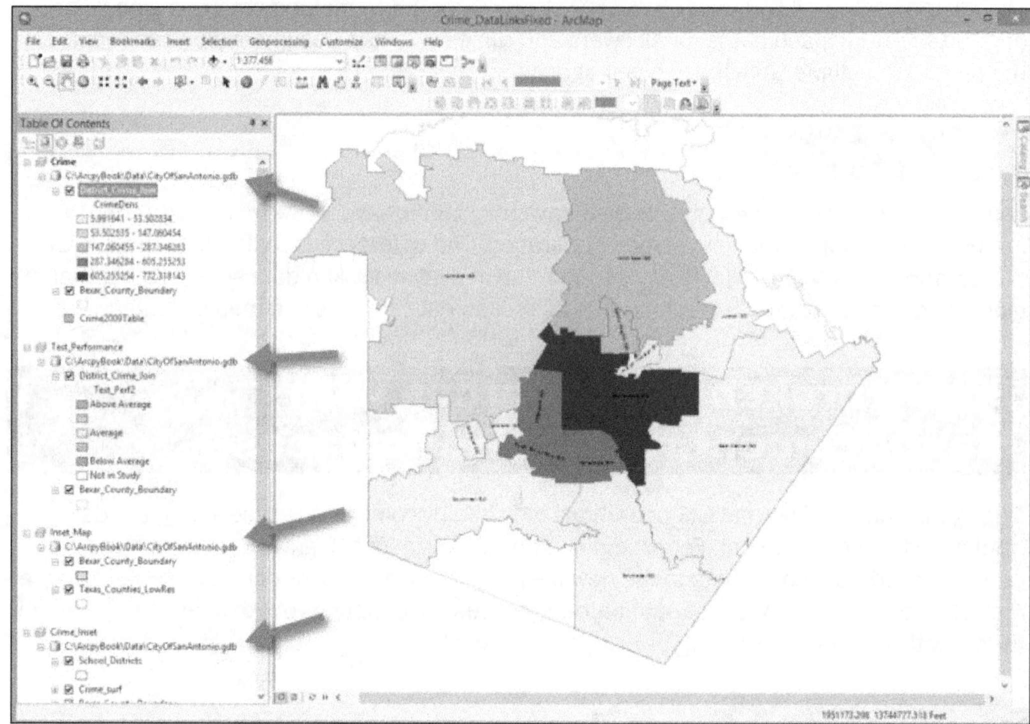

3. Open **IDLE** and create a new script window.
4. Import the `arcpy.mapping` module:

```
import arcpy.mapping as mapping
```

5. Reference the `Crime_DataLinksFixed.mxd` map document file:

```
mxd =
mapping.MapDocument(r
"c:\ArcpyBook\Ch3\Crime_DataLinksFixed.mxd")
```

6. Call the `replaceWorkspaces()` method, passing a reference to the old geodatabase type as well as the new geodatabase type:

```
mxd.replaceWorkspaces(r"c:\ArcpyBook
\data\CityOfSanAntonio.gdb",
"FILEGDB_WORKSPACE",r"c:\ArcpyBook
\new_data\CityOfSanAntonio_Personal.mdb","ACCESS_WORKSPACE"
)
```

7. Save a copy of the map document file:

```
mxd.saveACopy(r
"c:\ArcpyBook\Ch3\Crime_DataLinksUpdated.mxd")
```

8. Save the script as `c:\ArcpyBook\Ch3\MapDocumentReplaceWorkspaces.py`.
9. You can check your work by examining the `c:\ArcpyBook\code\Ch3\MapDocumentReplaceWorkspaces.py` solution file.
10. Run the script.
11. In ArcMap, open the `c:\ArcpyBook\Ch3\Crime_DataLinksUpdated.mxd` file. As shown in the following screenshot, all data sources now reference a personal geodatabase (note the `.mdb` extension):

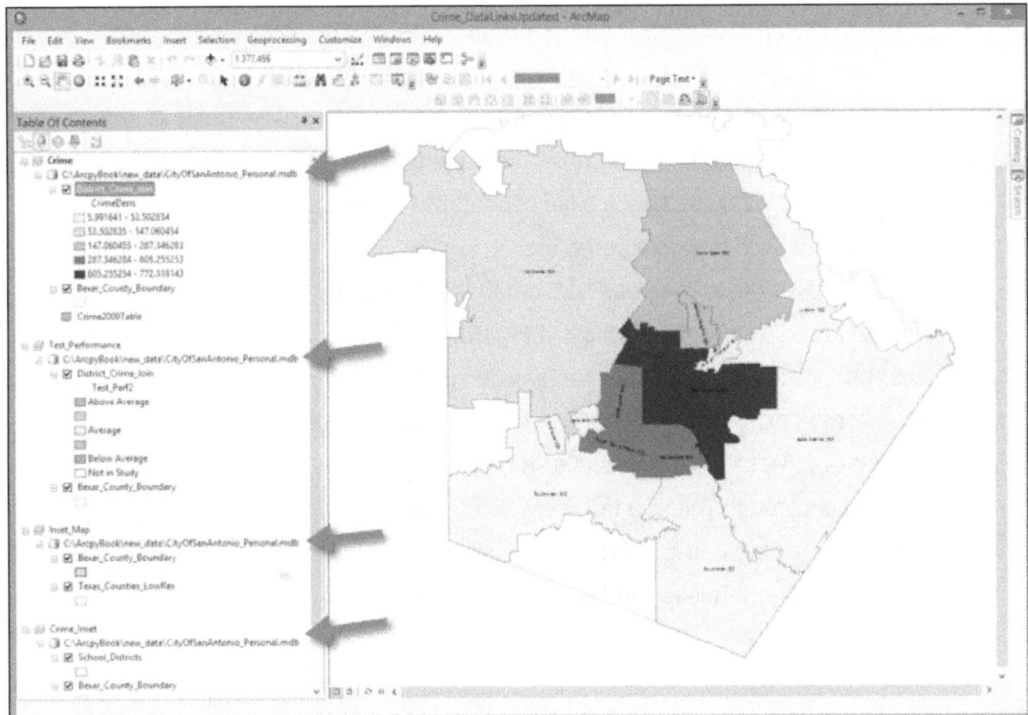

How it works...

The `MapDocument.replaceWorkspaces()` method accepts several parameters including old and new workspace paths along with the old and new workspace types. Paths to the workspaces are self-explanatory, but some discussion of the workspace types is helpful. The workspace types are passed into the method as string keywords. In this case, the old workspace type was a file geodatabase so its keyword is `FILEGDB_WORKSPACE`. The new workspace type is `ACCESS_WORKSPACE`, which indicates a personal geodatabase. Personal geodatabases are stored in Microsoft Access files. There are a number of different workspace types that can store GIS data. Make sure you provide the workspace type that is appropriate for your dataset. The following is a list of valid workspace types (many people still work with shapefiles so, in this case, the workspace type would be `SHAPEFILE_WORKSPACE`):

- `ACCESS_WORKSPACE`: This is a personal geodatabase or Access workspace
- `ARCINFO_WORKSPACE`: This is an ArcInfo coverage workspace
- `CAD_WORKSPACE`: This is a CAD file workspace
- `EXCEL_WORKSPACE`: This is an Excel file workspace
- `FILEGDB_WORKSPACE`: This is a file geodatabase workspace
- `NONE`: This is used to skip a parameter
- `OLEDB_WORKSPACE`: This is an OLE database workspace
- `PCCOVERAGE_WORKSPACE`: This is a PC ARC/INFO Coverage workspace
- `RASTER_WORKSPACE`: This is a raster workspace
- `SDE_WORKSPACE`: This is an SDE geodatabase workspace
- `SHAPEFILE_WORKSPACE`: This is a shapefile workspace
- `TEXT_WORKSPACE`: This is a text file workspace
- `TIN_WORKSPACE`: This is a TIN workspace
- `VPF_WORKSPACE`: This is a VPF workspace

When switching workspaces via the `replaceWorkspaces()` method, the dataset names must be identical. For example, a shapefile called `Highways.shp` can be redirected to a file geodatabase workspace only if the dataset name in the file geodatabase is also called `Highways`. Use the `replaceDataSource()` method on the `layer` or `TableView` objects if the dataset name is different.

Fixing individual layer and table objects with replaceDataSource()

The previous recipes in this chapter have used various methods on the `MapDocument` object to fix broken data links. The `Layer` and `TableView` objects also have methods that can be used to fix broken data links at the individual object level rather than working on all datasets in a map document file. This recipe discusses the repairing of `Layer` and `TableView` objects.

Getting ready

Both the `Layer` and `TableView` classes have a `replaceDataSource()` method. This method changes the workspace path, workspace type, and/or dataset name for a single layer or table. In this recipe, you'll write a script that changes the workspace path and workspace type for a single layer. The `replaceDataSource()` method is available for the `Layer` and `TableView` classes. In the case of a layer, it can either be in a map document or layer file. For a table, it can refer to the map document only, since `TableView` objects can't be contained inside a layer file.

How to do it...

Follow these steps to learn how to fix individual `Layer` and `TableView` objects in a map document using `replaceDataSource()`:

Open `c:\ArcpyBook\Ch3\Crime_DataLinksLayer.mxd` in ArcMap. The Crime data frame contains a layer called **Burglary**, which is a feature class in the `CityOfSanAntonio` file geodatabase. You're going to replace this feature class with a shapefile layer containing the same data:

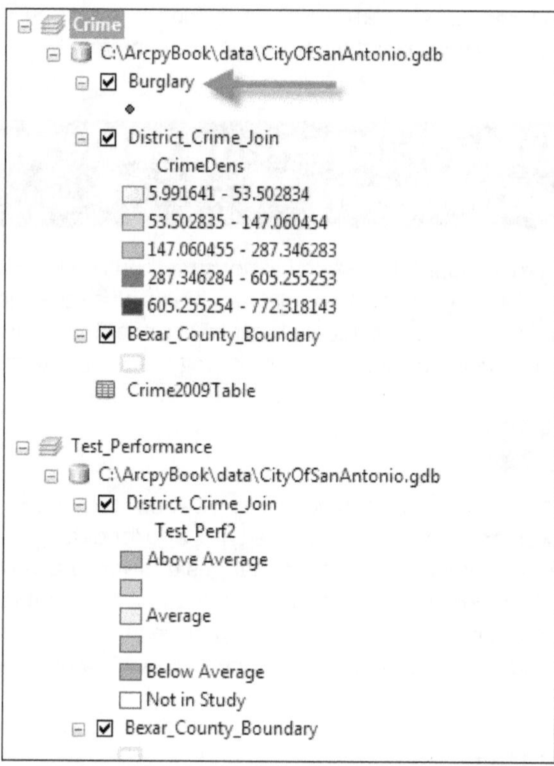

1. Open **IDLE** and create a new script window.
2. Import the `arcpy.mapping` module:

   ```
   import arcpy.mapping as mapping
   ```

3. Reference the `Crime_DataLinksLayer.mxd` map document file:

   ```
   mxd = mapping.MapDocument(r"c:\ArcpyBook\Ch3\
   Crime_DataLinksLayer.mxd")
   ```

4. Get a reference to the `Crime` data frame:

   ```
   df = mapping.ListDataFrames(mxd,"Crime")[0]
   ```

5. Find the **Burglary** layer and store it in a variable:

   ```
   lyr = mapping.ListLayers(mxd,"Burglary",df)[0]
   ```

6. Call the `replaceDataSource()` method on the `Layer` object and pass the path to the shapefile. A keyword will indicate that this will be a shapefile workspace, and it also indicates the name of the shapefile:

```
lyr.replaceDataSource(r"c:\ArcpyBook\data","SHAPEFILE_
WORKSPACE","Burglaries_2009")
```

7. Save the results to a new map document file:

```
mxd.saveACopy(
r"c:\ArcpyBook\Ch3\Crime_DataLinksNewLayer.mxd")
```

8. Save the script as `c:\ArcpyBook\Ch3\LayerReplaceDataSource.py`.
9. You can check your work by examining the `c:\ArcpyBook\code\Ch3\LayerReplaceDataSource.py` solution file.
10. Run the script.
11. Open `C:\ArcpyBook\Ch3\Crime_DataLinksNewLayer.mxd` in ArcMap. You should see that the **Burglary** layer now references a new workspace:

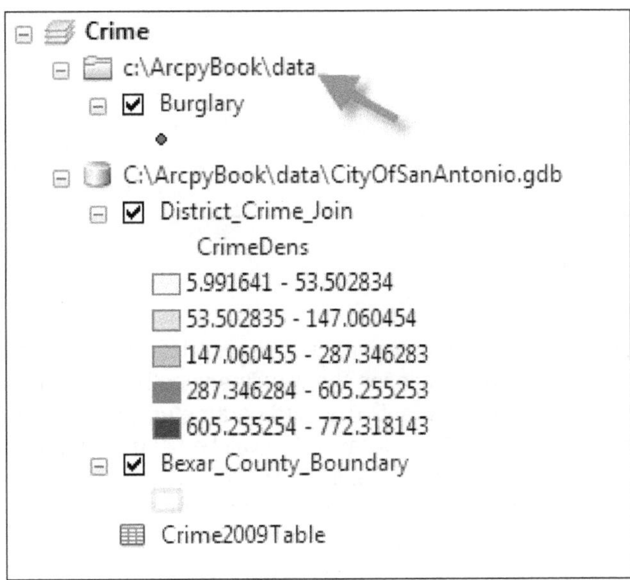

12. Right-click on the **Burglary** layer and select **Properties**.

13. Click on the **Source** tab and note the new workspace, workspace type, and dataset name:

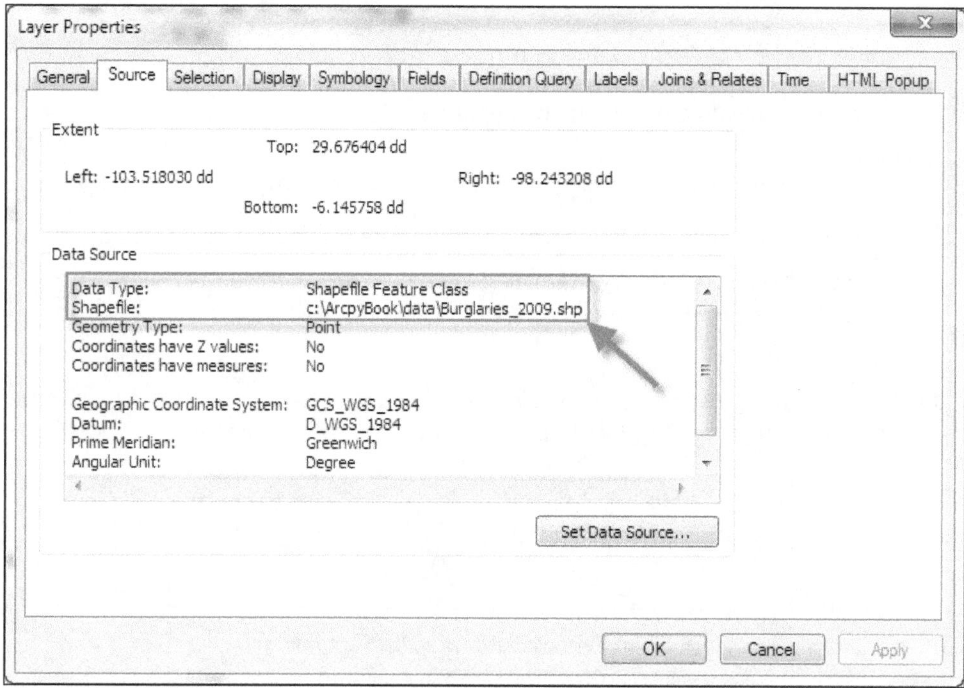

How it works...

The `replaceDataSource()` method accepts two required parameters and two optional parameters. The first two parameters define the workspace path and workspace type for the layer that will be used as the replacement. The third parameter, `dataset_name`, is an optional parameter that defines the name of the dataset that will be used as the replacement layer. This name must be an exact match. For example, in this recipe, we passed in a `dataset_name` attribute as `Burglaries_2009`, which is the name of the shapefile that will now be used as the replacement layer in the data frame. If a name is not provided, the method will attempt to replace the dataset by finding a table with the same name as the current layer's dataset property. The final optional parameter is `validate`. By default, this value is set to `True`. When set to `True`, a workspace will only be updated if the `workspace_path` value is a valid workspace. If it is not a valid workspace, then the workspace will not be replaced. If it's set to `False`, the method will set the source to match `workspace_path`, regardless of whether it is a valid match or not. This can result in a broken data source, but can be useful if you are creating or modifying a map document in preparation for data that does not yet exist.

There's more...

The `Layer` and `TableView` classes also contain a `findAndReplaceWorkspacePath()` method. This method is very similar to the `MapDocument.findAndReplaceWorkspacePaths()` method. The only difference is that it works against a single `Layer` or `TableView` class instead of iterating the entire map document or layer file.

Finding broken data sources in all map documents in a folder

A common scenario in many organizations involves the movement of data from one workspace to another or from one workspace type to another. When this happens, any map documents or layers that reference these data sources become broken. Finding each of these data sources can be a huge task if undertaken manually. Fortunately, you can create a geoprocessing script that will find all broken data sources in a folder or list of folders.

Getting ready

In this recipe, you will learn how to recursively search directories for map document files, find any broken data sources within these map documents, and write the names of the broken data layers to a file.

How to do it...

Follow these steps to learn how to find all broken data sources in all map documents in a folder:

1. Open **IDLE** and create a new script window.
2. Import the `arcpy` and `os` packages:
   ```
   import arcpy.mapping as mapping, os
   ```
3. Open a file that you will use to write the broken layer names:
   ```
   f = open('BrokenDataList.txt', 'w')
   ```
4. Pass a path to the `c:\ArcpyBook` folder to use in the `os.walk()` method along with a `for` loop to walk the directory tree:
   ```
   for root,dirs,files in os.walk("C:\ArcpyBook"):
   ```

5. Inside the `for` loop, create a second `for` loop that loops through all the files returned and create a new `filename` variable. Remember to indent the `for` loop inside the first `for` loop:

```
for name in files:
    filename = os.path.join(root, name)
```

6. Following the last line of code that you added, test the file extension to see if it is a map document file. If so, create a new map document object instance using the path, write the map document name, get a list of broken data sources, loop through each of the broken data sources, and write to the file:

```
if ".mxd" in filename:
    mxd = mapping.MapDocument(filename)
    f.write("MXD: " + filename + "\n")
    brknList = mapping.ListBrokenDataSources(mxd)
    for brknItem in brknList:
        print "Broken data item: " + brknItem.name + " in " +
        filename
        f.write("\t" + brknItem.name + "\n")
```

7. Add a `print` statement to indicate that you are done and close the file:

```
print("All done")
f.close()
```

8. The entire script should appear as follows:

```
import arcpy.mapping as mapping, os
f = open('BrokenDataList.txt', 'w')
for root, dirs, files in os.walk("c:\ArcpyBook"):
    for name in files:
        filename = os.path.join(root, name)
        if ".mxd" in filename:
            mxd = mapping.MapDocument(filename)
            f.write("MXD: " + filename + "\n")
            brknList = mapping.ListBrokenDataSources(mxd)
            for brknItem in brknList:
                print("Broken data item: " +  brknItem.name + " in " + filename)
                f.write("\t" + brknItem.name + "\n")
print("All done")
f.close()
```

9. You can check your work by examining the `c:\ArcpyBook\code\Ch3\ListBrokenDataSources.py` solution file.
10. Run the script to generate the file.

11. Open the file to see the results. Your output will vary depending upon the path you've defined. The following screenshot shows my output file:

```
MXD: Crime.mxd
MXD: Crime_BrokenDataLinks.mxd
      District_Crime_Join
      Bexar_County_Boundary
      District_Crime_Join
      Bexar_County_Boundary
      Bexar_County_Boundary
      Texas_Counties_LowRes
      School_Districts
      Crime_surf
      Bexar_County_Boundary
      Crime2009Table
MXD: TravisCounty.mxd
```

How it works...

This script uses a combination of methods from the Python `os` package and the `arcpy.mapping` package. The `os.walk()` method walks a directory tree and returns the path, a list of directories, and a list of files for each directory starting with a root directory that you have defined as the `c:\ArcpyBook` directory. This root directory could have been any directory. The `os.walk()` method returns a three item tuple consisting of the root directory, a list of directories immediately contained within that root, as well as a list of files immediately contained within the root. We then loop through this list of files and test each one to see if it contains the `.mxd` string, which indicates a map document file. Files identified as map documents have their filenames written to a text file, and a new `MapDocument` object instance is created. The `ListBrokenDataSources()` method is then used with a reference to the map document to generate a list of broken data sources within the file, and these broken data sources are written to the file as well.

4

Automating Map Production and Printing

In this chapter, we will cover the following recipes:

- Creating a list of layout elements
- Assigning a unique name to layout elements
- Restricting the layout elements returned by ListLayoutElements()
- Updating the properties of layout elements
- Getting a list of available printers
- Printing maps with PrintMap()
- Exporting a map to a PDF file
- Exporting a map to an image file
- Exporting a report
- Building a map book with Data Driven Pages and ArcPy mapping
- Publishing a map document to an ArcGIS Server service

Introduction

The `arcpy.mapping` module, released with ArcGIS 10, provides a number of capabilities related to the automation of map production. The `arcpy.mapping` module can be used to automate map production, build map books, export maps to image or PDF files, and create and manage PDF files. In this chapter, you'll learn how to use the `arcpy.mapping` module to automate various geoprocessing tasks related to map production and printing.

Creating a list of layout elements

Often, the first step in a geoprocessing script that automates the production of maps is to generate a list of the available layout elements. For example, you might need to update the title of your map before printing or creating a PDF file. In this case, the title is likely be stored in a `TextElement` object. You can generate a list of `TextElement` objects in your map layout view and then change the title. The first step is to generate a list of `TextElement` objects.

Getting ready

In ArcMap, two views are available, namely data view and layout view. **Data view** is used to view geographic and tabular data, analyze data, symbolize layers, and manage data without regard for any particular map page size or layout. **Layout view** shows the map as printed on a page, and is used to create production quality maps through the addition of map elements. These elements include map frames, layers, legends, titles, north arrows, scale bars, and title blocks. Each object in the layout is represented in `arcpy.mapping` as a layout element class. Examples of many of these layout element classes are displayed in the following screenshot:

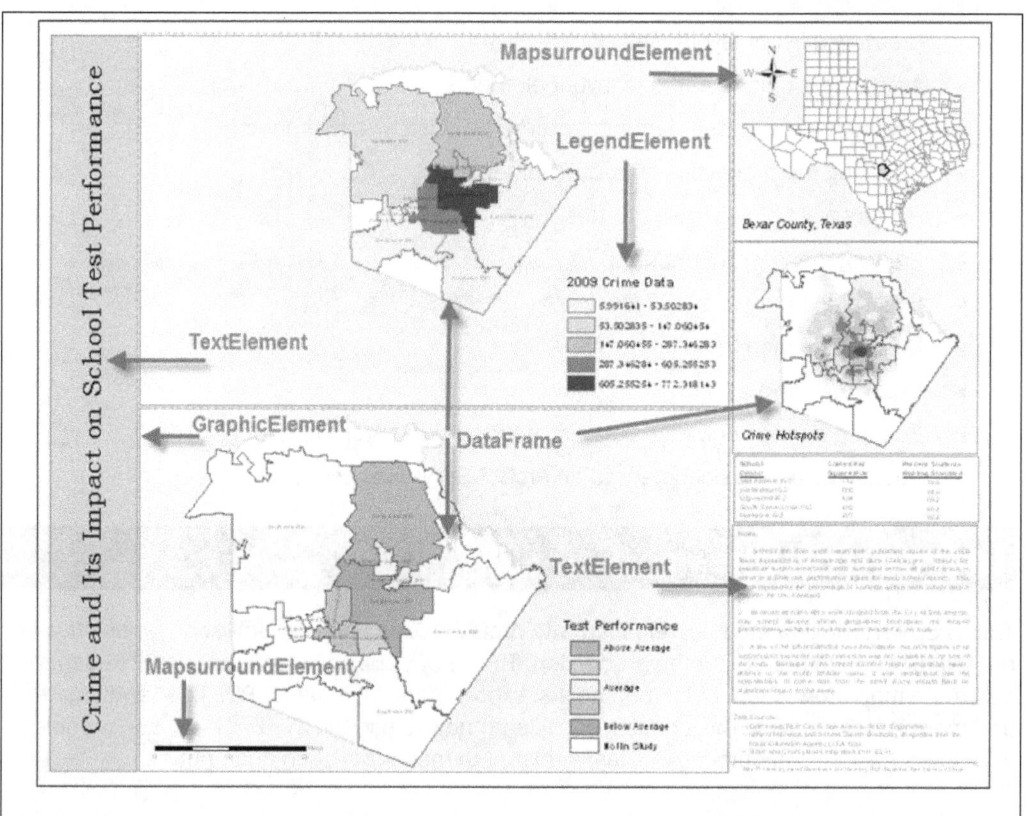

Each element can be assigned a unique name that can then be used to access the element programmatically. This unique name is defined in ArcMap. The `arcpy.mapping` module provides a `ListLayoutElements()` function that returns a list of all these elements. In this recipe, you will learn how to use the `ListLayoutElements()` function to generate a list of map layout elements.

How to do it...

Follow these steps to learn how to generate a list of layout elements:

1. Open `C:\ArcpyBook\Ch4\Crime_Ch4.mxd` in ArcMap.
2. Open the Python window.
3. Import the `arcpy.mapping` module:
   ```
   import arcpy.mapping as mapping
   ```
4. Reference the currently active document (`Crime_Ch4.mxd`) and assign this reference to a variable:
   ```
   mxd = mapping.MapDocument("CURRENT")
   ```
5. Generate a list of layout elements and print them to the screen if the name property is not empty:
   ```
   for el in mapping.ListLayoutElements(mxd):
     if el.name != '':
       print(el.name)
   ```
6. The entire script should appear as follows:
   ```
   import arcpy.mapping as mapping
   mxd = mapping.MapDocument("CURRENT")
   for el in mapping.ListLayoutElements(mxd):
     if el.name != '':
       print(el.name)
   ```
7. You can check your work by examining the `c:\ArcpyBook\code\Ch4\CreateListLayoutElements.py` solution file.
8. Run the script to see the following output:
   ```
   Crime_Inset
   Alternating Scale Bar
   Legend Test Performance
   Crime Legend
   North Arrow
   Inset_Map
   Test_Performance
   Crime
   ```

How it works...

`ListLayoutElements()` returns a list of layout elements in the form of various layout classes. Each element can be one of the `GraphicElement`, `LegendElement`, `PictureElement`, `TextElement`, or `MapSurroundElement` object instances. Each element can have a unique name. You don't have to assign a name to each element, but it is helpful to do so if you plan to access these elements programmatically in your scripts. In this script, we first made sure that the element had a name assigned to it before printing the name. This was done because ArcMap does not require that an element be assigned a name.

Assigning a unique name to layout elements

It's a good practice to assign a unique name to all your layout elements using ArcMap. This is important in the event that your geoprocessing scripts need to access a particular element to make changes. For example, you might need to update the icon that displays your corporate logo. Rather than making this change manually in all your map document files, you could write a geoprocessing script that updates all your map document files programmatically with the new logo. However, in order for this to be possible, a unique name will need to be assigned to your layout elements. This gives you the ability to access the elements of your layout individually.

Getting ready

As I mentioned in the previous recipe, each layout element will be one of a number of element types and each can be assigned a name. This element name can then be used when you need to reference a particular element in your Python script. You can use ArcMap to assign unique names to each layout element. In this recipe, you will use ArcMap to assign names to the elements.

How to do it...

Follow these steps to learn how to assign unique names to each layout element using ArcMap:

1. Open `C:\ArcpyBook\Ch4\Crime_Ch4.mxd` in ArcMap.

2. Switch to the layout view and you should see something similar to this screenshot:

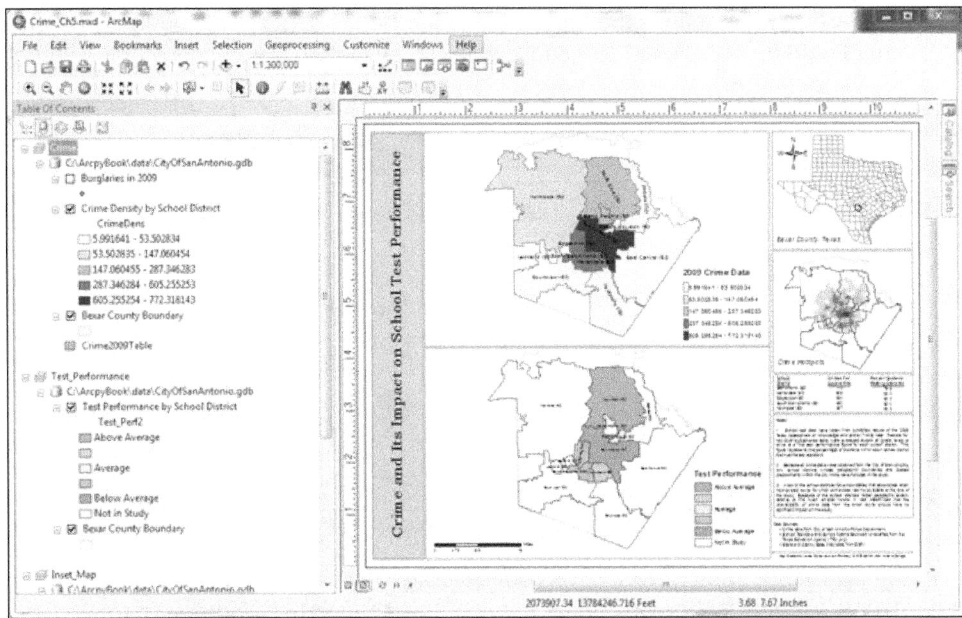

3. Names are assigned differently depending on the element type. Click on the uppermost data frame, which should be **Crime**, to select it. The selection handles should appear as follows:

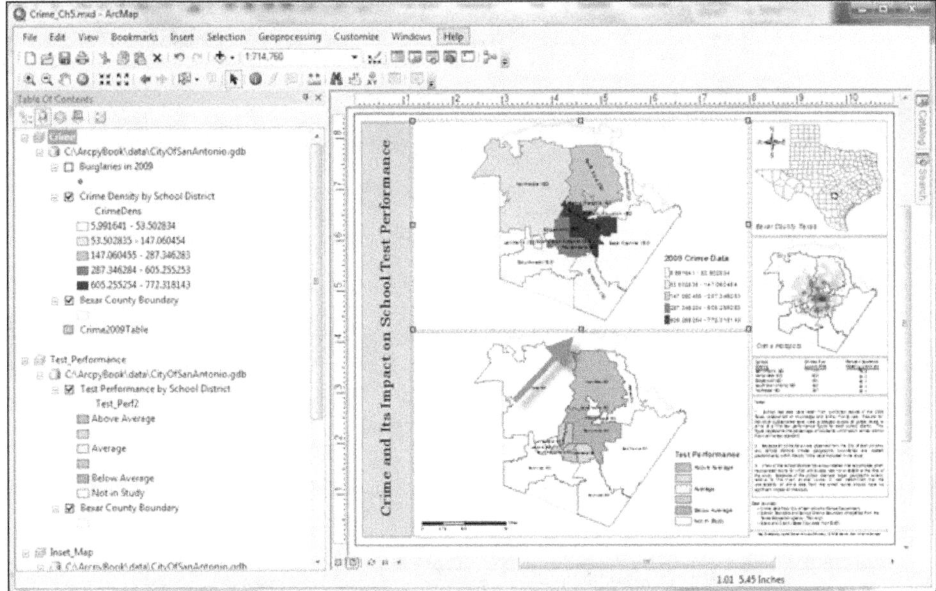

4. Right-click on the upper data frame and select **Properties** to display the **Data Frame Properties** window, as shown in the following screenshot. The **Element Name** property is what defines the unique name for the element and is found on the **Size and Position** tab as seen in the following screenshot. In this case, set the element name to `Crime`:

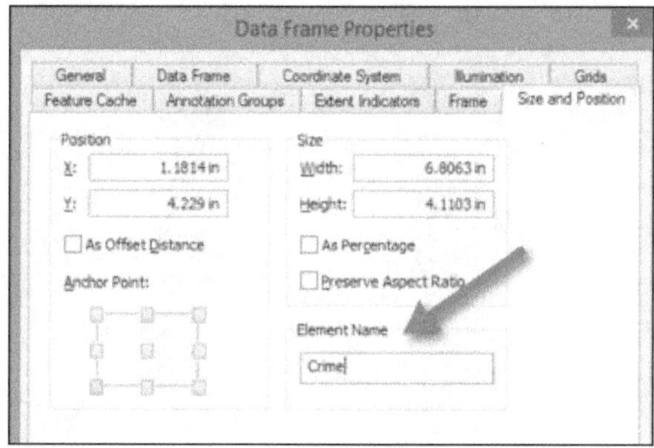

5. Close the **Data Frame Properties** window.
6. Select **2009 Crime Data legend** and open the **Properties** window by right-clicking on the legend and selecting **Properties**.
7. Click on the **Size and Position** tab.
8. Change the **Element Name** value to `Crime Legend`, as shown in the following screenshot:

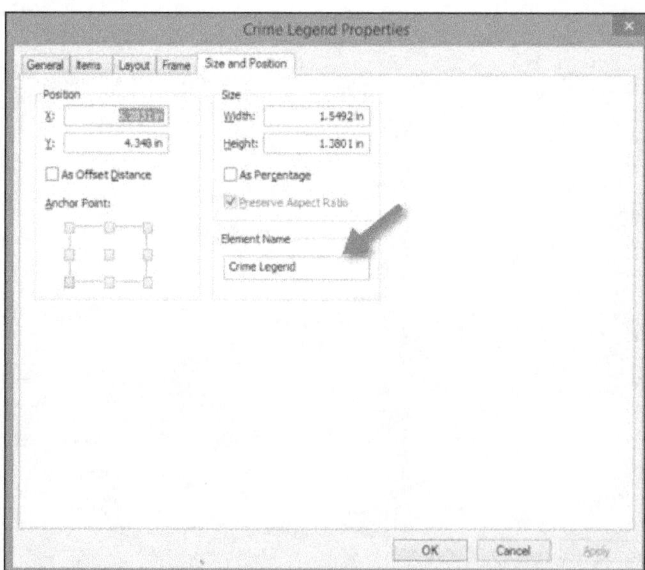

9. You can also define unique names for text elements. Select the title element (`Crime and Its Impact on School Test Performance`), right-click on the element, and select **Properties**.
10. Select the **Size and Position** tab and define a unique name for this element, as shown in the following screenshot:

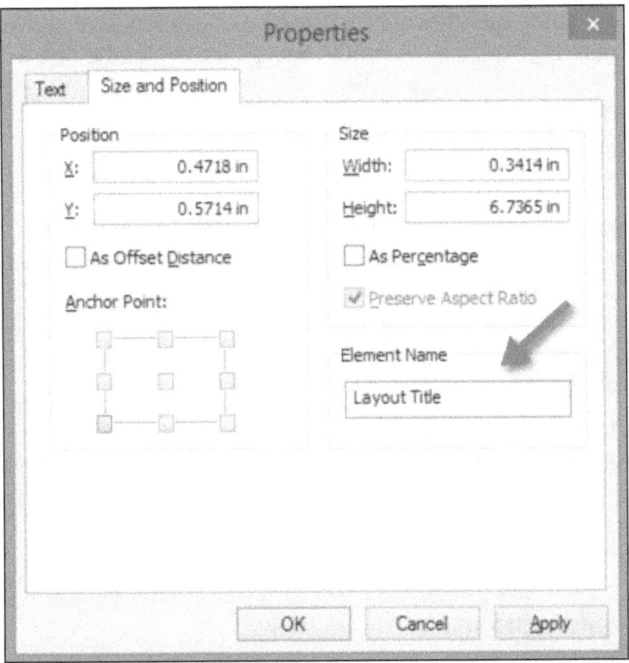

How it works...

Each element in the layout view can be assigned a name, which can then be used in your geoprocessing script to retrieve the specific element. You should strive to define unique names for each element. It isn't required that you define a unique name for each element, nor is it required that you even define a name at all. However, it is a best practice to give each element a name and ensure that each name is unique if you intend to access these elements from your Python scripts. In terms of naming practices for your elements, you should strive to include only letters and underscores in the name.

There's more...

You can use element names in conjunction with the `ListLayoutElements()` function to restrict the elements that are returned by the function through the use of a wildcard parameter. In the next recipe, you'll learn how to restrict the list of layout elements that are returned through the use of wildcards and element types.

Restricting the layout elements returned by ListLayoutElements()

Layouts can contain a large number of elements, many of which you won't need for a particular geoprocessing script. The `ListLayoutElements()` function can restrict the layout elements returned, by passing a parameter that defines the type of element that should be returned along with an optional wildcard, which finds elements using a portion of the name.

Getting ready

There are many different types of layout elements, including graphics, legends, pictures, text, and data frames. When you return a list of layout elements, you can restrict (filter) the types of elements that are returned. In this recipe, you will write a script that filters the layout elements returned by element type and wildcard.

How to do it...

Follow these steps to learn how to restrict the list of layers returned by the `ListLayoutElements()` function through the use of optional parameters, which define the type of element that should be returned along with a wildcard that can also restrict the elements that are returned:

1. Open `C:\ArcpyBook\Ch4\Crime_Ch4.mxd` in ArcMap.
2. Open the Python window.
3. Import the `arcpy.mapping` module:

   ```
   import arcpy.mapping as mapping
   ```

4. Reference the currently active document (`Crime_Ch4.mxd`) and assign this reference to a variable:

   ```
   mxd = mapping.MapDocument("CURRENT")
   ```

5. Use the `ListLayoutElements()` function with a restriction of only legend elements, as well as a wildcard that returns elements with a name containing the `Crime` text anywhere in the name:

   ```
   for el in mapping.ListLayoutElements(mxd,"LEGEND_
   ELEMENT","*Crime*"):
     print(el.name)
   ```

6. You can check your work by examining the `c:\ArcpyBook\code\Ch4\RestrictLayoutElements.py` solution file.
7. Run the script. In this case, only a single layout element will be returned:

   ```
   Crime Legend
   ```

How it works...

`ListLayoutElements()` is a versatile function, which in its most basic form is used to return a list of all the layout elements on the page layout of a map document. However, there are two optional parameters that you can supply to filter this list. The first type of filter is an element type filter in which you specify that you only want to return one of the layout element types. You can also apply a wildcard to filter the returned list. These two types of filters can be used in combination. For example, in this recipe, we are specifying that we only want to return `LEGEND_ELEMENT` objects with the `Crime` text anywhere in the element name. This results in a highly filtered list that only contains a single layout element.

> `ListLayoutElements()` can be filtered using one of these element types: `DATAFRAME_ELEMENT`, `GRAPHIC_ELEMENT`, `LEGEND_ELEMENT`, `MAPSURROUND_ELEMENT`, `PICTURE_ELEMENT`, or `TEXT_ELEMENT`.

Updating the properties of layout elements

Each layout element has a set of properties that you can update programmatically. For example, `LegendElement` includes properties that allow you to change the position of the legend on the page, update the legend title, and access legend items.

Getting ready

There are many different types of layout elements, including graphics, legends, text, maps, and pictures. Each of these elements is represented by a class in the `arcpy.mapping` package. These classes provide various properties that you can use to programmatically alter the element.

The `DataFrame` class provides access to the data frame properties in the map document file. This object can work with both map units and page layout units, depending on the property being used. Page layout properties, such as positioning and sizing, can be applied to the properties, including `elementPositionX`, `elementPositionY`, `elementWidth`, and `elementHeight`.

The `GraphicElement` object is a generic object for various graphics that can be added to the page layout, including tables, graphs, neatlines, markers, lines, and area shapes. You'll want to make sure that you set the `name` property for each graphic element (and any other element for that matter), if you intend to access it through a Python script.

`LegendElement` provides operations to position the legend on the page layout, modification of the legend title, and also provides access to the legend items and the parent data frame. `LegendElement` can only be associated with a single data frame.

`MapSurroundElement` can refer to north arrows, scale bars, and scale text. It is similar to `LegendElement` and is associated with a single data frame. Properties on this object enable repositioning of the element on the page.

`PictureElement` represents a raster or image on the page layout. The most useful property of this object enables acquiring and setting the data sources, which can be extremely helpful when you need to change a picture, such as a logo, in multiple map documents. For example, you could write a script that iterates through all your map document files and replaces the current logo with a new logo. You can also reposition or resize the object.

`TextElement` represents text on a page layout, including inserted text, callouts, rectangle text, and titles, but does not include legend titles or texts that are part of a table or chart. Properties enable the modification of a text string, which can be extremely useful in situations where you need to make the same text string change in multiple places in the page layout or over multiple map documents, and of course, repositioning of the object is also available.

Each element in the page layout is returned as an instance of one of the element objects. In this recipe, we're going to use the `title` property of the `Legend` object to programmatically change the title of the `Crime` legend and obtain a list of the layers that are part of the legend.

How to do it...

Follow these steps to learn how to update the properties of a layout element:

1. Open `C:\ArcpyBook\Ch4\Crime_Ch4.mxd` in ArcMap.
2. Open the Python window.
3. Import the `arcpy.mapping` module:
   ```
   import arcpy.mapping as mapping
   ```
4. Reference the currently active document (`Crime_Ch4.mxd`), and assign this reference to a variable:
   ```
   mxd = mapping.MapDocument("CURRENT")
   ```
5. Use the `ListLayoutElements()` method with a wildcard and restriction of only legend elements to return only the `Crime` legend and store it in a variable:
   ```
   elLeg = mapping.ListLayoutElements(mxd,
   "LEGEND_ELEMENT","*Crime*")[0]
   ```
6. Use the `title` property to update the title of the legend:
   ```
   elLeg.title = "Crimes by School District"
   ```
7. Get a list of the layers that are a part of the legend and print the names:
   ```
   for item in elLeg.listLegendItemLayers():
     print(item.name)
   ```

8. The entire script should appear as follows:

```
import arcpy.mapping as mapping
mxd = mapping.MapDocument("CURRENT")
elLeg = mapping.ListLayoutElements(mxd,
"LEGEND_ELEMENT","*Crime*")[0]
elLeg.title = "Crimes by School District"
for item in elLeg.listLegendItemLayers():
  print(item.name)
```

9. You can check your work by examining the `c:\ArcpyBook\code\Ch4\UpdateLayoutElementProperties.py` solution file.
10. Run the script. You should see the following layers printed:

```
Burglaries in 2009
Crime Density by School District
```

11. The change is displayed in the following screenshot:

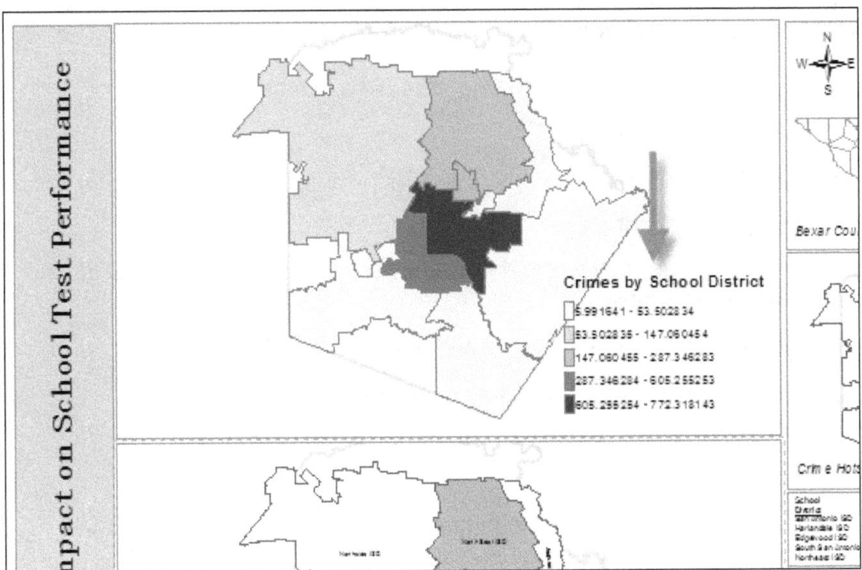

How it works...

Each of the layout elements has a set of properties and methods. In this particular case, we've used the `title` property on the `Legend` object. Other properties of this object allow you to set the width and height, positioning, and so on. Methods used for the `Legend` object give you the ability to adjust the column count, list the legend items, and remove and update items.

Getting a list of available printers

Yet another list function provided by `arcpy` is `ListPrinterNames()`, which generates a list of the available printers. As is the case with the other list functions that we've examined, `ListPrinterNames()` is often called a preliminary step in a multistep script.

Getting ready

Before printing maps with the `PrintMap()` function, it is a common practice to call the `ListPrinterNames()` function, which returns a list of the available printers for the local computer. A particular printer can then be found by iterating the list of printers and using it as an input for the `PrintMap()` function.

How to do it...

Follow these steps to learn how to use the `ListPrinterNames()` function to return a list of the available printers for your script:

1. Open `C:\ArcpyBook\Ch4\Crime_Ch4.mxd` in ArcMap.
2. Open the Python window.
3. Import the `arcpy.mapping` module:
   ```
   import arcpy.mapping as mapping
   ```
4. Reference the currently active document (`Crime_Ch4.mxd`) and assign this reference to a variable:
   ```
   mxd = mapping.MapDocument("CURRENT")
   ```
5. Call the `ListPrinterNames()` function and print each printer:
   ```
   for printerName in mapping.ListPrinterNames():
     print(printerName)
   ```
6. You can check your work by examining the `c:\ArcpyBook\code\Ch4\GetListOfPrinters.py` solution file.
7. Run the script. The output will vary depending upon the list of available printers for your computer. However, it should print something similar to the following code snippet:
   ```
   HP Photosmart D110 series
   HP Deskjet 3050 J610 series (Network)
   HP Deskjet 3050 J610 series (Copy 1)
   HP Deskjet 3050 J610 series
   Dell 968 AIO Printer
   ```

How it works...

The `ListPrinterNames()` function returns a Python list containing all the printers available to use in your script. You can then use the `PrintMap()` function, which we'll examine in the next recipe, to send a print job to a particular printer that is available for your computer.

Printing maps with PrintMap()

Sending your map layout to a printer is easy with the `PrintMap()` function. By default, the print job will be sent to the default printer saved with the map document, but you can also define a specific printer to which the job should be sent.

Getting ready

The `arcpy.mapping` module provides a `PrintMap()` function to print page layouts or data frames from ArcMap. Before calling `PrintMap()`, it is a common practice to call the `ListPrinterNames()` function, which returns a list of the available printers for the local computer. A particular printer can then be found by iterating the list of printers that can be used as an input for the `PrintMap()` function.

`PrintMap()` can print either a specific data frame or the page layout of a map document. By default, this function will use the printer saved with the map document or, the default system printer in the map document. As I mentioned earlier, you can also use `ListPrinterNames()` to get a list of the available printers, and select one of these printers as an input for `PrintMap()`. In this recipe, you will learn how to use the `PrintMap()` function to print the layout.

How to do it...

Follow these steps to learn how to use the `PrintMap()` function to print the layout view in ArcMap:

1. Open `C:\ArcpyBook\Ch4\Crime_Ch4.mxd` in ArcMap.
2. Open the Python window.
3. Import the `arcpy.mapping` module:

   ```
   import arcpy.mapping as mapping
   ```

4. Reference the currently active document (`Crime_Ch4.mxd`), and assign this reference to a variable:

   ```
   mxd = mapping.MapDocument("CURRENT")
   ```

5. Look for the `Test_Performance` data frame and print it if it's found:

```
for df in mapping.ListDataFrames(mxd):
  if df.name == "Test_Performance":
    mapping.PrintMap(mxd,"",df)
```

6. You can check your work by examining the `c:\ArcpyBook\code\Ch4\PrintingWithPrintMap.py` solution file.
7. Run the script. The script should send the data frame to the default printer.

How it works...

The `PrintMap()` function accepts one required parameter and a handful of optional parameters. The required parameter is a reference to the map document. The first optional parameter is the printer name. In this case, we haven't specified a particular printer to use. Since we haven't provided a specific printer; it will use the printer saved with the map document or the default system printer if a printer is not part of the map document. The second optional parameter is the data frame that we'd like to print, which in this instance is `Test_Performance`. Other optional parameters, not supplied in this case, are an output print file and image quality.

Exporting a map to a PDF file

Rather than sending your map or layout view to a printer, you may want to simply create PDF files that can be shared. ArcPy mapping provides an `ExportToPDF()` function, which you can use to do this.

Getting ready

PDF is a very popular interchange format designed to be viewable and printable from many different platforms. The ArcPy mapping `ExportToPDF()` function can be used to export data frames or the page layout to a PDF format. By default, the `ExportToPDF()` function exports the page layout, but you can pass an optional parameter that references a particular data frame, which can be printed instead of the page layout. In this recipe, you will learn how to export the page layout as well as a specific data frame to a PDF file.

How to do it...

Follow these steps to learn how to export a map to a PDF file:

1. Open `C:\ArcpyBook\Ch4\Crime_Ch4.mxd` in ArcMap.
2. Open the Python window.

3. Import the `arcpy.mapping` module:

```
import arcpy.mapping as mapping
```

4. Reference the currently active document (`Crime_Ch4.mxd`), and assign this reference to a variable:

```
mxd = mapping.MapDocument('CURRENT')
```

5. Export the page layout with the `ExportToPDF()` function:

```
mapping.ExportToPDF(mxd,r"c:\ArcpyBook\Ch4\Map_PageLayout.pdf")
```

6. You can check your work by examining the `c:\ArcpyBook\code\Ch4\ExportToPDF_Step1.py` solution file.
7. Run the script.
8. Open the `Map_PageLayout.pdf` file that was created, and you should see something similar to the following screenshot:

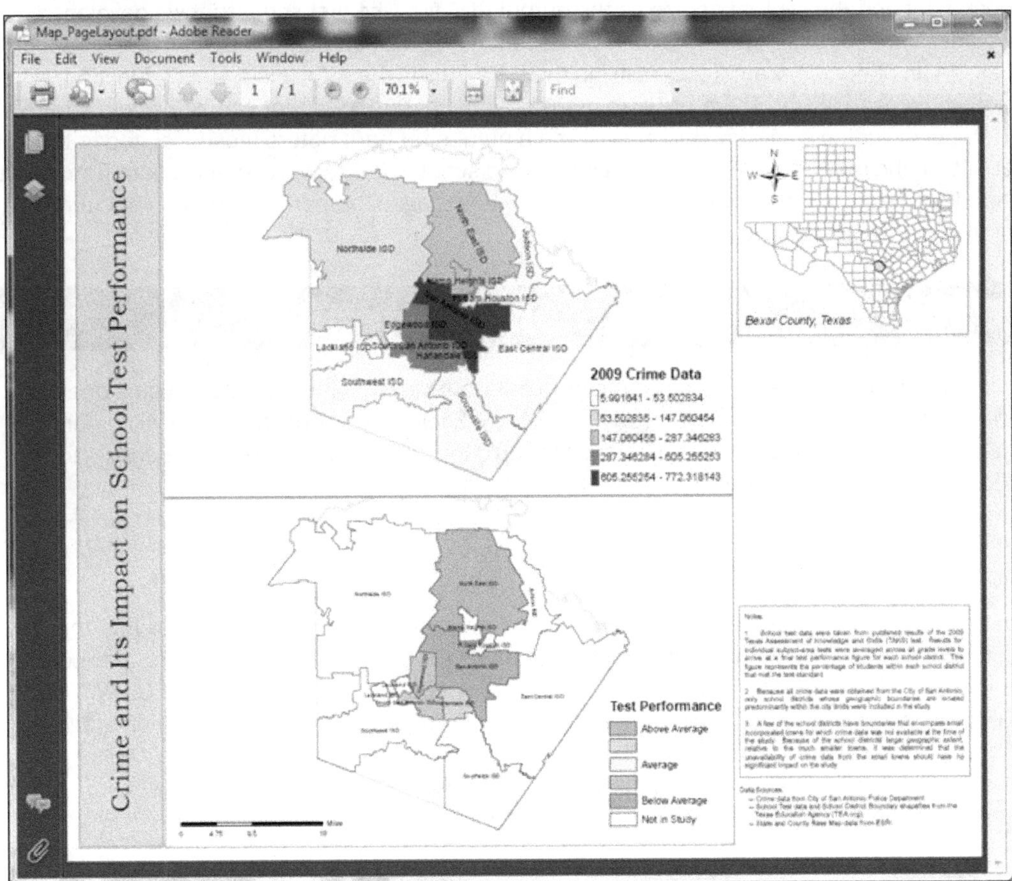

9. Now, we'll print a specific data frame from our map document file. Alter your script, so that it appears as follows. You can check your work by examining the `c:\ArcpyBook\code\Ch4\ExportToPDF_Step2.py` solution file.

```
import arcpy.mapping as mapping
mxd = mapping.MapDocument("CURRENT")
for df in mapping.ListDataFrames(mxd):
    if df.name == "Crime":
        df.referenceScale = df.scale
        mapping.ExportToPDF(mxd,r"c:\ArcpyBook\Ch4\DataFrameCrime.pdf",df)
```

10. Run the script and examine the output of the PDF file.

How it works...

The `ExportToPDF()` function requires two parameters, including a reference to the map document and the file that serves as the output PDF file. The first script that we developed was passed in a reference to the map document along with an output PDF file. Since we didn't pass in an optional parameter specifying the data frame, the `ExportToPDF()` function will export the page layout. There are also many optional parameters that can be passed into this method, including a specific data frame and a number of parameters mostly related to the quality of the output content and file. Our second script is passed in a specific data frame that should be exported. You can refer to the ArcGIS help pages for more information about each of the optional parameters.

Exporting a map to an image file

You can also export the contents of the map or layout view to an image file by using one of the many functions provided by `arcpy.mapping`. Each image export function will differ in its name depending upon the type of image file you'd like to create. The parameters passed into the function will also vary slightly.

Getting ready

In addition to providing the ability to export data frames and the page layout to a PDF format, you can also use one of the many export functions provided by `arcpy.mapping` to export an image file. Some of the available formats include AI, BMP, EMF, EPS, GIF, JPEG, SVG, and TIFF. The parameters provided for each function will vary depending on the type of image. Some examples of these function names include `ExportToJPEG()`, `ExportToGIF()`, and `ExportToBMP()`. In this recipe, you'll learn how to export your maps to images.

How to do it...

Follow these steps to learn how to export your data or layout view to an image file:

1. Open `C:\ArcpyBook\Ch4\Crime_Ch4.mxd` in ArcMap.
2. Open the Python window.
3. Import the `arcpy.mapping` module:

    ```
    import arcpy.mapping as mapping
    ```

4. Reference the currently active document (`Crime_Ch4.mxd`), and assign this reference to a variable:

    ```
    mxd = mapping.MapDocument("CURRENT")
    ```

5. Get a list of data frames in the map document and find the data frame with the name "`Crime`".

    ```
    for df in mapping.ListDataFrames(mxd):
        if df.name == "Crime":
    ```

6. Export the `Crime` data frame as a JPEG image. Your entire script should now appear as follows:

```
import arcpy.mapping as mapping
mxd = mapping.MapDocument("CURRENT")
for df in mapping.ListDataFrames(mxd):
    if df.name == "Crime":
        mapping.ExportToJPEG(mxd,r"c:\ArcpyBook\Ch4\DataFrameCrime.jpg",df)
```

7. You can check your work by examining the `c:\ArcpyBook\code\Ch4\ExportMapImageFile.py` solution file.
8. Run the script and examine the output file.

How it works...

Note that the `ExportToJPEG()` function looks virtually the same as `ExportToPDF()`. Keep in mind though that the optional parameters will be different for all the export functions. Each `ExportTo<Type>` function will vary depending on the parameters that can be used in the creation of the image file.

Exporting a report

Reports in ArcGIS provide you with a way of presenting information about your data or analysis. Information in a report is displayed by using information pulled directly from an attribute table in a feature class or a standalone table. Reports can contain attribute information, maps, pictures, graphics, and other supporting information. ArcMap includes a **Report Wizard** and **Report Designer** that you can use to create and modify reports. You can also save the format of a report to a template file. This template file can be used repeatedly to generate new reports based on any changes in your data. Using a combination of a report template along with `arcpy.mapping`, you can automate the production of reports.

Getting ready

The **Report Wizard** in ArcGIS can be used to create reports. There are two native data formats for ArcGIS reports: **Report Document File** (**RDF**) and **Report Layout File** (**RLF**). RDF reports provide a static report of your data. A one-time snapshot, if you will. A RLF is a template file and is created using **Report Designer**. The report template file can be used repeatedly and includes all the fields in the report along with how they are grouped, sorted, and formatted. It also includes any layout elements, such as graphics or maps. When the report is rerun, the report regenerates based on the source data that is connected to the template. The `arcpy.mapping ExportReport()` function can be used to connect a data source to a template file to automate the creation of a report. In this recipe, you will learn how to use the `ExportReport()` function with the `PDFDocument` class to create a report that contains crime information for school districts. The report will include attribute information and a map of the boundaries of the school district.

How to do it...

To save some time on this recipe, I have precreated a report template (RLF) file for you to use. This file, called `CrimeReport.rlf`, is located in the `c:\ArcpyBook\Ch4` folder and contains attribute columns for the name of the school district, number of crimes, crime density, and test performance scores. In addition to this, a placeholder for a map containing the boundaries of the school district has also been added to the template.

Follow these steps to learn how to automate the production of reports using the `arcpy.mapping ExportReport()` function and the `PDFDocument` class:

1. Create a new script file in IDLE or your favorite Python editor and save it as `c:\ArcpyBook\Ch4\CreateReport.py`.
2. Import the `arcpy` and `os` modules and get the current working directory:

```
import arcpy
import os
path = os.getcwd()
```

3. Create the output PDF file:

```
#Create PDF and remove if it already exists
pdfPath = path + r"\CrimeReport.pdf"
if os.path.exists(pdfPath):
  os.remove(pdfPath)
pdfDoc = arcpy.mapping.PDFDocumentCreate(pdfPath)
```

4. Create a list of school districts. We'll loop through this list to create reports for each district:

```
districtList = ["Harlandale", "East Central", "Edgewood",
                "Alamo Heights", "South San Antonio",
                "Southside", "Ft Sam Houston",
                "North East", "Northside", "Lackland",
                "Southwest", "Judson", "San Antonio"]
```

5. Get references to the map document, data frame, and layer:

```
mxd = arcpy.mapping.MapDocument(path + r"\Crime_Ch4.mxd")
df = arcpy.mapping.ListDataFrames(mxd)[0]
lyr = arcpy.mapping.ListLayers(mxd, "Crime Density by
School District")[0]
```

6. Start a loop through the school districts and apply a `where` clause that acts as the definition query so that only the individual school district will be displayed:

```
pageCount = 1
for district in districtList:
  #Generate image for each district
  whereClause = "\"NAME\" = '" + district + " ISD'"
  lyr.definitionQuery = whereClause
```

7. Select the individual school district, set the data frame extent to the extent of the school district, and clear the selection set:

```
arcpy.SelectLayerByAttribute_management(lyr, "NEW_SELECTION",
whereClause)
df.extent = lyr.getSelectedExtent()
arcpy.SelectLayerByAttribute_management(lyr, "CLEAR_SELECTION")
```

8. Export the data frame to a bitmap (`.bmp`) file:

```
arcpy.mapping.ExportToBMP(mxd, path +
"\DistrictPicture.bmp", df) #single file
```

9. Call the `ExportReport()` function to create the report:

```
#Generate report
print("Generating report for: " + district + " ISD")
```

```
arcpy.mapping.ExportReport(report_source=lyr,
   report_layout_file=path +
r"\CrimeLayout.rlf",output_file=path + r"\temp" +
str(pageCount) + ".pdf", starting_page_number=pageCount)
```

10. Append the report to the PDF file:

```
#Append pages into final output
print("Appending page: " + str(pageCount))
pdfDoc.appendPages(path + r"\temp" + str(pageCount) +
".pdf")
```

11. Remove the temporary PDF report:

```
os.remove(path + r"\temp" + str(pageCount) + ".pdf")
pageCount = pageCount + 1
```

12. Save the PDF document:

```
pdfDoc.saveAndClose()
```

13. The entire script should appear as follows:

```
import arcpy
import os
path = os.getcwd()

#Create PDF and remove if it already exists
pdfPath = path + r"\CrimeReport.pdf"
if os.path.exists(pdfPath):
  os.remove(pdfPath)
pdfDoc = arcpy.mapping.PDFDocumentCreate(pdfPath)

districtList = ["Harlandale", "East Central", "Edgewood", "Alamo Heights",
                "South San Antonio", "Southside", "Ft Sam Houston", "North East",
                "Northside", "Lackland", "Southwest", "Judson", "San Antonio"]

mxd = arcpy.mapping.MapDocument(path + r"\Crime_Ch4.mxd")
df = arcpy.mapping.ListDataFrames(mxd)[0]
lyr = arcpy.mapping.ListLayers(mxd, "Crime Density by School District")[0]

pageCount = 1
for district in districtList:
  #Generate image for each district
  whereClause = "\"NAME\" = '" + district + " ISD'"
  lyr.definitionQuery = whereClause
  arcpy.SelectLayerByAttribute_management(lyr, "NEW_SELECTION", whereClause)
  df.extent = lyr.getSelectedExtent()
  arcpy.SelectLayerByAttribute_management(lyr, "CLEAR_SELECTION")
  arcpy.mapping.ExportToBMP(mxd, path + "\DistrictPicture.bmp", df) #single file

  #Generate report
  print("Generating report for: " + district + " ISD")
  arcpy.mapping.ExportReport(report_source=lyr,
                             report_layout_file=path + r"\CrimeLayout.rlf",
                             output_file=path + r"\temp" + str(pageCount) + ".pdf",
                             starting_page_number=pageCount)
  #Append pages into final output
  print("Appending page: " + str(pageCount))
  pdfDoc.appendPages(path + r"\temp" + str(pageCount) + ".pdf")
  os.remove(path + r"\temp" + str(pageCount) + ".pdf")
  pageCount = pageCount + 1

pdfDoc.saveAndClose()
del mxd
```

14. You can check your work by examining the `c:\ArcpyBook\code\Ch4\CreateReport.py` solution file.
15. Save and run your script. This will create a file called `CrimeReport.pdf` in your `c:\ArcpyBook\ch4` folder. The contents will contain one report page for each school district, as seen in this screenshot:

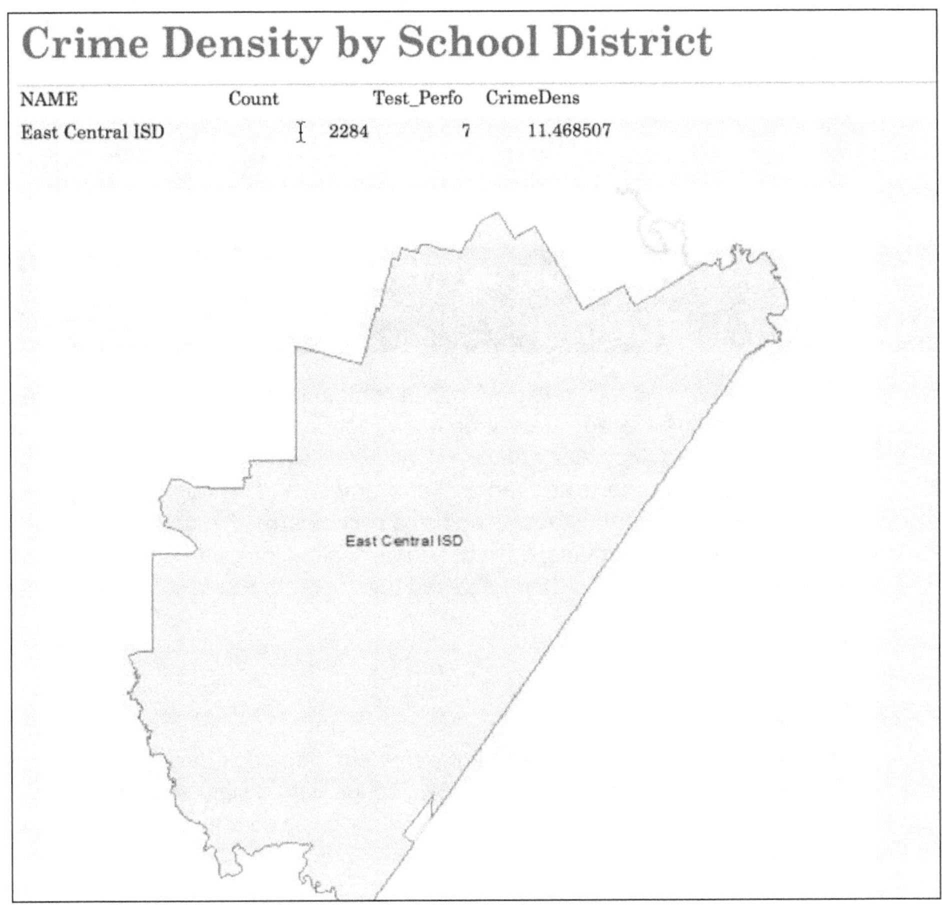

How it works...

In this recipe, we used several functions and classes that are part of the `arcpy.mapping` module, including `PDFDocument`, `ExportToReport()` and `ExportToBMP()`. Initially, we used the `PDFDocumentCreate()` function to create an instance of `PDFDocument`, which holds a pointer to the `CrimeReport.pdf` file that we'll create. Next, we created a list of school districts and began a loop through each of them. Inside the loop, for each district, we set a definition query on the layer, selected the district, and returned the extent of the district that was used to set the extent of the data frame. A bitmap file was then created using the `ExportToBMP()` function and the report was generated with the `ExportReport()` function. Finally, each page was appended to the `CrimeReport.pdf` file and the document was saved.

Building a map book with Data Driven Pages and ArcPy mapping

Many organizations have a need to create map books containing a series of individual maps that cover a larger geographical area. These map books contain a series of maps and some optional and additional pages, including title pages, an overview map, and some other ancillary information, such as reports and tables. For example, a utility company might want to generate a map book detailing their assets across a service area. A map book for this utility company could include a series of maps, each at a large scale, along with a title page and an overview map. These resources would then be joined together into a single document that could be printed or distributed as a PDF file.

Getting ready

ArcGIS for Desktop provides the ability to efficiently create a map book through a combination of Data Driven Pages along with an `arcpy.mapping` script. With a single map document file, you can use the **Data Driven Pages** toolbar to create a basic series of maps using the layout view along with your operational data and an `index` layer. The `index` layer contains features that will be used to define the extent of each map in the series. However, if you need to include additional pages in the map book, including a title page, an overview map, and other ancillary pages, you'll need to combine the output from the Data Driven Pages toolbar with the functionality provided by the `arcpy.mapping` module. With the `arcpy.mapping` module, you can automate the export of the map series and append the ancillary files to a single map book document. While it is certainly possible to programmatically generate the entire map book using only Python and the `arcpy.mapping` module, it is more efficient to use a combination of programming and the Data Driven Pages toolbar. In this recipe, you'll learn how to create a map book that includes a series of maps along with a title page and an overview map page.

How to do it...

To save some time on this recipe, I have precreated a map document file for you that contains the data and Data Driven Pages functionality to create a series of topographic maps for King County, Washington. This map document file, called `Topographic.mxd`, can be found in the `c:\ArcpyBook\Ch4` folder. You may want to take a few moments to open this file in ArcGIS for Desktop and examine the data. The Data Driven Pages functionality has already been enabled for you. Additionally, a map title page (`TitlePage.pdf`) and an overview map page (`MapIndex.pdf`) have also been created for you. These files are also located in your `c:\ArcpyBook\Ch4` folder.

The steps to generate a map series can be somewhat lengthy, and are beyond the scope of this book. However, if you'd like an overview of the process, go to the **ArcGIS Desktop Help** system, navigate to **Desktop** | **Mapping** | **Page layouts** | **Creating a Map Book**, and follow the first seven items under this folder. This includes building map books with ArcGIS through adding dynamic text to your map book.

Follow these steps to learn how to use the Data Driven Pages functionality and the `arcpy.mapping` module to create a map book:

1. Create a new IDLE script and save it as `c:\ArcpyBook\Ch4\DataDrivenPages_MapBook.py`.
2. Import the `arcpy` and `os` modules:

```
import arcpy
import os
```

3. Create an output directory variable:

```
# Create an output directory variable
outDir = r"C:\ArcpyBook\Ch4"
```

4. Create a new, empty PDF document in the specified output directory:

```
# Create a new, empty pdf document in the specified output
directory
finalpdf_filename = outDir + r"\MapBook.pdf"
if os.path.exists(finalpdf_filename):
  os.remove(finalpdf_filename)
finalPdf =
arcpy.mapping.PDFDocumentCreate(finalpdf_filename)
```

5. Add the title page to the PDF:

```
# Add the title page to the pdf
print("Adding the title page  \n")
finalPdf.appendPages(outDir + r"\TitlePage.pdf")
```

6. Add the index map to the PDF:

```
# Add the index map to the pdf
print("Adding the index page  \n")
finalPdf.appendPages(outDir + r"\MapIndex.pdf")
```

7. Export the Data Driven Pages to a temporary PDF and then add it to the final PDF:

```
# Export the Data Driven Pages to a temporary pdf and then add it
to the
# final pdf. Alternately, if your Data Driven Pages have already
been
# exported, simply append that document to the final pdf.
mxdPath = outDir + r"\Topographic.mxd"
mxd = arcpy.mapping.MapDocument(mxdPath)
print("Creating the data driven pages \n")
ddp = mxd.dataDrivenPages
temp_filename = outDir + r"\tempDDP.pdf"

if os.path.exists(temp_filename):
  os.remove(temp_filename)
ddp.exportToPDF(temp_filename, "ALL")
print("Appending the map series  \n")
finalPdf.appendPages(temp_filename)
```

8. Update the properties of the final PDF:

```
# Update the properties of the final pdf.
finalPdf.updateDocProperties(pdf_open_view="USE_THUMBS",
                             pdf_layout="SINGLE_PAGE")
```

9. Save the PDF:

```
# Save your result
finalPdf.saveAndClose()
```

10. Remove the temporary Data Driven Pages file:

```
# remove the temporary data driven pages file
if os.path.exists(temp_filename):
    os.remove(temp_filename)
```

11. The entire script should appear as follows:

```
import arcpy
import os

# Create an output directory variable
outDir = r"C:\ArcpyBook\Ch4"

# Create a new, empty pdf document in the specified output directory
finalpdf_filename = outDir + r"\MapBook.pdf"
if os.path.exists(finalpdf_filename):
  os.remove(finalpdf_filename)
finalPdf = arcpy.mapping.PDFDocumentCreate(finalpdf_filename)

# Add the title page to the pdf
print("Adding the title page  \n")
finalPdf.appendPages(outDir + r"\TitlePage.pdf")

# Add the index map to the pdf
print("Adding the index page  \n")
finalPdf.appendPages(outDir + r"\MapIndex.pdf")

# Export the Data Driven Pages to a temporary pdf and then add it to the
# final pdf. Alternately, if your Data Driven Pages have already been
# exported, simply append that document to the final pdf.
mxdPath = outDir + r"\Topographic.mxd"
mxd = arcpy.mapping.MapDocument(mxdPath)
print("Creating the data driven pages \n")
ddp = mxd.dataDrivenPages
temp_filename = outDir + r"\tempDDP.pdf"

if os.path.exists(temp_filename):
  os.remove(temp_filename)
ddp.exportToPDF(temp_filename, "ALL")
print("Appending the map series  \n")
finalPdf.appendPages(temp_filename)

# Update the properties of the final pdf
finalPdf.updateDocProperties(pdf_open_view="USE_THUMBS",
                             pdf_layout="SINGLE_PAGE")

# Save your result
finalPdf.saveAndClose()
```

12. You can check your work by examining the `c:\ArcpyBook\code\Ch4\DataDrivenPages_MapBook.py` solution file.

13. Save and execute your script. If the script successfully executes, you should find a new file called `MapBook.pdf` in the `c:\ArcpyBook\Ch4` folder. When you open this file, you should see this screenshot:

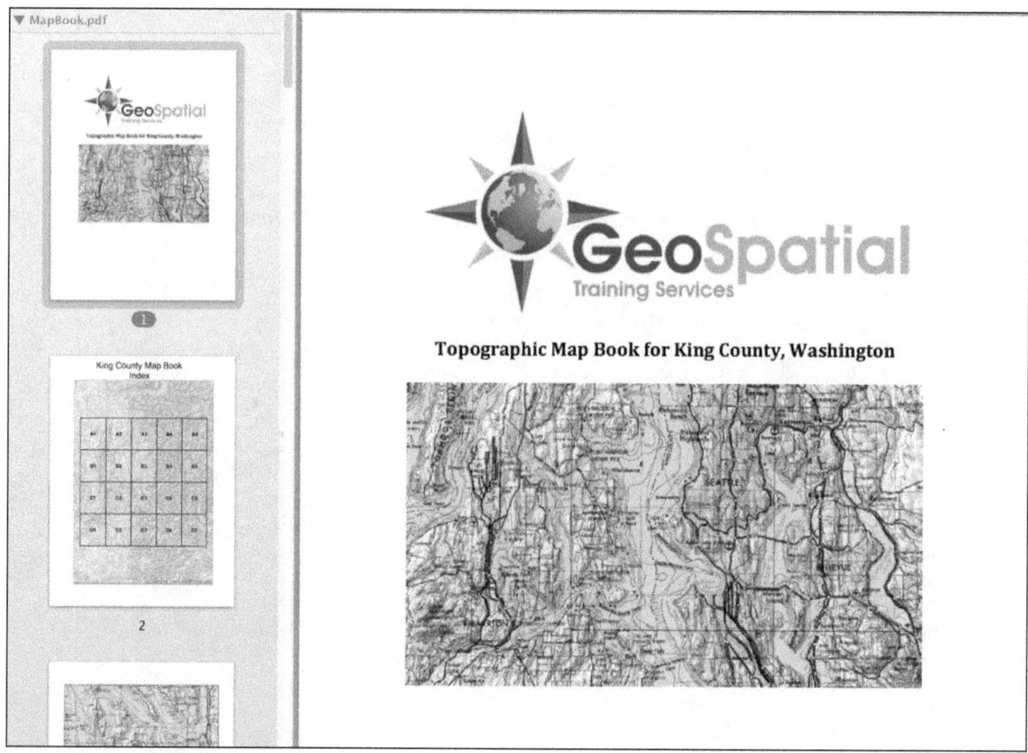

How it works...

The `PDFDocument` class in the `arcpy.mapping` module is frequently used to create map books. In this recipe, we used the `PDFDocumentCreate()` function to create an instance of `PDFDocument`. A path to the output PDF file was passed into the `PDFDocumentCreate()` function. With this instance of `PDFDocument`, we then called the `PDFDocument.appendPages()` method twice, inserting the title page and map index files that already existed as PDF files. Next, we retrieved a `dataDrivenPages` object from the map document file and exported each of the pages to a single PDF document. This document was then appended to our final output PDF file that already contained the title page and map index page. Finally, we updated the `PDFDocument` properties to use thumbs and a single page view, saved the entire file, and removed the temporary data drive page document.

Publishing a map document to an ArcGIS Server service

Using the `arcpy.mapping` module, it is possible to publish your map document files to **ArcGIS Server** as map services. ArcGIS Server is a platform to distribute maps and data on the Web. Using the ArcGIS JavaScript API, web and mobile applications can be created from services created in ArcGIS Server. For more information about ArcGIS Server, please visit the esri ArcGIS Server site at `http://www.esri.com/software/arcgis/arcgisserver`. There are several steps involved in creating a map service from a map document file. The map document file must first be analyzed for suitability and performance issues and any resulting errors must be fixed before final publication to ArcGIS Server. This process involves several steps including a call to an `arcpy.mapping` function along with the use of a couple of tools in `ArcToolbox` that can be called from your script. After errors have been fixed, you can then upload the resulting **Service Definition Draft** file to ArcGIS Server as a service.

Getting ready

The publication of a map document to ArcGIS Server with Python is a three-step process. The first step is to call the `CreateMapSDDraft()` `arcpy.mapping` function. This will convert a map document file to a Service Definition Draft file. This file contains a combination of a map document, information about the server, and a set of service properties. Information about the server includes the server connection or server type being published to, the type of service being published, metadata for the service, and data references. The draft service definition file does not contain data. `CreateMapSDDraft()` also generates a Python dictionary containing errors and warnings that could cause problems with the publication of the service.

The second step is to call the **StageService Tool(.sd)**. Staging compiles the information needed to successfully publish the GIS resources. If your data is not registered with the server, it will be added when Service Definition Draft is staged. Finally, the Service Definition Draft file can be uploaded and published as a GIS service to a specified GIS server by using the **UploadServiceDefinition Tool**. This step takes the Service Definition file, copies it onto the server, extracts the required information, and publishes the GIS resource. Here is an illustration of this process:

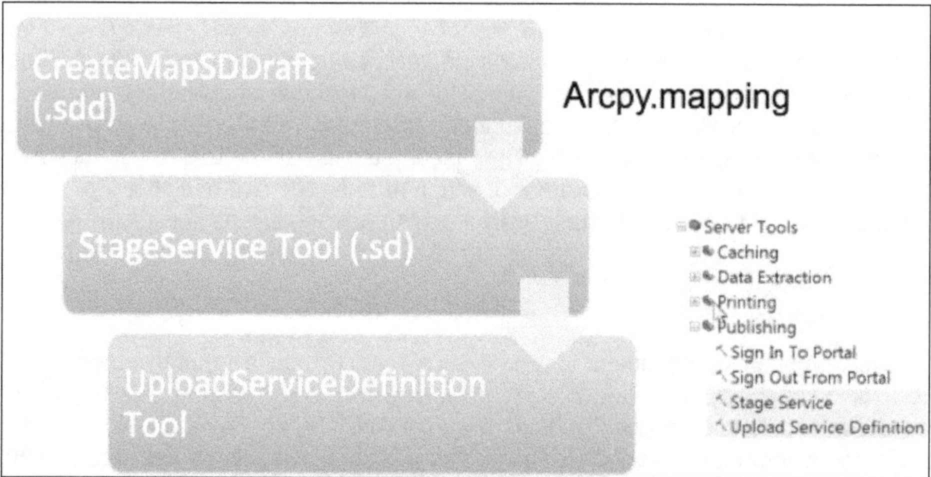

Note that you will need to have access to an ArcGIS Server instance and also have the necessary privileges to publish a service to complete this exercise. In this recipe, you will learn how to publish a map document file to an ArcGIS Server map service.

How to do it...

Follow these steps to analyze a map document for suitability for publication to ArcGIS Server and then publish it as a map service:

1. Create a new IDLE script and save it as `c:\ArcpyBook\Ch4\PublishMapService.py`.
2. Import the `arcpy.mapping` module:

   ```
   import arcpy.mapping as mapping
   ```

3. Set the current workspace:

   ```
   wrkspc = r'c:\ArcpyBook\Ch4'
   ```

4. Get a reference to the map document:

   ```
   mxd = mapping.MapDocument(wrkspc + r"\Crime.mxd")
   ```

5. Define variables for the service name and Service Draft Definition file:

```
service = 'Crime'
sddraft = wrkspc + service + '.sddraft'
```

6. Create the Service Definition Draft file:

```
mapping.CreateMapSDDraft(mxd, sddraft, service)
```

7. Analyze the draft file:

```
analysis = mapping.AnalyzeForSD(wrkspc + "Crime.sddraft")
```

8. Create a looping structure that will loop through all the potential messages, warnings, and errors, and print out the information:

```
for key in ('messages', 'warnings', 'errors'):
    print("----" + key.upper() + "----")
    vars = analysis[key]
    for ((message, code), layerlist) in vars.iteritems():
        print "    ", message, " (CODE %i)" % code
        print("     applies to:",)
        for layer in layerlist:
            print(layer.name)
```

9. The entire script should appear as follows:

```
import arcpy.mapping as mapping
wrkspc = r'c:\ArcpyBook\ch4'
mxd = mapping.MapDocument(wrkspc + r"\Crime.mxd")

service = 'Crime'
sddraft = wrkspc + service + '.sddraft'
mapping.CreateMapSDDraft(mxd, sddraft, service)
analysis = mapping.AnalyzeForSD(wrkspc + "Crime.sddraft")

for key in ('messages', 'warnings', 'errors'):
    print("----" + key.upper() + "----")
    vars = analysis[key]
    for ((message, code), layerlist) in vars.iteritems():
        print "    ", message, " (CODE %i)" % code
        print("     applies to:")
        for layer in layerlist:
            print(layer.name)
```

10. You can check your work by examining the `c:\ArcpyBook\code\Ch4\PublishMapService.py` solution file.

11. Save and run your code to see this output:

```
----MESSAGES----
     Layer draws at all scale ranges  (CODE 30003)
     applies to: District_Crime_Join
Bexar_County_Boundary
District_Crime_Join
Bexar_County_Boundary
Bexar_County_Boundary
Texas_Counties_LowRes
School_Districts
Crime_surf
Bexar_County_Boundary
----WARNINGS----
     Layer's data source has a different projection [GCS_WGS_1984]
than the data frame's projection  (CODE 10001)
     applies to: District_Crime_Join
Bexar_County_Boundary
District_Crime_Join
Bexar_County_Boundary
Bexar_County_Boundary
Texas_Counties_LowRes
School_Districts
Crime_surf
Bexar_County_Boundary
     Missing Tags in Item Description  (CODE 24059)
     applies to:      Missing Summary in Item Description
 (CODE 24058)
     applies to:
----ERRORS----
     Data frame uses a background symbol that is not a solid
fill  (CODE 18)
```

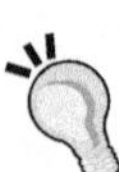

You'll want to pay particular attention to the Errors section. Errors must be fixed before the service can be created. Warnings can indicate problems related to the performance of the service but they won't stop a service from being published. In this case, the error indicates that the data frame uses a background symbol that is not a solid fill. This will need to be corrected in ArcGIS before we can proceed.

12. In ArcMap, open `crime.mxd` in the `c:\ArcpyBook\ch4` folder and right-click on the **Crime** data frame and select **Properties**.
13. Select the **Frame** tab, as seen in this screenshot:

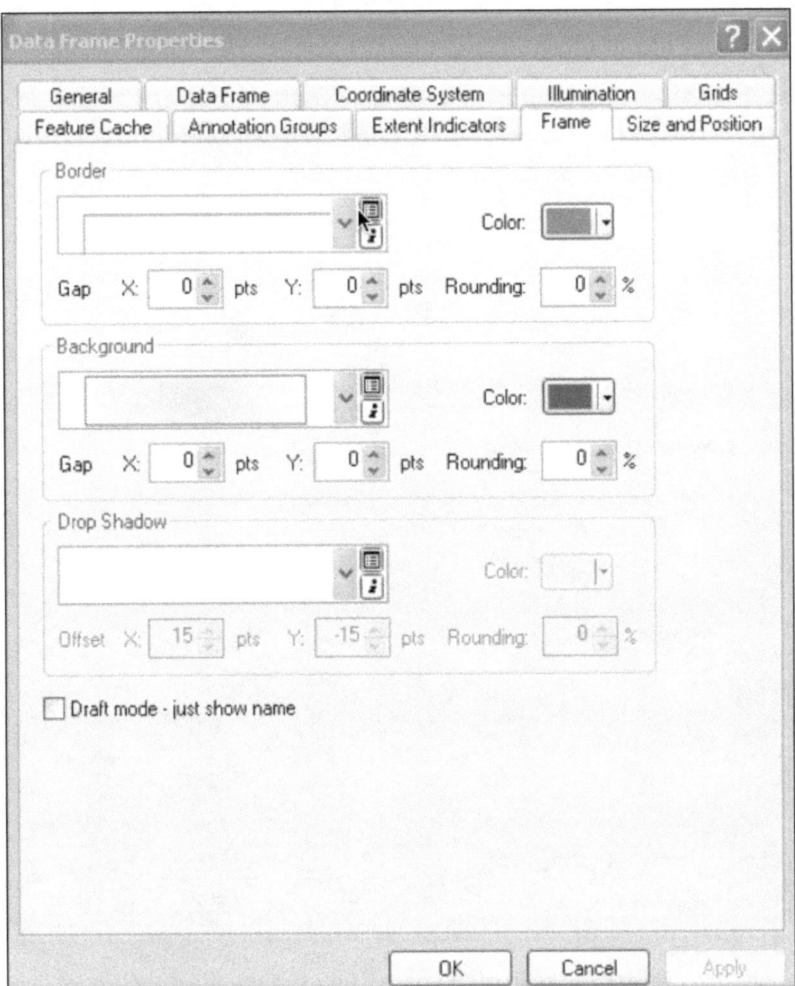

14. Change the **Background** from the current symbol to none and click on **OK**:

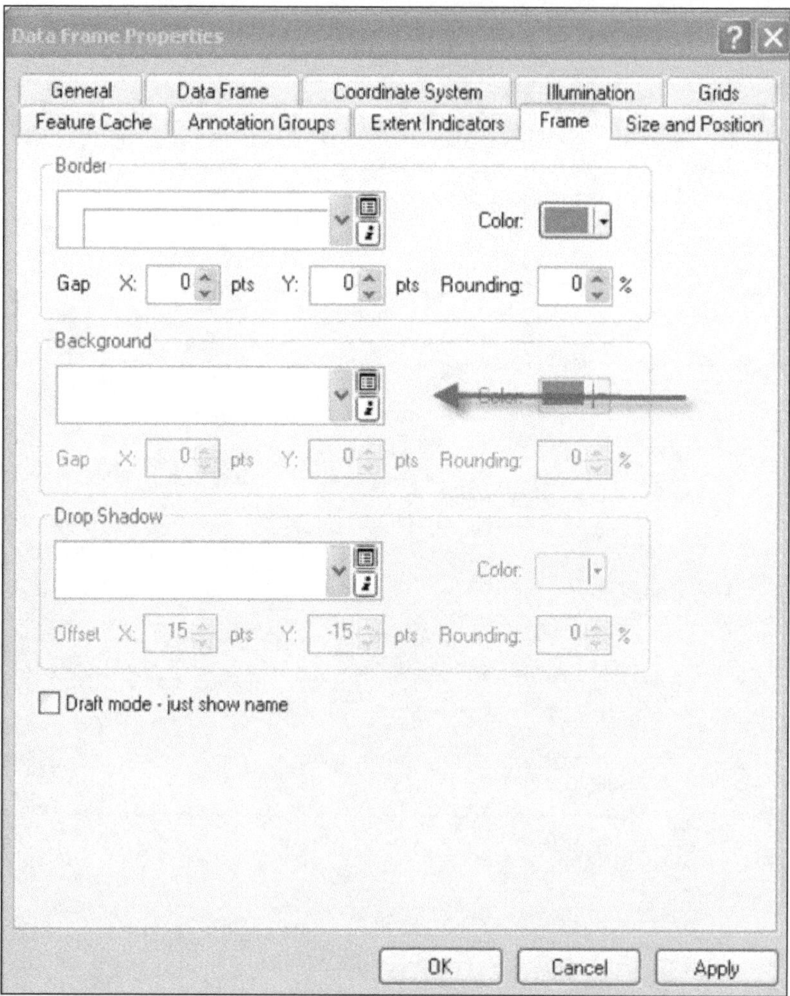

15. Repeat this process for each of the data frames in the map document.
16. Rerun the script you just wrote. This time, you shouldn't see any errors. You do still have a warning that should probably be fixed as well, but warnings won't stop your map document from being published as a service.
17. With all our errors fixed, we'll now convert the `Crime.mxd` file into a `Crime.sd` file. Delete the looping structure that you added in step 6.

18. Add the following `if/else` block of code. Note that I have commented on the line of code that calls the `UploadServiceDefinition` tool. If you have access to an ArcGIS Server instance and have the appropriate privileges and connection information, you can uncomment this line to have it upload the file as a map service. You would also need to add the connection parameters for the instance in the `con` variable, which is passed as the second parameter for this tool. Save and execute the script to see the results:

```
if analysis['errors'] == {}:
    #execute StageService
    arcpy.StageService_server(sddraft,sd)
    #execute UploadServiceDefinition
    #arcpy.UploadServiceDefinition_server(sd, con)
else:
    #if the sddraft analysis contained errors, display them
    print(analysis['errors'])
```

19. Your entire script should appear as follows:

```
import arcpy.mapping as mapping
wrkspc = r'c:\ArcpyBook\ch4'
mxd = mapping.MapDocument(wrkspc + r"\Crime.mxd")

service = 'Crime'
sddraft = wrkspc + service + '.sddraft'
mapping.CreateMapSDDraft(mxd, sddraft, service)
analysis = mapping.AnalyzeForSD(wrkspc + "Crime.sddraft")

if analysis['errors'] == {}:
    #execute StageService
    arcpy.StageService_server(sddraft,sd)
    #execute UploadServiceDefinition
    #arcpy.UploadServiceDefinition_server(sd, con)
else:
    #if the sddraft analysis contained errors, display them
    print(analysis['errors'])
```

20. You can check your work by examining the `c:\ArcpyBook\code\Ch4\PublishMapService2.py` solution file.

21. If you have access to an ArcGIS Server instance and have the necessary privileges, you can uncomment the `UploadServiceDefinition` tool and execute the script.

How it works...

The `CreateMapSDDraft()` function creates a Service Definition Draft file from a map document file. Next, we call the `AnalyzeForSD()` function and examine the results that are returned for any messages, warnings, or errors. Any errors that are identified must then be fixed before the map service can be created. Finally, if no errors are present, we call the `StageService` tool that creates a Service Definition Draft file that can then be passed into the `UploadServiceDefinition` tool for publication to ArcGIS Server.

5

Executing Geoprocessing Tools from Scripts

In this chapter, we will cover the following recipes:

- Finding geoprocessing tools
- Retrieving a toolbox alias
- Executing geoprocessing tools from a script
- Using the output of a tool as an input to another tool

Introduction

ArcGIS for Desktop contains over 800 geoprocessing tools, which can be used in your Python scripts. Using geoprocessing tools from your Pythons scripts enables you to execute complex workflows and perform batch geoprocessing tasks. In this chapter, you will learn how to use these tools in your scripts. Each tool has unique characteristics. The syntax to execute each will differ depending upon the type of input required to successfully execute the tool. We'll examine how you can determine the input parameters for any tool by using the ArcGIS for Desktop help system. The execution of a tool results in the creation of one or more output datasets along with a set of messages that are generated while the tool is running. We'll examine how you can use these messages.

Finding geoprocessing tools

Before using a tool in your geoprocessing script, you will need to make sure that you have access to this tool, based on the current license level of ArcGIS for Desktop that you are running or that your end users will run. In addition to this, any extensions you have licensed and enabled must be taken into consideration as well. This information is contained within the ArcGIS for Desktop help system.

Getting ready

The availability of geoprocessing tools for your script is dependent on the level of the ArcGIS license you are using. In version 10.3 of ArcGIS for Desktop, there are three license levels, namely basic, standard, and advanced. These were formerly known as **ArcView**, **ArcEditor**, and **ArcInfo**, respectively. It is important for you to understand the license level required for the tool that you want to use in your script. In addition to this, the use of extensions in ArcGIS for Desktop can result in the availability of additional tools for your script. There are two primary ways to find tools in ArcGIS for Desktop. The first is to use the search window and the second is to simply browse the contents of **ArcToolbox**. In this recipe, you will learn how to use the search window to find available geoprocessing tools that can be used in your scripts.

How to do it...

1. Open `C:\ArcpyBook\Ch5\Crime_Ch5.mxd` in ArcMap.
2. From the **Geoprocessing** menu item, select **Search For Tools**. This will display the **Search** window, as shown in the following screenshot. By default, you will be searching for **Tools**:

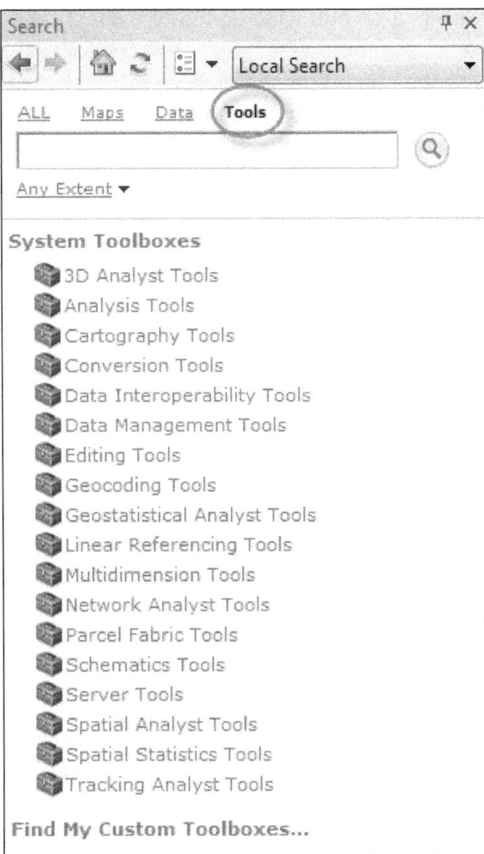

3. Type the `Clip` term into the search textbox. As you begin typing this word, the search textbox will automatically filter the results based on the first few letters you type. You'll notice that for `Clip`, there are three possible tools: `clip(analysis)`, `clip(coverage)`, and `clip(data_management)`. There are a number of cases where there are several geoprocessing tools with the same name. To uniquely define a tool, the toolbox alias is attached to the tool name. We'll examine toolbox aliases in greater detail in the next recipe.

4. For now, click on the search button to generate a list of matching tools. The search should generate a list similar to what you see in the following screenshot. Tools are indicated by a hammer icon in the search results. You'll also see a couple of other icons in the search results. The scroll icon indicates a Python script, and an icon containing multicolored squares indicates a model:

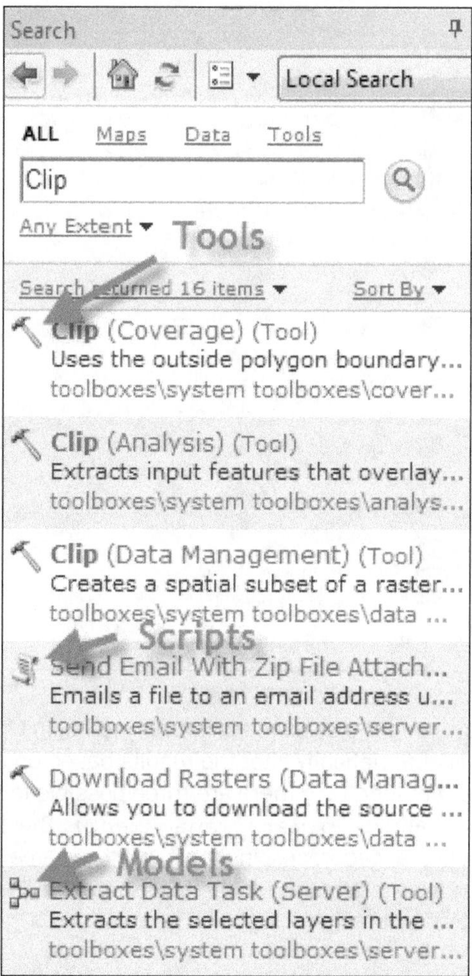

5. Select the **Clip (Analysis)** tool. This will open the dialog box for **the Clip (Analysis)** tool. This isn't all that useful to you as a script programmer. You will probably be more interested in the help provided by ArcGIS for Desktop for a particular tool.

6. Click on the **Tool Help** button at the bottom of the tool dialog box to display detailed information about this particular tool:

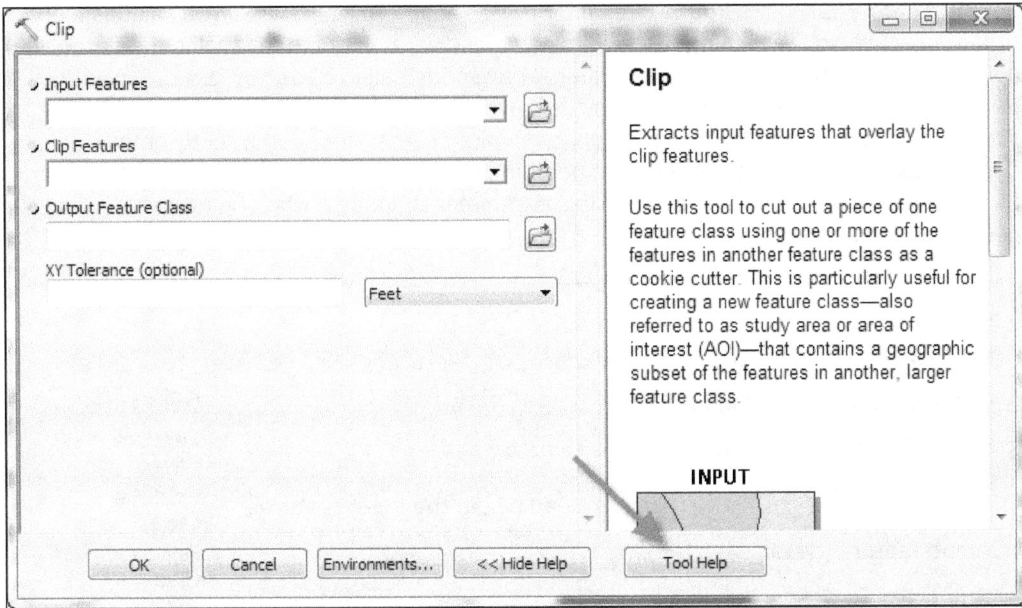

7. Scroll down to the bottom of the help page for the **Clip** tool to examine the syntax for this particular tool.

How it works...

The help system contains a summary, illustration, usage, syntax, code samples, available environment variables, related topics, and licensing information for each tool. As a geoprocessing script programmer, you will primarily be interested in the syntax, code samples, and licensing information sections near the bottom.

[You should always examine the licensing information section at the bottom of the help documentation for each tool, to make sure you have the appropriate license level to use the tool.]

The syntax section contains information about how this tool should be called from your Python script, including the name of the tool and the required and optional input parameters. All the parameters will be enclosed within parentheses. The required parameters for the `Clip` tool are `in_features`, `clip_features`, and `out_feature_class`. When you call this tool from your script, you will be required to provide these parameters to the tool for it to execute correctly. The fourth parameter is an optional parameter called `cluster_tolerance`. Parameters marked as optional in the syntax are surrounded by curly braces. The following screenshot provides an example of an optional parameter surrounded by curly braces. This doesn't mean that you enclose the parameter in curly braces when you call the tool. It is in the help section simply to indicate that this parameter is optional when being called from your geoprocessing script:

Syntax

Clip_analysis (in_features, clip_features, out_feature_class, {cluster_tolerance})

Parameter	Explanation	Data Type
in_features	The features to be clipped.	Feature Layer
clip_features	The features used to clip the input features.	Feature Layer
out_feature_class	The feature class to be created.	Feature Class
cluster_tolerance (Optional)	The minimum distance separating all feature coordinates as well as the distance a coordinate can move in X or Y (or both). Set the value to be higher for data with less coordinate accuracy and lower for data with extremely high accuracy.	Linear unit

Retrieving a toolbox alias

All toolboxes have an alias which, when combined with the tool name, provides a unique reference to any tool in ArcGIS for Desktop. This alias is necessary because a number of tools have the same name. When referencing a tool from your Python script, it is necessary to reference both the tool name and alias.

Getting ready

In the last recipe, we looked at the **Clip** tool. There are actually three **Clip** tools, which can be found in the **Analysis Tools**, **Coverage Tools**, and **Data Management Tools** toolboxes. Each **Clip** tool performs a different function. For instance, the **Clip** tool in the **Analysis Tools** toolbox clips a vector feature class using an input feature, while the **Clip** tool in the **Data Management Tools** toolbox is used to create a spatial subset of a raster. Since it is possible to have multiple tools with the same name, we can uniquely identify a particular tool by providing both the tool name and the toolbox alias in which the tool resides. In this recipe, you will learn how to find the alias of a toolbox.

How to do it...

1. Open `C:\ArcpyBook\Ch5\Crime_Ch5.mxd` in ArcMap.
2. If necessary, open **ArcToolbox**.
3. Find the **Analysis Tools** toolbox, as shown in the following screenshot:

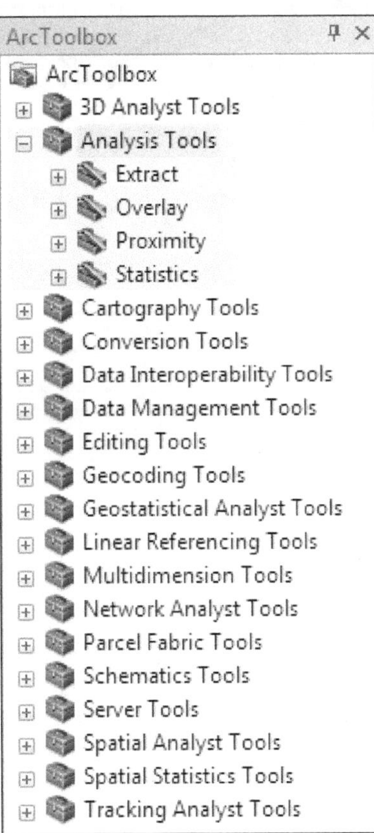

4. Right-click on the **Analysis Tools** toolbox and select **Properties**. This will display the **Analysis Tools Properties** dialog box, as shown in the following screenshot. The **Alias:** textbox will contain the alias:

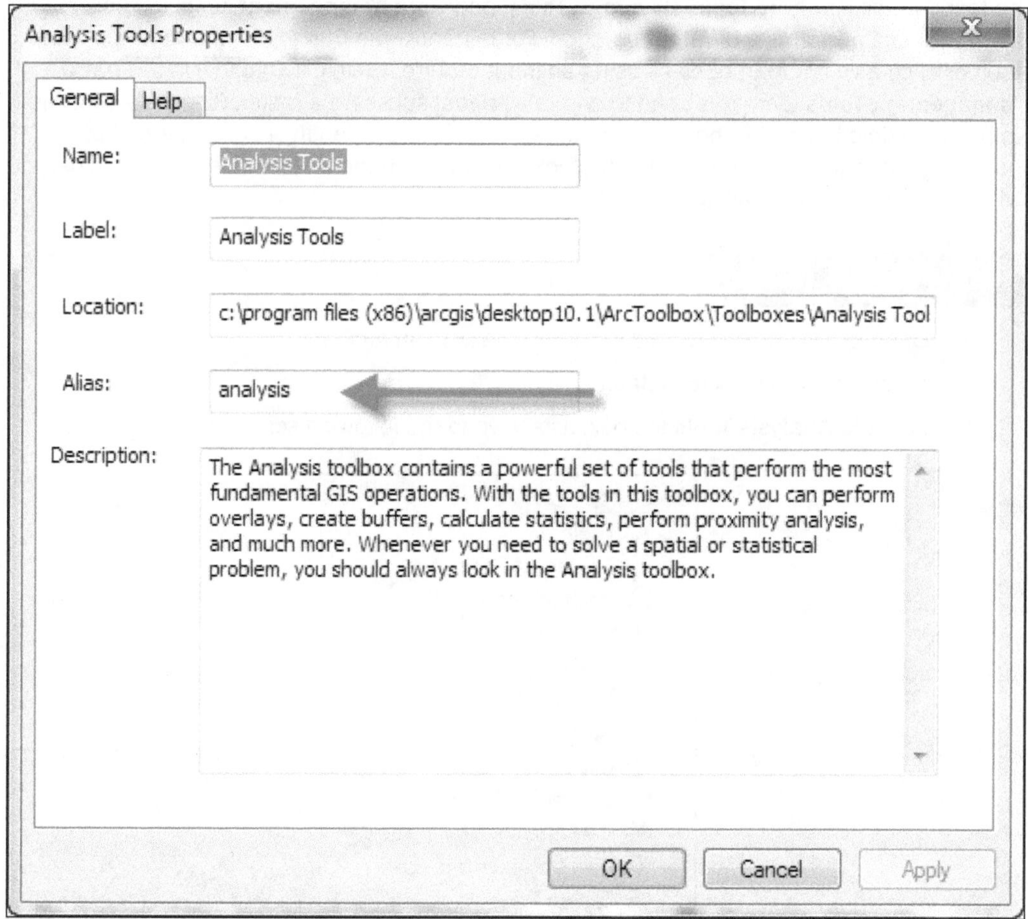

How it works...

You can follow this process to find the alias name of any toolbox. In a Python script, you can execute a tool by referring to the tool with the `<toolname>_<toolbox alias>` syntax. For example, if you were calling the **Buffer** tool, it would be `Buffer_analysis`. Toolbox aliases are invariably simple. They are typically one word and do not include dashes or special characters. In the next recipe, we'll create a simple script that follows this format to execute a tool.

Executing geoprocessing tools from a script

Once you have determined the toolbox alias and then verified the accessibility of the tool based on your current license level, you are ready to add the execution of the tool to a script.

Getting ready

Now that you understand how to find the tools that are available and how to uniquely reference them, the next step is to put this together and execute a tool from a geoprocessing script. In this recipe, you can then execute the tool from your script.

How to do it...

1. Open `C:\ArcpyBook\Ch5\Crime_Ch5.mxd` in ArcMap.
2. Click on the **Add Data** button and add the `EdgewoodSD.shp` file to the table of contents from the `c:\ArcpyBook\Ch5` folder.
3. If needed, turn off the **Crime Density by School District** and **Burglaries in 2009** layers to get a better view of the **EdgewoodSD** layer. There is only one polygon feature in this file. It represents the **Edgewood School District**. Now, we're going to write a script that clips the **Burglaries in 2009** features to this school district.
4. Open the Python window in ArcMap.
5. Import the `arcpy` module:

   ```
   import arcpy
   ```

6. Create a variable that references the input feature class to be clipped:

   ```
   in_features =
   "c:/ArcpyBook/data/CityOfSanAntonio.gdb/Burglary"
   ```

7. Create a variable that references the layer to be used for the clip:

   ```
   clip_features = "c:/ArcpyBook/Ch5/EdgewoodSD.shp"
   ```

8. Create a variable that references the output feature class:

   ```
   out_feature_class = "c:/ArcpyBook/Ch5/ClpBurglary.shp"
   ```

9. Execute the **Clip** tool from the **Analysis Tools** toolbox:

   ```
   arcpy.Clip_analysis(in_features,clip_features,
   out_feature_class)
   ```

10. You can check your work by examining the `c:\ArcpyBook\code\Ch5\ExecuteGeoprocessingTools.py` solution file.

11. Run the script. The output feature class containing only those burglary points within the **EdgewoodSD** school district should be added to the data frame, as shown in the following screenshot:

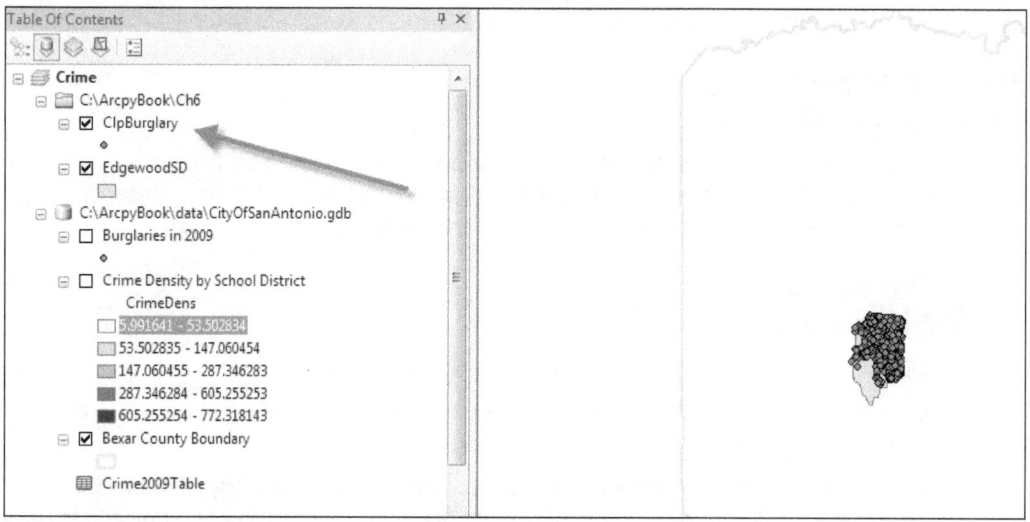

How it works...

The primary line of code of interest in this recipe is the final line that executes the **Clip** tool. Notice that we called this tool by specifying a syntax of `Clip_analysis`, which gives us a reference to the **Clip** tool in the **Analysis Tools** toolbox, which has an alias of `analysis`. We've also passed three parameters that reference the input feature class, clip feature class, and output feature class. I should point out that we hardcoded the paths to each of the datasets. This is not a good programming practice, but in this particular instance, I just wanted to illustrate how to execute a tool. A future chapter will show how you can remove the hardcoding in your scripts and make them much more versatile.

Most tools that you use will require paths to data sources. This path must be the same as the path reported on the ArcCatalog **Location:** toolbar, as shown in the following screenshot:

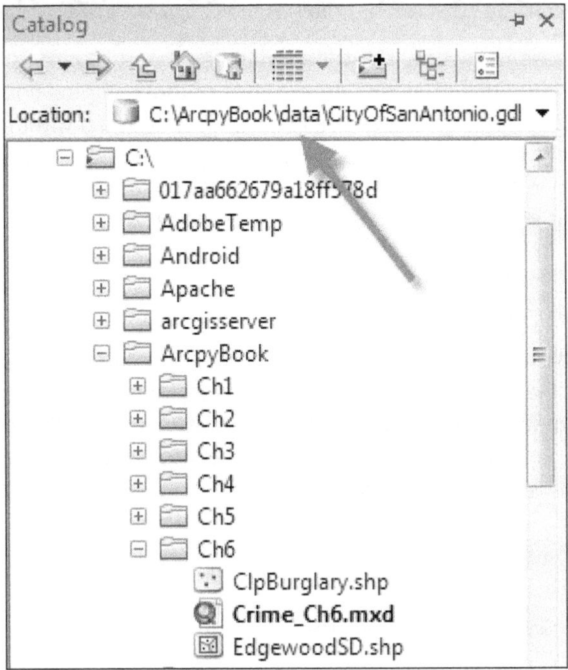

Tools use ArcCatalog to find geographic data using an ArcCatalog path. This path is a string and is unique to each dataset. The path can include folder locations, database connections, or a URL. So, it is important to check the path using ArcCatalog before attempting to write Python scripts against the data. ArcSDE paths require special consideration. Many ArcSDE users do not have standardized connection names, which can cause issues when running models or scripts.

There's more...

Geoprocessing tools are organized in two ways. You can access tools as functions on `arcpy` or as modules matching the toolbox alias name. In the first case, when tools are accessible as functions from `arcpy`, they are called in the format that you followed in this recipe. The tool name is followed by an underscore and then the toolbox alias. In the second form, tools are called as functions of a module, which takes the name of the toolbox alias. Here, `analysis` is the toolbox alias, so it becomes a module. `Clip` is a function of this module and is called as follows:

```
arcpy.analysis.Clip(in_features,clip_features,out_feature_class)
```

Which method you use is really a matter of preference. They both accomplish the same thing, which is the execution of a geoprocessing tool.

Using the output of a tool as an input to another tool

There will be many occasions when you will need to use the output of one tool as input to another tool. This is called tool chaining. An example of tool chaining could involve buffering a `stream` layer and then finding all residential properties that fall within the buffer. In this case, the `Buffer` tool would output a new layer, which would then be used as an input to the `Select by Location` tool or one of the other overlay tools. In this recipe, you will learn how to obtain the output of a tool and use it as input to another tool.

Getting ready

The `Buffer` tool creates an output feature class from an input feature layer using a specified distance. This output feature class can be stored in a variable, which can then be used as an input to another tool, such as the **Select Layer by Location** tool. In this recipe, you will learn how to use the output from the `Buffer` tool as an input to the **Select Layer by Location** tool to find schools that are within a half mile of a stream.

How to do it...

Follow these steps to learn how to access the currently active map document in ArcMap:

1. Open ArcMap with a new map document file (`.mxd`).
2. Click on the **Add Data** button and add the streams and schools shapefiles from `c:\ArcpyBook\data\TravisCounty`.
3. Click on the Python window button.
4. Import the `arcpy` module:

   ```
   import arcpy
   ```

5. Set the workspace:

   ```
   arcpy.env.workspace = "c:/ArcpyBook/data/TravisCounty"
   ```

6. Start a `try` statement and add variables for the streams, buffered streams layer, distance, and schools:

   ```
   try:
     # Buffer areas of impact around major roads
     streams = "Streams.shp"
     streamsBuffer = "StreamsBuffer.shp"
     distance = "2640 Feet"
     schools2mile = "Schools.shp"
     schoolsLyrFile = 'Schools2Mile_lyr'
   ```

7. Execute the Buffer tool by passing in the input feature class, output feature class, distance, and several optional variables that control the look of the output buffer.

```
arcpy.Buffer_analysis(streams, streamsBuffer,
distance,'FULL','ROUND','ALL')
```

8. Create a temporary layer for the schools by using the `MakeFeatureLayer` tool:

```
arcpy.MakeFeatureLayer_management(schools2mile,
schoolsLyrFile)
```

9. Select all schools within a half mile of a stream by using the `SelectLayerByLocation` tool:

```
arcpy.SelectLayerByLocation_management(schoolsLyrFile,
'intersect', streamsBuffer)
```

10. Add the `except` block to catch any errors:

```
except Exception as e:
  print(e.message)
```

11. The entire script should appear as follows:

```
import arcpy
arcpy.env.workspace = "c:/ArcpyBook/data/TravisCounty"
try:
    # Buffer areas of impact around major roads
    streams = "Streams.shp"
    streamsBuffer = "StreamsBuffer"
    distance = "2640 Feet"
    schools2mile = "Schools.shp"
    schoolsLyrFile = 'Schools2Mile_lyr'

    arcpy.Buffer_analysis(streams, streamsBuffer, distance,'FULL','ROUND','ALL')

    # Make a layer
    arcpy.MakeFeatureLayer_management(schools2mile, schoolsLyrFile)
    arcpy.SelectLayerByLocation_management(schoolsLyrFile, 'intersect', streamsBuffer)
except Exception as e:
    print(e.message)
```

12. You can check your work by examining the `c:\ArcpyBook\code\Ch5\ToolOutputUsedAsInput.py` solution file.

13. Run the script to view the results shown in the following screenshot:

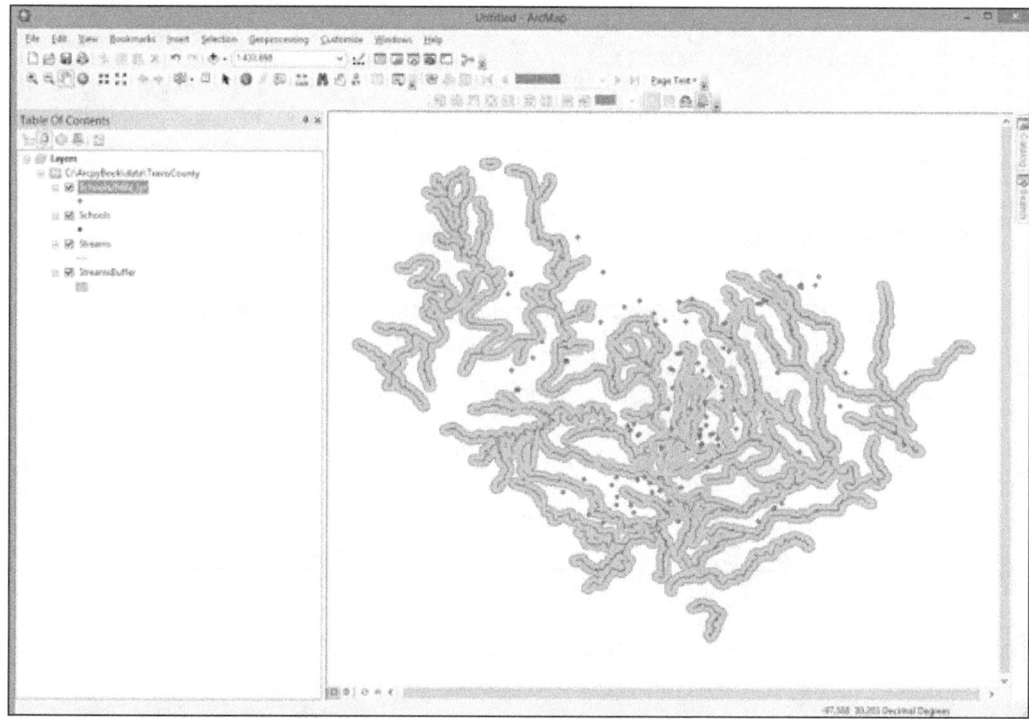

How it works...

The `Buffer` tool creates an output feature class, which we call `StreamsBuffer.shp` and is stored in a variable called `streamsBuffer`. The `streamsBuffer` variable is then used as an input to the `SelectLayerByLocation` tool as the third parameter being passed to the function. The creation of the `Schools2Mile_lyr` layer file accomplishes this output as an input parameter as well. Using the output of one tool simply requires that you create a variable to hold the output data and then it can be reused as needed in other tools.

6

Creating Custom Geoprocessing Tools

In this chapter, we will cover the following recipes:

- Creating a custom geoprocessing tool
- Creating a Python toolbox

Introduction

In addition to accessing the system tools provided by ArcGIS, you can also create your own custom tools. These tools work in the same way as system tools and can be used in ModelBuilder, a Python window, or standalone Python scripts. Many organizations build their own library of tools that perform geoprocessing operations specific to their data.

Creating a custom geoprocessing tool

Along with being able to execute any of the available tools in your scripts, you can also create your own custom tools, which can also be called from a script. Custom tools are frequently created to handle geoprocessing tasks that are specific to an organization. These tools can be easily shared as well.

Getting ready

In this recipe, you will learn how to create custom geoprocessing script tools by attaching a Python script to a custom toolbox in ArcToolbox. There are a number of advantages of creating a custom script tool. When you take this approach, the script becomes a part of the geoprocessing framework, which means that it can be run from a model, command line, or another script. Also, the script has access to the environment settings and help documentation of ArcMap. Other advantages include a nice, easy-to-use user interface and error prevention capabilities. Error prevention capabilities that are provided include a dialog box that informs the user of certain errors.

These custom developed script tools must be added to a custom toolbox that you create, because the system toolboxes provided with ArcToolbox are read-only toolboxes, and thus can't accept new tools.

In this recipe, you are going to be provided with a prewritten Python script that reads wildfire data from a comma-delimited text file, and writes this information to a point feature class called `FireIncidents`. References to these datasets have been hardcoded, so you are going to have to alter the script to accept dynamic variable inputs. You'll then attach the script to a custom tool in ArcToolbox to give your end users a visual interface to use the script.

How to do it...

The custom Python geoprocessing scripts that you write can be added to ArcToolbox inside custom toolboxes. You are not allowed to add your scripts to any of the system toolboxes, such as **Analysis** or **Data Management**. However, by creating a new custom toolbox, you can add scripts in this way:

1. Open ArcMap with an empty map document file and open the ArcToolbox window.
2. Right-click anywhere in the white space area of ArcToolbox and select **Add Toolbox**.
3. Navigate to the `C:\ArcpyBook\Ch6` folder.
4. In the **Add Toolbox** dialog box, click on the new toolbox button. This will create a new toolbox with a default name of `Toolbox.tbx`; you will rename the toolbox in the next step:

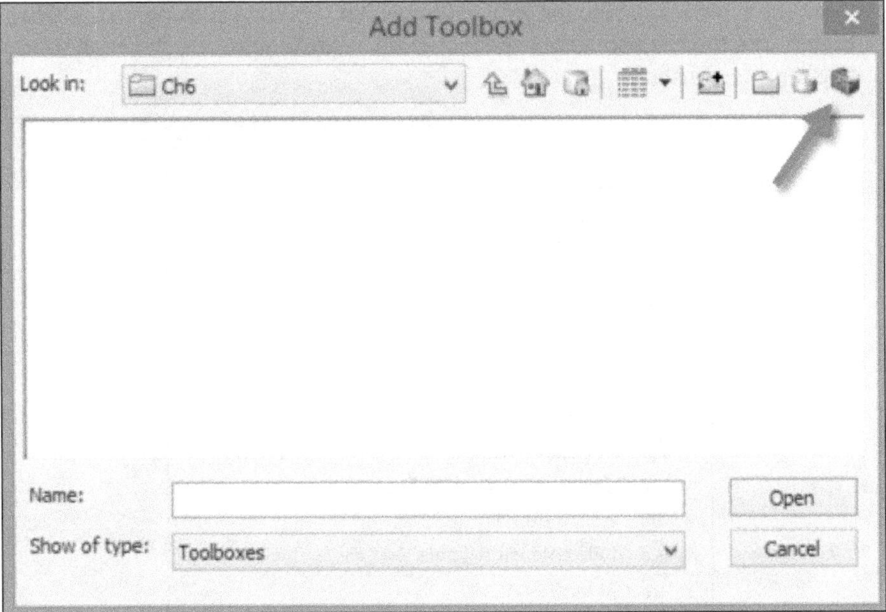

5. Name the toolbox `WildfireTools.tbx`:

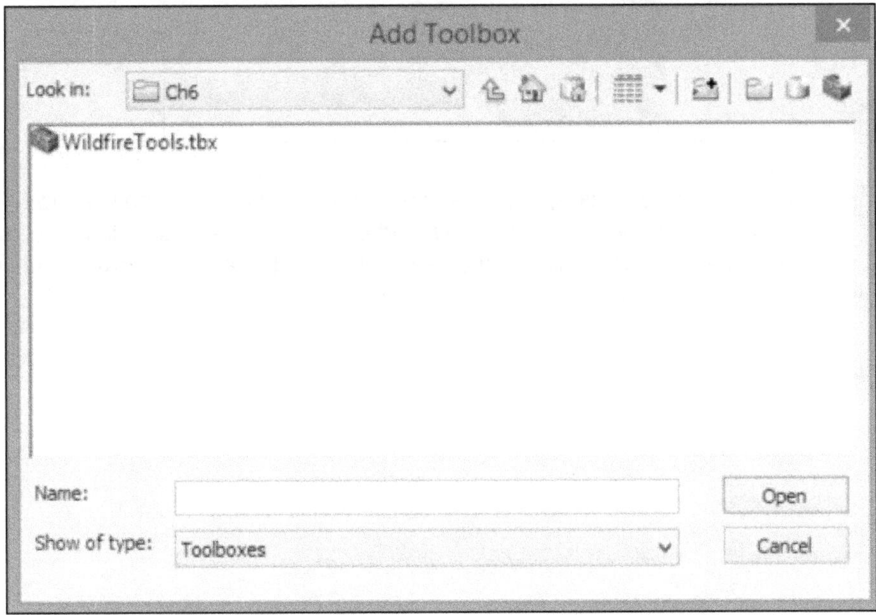

6. Open the toolbox by selecting `WildfireTools.tbx` and clicking on the **Open** button. The toolbox should now be displayed in **ArcToolbox**, as shown in the following screenshot:

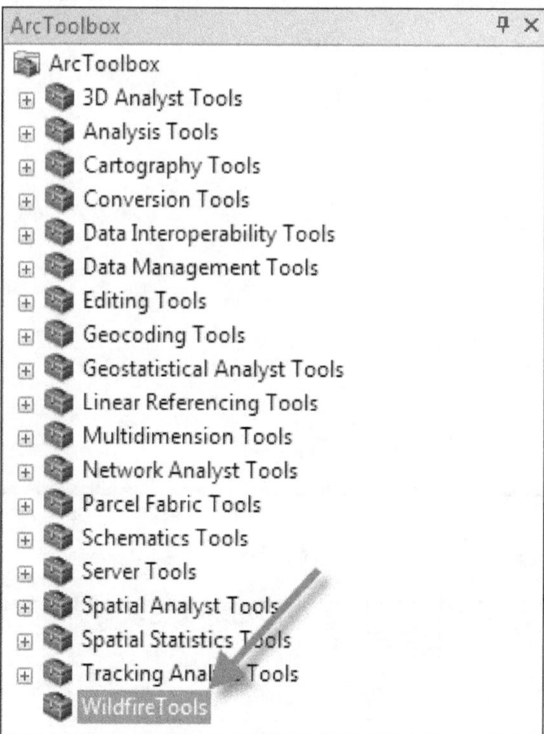

7. Each toolbox should be given a name and an alias. The alias will be used to uniquely define your custom tool. Alias names should be kept short and should not include any special characters. Right-click on the new toolbox and select **Properties**. Add an alias of `wildfire`, as shown in the following screenshot:

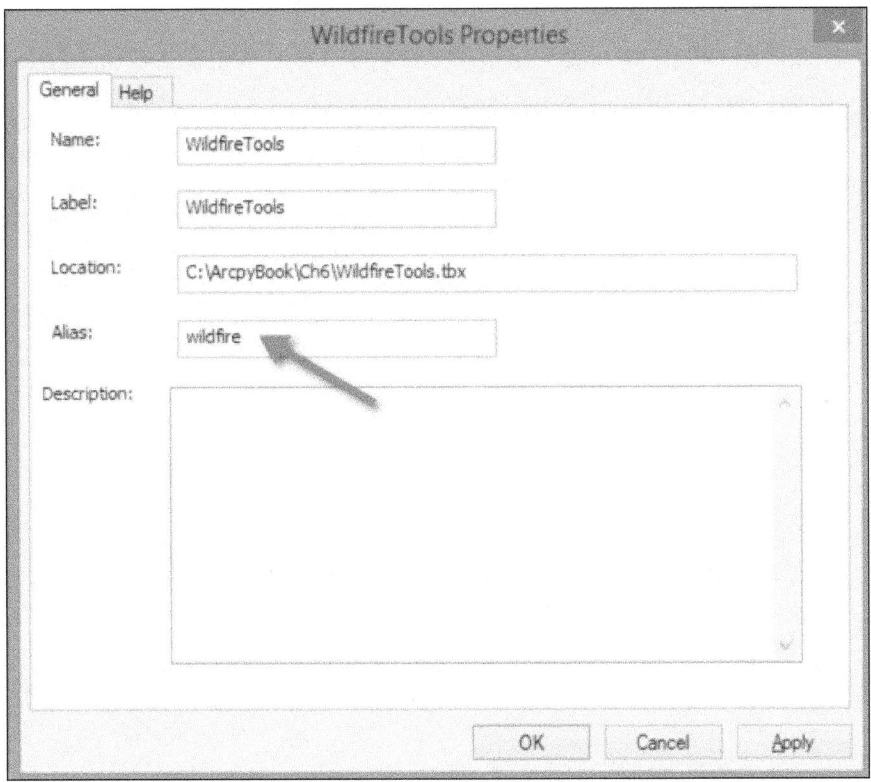

You can optionally create a new toolset inside this toolbox by right-clicking on the toolbox and navigating to **New | Toolset**. Toolsets allow you to functionally group your scripts. In this example, it won't be necessary to do this, but if you need to group your scripts in the future, then this is how you can accomplish it.

8. In this next step, we will alter an existing Python script called `InsertWildfires.py` to accept dynamic inputs that will be provided by the user of the tool through the ArcToolbox interface. Open `c:\ArcpyBook\Ch6\InsertWildfires.py` in IDLE.

   Notice that we have hardcoded the path to our workspace as well as the comma-delimited text file containing the wildland fire incidents:

```
arcpy.env.workspace =
"C:/ArcpyBook/data/Wildfires/WildlandFires.mdb"
f =
open("C:/ArcpyBook/data/Wildfires/NorthAmericaWildfires_2007275.
txt","r")
```

9. Delete the preceding two lines of code.

   In addition to this, we have also hardcoded the name of the output feature class:

   ```
   cur = arcpy.InsertCursor("FireIncidents")
   ```

   This hardcoding limits the usefulness of our script. If the datasets move or are deleted, the script will no longer run. Additionally, the script lacks the flexibility to specify different input and output datasets. In the next step, we will remove this hardcoding and replace it with the ability to accept dynamic input.

10. We will use the `GetParameterAsText()` function found in `arcpy` to accept dynamic input from the user. Add the following lines of code to the try block, so that your code appears as follows:

    ```
    try:
      #the output feature class name
      outputFC = arcpy.GetParameterAsText(0)

      # template featureclass that defines the attribute schema
      fClassTemplate = arcpy.GetParameterAsText(1)

      # open the file to read
      f = open(arcpy.GetParameterAsText(2),'r')


      arcpy.CreateFeatureclass_management
      (os.path.split(outputFC)[0], os.path.split(outputFC)[1],
      "point", fClassTemplate)
    ```

    Notice that we call the `CreateFeatureClass` tool, found in the **Data Management Tools** toolbox, passing the `outputFC` variable along with the template feature class (`fClassTemplate`). This tool will create the empty feature class containing the output feature class defined by the user.

11. You will also need to alter the line of code that creates an `InsertCursor` object. Change the line as follows:

    ```
    with arcpy.da.InsertCursor(outputFC) as cur:
    ```

12. The entire script should appear as follows:

    ```
    #Script to Import data to a feature class within a geodatabase
    import arcpy, os
    try:
        outputFC = arcpy.GetParameterAsText(0)
        fClassTemplate = arcpy.GetParameterAsText(1)
    ```

```
    f = open(arcpy.GetParameterAsText(2),'r')
    arcpy.CreateFeatureclass_management(os.path.split(outputFC)
    [0], os.path.split(outputFC)[1],"point",fClassTemplate)
    lstFires = f.readlines()
    with arcpy.da.InsertCursor(outputFC) as cur:
        cntr = 1
        for fire in lstFires:
            if 'Latitude' in fire:
                continue
            vals = fire.split(",")
            latitude = float(vals[0])
            longitude = float(vals[1])
            confid = int(vals[2])
            pnt = arcpy.Point(longitude, latitude)
            feat = cur.newRow()
            feat.shape = pnt
            feat.setValue("CONFIDENCEVALUE", confid)
            cur.insertRow(feat)
            arcpy.AddMessage("Record number" + str(cntr) +
            "written to feature class")
            cntr = cntr + 1
except:
    print arcpy.GetMessages()
finally:
    f.close()
```

13. You can check your work by examining the `c:\ArcpyBook\code\Ch6\InsertWildfires.py` solution file.
14. In the next step, we will add the script that we just created to the **Wildfire Tools** toolbox as a script tool.
15. In ArcToolbox, right-click on the **Wildfire Tools** custom toolbox that you created earlier and navigate to **Add** | **Script**. This will display the **Add Script** dialog, as shown in the following screenshot. Give your script a name, label, and description. The **Name:** field can not contain any spaces or special characters. The **Label:** field is the name that shows up next to the script. For this example, give it a label of `Load Wildfires From Text`. Finally, add some descriptive information that details the operations that the script will perform.

16. The details relating to **Name:**, **Label:**, and **Description:** are shown in the following screenshot:

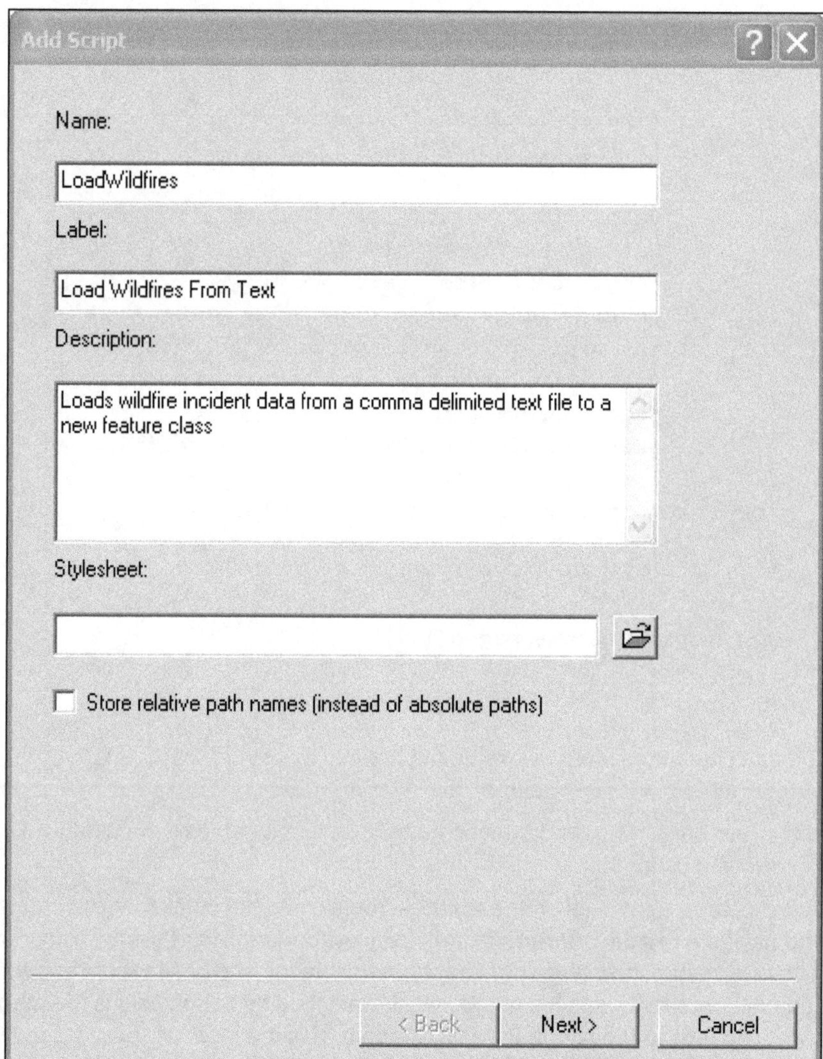

17. Click on **Next** to display the next input dialog box for **Add Script**.
18. In this dialog box, you will specify the script that will be attached to the tool. Navigate to `c:\ArcpyBook\Ch6\InsertWildfires.py` and add `InsertWildfires.py` as the script.

19. You will also want to make sure that the **Run Python script in process** checkbox is selected, as shown in the following screenshot. Running a Python script *in process*. increases the performance of your script.

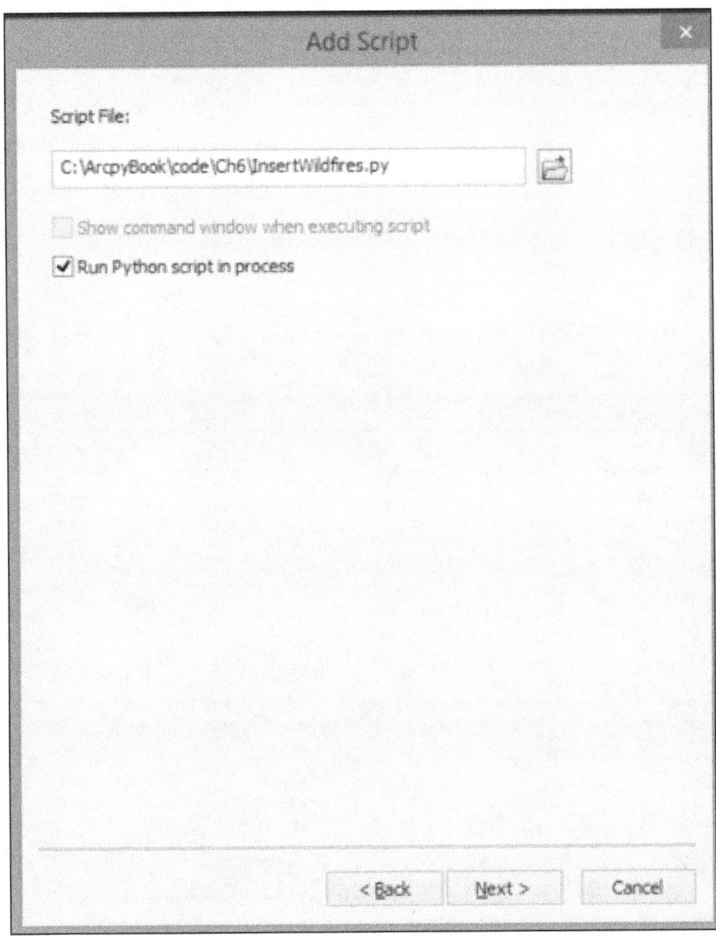

Running a script out of process requires ArcGIS to create a separate process to execute the script. The time it takes to start this process and execute the script leads to performance problems. Always run your scripts in process. Running a script in process means that ArcGIS does not have to spawn a second process to run the script. It runs in the same process space as ArcGIS.

20. Click on **Next** to display the parameter window, as shown in the following screenshot:

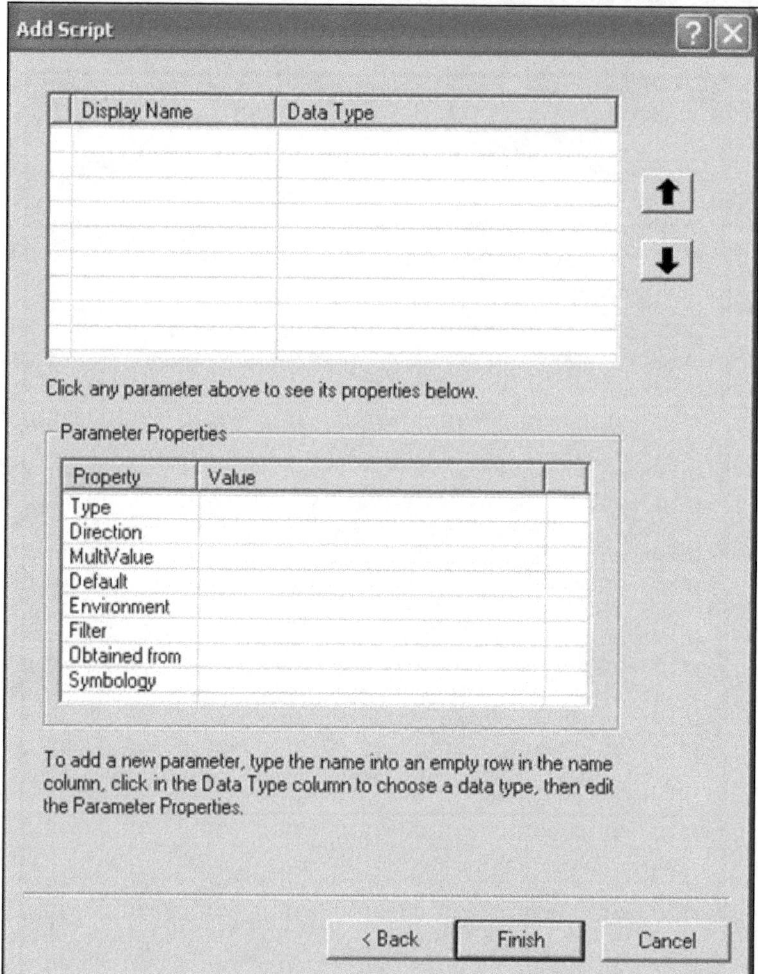

Each parameter that you enter in this dialog box corresponds to a single call to `GetParameterAsText()`. Earlier, you altered your script to accept dynamic parameters through the `GetParameterAsText()` method. The parameters should be entered in this dialog box in the same order that your script expects to receive them. For instance, you inserted the following line of code in your code:

```
outputFC = arcpy.GetParameterAsText(0)
```

The first parameter that you add to the dialog box will need to correspond to this line. In our code, this parameter represents the feature class that will be created as a result of this script. You add parameters by clicking on the first available row under **Display Name**. You can enter any text in this row. This text will be displayed to the user. You will also need to select a corresponding data type for the parameter. In this case, Data Type should be set to **Feature Class**, since this is the expected data that will be gathered from the user. Each parameter also has a number of properties that can be set. Some of the more important properties include **Type**, **Direction**, and **Default**.

21. Enter the information, as shown in the following screenshot, into your dialog box, for the output feature class. Make sure that you set **Direction** to `Output`:

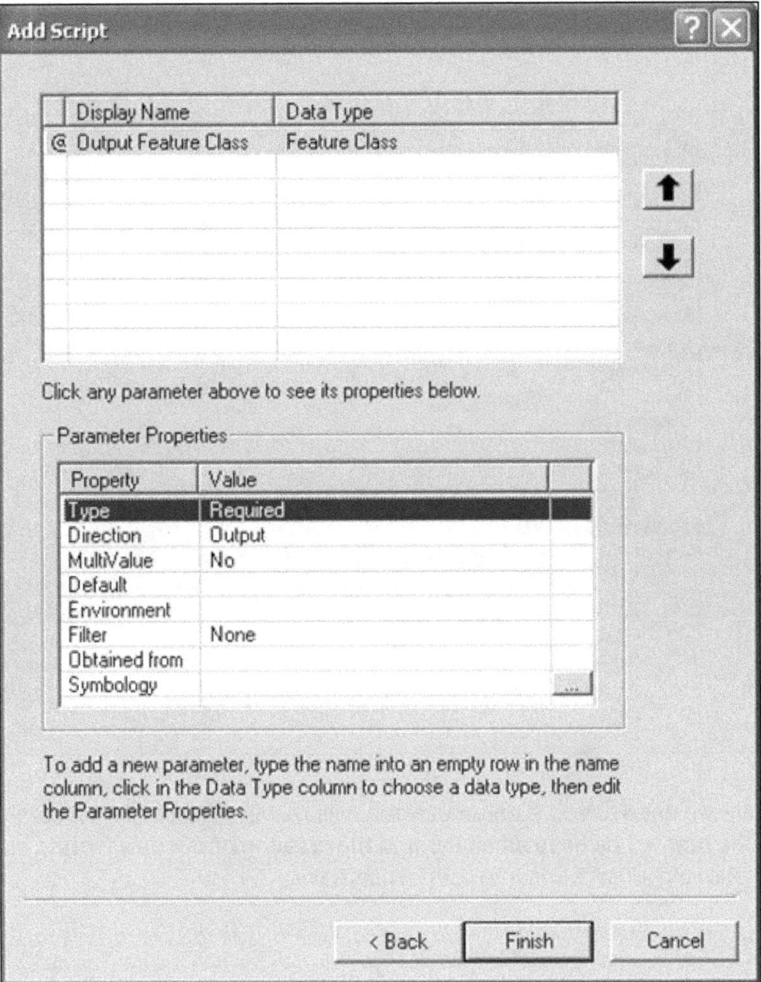

22. Next, we need to add a parameter that defines the feature class that will be used as the attribute template for our new feature class. Enter the following information in your dialog box:

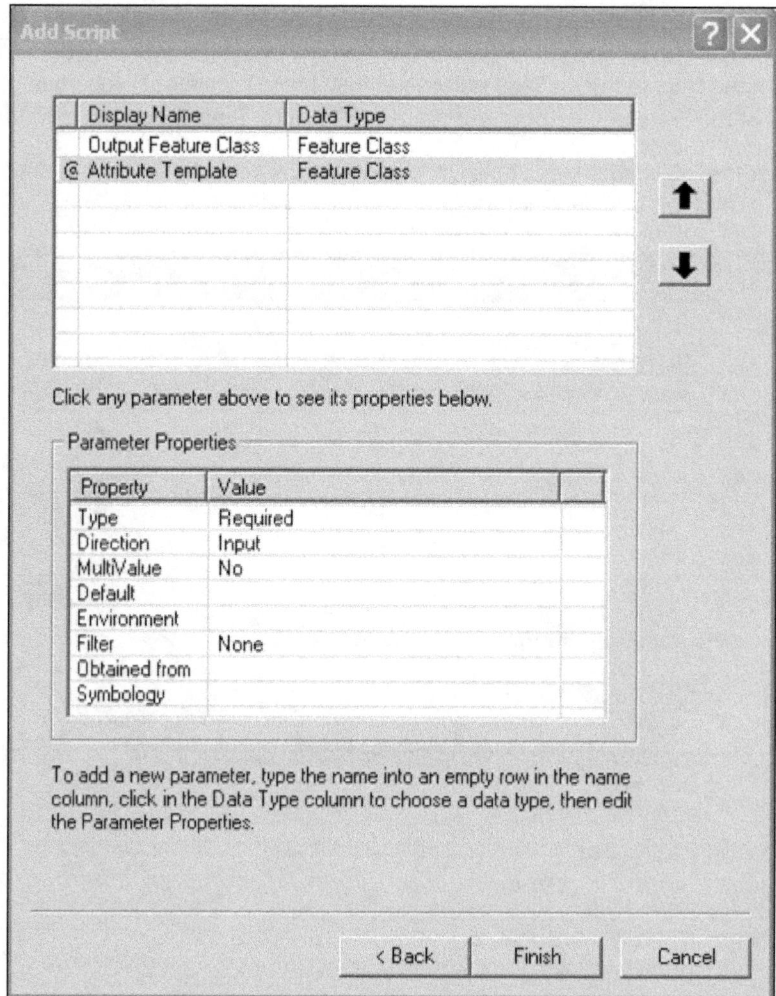

23. Finally, we need to add a parameter that will be used to specify the comma-delimited text file that will be used as an input in the creation of our new feature class. Enter the following information into your dialog box:

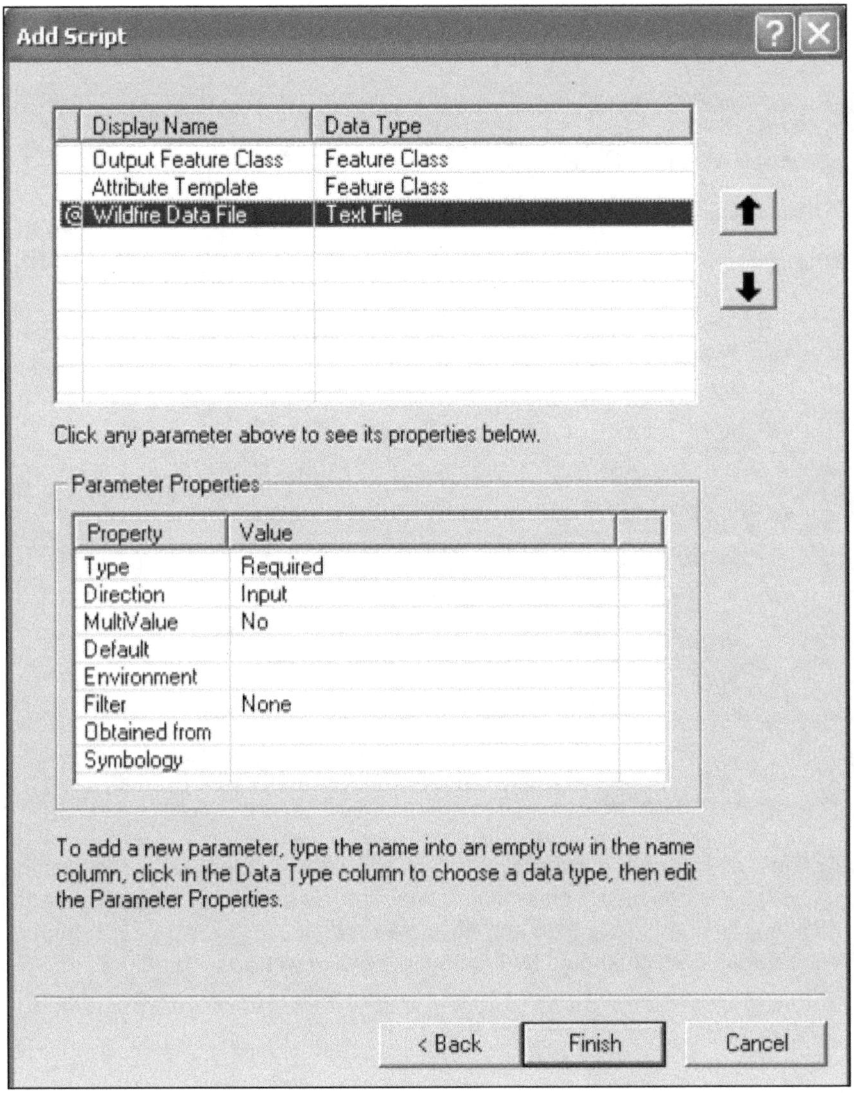

Add Script
Display Name
Data Type
Output Feature Class
Feature Class
Attribute Template
Feature Class
Wildfire Data File
Text File
Click any parameter above to see its properties below.
Parameter Properties
Property
Value
Type
Required
Direction
Input
MultiValue
No
Default
Environment
Filter
None
Obtained from
Symbology
To add a new parameter, type the name into an empty row in the name column, click in the Data Type column to choose a data type, then edit the Parameter Properties.
< Back
Finish
Cancel

24. Click on **Finish**. The new script tool will be added to your **Wildfire Tools** toolbox, as shown in the following screenshot:

Wildfire Tools
Load Wildfires From Text

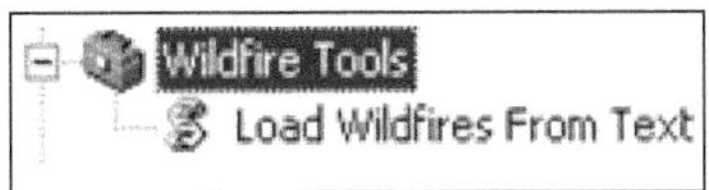

25. Now, we'll test the tool to make sure it works. Double-click on the script tool to display the dialog box, as shown in the following screenshot:

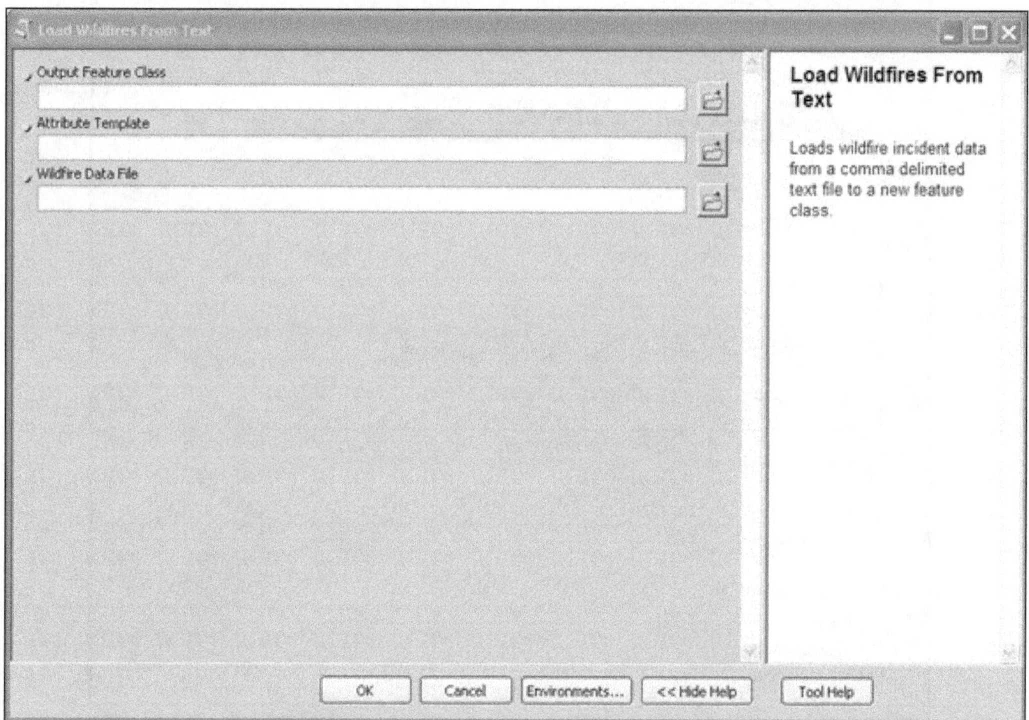

26. Define a new output feature class, which should be loaded inside the existing `WildlandFires.mdb` personal geodatabase, as shown in the next screenshot. Click on the open folder icon and navigate to the `WildlandFires.mdb` personal geodatabase, which should be located in `c:\ArcpyBook\data\Wildfires`.

27. You will also need to give your new feature class a name. In this case, we'll name the feature class `TodaysWildfires`, but the name can be whatever you'd like. In the following screenshot, you can see an example of how this should be done. Click on the **Save** button:

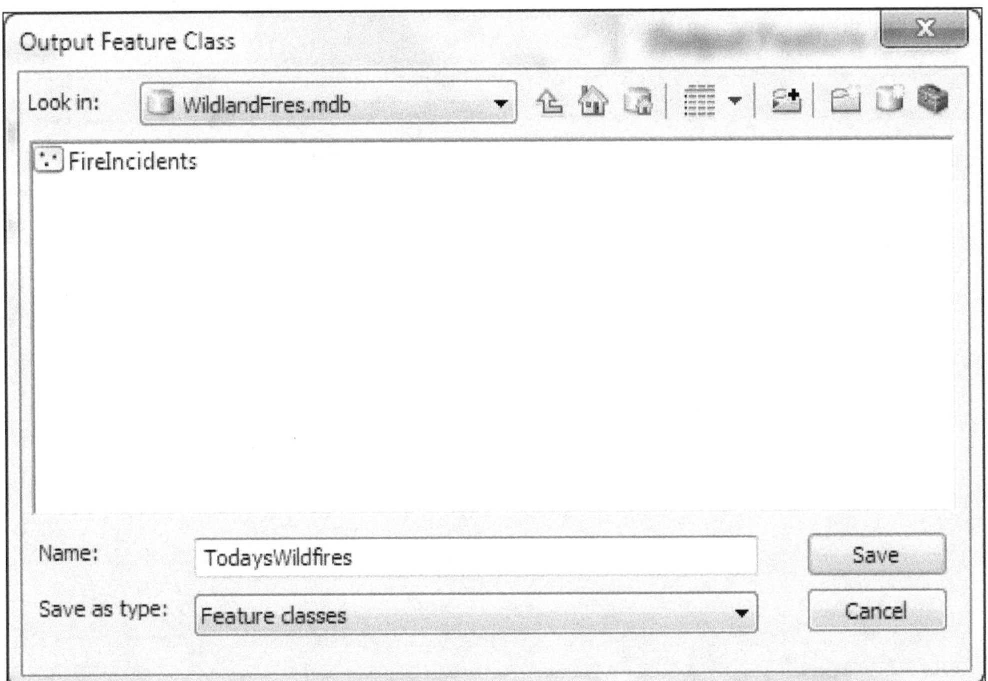

28. For the attribute template, you will want to point to the `FireIncidents` feature class that has already been created for you. This feature class contains a field called `CONFIDENCEVAL`. This field will be created in our new feature class. Click on the **Browse** button, navigate to `c:\ArcpyBook\data\Wildfires\WildlandFires.mdb`, and you should see the `FireIncidents` feature class. Select it and click on **Add**.

29. Finally, the last parameter needs to point to our comma-delimited text file containing wildland fires. This file can be found at `c:\ArcpyBook\data\Wildfires\NorthAmericaWildfires_2007275.txt`. Click on the **Browse** button and navigate to `c:\ArcpyBook\data\Wildfires`. Click on `NorthAmericaWildfires_2007275.txt` and click on the **Add** button. Your tool should appear as follows:

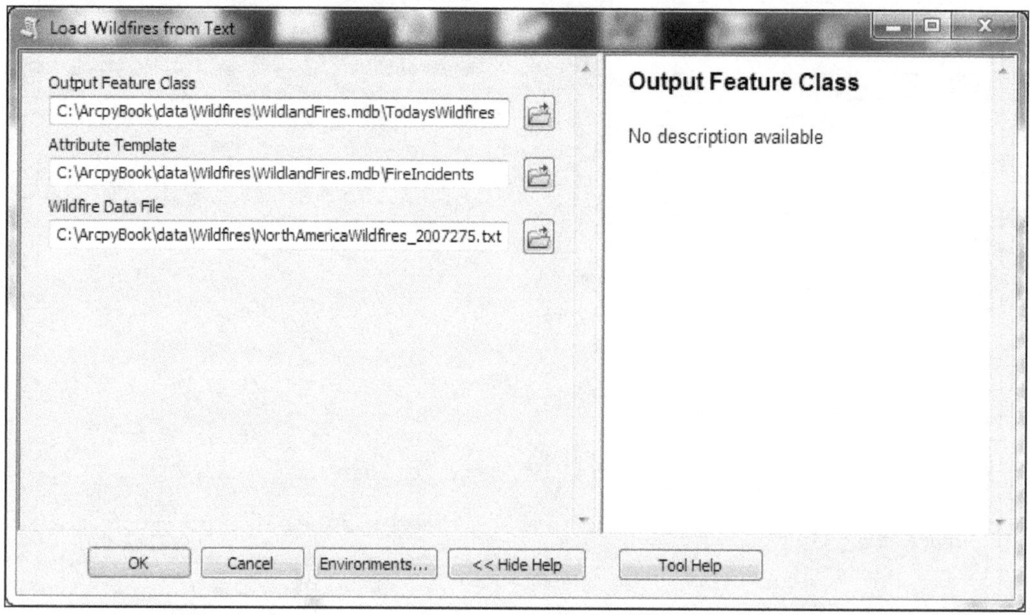

30. Click on **OK** to execute the tool. Any messages will be written to the dialog box shown in the following screenshot. This is a standard dialog box for any geoprocessing tool.

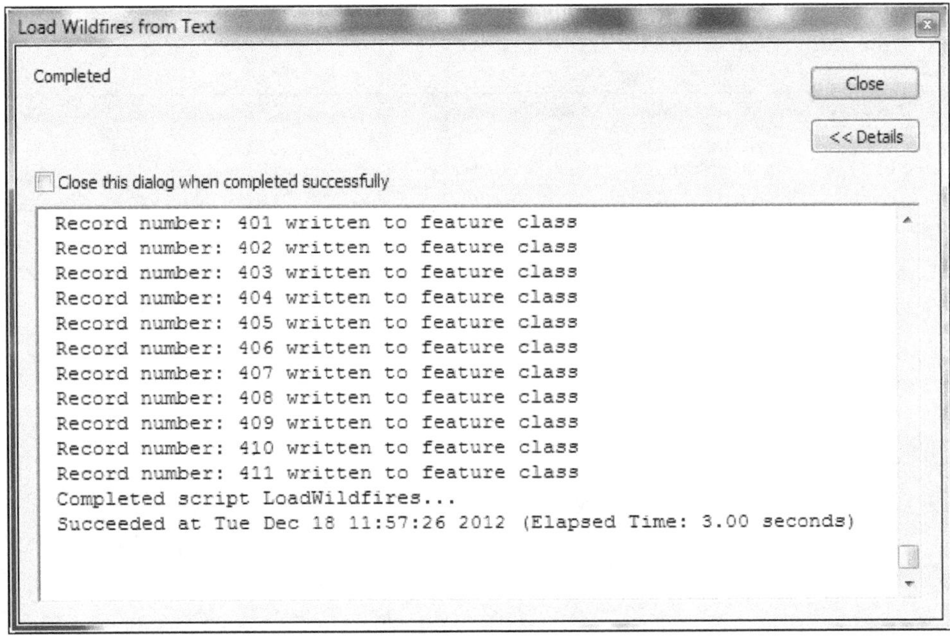

31. If everything is set up correctly, you should see the following screenshot, which shows that a new feature class will be added to the ArcMap display:

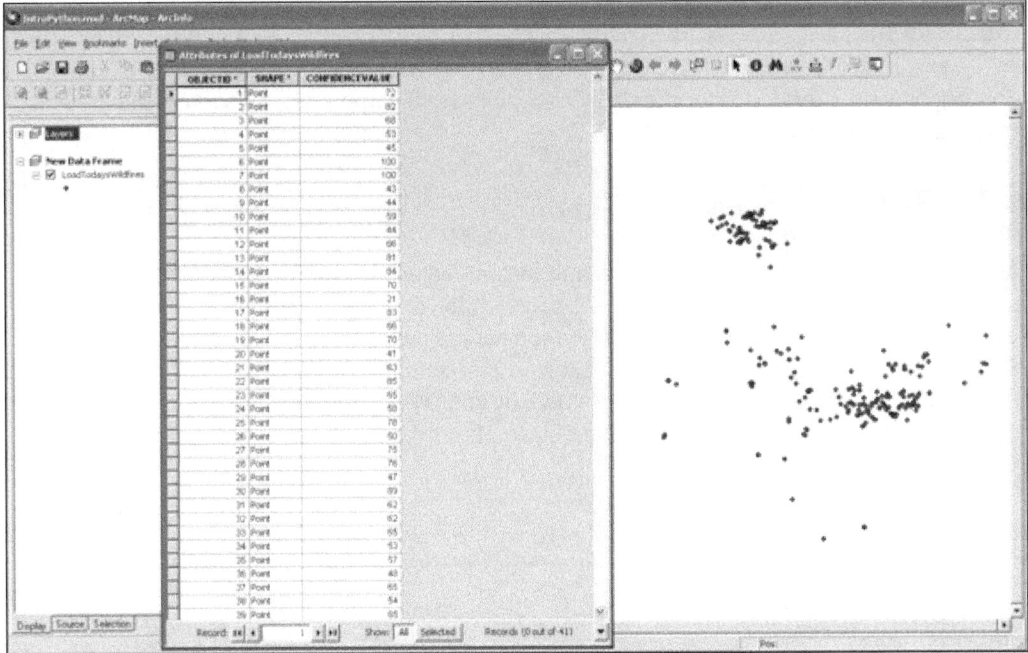

32. In ArcMap, select **add basemap** and then choose the Topographic `basemap`. Click on the **Add** button to add the `basemap` layer.

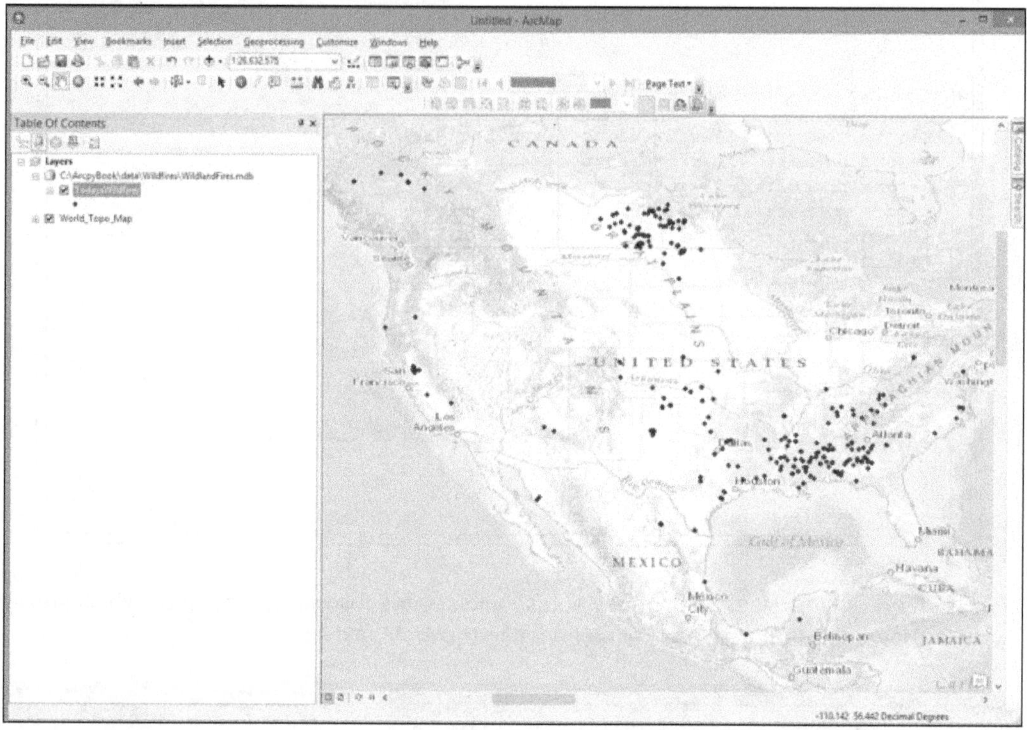

This will provide a reference for the data that you have just imported, as seen in the preceding screenshot.

How it works...

Almost all script tools have parameters, and the values are set for the tool dialog box. When the tool is executed, the parameter values are sent to your script. Your script reads these values and then proceeds with its work. Python scripts can accept parameters as input. Parameters, also known as arguments, allow your scripts to become dynamic. Up to this point, all of our scripts have used hardcoded values. By specifying input parameters for a script, you are able to supply the name of the feature class at runtime. This capability makes your scripts more versatile.

The `GetParameterAsText()` method, which is used to capture parameter input, is zero-based with the first parameter entered occupying a `0` index and each successive parameter is incremented by `1`. The output feature class that will be created by reading the comma-delimited text file is specified in the `outputFC` variable, which is retrieved by `GetParameterAsText(0)`. With `GetParameterAsText(1)`, we capture a feature class that will act as a template for the output feature class attribute schema. The attribute fields in the template feature class are used to define the fields that will populate our output feature class. Finally, `GetParameterAsText(2)` is used to create a variable called `f`, which will hold the comma-delimited text file that will be read.

There's more...

The `arcpy.GetParameterAsText()` method is not the only way to capture information passed into your script. When you call a Python script from the command line, you can pass in a set of arguments. When passing arguments to a script, each word must be separated by a space. These words are stored in a zero-based list object called `sys.argv`. With `sys.argv`, the first item in the list, referenced by the `0` index, stores the name of the script. Each successive word is referenced by the next integer. Therefore, the first parameter will be stored in `sys.argv[1]`, the second in `sys.argv[2]`, and so on. These arguments can then be accessed from within your script.

It is recommended that you use the `GetParameterAsText()` function rather than `sys.argv`, because `GetParameterAsText()` does not have a character limit, whereas `sys.argv` has a limit of 1,024 characters per parameter. In either case, once the parameters have been read into the script, your script can continue execution using the input values.

Creating a Python toolbox

There are two ways to create toolboxes in ArcGIS: script tools in custom toolboxes that we covered in the last recipe, and script tools in Python toolboxes. Python toolboxes were introduced in version 10.1 of ArcGIS and they encapsulate everything in one place: parameters, validation code, and source code. This is not the case with custom toolboxes, which are created using a wizard and a separate script that processes business logic.

Getting ready

A **Python Toolbox** is similar to any other toolbox in **ArcToolbox**, but it is created entirely in Python and has a file extension of `.pyt`. It is created programmatically as a class named `Toolbox`. In this recipe, you will learn how to create a **Python Toolbox** and add a custom tool. After creating the basic structure of `Toolbox` and `Tool`, you'll complete the functionality of the tool by adding code that connects to an **ArcGIS Server** map service, downloads real-time data, and inserts it into a feature class.

How to do it...

Complete these steps to create a **Python Toolbox** and create a custom tool that connects to an **ArcGIS Server** map service, downloads real-time data, and inserts it into a feature class:

1. Open **ArcCatalog**. You can create a python toolbox in a folder by right-clicking on the folder and selecting **New** | **Python Toolbox**. In ArcCatalog, there is a folder called **Toolboxes** and inside it is a **My Toolboxes** folder, as seen in this screenshot:

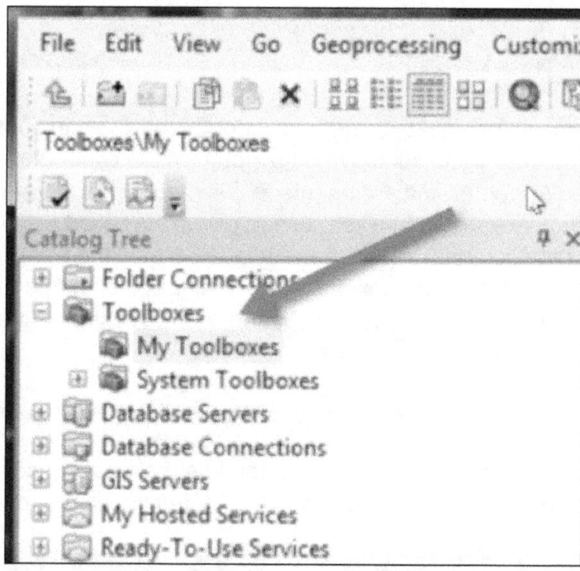

2. Right-click on this folder and select **New** | **Python Toolbox**.
3. The name of the toolbox is controlled by the file name. Name the toolbox `InsertWildfires.pyt`:

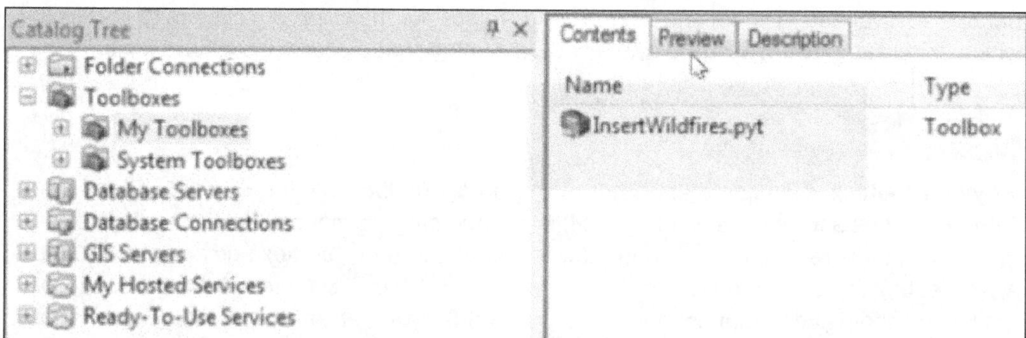

4. The **Python Toolbox** file (`.pyt`) can be edited in any text or code editor. By default, the code will open in **Notepad**. You can change this by setting the default editor for your script by going to **Geoprocessing** | **Geoprocessing Options** and going to the **Editor** section. You'll notice in the following screenshot that I have set my editor to **PyScripter**, which is my preferred environment. You may want to change this to **IDLE** or whatever development environment you are currently using. Please note that this step is not required though. As mentioned, by default, it will open your code in Notepad.

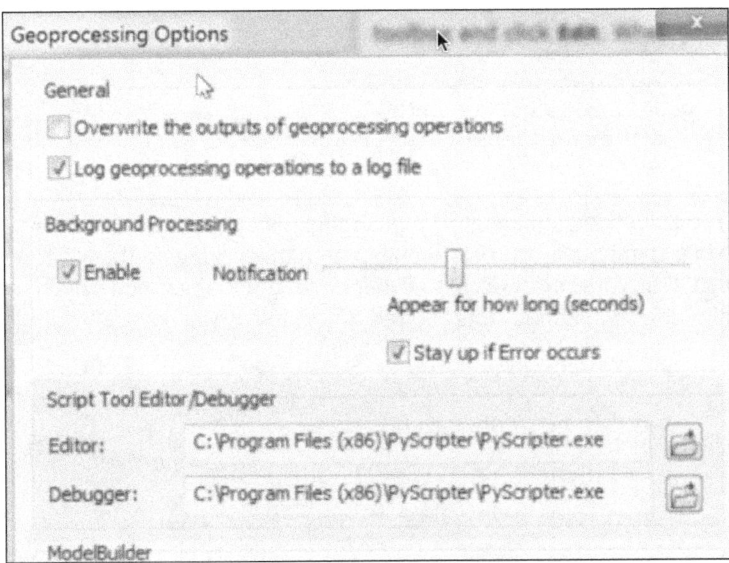

5. Right-click on `InsertWildfires.pyt` and select **Edit**. This will open your development environment. Your development environment will vary depending on the editor that you have defined.
6. Remember that you will not be changing the name of the class, which is `Toolbox`. However, you will rename the `Tool` class to reflect the name of the tool you want to create. Each tool will have various methods, including `__init__()`, which is the constructor for the tool along with `getParameterInfo()`, `isLicensed()`, `updateParameters()`, `updateMessages()`, and `execute()`. You can use the `__init__()` method to set initialization properties, such as the tool's label and description. Look for the `Tool` class and change the name to `USGSDownload`. Also, set the label, and description, as seen in this code:

```
class USGSDownload(object):
    def __init__(self):
        """Define the tool (tool name is the name of the
class)."""
        self.label = "USGS Download"
        self.description = "Download from USGS ArcGIS
Server instance"
```

7. You can use the `Tool` class as a template for other tools you'd like to add to the toolbox by copying and pasting the class and its methods. We're not going to do this in this particular exercise, but I wanted you to be aware of this fact. You will need to add each tool to the `tools` property of `Toolbox`. Add the `USGS Download` tool, as seen in this code:

```
class Toolbox(object):
    def __init__(self):
        """Define the toolbox (the name of the toolbox is the name
of the
        .pyt file)."""
        self.label = "Toolbox"
        self.alias = ""
        # List of tool classes associated with this toolbox
        self.tools = [USGSDownload]
```

8. When you close the code editor, your **Toolboxes** should automatically be refreshed. You can also manually refresh a toolbox by right-clicking on the toolbox and selecting **Refresh**. If a syntax error occurs in your code, the toolbox icon will change, as seen in the following screenshot. Note the red **X** next to the toolbox.

9. You shouldn't have any errors at this time, but if you do, right-click on the toolbox and select Check Syntax to display the errors, as seen in the following screenshot. Note that if you have an error, it may be different from the following example:

Python Errors

```
Traceback (most recent call last):
  File "<string>", line 12, in __init__
NameError: global name 'Tool' is not defined
```

Edit Toolbox...

10. Assuming that you don't have any syntax errors, you should see the following Toolbox/Tool structure:

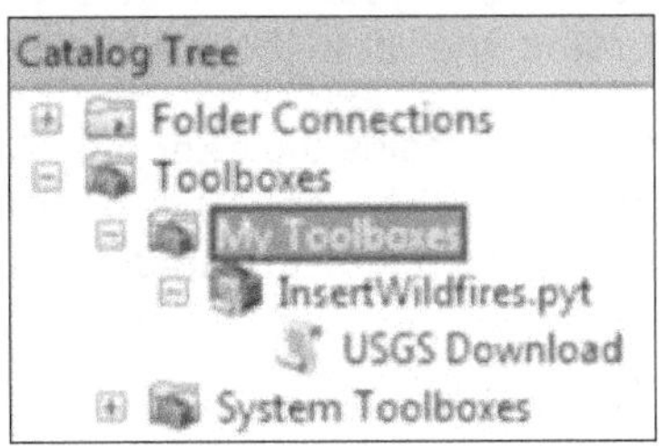

11. Almost all tools have parameters, and you set their values in the tool dialog box or within a script. When the tool is executed, the parameter values are sent to your tool's source code. Your tool reads these values and proceeds with its work. You use the `getParameterInfo()` method to define the parameters for your tool. Individual `Parameter` objects are created as part of this process. Add the following parameters in the `getParameterInfo()` method and then we'll discuss them:

```
def getParameterInfo(self):

    """Define parameter definitions"""
    # First parameter
    param0 = arcpy.Parameter(
        displayName="ArcGIS Server Wildfire URL",
        name="url",
        datatype="GPString",
        parameterType="Required",
        direction="Input")
    param0.value = "http://wildfire.cr.usgs.gov/arcgis/rest/services/geomac_dyn/MapServer/0/query"

    # Second parameter
    param1 = arcpy.Parameter(
        displayName="Output Feature Class",
        name="out_fc",
        datatype="DEFeatureClass",
        parameterType="Required",
        direction="Input")

    params = [param0, param1]
    return params
```

Each `Parameter` object is created using `arcpy.Parameter` and is passed a number of arguments that define the object.

For the first `Parameter` object (`param0`), we are going to capture a URL for an ArcGIS Server map service containing current wildfire data. We give it a display name (ArcGIS Server Wildfire URL), which will be displayed in the dialog box for the tool, a name for the parameter, data type, parameter type (this is mandatory), and direction.

In the case of the first parameter (`param0`), we also assign an initial value, which is the URL for an existing map service containing wildfire data.

For the second parameter, we define an output feature class where the wildfire data that is read from the map service will be written. An empty feature class to store the data has already been created for you. Finally, we added both parameters to a Python list called `params` and return the list to the calling function

12. The main work of a tool is done inside the `execute()` method. This is where the geoprocessing of your tool takes place. The `execute()` method, seen in the following code, can accept a number of arguments, including the tool (self), parameters, and messages:

    ```
    def execute(self, parameters, messages):
          """The source code of the tool. """
          return
    ```

13. To access the parameter values that are passed into the tool, you can use the `valueAsText()` method. Add the following code to access the parameter values that will be passed into your tool. Remember, as seen in a previously mentioned step, that the first parameter will contain a URL for a map service containing wildfire data, and the second parameter is the output feature class where the data will be written:

    ```
    def execute(self, parameters, messages):
            inFeatures = parameters[0].valueAsText
            outFeatureClass = parameters[1].valueAsText
    ```

14. At this point, you have created a Python toolbox, added a tool, defined the parameters for the tool, and created variables that will hold the parameter values that the end user has defined. Ultimately, this tool will use the URL that is passed into the tool to connect to an ArcGIS Server map service, download the current wildfire data, and write the wildfire data to a feature class. We'll do this next.

15. Note that to complete the remainder of this exercise, you will need to install the Python `requests` (refer to `http://docs.python-requests.org/en/latest/`) module using `pip` (refer to `https://pip.pypa.io/en/latest/installing.html`). Do this now before proceeding to the next step. Installation instructions for both `pip` and `requests` can be found at the links provided.

16. Next, add the code that connects to the wildfire map service to perform a query. In this step, you will also define the `QueryString` parameters that will be passed into the query of the map service. First, we'll import the `requests` and `json` modules by adding this code:

    ```
    import requests
    import json
    ```

17. Then, create the payload variable that will hold the `QueryString` parameters. Notice that in this case we have defined a `where` clause so that only the fires greater than `5` acres in size will be returned. The `inFeatures` variable holds the URL:

    ```
    def execute(self, parameters, messages):
            inFeatures = parameters[0].valueAsText
    ```

```
        outFeatureClass = parameters[1].valueAsText

        agisurl = inFeatures

        payload = { 'where': 'acres > 5','f': 'pjson',
'outFields': 'latitude,longitude,fire_name,acres'}
```

18. Submit the request to the ArcGIS Server instance and the response should be stored in a variable called `r`. Print a message to the dialog indicating the response:

```
def execute(self, parameters, messages):
        inFeatures = parameters[0].valueAsText
        outFeatureClass = parameters[1].valueAsText

        agisurl = inFeatures

        payload = { 'where': 'acres > 5','f': 'pjson',
'outFields': 'latitude,longitude,fire_name,acres'}

        r = requests.get(inFeatures, params=payload)
```

19. Let's test the code to make sure we're on the right track. Save the file and refresh your toolbox in ArcCatalog. Execute the tool and leave the default URL. If everything works as expected, you should see a JSON object output of the progress dialog. Your output will probably vary somewhat.

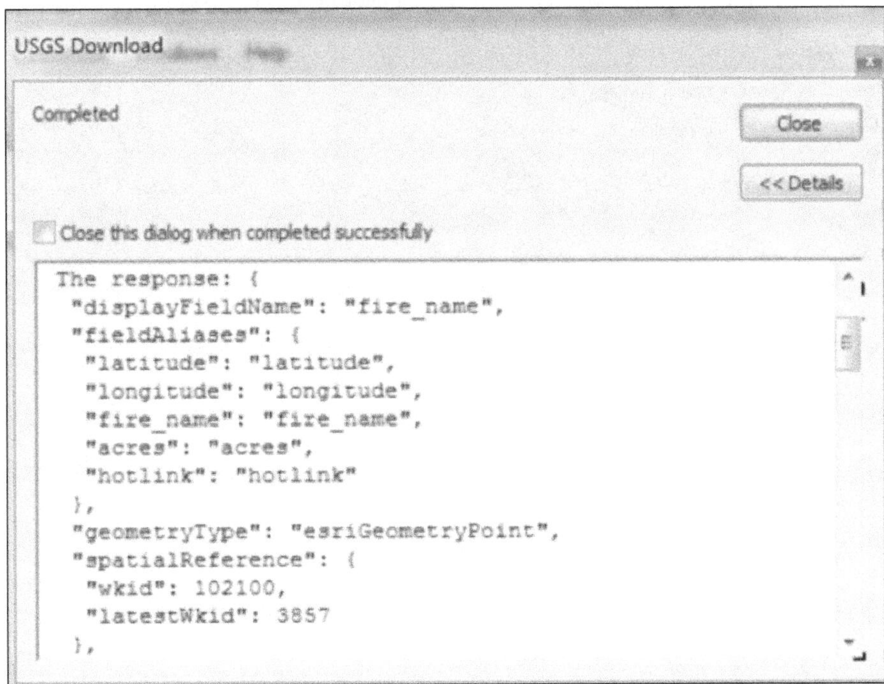

20. Return to the `execute()` method and convert the JSON object to a Python dictionary:

```
def execute(self, parameters, messages):
    inFeatures = parameters[0].valueAsText
    outFeatureClass = parameters[1].valueAsText

    agisurl = inFeatures

    payload = { 'where': 'acres > 5','f': 'pjson',
'outFields': 'latitude,longitude,fire_name,acres'}

    r = requests.get(inFeatures, params=payload)


    decoded = json.loads(r.text)
```

21. Create an `InsertCursor` by passing the output feature class defined in the tool dialog along with the fields that will be populated. We then start a `for` loop that loops through each of the features (wildfires) that have been returned from the request to the ArcGIS Server map service. The `decoded` variable is a Python dictionary. Inside the `for` loop, we retrieve the fire name, latitude, longitude, and acres from the `attributes` dictionary. Finally, we call the `insertRow()` method to insert a new row into the feature class along with the fire name and acres as attributes. The progress information is written to **Progress Dialog** and the counter is updated. The `execute()` method should now appear as follows:

```
def execute(self, parameters, messages):
    inFeatures = parameters[0].valueAsText
    outFeatureClass = parameters[1].valueAsText

    agisurl = inFeatures

    payload = { 'where': 'acres > 5','f': 'pjson', 'outFields': 'latitude,longitude,fire_name,acres'}

    r = requests.get(inFeatures, params=payload)
    decoded = json.loads(r.text)

    with arcpy.da.InsertCursor(outFeatureClass, ("SHAPE@XY", "NAME", "ACRES")) as cur:
        cntr = 1
        for rslt in decoded['features']:
            fireName = rslt['attributes']['fire_name']
            latitude = rslt['attributes']['latitude']
            longitude = rslt['attributes']['longitude']
            acres = rslt['attributes']['acres']
            cur.insertRow([(longitude,latitude),fireName, acres])
            arcpy.AddMessage("Record number: " + str(cntr) + " written to feature class")
            cntr = cntr + 1
```

22. Save the file and refresh your **Python Toolbox** if needed.
23. You can check your work by examining the `c:\ArcpyBook\code\Ch6\InsertWildfires_PythonToolbox.py` solution file.
24. Double-click on the **USGS Download** tool.
25. Leave the default URL and select the **RealTimeFires** feature class in the **WildlandFires** geodatabase found in `c:\ArcpyBook\data`. The **RealTimeFires** feature class is empty and has fields for `NAME` and `ACRES`.
26. Click on **OK** to execute the tool. The number of features written to the feature class will vary depending on the current wildfire activity. Most of the time, there is at least a little bit of activity, but it is possible (though not likely) that there wouldn't be any wildfires in the U.S:

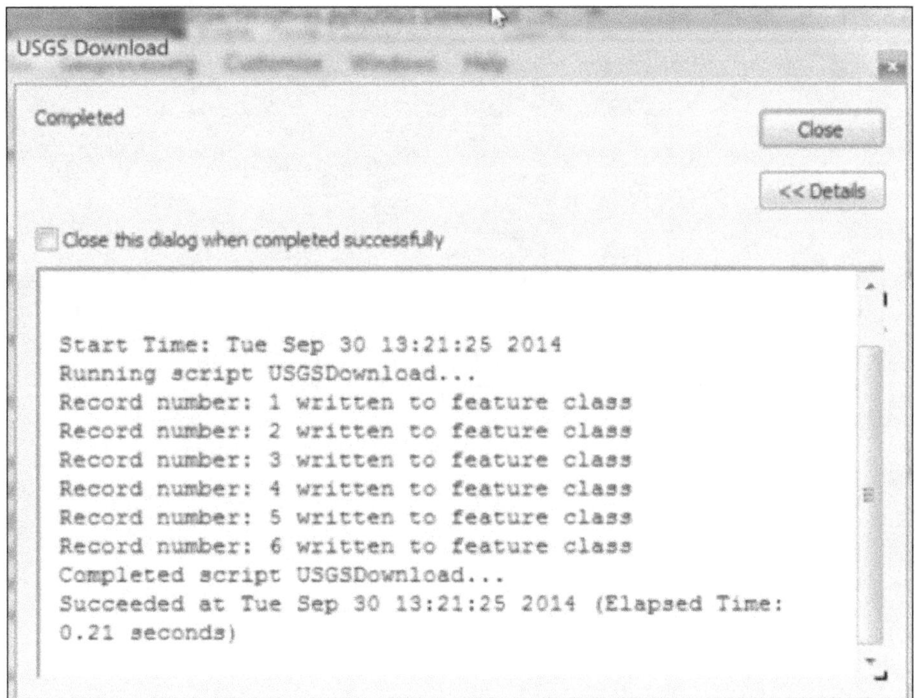

27. View the feature class in **ArcMap** to see its features. You may want to add a `basemap` layer to provide a reference, as seen in this screenshot:

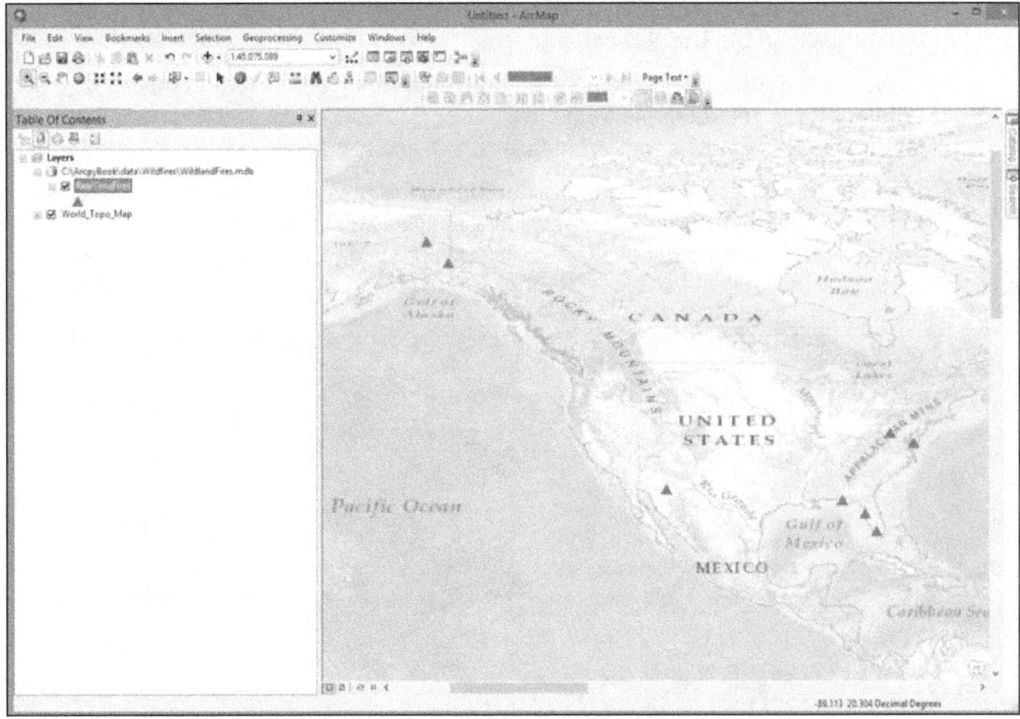

How it works...

The newer style ArcGIS Python Toolbox provides a Python-centric way of creating your custom script tools. The older style of creating custom script tools in ArcGIS for Desktop uses a combination of Python along with a wizard-based approach to define various aspects of the tool. The newer approach provides a more straightforward method for creating your tools. All the tools that you create are contained within a `Toolbox` class that should not be renamed. By default, a single `Tool` class will be created inside `Toolbox`. This `Tool` class should be renamed. In this recipe, we renamed it `USGSDownload`. Inside the `USGSDownload` class, the `getParameterInfo()` and `execute()` methods are present, among others. Using the `getParameterInfo()` method, `Parameter` objects can be defined to hold input data. In this tool, we defined a `Parameter` to capture a URL for an ArcGIS Server map service containing live wildfire data and a second `Parameter` object to reference a local feature class to hold the data. Finally, the `execute()` method is triggered when the user clicks on the **OK** button in the tool. Parameter information is sent as an argument to the `execute()` method in the form of the `parameters` variable. Inside this method, a request to obtain the wildfire data from the remove ArcGIS Server instance is submitted using the Python `requests` module. The response is returned as a `json` object that is converted into a Python dictionary stored in a variable called **decoded**. The fire name, latitude, longitude, and acres are pulled out of the decoded variable and written to the local feature class using an `InsertCursor` object from the `arcpy.da` module. We'll cover the `arcpy.da` module in great detail in a later chapter of the book.

7

Querying and Selecting Data

In this chapter, we will cover the following recipes:

- Constructing a proper attribute query syntax
- Creating feature layers and table views
- Selecting features and rows with the Select Layer by Attribute tool
- Selecting features with the Select by Location tool
- Combining a spatial and attribute query with the Select by Location tool

Introduction

Selecting features from a geographic layer or rows from a standalone attribute table is one of the most common GIS operations. Queries are created to enable these selections, and can be either attribute or spatial queries. **Attribute queries** use SQL statements to select features or rows through the use of one or more fields or columns in a dataset. An example attribute query would be "Select all land parcels with a property value greater than $500,000". **Spatial queries** are used to select features based on some type of spatial relationship. An example might be "Select all land parcels that intersect a school district" or perhaps "Select all streets that are completely within Travis County, Texas." It is also possible to combine attribute and spatial queries. An example might be "Select all land parcels that intersect the 100 year floodplain and have a property value greater than $500,000".

Constructing a proper attribute query syntax

The construction of property attribute queries is critical to your success in creating geoprocessing scripts that query data from feature classes and tables. All attribute queries that you execute against feature classes and tables will need to have the correct SQL syntax and also follow various rules depending upon the data type that you execute the queries against.

Getting ready

Creating the syntax for attribute queries is one of the most difficult and time-consuming tasks that you'll need to master when creating Python scripts that incorporate the use of the **Select by Attributes** tool. These queries are basically SQL statements along with a few idiosyncrasies that you'll need to master. If you already have a good understanding of creating queries in ArcMap or perhaps experience in creating SQL statements in other programming languages, then this will be a little easier for you. In addition to creating valid SQL statements, you also need to be aware of some specific Python syntax requirements and some data type differences that will result in a slightly altered formatting of your statements for some data types. In this recipe, you'll learn how to construct valid query syntax and understand the nuances of how different data types alter the syntax as well as some Python-specific constructs.

How to do it...

Initially, we're going to take a look at how queries are constructed in ArcMap, so that you can get a feel of how they are structured.

1. In ArcMap, open `C:\ArcpyBook\Ch7\Crime_Ch7.mxd`.
2. Right-click on the **Burglaries in 2009** layer and select **Open Attribute Table**. You should see an attribute table similar to the following screenshot. We're going to be querying the **SVCAREA** field:

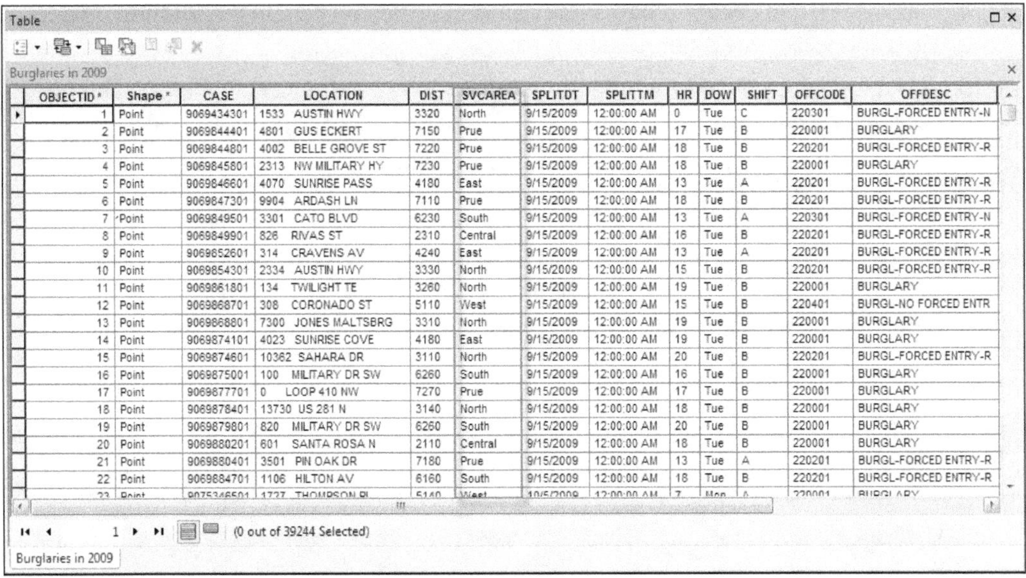

Table

Burglaries in 2009

OBJECTID *	Shape *	CASE	LOCATION	DIST	SVCAREA	SPLITDT	SPLITTM	HR	DOW	SHIFT	OFFCODE	OFFDESC
1	Point	9069434301	1533 AUSTIN HWY	3320	North	9/15/2009	12:00:00 AM	0	Tue	C	220301	BURGL-FORCED ENTRY-N
2	Point	9069844401	4801 GUS ECKERT	7150	Prue	9/15/2009	12:00:00 AM	17	Tue	B	220001	BURGLARY
3	Point	9069844801	4002 BELLE GROVE ST	7220	Prue	9/15/2009	12:00:00 AM	18	Tue	B	220201	BURGL-FORCED ENTRY-R
4	Point	9069845801	2313 NW MILITARY HY	7230	Prue	9/15/2009	12:00:00 AM	18	Tue	B	220001	BURGLARY
5	Point	9069846601	4070 SUNRISE PASS	4180	East	9/15/2009	12:00:00 AM	13	Tue	A	220201	BURGL-FORCED ENTRY-R
6	Point	9069847301	9904 ARDASH LN	7110	Prue	9/15/2009	12:00:00 AM	18	Tue	B	220201	BURGL-FORCED ENTRY-R
7	Point	9069849501	3301 CATO BLVD	6230	South	9/15/2009	12:00:00 AM	13	Tue	A	220301	BURGL-FORCED ENTRY-N
8	Point	9069849901	826 RIVAS ST	2310	Central	9/15/2009	12:00:00 AM	16	Tue	B	220201	BURGL-FORCED ENTRY-R
9	Point	9069852601	314 CRAVENS AV	4240	East	9/15/2009	12:00:00 AM	13	Tue	A	220201	BURGL-FORCED ENTRY-R
10	Point	9069854301	2334 AUSTIN HWY	3330	North	9/15/2009	12:00:00 AM	15	Tue	B	220201	BURGL-FORCED ENTRY-R
11	Point	9069861801	134 TWILIGHT TE	3260	North	9/15/2009	12:00:00 AM	19	Tue	B	220001	BURGLARY
12	Point	9069868701	308 CORONADO ST	5110	West	9/15/2009	12:00:00 AM	15	Tue	B	220401	BURGL-NO FORCED ENTR
13	Point	9069868801	7300 JONES MALTSBRG	3310	North	9/15/2009	12:00:00 AM	19	Tue	B	220001	BURGLARY
14	Point	9069874101	4023 SUNRISE COVE	4180	East	9/15/2009	12:00:00 AM	19	Tue	B	220001	BURGLARY
15	Point	9069874601	10362 SAHARA DR	3110	North	9/15/2009	12:00:00 AM	20	Tue	B	220201	BURGL-FORCED ENTRY-R
16	Point	9069875001	100 MILITARY DR SW	6260	South	9/15/2009	12:00:00 AM	16	Tue	B	220001	BURGLARY
17	Point	9069877701	0 LOOP 410 NW	7270	Prue	9/15/2009	12:00:00 AM	17	Tue	B	220001	BURGLARY
18	Point	9069878401	13730 US 281 N	3140	North	9/15/2009	12:00:00 AM	18	Tue	B	220001	BURGLARY
19	Point	9069879801	820 MILITARY DR SW	6260	South	9/15/2009	12:00:00 AM	20	Tue	B	220001	BURGLARY
20	Point	9069880201	601 SANTA ROSA N	2110	Central	9/15/2009	12:00:00 AM	18	Tue	B	220001	BURGLARY
21	Point	9069880401	3501 PIN OAK DR	7180	Prue	9/15/2009	12:00:00 AM	13	Tue	A	220201	BURGL-FORCED ENTRY-R
22	Point	9069884701	1106 HILTON AV	6160	South	9/15/2009	12:00:00 AM	18	Tue	B	220201	BURGL-FORCED ENTRY-R
23	Point	9075346501	1727 THOMPSON PL	5140	West	10/5/2009	12:00:00 AM	7	Mon	A	220001	BURGLARY

(0 out of 39244 Selected)

Burglaries in 2009

3. With the attribute table open, select the **Table Options** button and then **Select by Attributes** to display a dialog box that will allow you to construct an attribute query.

   Notice the **Select * FROM Burglary WHERE**: statement on the query dialog box (shown in the following screenshot). This is a basic SQL statement that will return all the columns from the attribute table for **Burglary** that meet the condition that we define through the query builder. The asterisk (*) simply indicates that all fields will be returned:

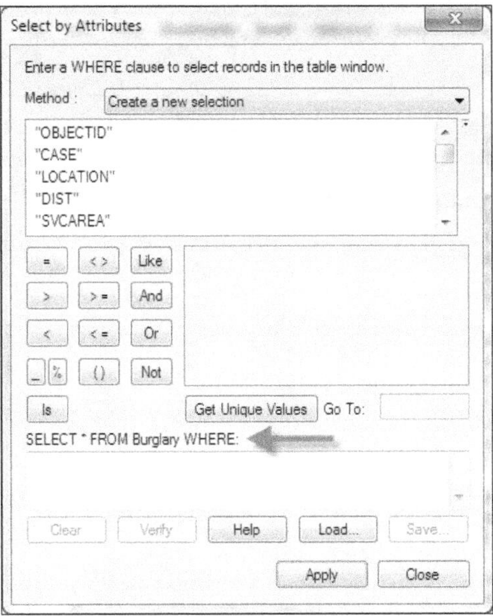

4. Make sure that **Create a new selection** is the selected item in the **Method** dropdown list. This will create a new selection set.
5. Double-click on **SVCAREA** from the list of fields to add the field to the SQL statement builder, as follows:

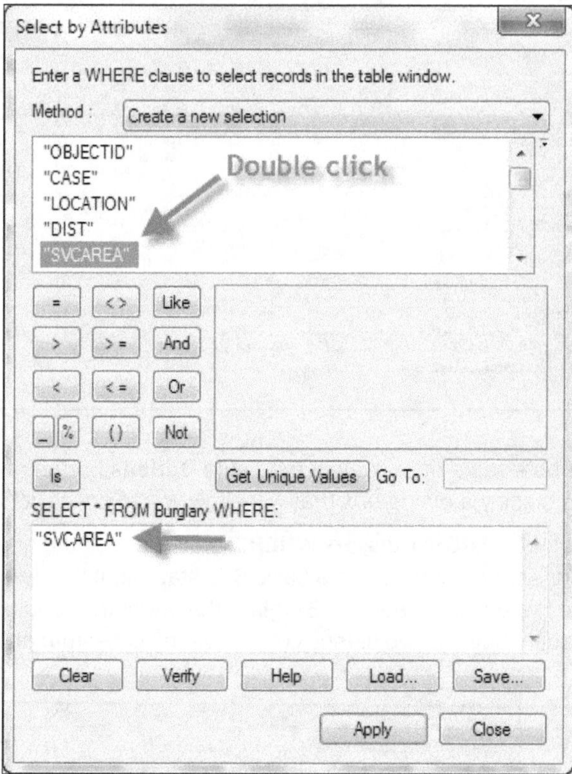

6. Click on the **=** button.
7. Click on the **Get Unique Values** button.

8. From the list of values generated, double-click on **'North'** to complete the SQL statement, as shown in the following screenshot:

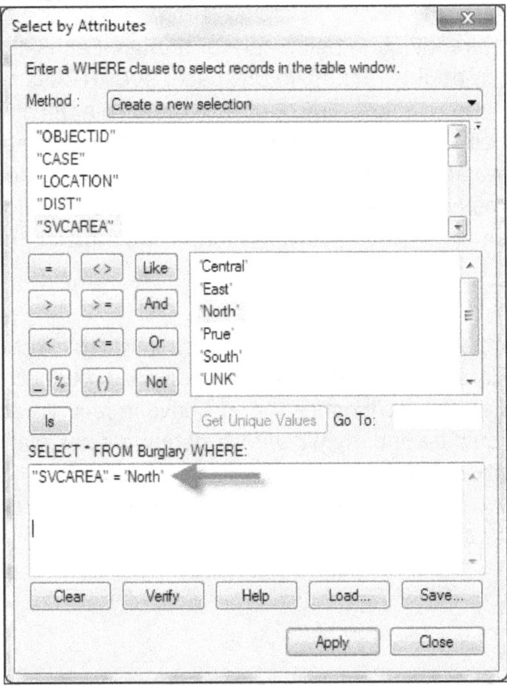

9. Click on the **Apply** button to execute the query. This should select 7520 records.

   Many people mistakenly assume that you can simply take a query that has been generated in this fashion and paste it into a Python script. That is not the case. There are some important differences that we'll cover next.

10. Close the **Select by Attributes** window and the **Burglaries** in 2009 table.
11. Clear the selected feature set by navigating to **Selection | Clear Selected Features**.
12. Open the Python window and add the code to import `arcpy`:

    ```
    import arcpy
    ```

13. Create a new variable to hold the query and add the same statement that you created earlier:

    ```
    qry = "SVCAREA" = 'North'
    ```

14. Press *Enter* on your keyboard and you should see an error message similar to the following:

    ```
    Runtime error SyntaxError: can't assign to literal
    (<string>, line 1)
    ```

Python interprets **SVCAREA** and **North** as strings, but the equal to sign between the two is not part of the string used to set the `qry` variable. There are several things we need to do to generate a syntactically correct statement for the Python interpreter.

One important thing has already been taken care of though. Each field name used in a query needs to be surrounded by double quotes. In this case, **SVCAREA** is the only field used in the query and it has already been enclosed by double quotes. This will always be the case when you're working with shapefiles, file geodatabases, or ArcSDE geodatabases. Here is where it gets a little confusing though. If you're working with data from a personal geodatabase, the field names will need to be enclosed by square brackets instead of double quotes, as shown in the following code example. This can certainly leads to confusion for script developers:

```
qry = [SVCAREA] = 'North'
```

Now, we need to deal with the single quotes surrounding **'North'**. When querying data from fields that have a `text` data type, the string being evaluated must be enclosed by quotes. If you examine the original query, you'll notice that we have in fact already enclosed `North` with quotes, so everything should be fine, right? Unfortunately, it's not that simple with Python. Quotes along with a number of other characters must be escaped with a forward slash followed by the character being escaped. In this case, the escape sequence would be `\'` as shown in the following steps:

15. Alter your query syntax to incorporate the escape sequence:

    ```
    qry = "SVCAREA" = \'North\'
    ```

16. Finally, the entire query statement should be enclosed with quotes:

    ```
    qry = '"SVCAREA" = \'North\''
    ```

In addition to the `=` sign, which tests for equality, there are a number of additional operators that you can use with strings and numeric data, including not equal (`< >`), greater than (`>`), greater than or equal to (`>=`), less than (`<`), and less than or equal to (`<=`).

Wildcard characters, including `%` and _, can also be used for shapefiles, file geodatabases, and ArcSDE geodatabases. These include `%` that represents any number of characters. The `LIKE` operator is often used with wildcard characters to perform partial string matching. For example, the following query would find all records with a service area that begins with `N` and has any number of characters after it:

```
qry = '"SVCAREA" LIKE \'N%\''
```

The (_) underscore character can be used to represent a single character. For personal geodatabases, the (`*`) asterisk is used to represent a wildcard character for any number of characters, while (`?`) represents a single character.

You can also query for the absence of data, also known as NULL values. A NULL value is often mistaken for a value of zero, but this does not always hold true. The NULL values indicate the absence of data, which is different from a value of zero. Null operators include **IS NULL** and **IS NOT NULL**. The following code example will find all the records where the SVCAREA field contains no data:

```
qry = '"SVCAREA" IS NULL'
```

The final topic that we'll cover in this section are operators used to combine expressions where multiple query conditions need to be met. The AND operator requires that both query conditions be met for the query result to be true, resulting in selected records. The OR operator requires that at least one of the conditions be met.

How it works...

The creation of syntactically correct queries is one of the most challenging aspects of programming ArcGIS with Python. However, once you understand some basic rules, it gets a little easier. In this section, we'll summarize these rules. One of the more important things to keep in mind is that field names must be enclosed with double quotes for all datasets, with the exception of personal geodatabases, which require braces surrounding field names.

There is also an AddFieldDelimiters() function that you can use to add the correct delimiter to a field based on the datasource supplied as a parameter to the function. The syntax for this function is as follows:

```
AddFieldDelimiters(dataSource,field)
```

Additionally, most people, especially those new to programming with Python, struggle with the issue of adding single quotes to string values being evaluated by the query. In Python, quotes have to be escaped with a single forward slash followed by the quote. Using this escape sequence will ensure that Python does in fact see this as a quote rather than the end of the string.

Finally, take some time to familiarize yourself with the wildcard characters. For datasets other than personal geodatabases, you'll use the % character for multiple characters and an underscore character for a single character. If you're using a personal geodatabase, the * character is used to match multiple characters and the ? character is used to match a single character. Obviously, the syntax differences between personal geodatabases and all other types of datasets can lead to some confusion.

Creating feature layers and table views

Feature layers and table views serve as intermediate datasets held in memory specifically for use with tools, such as **Select by Location** and **Select Attributes**. Although these temporary datasets can be saved, they are not needed in most cases.

Getting ready

Feature classes are physical representations of geographic data and are stored as files (shapefiles, personal geodatabases, and file geodatabases) or within a geodatabase. **Environmental Systems Research Institute** (**Esri**) defines a feature class as "a collection of features that shares a common geometry (point, line, or polygon), attribute table, and spatial reference."

Feature classes can contain default and user-defined fields. Default fields include the `SHAPE` and `OBJECTID` fields. These fields are maintained and updated automatically by ArcGIS. The `SHAPE` field holds the geometric representation of a geographic feature, while the `OBJECTID` field holds a unique identifier for each feature. Additional default fields will also exist depending on the type of feature class. A line feature class will have a `SHAPE_LENGTH` field. A polygon feature class will have both, a `SHAPE_LENGTH` and a `SHAPE_AREA` field.

Optional fields are created by end users of ArcGIS and are not automatically updated by GIS. These contain attribute information about the features. These fields can also be updated by your scripts.

Tables are physically represented as standalone **DBF** (also known as **dBase File Format**) tables or within a geodatabase. Both, tables and feature classes, contain attribute information. However, a table contains only attribute information. There isn't a `SHAPE` field associated with a table, and they may or may not contain an `OBJECTID` field.

Standalone Python scripts that use the **Select by Attributes** or **Select by Location** tool require that you create an intermediate dataset rather than using feature classes or tables. These intermediate datasets are temporary in nature and are called **feature layers** or **table views**. Unlike feature classes and tables, these temporary datasets do not represent actual files on disk or within a geodatabase. Instead, they are an in-memory representation of feature classes and tables. These datasets are active only while a Python script is running. They are removed from memory after the tool has been executed. However, if the script is run from within ArcGIS as a script tool, then the temporary layer can be saved either by right-clicking on the layer in the table of contents and selecting **Save As Layer File** or simply by saving the map document file.

Feature layers and table views must be created as a separate step in your Python scripts before you can call the **Select by Attributes** or **Select by Location** tools. The **Make Feature Layer** tool generates the in-memory representation of a feature class, which can then be used to create queries and selection sets as well as join tables. After this step has been completed, you can use the **Select by Attributes** or **Select by Location** tool. Similarly, the **Make Table View** tool is used to create an in-memory representation of a table. The function of this tool is the same as **Make Feature Layer**. Both the **Make Feature Layer** and **Make Table View** tools require an input dataset, an output layer name, and an optional query expression, which can be used to limit the features or rows that are a part of the output layer. In addition to this, both tools can be found in the **Data Management Tools** toolbox.

The syntax to use the Make Feature Layer tool is as follows:

```
arcpy.MakeFeatureLayer_management(<input feature layer>, <output layer
name>,{where clause})
```

The syntax to use the **Make Table View** tool is as follows:

```
Arcpy.MakeTableView_management(<input table>, <output table name>,
{where clause})
```

In this recipe, you will learn how to use the **Make Feature Layer** and **Make Table View** tools. These tasks will be done inside ArcGIS, so that you can see the in-memory copy of the layer that is created.

How to do it...

Follow these steps to learn how to use the Make Feature Layer and Make Table View tools:

1. Open `c:\ArcpyBook\Ch7\Crime_Ch7.mxd` in ArcMap.
2. Open the Python window.
3. Import the `arcpy` module:

   ```
   import arcpy
   ```

4. Set the workspace:

   ```
   arcpy.env.workspace = "c:/ArcpyBook/data/CityOfSanAntonio.gdb"
   ```

5. Start a `try` block:

   ```
   try:
   ```

6. Make an in-memory copy of the **Burglary** feature class using the **Make Feature Layer** tool. Make sure you indent this line of code:

   ```
   flayer = arcpy.MakeFeatureLayer_management("Burglary","Burglary_
   Layer")
   ```

7. Add an `except` block and a line of code to print an error message in the event of a problem:

   ```
   except Exception as e:
     print(e.message)
   ```

8. The entire script should appear as follows:

```
import arcpy
arcpy.env.workspace = "c:/ArcpyBook/data/CityOfSanAntonio.gdb"
try:
  flayer = arcpy.MakeFeatureLayer_management("Burglary","Burglary_
Layer")
except Exception as e:
  print(e.message)
```

9. Save the script to `C:\ArcpyBook\Ch7\CreateFeatureLayer.py`.
10. You can check your work by examining the `c:\ArcpyBook\code\Ch7\CreateFeatureLayer.py` solution file.
11. Run the script. The new `Burglary_Layer` file will be added to the ArcMap table of contents:

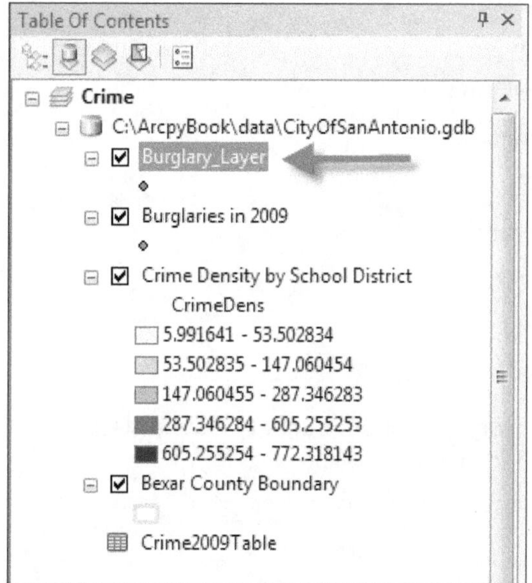

12. The functionality of the **Make Table View** tool is equivalent to the **Make Feature Layer** tool. The difference is that it works against standalone tables instead of feature classes.
13. Remove the following line of code:

```
flayer = arcpy.MakeFeatureLayer_management("Burglary","Burglary_
Layer")
```

14. Add the following line of code in its place:

```
tView = arcpy.MakeTableView_management("Crime2009Table","Crime2009
TView")
```

15. You can check your work by examining the `c:\ArcpyBook\code\Ch7\CreateTableView.py` solution file.
16. Run the script to see the table view added to the ArcMap table of contents.

How it works...

The Make Feature Layer and Make Table View tools create in-memory representations of feature classes and tables, respectively. Both, the Select by Attributes and Select by Location tools, require that these temporary, in-memory structures be passed as parameters when called from a Python script. Both tools also require that you pass a name for the temporary structures.

There's more...

You can also apply a query to either the Make Feature Layer or the Make Table View tools to restrict the records returned in the feature layer or table view. This is done through the addition of a `where` clause when calling either of the tools from your script. This query is similar to a situation where you set a definition query on the layer by navigating to **Layer Properties** | **Definition Query**.

The syntax to add a query is as follows:

```
MakeFeatureLayer(in_features, out_layer, where_clause)
MakeTableView(in_table, out_view, where_clause)
```

Selecting features and rows with the Select Layer by Attribute tool

Attribute queries can be executed against a feature class or table through the use of the Select Layer by Attribute tool. A `where` clause can be included to filter the selected records and various selection types can be included.

Getting ready

The **Select Layer by Attribute** tool, shown in the following screenshot, is used to select records from a feature class or table based on a query that you define. We covered the somewhat complex topic of queries in an earlier recipe in this chapter, so hopefully, you now understand the basic concepts of creating a query. You have also learned how to create a temporary, in-memory representation of a feature class or table, which is a pre-requisite to using either the **Select by Attributes** or **Select by Location** tool.

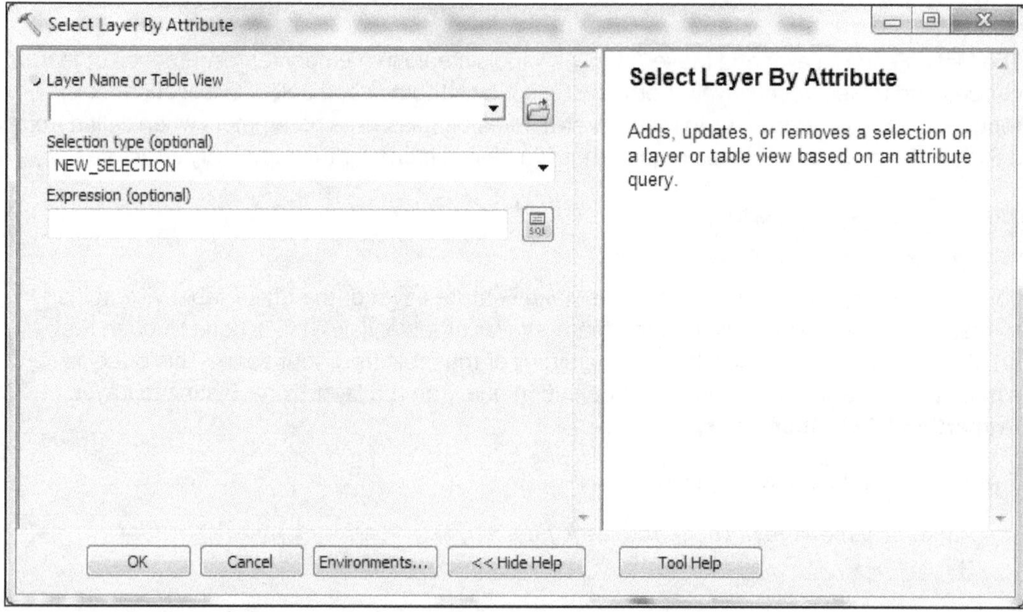

The **Select by Attributes** tool uses a query along with either a feature layer or table view and a selection method to select records. By default, the selection method will be a new selection set. Other selection methods include "add to selection", "remove from selection", "subset selection", "switch selection", and "clear selection". Each of the selection methods is summarized as follows:

- `NEW_SELECTION`: This is the default selection method and it creates a new selection set
- `ADD_TO_SELECTION`: This adds a selection set to the currently selected records based on a query
- `REMOVE_FROM_SELECTION`: This removes records from a selection set based on a query
- `SUBSET_SELECTION`: This combines selected records that are common to the existing selection set

- `SWITCH_SELECTION`: This selects records that are not selected currently and unselects the existing selection set
- `CLEAR_SELECTION`: This clears all records that are currently a part of the selected set

The syntax to call the **Select by Attributes** tool is as follows:

```
arcpy.SelectLayerByAttribute_management(<input feature layer or
table view>, {selection method}, {where clause})
```

In this recipe, you'll learn how to use the **Select by Attributes** tool to select features from a feature class. You'll use the skills you learned in previous recipes to build a query, create a feature layer, and finally call the **Select by Attributes** tool.

How to do it...

Follow these steps to learn how to select records from a table or feature class using the **Select Layer by Attributes** tool:

1. Open IDLE and create a new script window.
2. Save the script to `c:\ArcpyBook\Ch7\SelectLayerAttribute.py`.
3. Import the `arcpy` module:

   ```
   import arcpy
   ```

4. Set the workspace to the City of San Antonio geodatabase.

   ```
   arcpy.env.workspace = "c:/ArcpyBook/data/CityOfSanAntonio.gdb"
   ```

5. Start a `try` block:

   ```
   try:
   ```

6. Create the query that we used in the first recipe in this chapter. This will serve as a `where` clause that will select all the records with a service area of `North`. This line of code and the next four should be indented:

   ```
   qry = '"SVCAREA" = \'North\''
   ```

7. Make an in-memory copy of the `Burglary` feature class:

   ```
   flayer = arcpy.MakeFeatureLayer_management("Burglary","Burglary_
   Layer")
   ```

8. Call the **Select Layer by Attribute** tool by passing in a reference to the feature layer we just created. Define this as a new selection set and pass in a reference to the query:

   ```
   arcpy.SelectLayerByAttribute_management(flayer, "NEW_SELECTION",
   qry)
   ```

9. Print the number of selected records in the layer using the **Get Count** tool:

```
cnt = arcpy.GetCount_management(flayer)
print("The number of selected records is: " + str(cnt))
```

10. Add an `except` block and a line of code to print an error message in the event of a problem:

```
except Exception as e:
  print(e.message)
```

11. The entire script should appear as shown in the following code snippet. Please remember to include indentation with the `try` and `except` blocks:

```
import arcpy
arcpy.env.workspace = "c:/ArcpyBook/data/CityOfSanAntonio.gdb"
try:
  qry = '"SVCAREA" = \'North\''
  flayer =   arcpy.MakeFeatureLayer_
management("Burglary","Burglary_Layer")
  arcpy.SelectLayerByAttribute_management(flayer, "NEW_SELECTION",
qry)
  cnt = arcpy.GetCount_management(flayer)
  print("The number of selected records is: " + str(cnt))
except Exception as e:
  print(e.message)
```

12. Save the script.

13. You can check your work by examining the `c:\ArcpyBook\code\Ch7\SelectLayerAttribute.py` solution file.

14. Run the script. If everything has been done correctly, you should see a message indicating that `7520` records have been selected:

```
The total number of selected records is: 7520
```

How it works...

The **Select by Attributes** tool requires that either a feature layer or table view be passed as the first parameter. In this recipe, we passed a feature layer that was created by the **Make Feature Layer** tool in the preceding line. We used **Make Feature Layer** to create a feature layer from the `Burglary` feature class. This feature layer was assigned to the `flayer` variable, which is then passed into the **Select by Attribute** tool as the first parameter. In this script, we also passed in a parameter indicating that we'd like to create a new selection set along with the `final` parameter, which is a `where` clause. The `where` clause is specified in the `qry` variable. This variable holds a query that will select all the features with a service area of `North`.

Selecting features with the Select by Location tool

The Select Layer by Location tool, as shown in the next screenshot, can be used to select features based on some type of spatial relationship. Since it deals with spatial relationships, this tool only applies to feature classes and their corresponding in-memory feature layers.

Getting ready

There are many different types of spatial relationships that you can apply while selecting features using the **Select by Location** tool, including intersect, contains, within, boundary touches, is identical, and many others. If it's not specified, the default intersect spatial relationship will be applied. The input feature layer is the only required parameter, but there are a number of optional parameters, including the spatial relationship, search distance, a feature layer, or feature class to test against the input layer, and a selection type. In this recipe, you will learn how to use the **Select by Location** tool in a Python script to select features based on a spatial relationship. You'll use the tool to select burglaries that are within the boundaries of the Edgewood school district.

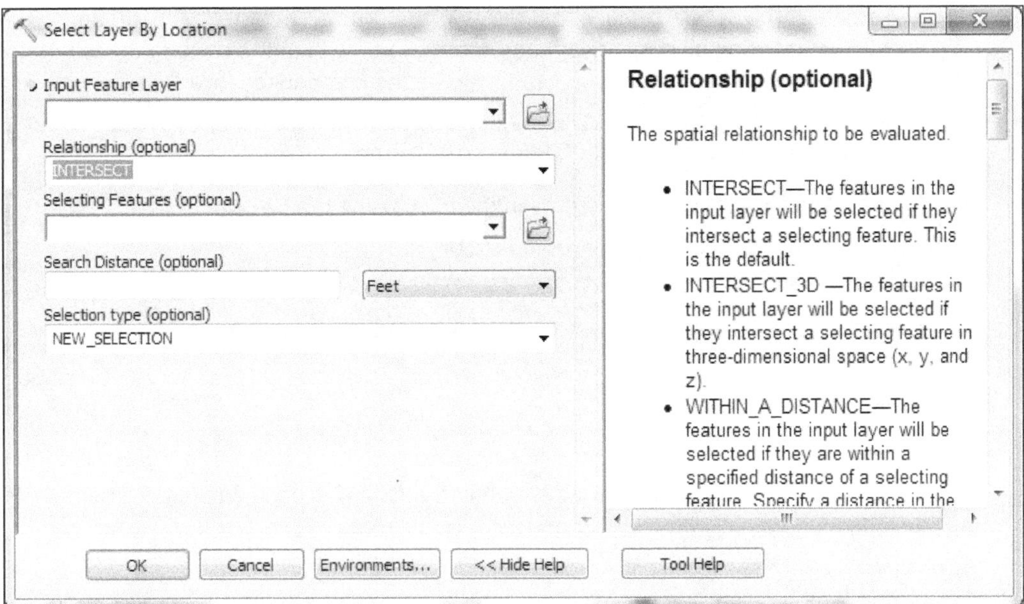

How to do it...

Follow these steps to learn how to perform a spatial query using the **Select by Location** tool:

1. Open IDLE and create a new script window.
2. Save the script to `c:\ArcpyBook\Ch7\SelectByLocation.py`.
3. Import the `arcpy` module:

   ```
   import arcpy
   ```

4. Set the workspace to the City of San Antonio geodatabase:

   ```
   arcpy.env.workspace = "c:/ArcpyBook/data/CityOfSanAntonio.gdb"
   ```

5. Start a `try` block:

   ```
   try:
   ```

6. Make an in-memory copy of the `Burglary` feature class:

   ```
   flayer = arcpy.MakeFeatureLayer_management("Burglary","Burglary_
   Layer")
   ```

7. Call the **Select Layer by Location** tool passing in a reference to the feature layer we just created. The spatial relationship test will be `COMPLETELY_WITHIN`, meaning that we want to find all burglaries that are completely within the boundaries of the comparison layer. Define `EdgewoodSD.shp` as the comparison layer:

   ```
   arcpy.SelectLayerByLocation_management (flayer, "COMPLETELY_
   WITHIN", "c:/ArcpyBook/Ch7/EdgewoodSD.shp")
   ```

8. Print the number of selected records in the layer using the **Get Count** tool:

   ```
   cnt = arcpy.GetCount_management(flayer)
   print("The number of selected records is: " + str(cnt))
   ```

9. Add an `except` block and a line of code to print an error message in the event of a problem:

   ```
   except Exception as e:
     print e.message
   ```

10. The entire script should appear as shown in the following code snippet. Remember to include indentation with the `try` and `except` blocks:

    ```
    import arcpy
    arcpy.env.workspace = "c:/ArcpyBook/data/CityOfSanAntonio.gdb"
    try:
      flayer =   arcpy.MakeFeatureLayer_
    management("Burglary","Burglary_Layer")
      arcpy.SelectLayerByLocation_management (flayer, "COMPLETELY_
    WITHIN", "c:/ArcpyBook/Ch7/EdgewoodSD.shp")
    ```

```
    cnt = arcpy.GetCount_management(flayer)
    print("The number of selected records is: " + str(cnt))
  except Exception as e:
    print("An error occurred during selection")
```

11. Save the script.
12. You can check your work by examining the `c:\ArcpyBook\code\Ch7\SelectByLocation_Step1.py` solution file.
13. Run the script. If everything was done correctly, you should see a message indicating that `1470` records have been selected:

    ```
    The total number of selected records is: 1470
    ```

    In this case, we did not define the optional search distance and selection type parameters. By default, a new selection will be applied as the selection type. We didn't apply a distance parameter in this case, but we'll do this now to illustrate how it works.

14. Update the line of code that calls the **Select Layer by Location** tool:

    ```
    arcpy.SelectLayerByLocation_management (flayer, "WITHIN_A_
    DISTANCE", "c:/ArcpyBook/Ch7/EdgewoodSD.shp","1 MILES")
    ```

15. Save the script.
16. You can check your work by examining the `c:\ArcpyBook\code\Ch7\SelectByLocation_Step2.py` solution file.
17. Run the script. If everything was done correctly, you should see a message indicating that `2976` records have been selected. This will select all burglaries within the boundaries of the Edgewood school district along with any burglaries within one mile of the boundary:

    ```
    The total number of selected records is: 2976
    ```

    The final thing you'll do in this section is use the **Copy Features** tool to write the temporary layer to a new feature class.

18. Comment out the two lines of code that get a count of the number of features and print them to the screen:

    ```
    ## cnt = arcpy.GetCount_management(flayer)
    ## print("The number of selected records is: " + str(cnt))
    ```

19. Add a line of code that calls the **Copy Features** tool. This line should be placed just below the line of code that calls the **Select Layer by Location** tool. The **Copy Features** tool accepts a feature layer as the first input parameter and an output feature class, which in this case will be a shapefile called `EdgewoodBurglaries.shp`:

    ```
    arcpy.CopyFeatures_management(flayer, 'c:/ArcpyBook/Ch7/
    EdgewoodBurglaries.shp')
    ```

20. The entire script should now appear as shown in the following code snippet. Remember to include indentation with the `try` and `except` blocks:

```
import arcpy
arcpy.env.workspace = "c:/ArcpyBook/data/CityOfSanAntonio.gdb"
try:
  flayer = arcpy.MakeFeatureLayer_management("Burglary","Burglary_
Layer")
  arcpy.SelectLayerByLocation_management (flayer, "WITHIN_A_
DISTANCE", "c:/ArcpyBook/Ch7/EdgewoodSD.shp","1 MILES")
  arcpy.CopyFeatures_management(flayer, 'c:/ArcpyBook/Ch7/
EdgewoodBurglaries.shp')
        #cnt = arcpy.GetCount_management(flayer)
 #print("The total number of selected records is: " + str(cnt))
except Exception as e:
  print(e.message)
```

21. Save the script.
22. You can check your work by examining the `c:\ArcpyBook\code\Ch7\SelectByLocation_Step3.py` solution file.
23. Run the script.
24. Examine your `c:\ArcpyBook\Ch7` folder to see the output shapefile.

How it works...

The **Select by Location** tool requires that a feature layer be passed as the first parameter. In this recipe, we pass a feature layer that was created by the **Make Feature Layer** tool in the preceding line. We used **Make Feature Layer** to create a feature layer from the `Burglary` feature class. This feature layer was assigned to the `flayer` variable, which is then passed into the **Select by Location** tool as the first parameter. In this script, we've also passed a parameter that indicates the spatial relationship that we'd like to apply. Finally, we've also defined a source layer to use for the comparison of the spatial relationship. Other optional parameters that can be applied include a search distance and a selection type.

Combining a spatial and attribute query with the Select by Location tool

There may be times when you may want to select features using a combined attribute and spatial query. For example, you might want to select all burglaries within the Edgewood school district that occurred on a Monday. This can be accomplished by running the **Select by Location** and **Select by Attributes** tools sequentially and applying a `SUBSET SELECTION` selection type.

Getting ready

This recipe will require that you create a feature layer that will serve as a temporary layer, which will be used with the **Select by Location** and **Select Layer by Attributes** tools. The **Select by Location** tool will find all burglaries that are within the Edgewood School District and apply a selection set to these features. The **Select Layer by Attributes** tool uses the same temporary feature layer and applies a `where` clause that finds all burglaries that occurred on a particular Monday. In addition to this, the tool also specifies that the selection should be a subset of the currently selected features found by the **Select by Location** tool. Finally, you'll print the total number of records that were selected by the combined spatial and attribute query.

How to do it...

1. Open IDLE and create a new script window.
2. Save the script as `c:\ArcpyBook\Ch7\SpatialAttributeQuery.py`.
3. Import the `arcpy` module:

   ```
   import arcpy
   ```

4. Set the workspace to the geodatabase of the City of San Antonio:

   ```
   arcpy.env.workspace = "c:/ArcpyBook/data/CityofSanAntonio.gdb"
   ```

5. Start a `try` block. You'll have to indent the following line up to the `except` block:

   ```
   try:
   ```

6. Create a variable for the query and define the `where` clause:

   ```
   qry = '"DOW" = \'Mon\''
   ```

7. Create the feature layer:

   ```
   flayer = arcpy.MakeFeatureLayer_management("Burglary","Burglary_
   Layer")
   ```

8. Execute the **Select by Location** tool to find all burglaries within the Edgewood School District:

   ```
   arcpy.SelectLayerByLocation_management (flayer, "COMPLETELY_
   WITHIN", "c:/ArcpyBook/Ch7/EdgewoodSD.shp")
   ```

9. Execute the **Select Layer by Attributes** tool to find all the burglaries that match the query we previously defined in the `qry` variable. This should be defined as a subset query:

   ```
   arcpy.SelectLayerByAttribute_management(flayer, "SUBSET_
   SELECTION", qry)
   ```

10. Print the number of records that were selected:

    ```
    cnt = arcpy.GetCount_management(flayer)
    print("The total number of selected records is: " + str(cnt))
    ```

11. Add the `except` block:

```
except Exception as e:
  print(e.message)
```

12. The entire script should appear as follows:

```
import arcpy
arcpy.env.workspace = "c:/ArcpyBook/data/CityOfSanAntonio.gdb"
try:
  qry = '"DOW" = \'Mon\''
  flayer = arcpy.MakeFeatureLayer_management("Burglary","Burglary_
Layer")
  arcpy.SelectLayerByLocation_management (flayer, "COMPLETELY_
WITHIN", "c:/ArcpyBook/Ch7/EdgewoodSD.shp")
  arcpy.SelectLayerByAttribute_management(flayer, "SUBSET_
SELECTION", qry)
  cnt = arcpy.GetCount_management(flayer)
  print("The total number of selected records is: " + str(cnt))
except Exception as e:
  print(e.message)
```

13. Save and run the script. If everything was done correctly, you should see a message indicating that `197` records have been selected. This will select all the burglaries within the boundaries of the Edgewood School District that occurred on a Monday:

```
The total number of selected records is: 197
```

14. You can check your work by examining the `c:\ArcpyBook\code\Ch7\SpatialAttributeQuery.py` solution file.

How it works...

A new feature layer is created with the **Make Feature Layer** tool and assigned to the variable `flayer`. This temporary layer is then used as an input to the **Select by Location** tool along with a `COMPLETELY_WITHIN` spatial operator, to find all the burglaries within the Edgewood School District. This same feature layer, with a selection set already defined, is then used as an input parameter to the **Select Layer by Attributes** tool. In addition to passing a reference to the feature layer, the **Select Layer by Attributes** tool is also passed a parameter that defines the selection type and a `where` clause. The selection type is set to `SUBSET_SELECTION`. This selection type creates a new selection that is combined with the existing selection. Only the records that are common to both remain selected. The `where` clause passed in as the third parameter is an attribute query to find all the burglaries that occurred on a Monday. The query uses the `DOW` field and looks for a value of `Mon`. Finally, the **Get Count** tool is used against the `flayer` variable to get a count of the number of selected records, and this is printed on the screen.

8
Using the ArcPy Data Access Module with Feature Classes and Tables

In this chapter, we will cover the following recipes:

- Retrieving features from a feature class with SearchCursor
- Filtering records with a where clause
- Improving cursor performance with geometry tokens
- Inserting rows with InsertCursor
- Updating rows with UpdateCursor
- Deleting rows with UpdateCursor
- Inserting and updating rows inside an edit session
- Reading geometry from a feature class
- Using Walk() to navigate directories

Introduction

We'll start this chapter with a basic question. What are cursors? **Cursors** are in-memory objects containing one or more rows of data from a table or feature class. Each row contains attributes from each field in a data source along with the geometry for each feature. Cursors allow you to search, add, insert, update, and delete data from tables and feature classes.

The `arcpy` data access module or `arcpy.da` was introduced in ArcGIS 10.1 and contains methods that allow you to iterate through each row in a cursor. Various types of cursors can be created depending on the needs of developers. For example, search cursors can be created to read values from rows. Update cursors can be created to update values in rows or delete rows, and insert cursors can be created to insert new rows.

There are a number of cursor improvements that have been introduced with the `arcpy` data access module. Prior to the development of ArcGIS 10.1, cursor performance was notoriously slow. Now, cursors are significantly faster. Esri has estimated that `SearchCursors` are up to 30 times faster, while `InsertCursors` are up to 12 times faster. In addition to these general performance improvements, the data access module also provides a number of new options that allow programmers to speed up processing. Rather than returning all the fields in a cursor, you can now specify that a subset of fields be returned. This increases the performance as less data needs to be returned. The same applies to geometry. Traditionally, when accessing the geometry of a feature, the entire geometric definition would be returned. You can now use geometry tokens to return a portion of the geometry rather than the full geometry of the feature. You can also use lists and tuples rather than using rows. There are also other new features, such as edit sessions and the ability to work with versions, domains, and subtypes.

There are three cursor functions in `arcpy.da`. Each returns a cursor object with the same name as the function. `SearchCursor()` creates a read-only `SearchCursor` object containing rows from a table or feature class. `InsertCursor()` creates an `InsertCursor` object that can be used to insert new records into a table or feature class. `UpdateCursor()` returns a cursor object that can be used to edit or delete records from a table or feature class. Each of these cursor objects has methods to access rows in the cursor. You can see the relationship between the cursor functions, the objects they create, and how they are used, as follows:

Function	**Object created**	**Usage**
`SearchCursor()`	`SearchCursor`	This is a read-only view of data from a table or feature class
`InsertCursor()`	`InsertCursor`	This adds rows to a table or feature class
`UpdateCursor()`	`UpdateCursor`	This edits or deletes rows in a table or feature class

The `SearchCursor()` function is used to return a `SearchCursor` object. This object can only be used to iterate through a set of rows returned for read-only purposes. No insertions, deletions, or updates can occur through this object. An optional `where` clause can be set to limit the rows returned.

Once you've obtained a cursor instance, it is common to iterate the records, particularly with `SearchCursor` or `UpdateCursor`. There are some peculiarities that you need to understand when navigating the records in a cursor. Cursor navigation is forward-moving only. When a cursor is created, the pointer of the cursor sits just above the first row in the cursor. The first call to `next()` will move the pointer to the first row. Rather than calling the `next()` method, you can also use a `for` loop to process each of the records without the need to call the `next()` method. After performing whatever processing you need to do with this row, a subsequent call to `next()` will move the pointer to row 2. This process continues as long as you need to access additional rows. However, after a row has been visited, you can't go back a single record at a time. For instance, if the current row is row 3, you can't programmatically back up to row 2. You can only go forward. To revisit rows 1 and 2, you would need to either call the `reset()` method or recreate the cursor and move back through the object. As I mentioned earlier, cursors are often navigated through the use of `for` loops as well. In fact, this is a more common way to iterate a cursor and a more efficient way to code your scripts. Cursor navigation is illustrated in the following diagram:

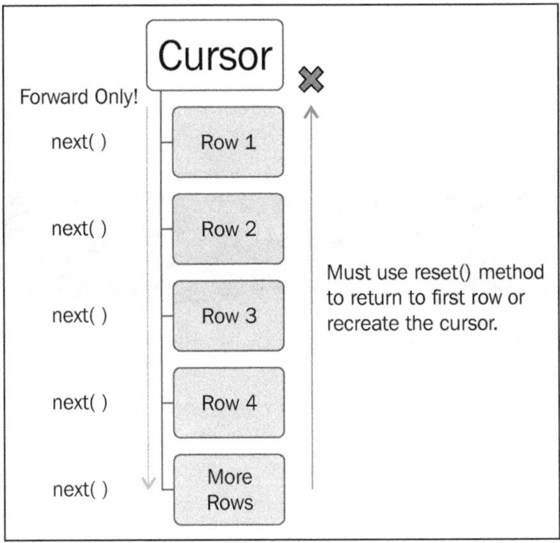

The `InsertCursor()` function is used to create an `InsertCursor` object that allows you to programmatically add new records to feature classes and tables. To insert rows, call the `insertRow()` method on this object. You can also retrieve a read-only tuple containing the field names in use by the cursor through the `fields` property. A lock is placed on the table or feature class being accessed through the cursor. Therefore, it is important to always design your script in a way that releases the cursor when you are done.

The `UpdateCursor()` function can be used to create an `UpdateCursor` object that can update and delete rows in a table or feature class. As is the case with `InsertCursor`, this function places a lock on the data while it's being edited or deleted. If the cursor is used inside a Python's `with` statement, the lock will automatically be freed after the data has been processed. This hasn't always been the case. Prior to ArcGIS 10.1, cursors were required to be manually released using the Python `del` statement. Once an instance of `UpdateCursor` has been obtained, you can then call the `updateCursor()` method to update records in tables or feature classes and the `deleteRow()` method to delete a row.

The subject of data locks requires a little more explanation. The `insert` and `update` cursors must obtain a lock on the data source they reference. This means that no other application can concurrently access this data source. Locks are a way of preventing multiple users from changing data at the same time and thus, corrupting the data. When the `InsertCursor()` and `UpdateCursor()` methods are called in your code, Python attempts to acquire a lock on the data. This lock must be specifically released after the cursor has finished processing so that the running applications of other users, such as `ArcMap` or `ArcCatalog`, can access the data sources. If this isn't done, no other application will be able to access the data. Prior to ArcGIS 10.1 and the `with` statement, cursors had to be specifically unlocked through Python's `del` statement. Similarly, `ArcMap` and `ArcCatalog` also acquire data locks when updating or deleting data. If a data source has been locked by either of these applications, your Python code will not be able to access the data. Therefore, the best practice is to close `ArcMap` and `ArcCatalog` before running any standalone Python scripts that use `insert` or `update` cursors.

In this chapter, we're going to cover the use of cursors to access and edit tables and feature classes. However, many of the cursor concepts that existed before ArcGIS 10.1 still apply.

Retrieving features from a feature class with SearchCursor

There are many occasions when you need to retrieve rows from a table or feature class for read-only purposes. For example, you might want to generate a list of all land parcels in a city with a value greater than $100,000. In this case, you don't have any need to edit the data. Your needs are met simply by generating a list of rows that meet some sort of criteria. A `SearchCursor` object contains a read-only copy of rows from a table or feature class. These objects can also be filtered through the use of a `where` clause so that only a subset of the dataset is returned.

Getting ready

The `SearchCursor()` function is used to return a `SearchCursor` object. This object can only be used to iterate a set of rows returned for read-only purposes. No insertions, deletions, or updates can occur through this object. An optional `where` clause can be set to limit the rows returned. In this recipe, you will learn how to create a basic `SearchCursor` object on a feature class through the use of the `SearchCursor()` function.

The `SearchCursor` object contains a `fields` property along with the `next()` and `reset()` methods. The `fields` property is a read-only structure in the form of a Python **tuple**, containing the fields requested from the feature class or table. You are going to hear the term tuple a lot in conjunction with cursors. If you haven't covered this topic before, tuples are a Python structure to store a sequence of data similar to Python lists. However, there are some important differences between Python tuples and lists. Tuples are defined as a sequence of values inside parentheses, while lists are defined as a sequence of values inside brackets. Unlike lists, tuples can't grow and shrink, which can be a very good thing in some cases when you want data values to occupy a specific position each time. This is the case with cursor objects that use tuples to store data from fields in tables and feature classes.

How to do it...

Follow these steps to learn how to retrieve rows from a table or feature class inside a `SearchCursor` object:

1. Open **IDLE** and create a new script window.
2. Save the script as `C:\ArcpyBook\Ch8\SearchCursor.py`.
3. Import the `arcpy.da` module:
   ```
   import arcpy.da
   ```
4. Set the workspace:
   ```
   arcpy.env.workspace = "c:/ArcpyBook/Ch8"
   ```
5. Use a Python `with` statement to create a cursor:
   ```
   with
   arcpy.da.SearchCursor("Schools.shp",("Facility","Name")) as
   cursor:
   ```
6. Loop through each row in `SearchCursor` and print the name of the school. Make sure you indent the `for` loop inside the `with` block:
   ```
   for row in sorted(cursor):
     print("School name: " + row[1])
   ```

7. The entire script should appear as follows:

```
import arcpy.da
arcpy.env.workspace = "c:/ArcpyBook/Ch8"
with
arcpy.da.SearchCursor("Schools.shp",("Facility","Name")) as
cursor:
    for row in sorted(cursor):
        print("School name: " + row[1])
```

8. Save the script.
9. You can check your work by examining the `C:\ArcpyBook\code\Ch8\SearchCursor_Step1.py` solution file.
10. Run the script. You should see the following output:

```
School name: ALLAN
School name: ALLISON
School name: ANDREWS
School name: BARANOFF
School name: BARRINGTON
School name: BARTON CREEK
School name: BARTON HILLS
School name: BATY
School name: BECKER
School name: BEE CAVE
```

How it works...

The `with` statement used with the `SearchCursor()` function will create, open, and close the cursor. So, you no longer have to be concerned with explicitly releasing the lock on the cursor as you did prior to ArcGIS 10.1. The first parameter passed into the `SearchCursor()` function is a feature class, represented by the `Schools.shp` file. The second parameter is a Python tuple containing a list of fields that we want returned in the cursor. For performance reasons, it is a best practice to limit the fields returned in the cursor to only those that you need to complete the task. Here, we've specified that only the `Facility` and `Name` fields should be returned. The `SearchCursor` object is stored in a variable called `cursor`.

Inside the `with` block, we use a Python `for` loop to loop through each school returned. We also use the Python `sorted()` function to sort the contents of the cursor. To access the values from a field on the row, simply use the index number of the field you want to return. In this case, we want to return the contents of the `Name` column, which will be the `1` index number, since it is the second item in the tuple of field names that are returned.

Filtering records with a where clause

By default, `SearchCursor` will contain all rows in a table or feature class. However, in many cases, you will want to restrict the number of rows returned by some sort of criteria. Applying a filter through the use of a `where` clause limits the records returned.

Getting ready

By default, all rows from a table or feature class will be returned when you create a `SearchCursor` object. However, in many cases, you will want to restrict the records returned. You can do this by creating a query and passing it as a `where` clause parameter when calling the `SearchCursor()` function. In this recipe, you'll build on the script you created in the previous recipe by adding a `where` clause that restricts the records returned.

How to do it...

Follow these steps to apply a filter to a `SearchCursor` object that restricts the rows returned from a table or feature class:

1. Open **IDLE** and load the `SearchCursor.py` script that you created in the previous recipe.
2. Update the `SearchCursor()` function by adding a `where` clause that queries the facility field for records that have the `HIGH SCHOOL` text:

   ```
   with
   arcpy.da.SearchCursor("Schools.shp",("Facility","Name"),
   '"FACILITY" = \'HIGH SCHOOL\'') as cursor:
   ```

3. You can check your work by examining the `C:\ArcpyBook\code\Ch8\SearchCursor_Step2.py` solution file.
4. Save and run the script. The output will now be much smaller and restricted to high schools only:

   ```
   High school name: AKINS
   High school name: ALTERNATIVE LEARNING CENTER
   High school name: ANDERSON
   High school name: AUSTIN
   High school name: BOWIE
   High school name: CROCKETT
   High school name: DEL VALLE
   High school name: ELGIN
   High school name: GARZA
   ```

```
High school name: HENDRICKSON
High school name: JOHN B CONNALLY
High school name: JOHNSTON
High school name: LAGO VISTA
```

How it works...

We covered the creation of queries in *Chapter 7, Querying and Selecting Data*, so hopefully you now have a good grasp of how these are created along with all the rules you need to follow when coding these structures. The `where` clause parameter accepts any valid SQL query, and is used in this case to restrict the number of records that are returned.

Improving cursor performance with geometry tokens

Geometry tokens were introduced in ArcGIS 10.1 as a performance improvement for cursors. Rather than returning the entire geometry of a feature inside the cursor, only a portion of the geometry is returned. Returning the entire geometry of a feature can result in decreased cursor performance due to the amount of data that has to be returned. It's significantly faster to return only the specific portion of the geometry that is needed.

Getting ready

A token is provided as one of the fields in the field list passed into the constructor for a cursor and is in the `SHAPE@<Part of Feature to be Returned>` format. The only exception to this format is the `OID@` token, which returns the object ID of the feature. The following code example retrieves only the `X` and `Y` coordinates of a feature:

```
with arcpy.da.SearchCursor(fc, ("SHAPE@XY","Facility","Name")) as
cursor:
```

The following table lists the available geometry tokens. Not all cursors support the full list of tokens. Check the ArcGIS help files for information about the tokens supported by each cursor type. The `SHAPE@` token returns the entire geometry of the feature. Use this carefully though, because it is an expensive operation to return the entire geometry of a feature and can dramatically affect performance. If you don't need the entire geometry, then do not include this token!

SHAPE@XY	• Feature centroid x,y
SHAPE@X	• Feature X coordinate
SHAPE@TRUECENTROID	• Feature true centroid
SHAPE@Y	• Feature Y coordinate
SHAPE@Z	• Feature Z coordinate
SHAPE@M	• Feature M value
SHAPE@	• Geometry object; Entire feature
SHAPE@AREA	• Feature Area
SHAPE@LENGTH	• Feature Length
OID@	• Value of ObjectID field

In this recipe, you will use a geometry token to increase the performance of a cursor. You'll retrieve the `X` and `Y` coordinates of each land parcel from the `parcels` feature class along with some attribute information about the parcel.

How to do it...

Follow these steps to add a geometry token to a cursor, which should improve the performance of this object:

1. Open **IDLE** and create a new script window.
2. Save the script as `C:\ArcpyBook\Ch8\GeometryToken.py`.
3. Import the `arcpy.da` module and the time module:

   ```
   import arcpy.da
   import time
   ```

4. Set the workspace:

   ```
   arcpy.env.workspace = "c:/ArcpyBook/Ch8"
   ```

5. We're going to measure how long it takes to execute the code using a geometry token. Add the `start` time for the script:

```
start = time.clock()
```

6. Use a Python `with` statement to create a cursor that includes the centroid of each feature as well as the ownership information stored in the `PY_FULL_OW` field:

```
with
arcpy.da.SearchCursor("coa_parcels.shp",("PY_FULL_OW","SHAPE@XY"))
as cursor:
```

7. Loop through each row in `SearchCursor` and print the name of the parcel and location. Make sure you indent the `for` loop inside the `with` block:

```
for row in cursor:
  print("Parcel owner: {0} has a location of:
{1}".format(row[0], row[1]))
```

8. Measure the elapsed time:

```
elapsed = (time.clock() - start)
```

9. Print the execution time:

```
print("Execution time: " + str(elapsed))
```

10. The entire script should appear as follows:

```
import arcpy.da
import time
arcpy.env.workspace = "c:/ArcpyBook/Ch9"
start = time.clock()
with arcpy.da.SearchCursor("coa_parcels.shp",("PY_FULL_OW",
"SHAPE@XY")) as cursor:
    for row in cursor:
        print("Parcel owner: {0} has a location of:
{1}".format(row[0], row[1]))
elapsed = (time.clock() - start)
print("Execution time: " + str(elapsed))
```

11. You can check your work by examining the `C:\ArcpyBook\code\Ch8\GeometryToken.py` solution file.
12. Save the script.
13. Run the script. You should see something similar to the following output. Note the execution time; your time will vary:

```
Parcel owner: CITY OF AUSTIN ATTN REAL ESTATE DIVISION has a
location of: (3110480.5197341456, 10070911.174956793)

Parcel owner: CITY OF AUSTIN ATTN REAL ESTATE DIVISION has a
location of: (3110670.413783513, 10070800.960865)
```

```
Parcel owner: CITY OF AUSTIN has a location of:
(3143925.0013213265, 10029388.97419636)

Parcel owner: CITY OF AUSTIN % DOROTHY NELL ANDERSON ATTN
BARRY LEE ANDERSON has a location of: (3134432.983822767,
10072192.047894118)

Execution time: 9.08046185109
```

Now, we're going to measure the execution time if the entire geometry is returned instead of just the portion of the geometry that we need:

1. Save a new copy of the script as `C:\ArcpyBook\Ch8\GeometryTokenEntireGeometry.py`.
2. Change the `SearchCursor()` function to return the entire geometry using `SHAPE@` instead of `SHAPE@XY`:

   ```
   with arcpy.da.SearchCursor("coa_parcels.shp",("PY_FULL_OW",
   "SHAPE@")) as cursor:
   ```

3. You can check your work by examining the `C:\ArcpyBook\code\Ch8\GeometryTokenEntireGeometry.py` solution file.
4. Save and run the script. You should see the following output. Your time will vary from mine, but notice that the execution time is slower. In this case, it's only a little over a second slower, but we're only returning 2600 features. If the feature class were significantly larger, as many are, this would be amplified:

   ```
   Parcel owner: CITY OF AUSTIN ATTN REAL ESTATE DIVISION has a
   location of: <geoprocessing describe geometry object object at
   0x06B9BE00>

   Parcel owner: CITY OF AUSTIN ATTN REAL ESTATE DIVISION has a
   location of: <geoprocessing describe geometry object object at
   0x2400A700>

   Parcel owner: CITY OF AUSTIN has a location of: <geoprocessing
   describe geometry object object at 0x06B9BE00>

   Parcel owner: CITY OF AUSTIN % DOROTHY NELL ANDERSON ATTN
   BARRY LEE ANDERSON has a location of: <geoprocessing describe
   geometry object object at 0x2400A700>

   Execution time: 10.1211390896
   ```

How it works...

A geometry token can be supplied as one of the field names supplied in the constructor for the cursor. These tokens are used to increase the performance of a cursor by returning only a portion of the geometry instead of the entire geometry. This can dramatically increase the performance of a cursor, particularly when you are working with large polyline or polygon datasets. If you only need specific properties of the geometry in your cursor, you should use these tokens.

Inserting rows with InsertCursor

You can insert a row into a table or feature class using an `InsertCursor` object. If you want to insert attribute values along with the new row, you'll need to supply the values in the order found in the attribute table.

Getting ready

The `InsertCursor()` function is used to create an `InsertCursor` object that allows you to programmatically add new records to feature classes and tables. The `insertRow()` method on the `InsertCursor` object adds the row. A row in the form of a list or tuple is passed into the `insertRow()` method. The values in the list must correspond to the field values defined when the `InsertCursor` object was created. Similar to instances that include other types of cursors, you can also limit the field names returned using the second parameter of the method. This function supports geometry tokens as well.

The following code example illustrates how you can use `InsertCursor` to insert new rows into a feature class. Here, we insert two new wildfire points into the `California` feature class. The row values to be inserted are defined in a `list` variable. Then, an `InsertCursor` object is created, passing in the feature class and fields. Finally, the new rows are inserted into the feature class by using the `insertRow()` method:

```
rowValues = [(Bastrop','N',3000,(-105.345,32.234)),
('Ft Davis','N', 456, (-109.456,33.468))]
fc = "c:/data/wildfires.gdb/California"
fields = ["FIRE_NAME", "FIRE_CONTAINED", "ACRES", "SHAPE@XY"]
with arcpy.da.InsertCursor(fc, fields) as cursor:
  for row in rowValues:
    cursor.insertRow(row)
```

In this recipe, you will use `InsertCursor` to add wildfires retrieved from a `.txt` file into a point feature class. When inserting rows into a feature class, you will need to know how to add the geometric representation of a feature into the feature class. This can be accomplished by using `InsertCursor` along with two miscellaneous objects: `Array` and `Point`. In this exercise, we will add point features in the form of wildfire incidents to an empty point feature class. In addition to this, you will use Python file manipulation techniques to read the coordinate data from a text file.

How to do it...

We will be importing the North American wildland fire incident data from a single day in October, 2007. This data is contained in a comma-delimited text file containing one line for each fire incident on this particular day. Each fire incident has a latitude, longitude coordinate pair separated by commas along with a confidence value. This data was derived by automated methods that use remote sensing data to derive the presence or absence of a wildfire. Confidence values can range from 0 to 100. Higher numbers represent a greater confidence that this is indeed a wildfire:

1. Open the file at `C:\ArcpyBook\Ch8\Wildfire Data\NorthAmericaWildfire_2007275.txt` and examine the contents.

   You will notice that this is a simple comma-delimited text file containing the longitude and latitude values for each fire along with a confidence value. We will use Python to read the contents of this file line by line and insert new point features into the `FireIncidents` feature class located in the `C:\ArcpyBook\Ch8 \WildfireData\WildlandFires.mdb` personal geodatabase.

2. Close the file.
3. Open `ArcCatalog`.
4. Navigate to `C:\ArcpyBook\Ch8\WildfireData`.

   You should see a personal geodatabase called `WildlandFires`. Open this geodatabase and you will see a point feature class called `FireIncidents`. Right now, this is an empty feature class. We will add features by reading the text file you examined earlier and inserting points.

5. Right-click on `FireIncidents` and select **Properties**.
6. Click on the **Fields** tab.

   The latitude/longitude values found in the file we examined earlier will be imported into the `SHAPE` field and the confidence values will be written to the `CONFIDENCEVALUE` field.

7. Open **IDLE** and create a new script.
8. Save the script to `C:\ArcpyBook\Ch8\InsertWildfires.py`.
9. Import the `arcpy` modules:

   ```
   import arcpy
   ```

10. Set the workspace:

    ```
    arcpy.env.workspace =
    "C:/ArcpyBook/Ch8/WildfireData/WildlandFires.mdb"
    ```

11. Open the text file and read all the lines into a list:

```
f =
open("C:/ArcpyBook/Ch8/WildfireData/NorthAmericaWildfires_2007275.
txt","r")
lstFires = f.readlines()
```

12. Start a `try` block:

```
try:
```

13. Create an `InsertCursor` object using a `with` block. Make sure you indent inside the `try` statement. The cursor will be created in the `FireIncidents` feature class:

```
with
arcpy.da.InsertCursor("FireIncidents",("SHAPE@
XY","CONFIDENCEVALUE")) as cur:
```

14. Create a counter variable that will be used to print the progress of the script:

```
cntr = 1
```

15. Loop through the text file line by line using a `for` loop. Since the text file is comma-delimited, we'll use the Python `split()` function to separate each value into a list variable called `vals`. We'll then pull out the individual latitude, longitude, and confidence value items and assign them to variables. Finally, we'll place these values into a list variable called `rowValue`, which is then passed into the `insertRow()` function for the `InsertCursor` object, and we then print a message:

```
for fire in lstFires:
      if 'Latitude' in fire:
        continue
      vals = fire.split(",")
      latitude = float(vals[0])
      longitude = float(vals[1])
      confid = int(vals[2])
      rowValue = [(longitude,latitude),confid]
      cur.insertRow(rowValue)
      print("Record number " + str(cntr) + " written to
      feature class")
      #arcpy.AddMessage("Record number" + str(cntr) + "
      written to feature class")
      cntr = cntr + 1
```

16. Add the `except` block to print any errors that may occur:

```
except Exception as e:
  print(e.message)
```

17. Add a `finally` block to close the text file:

```
finally:
  f.close()
```

18. The entire script should appear as follows:

```
import arcpy

arcpy.env.workspace = "C:/ArcpyBook/Ch8/WildfireData/
WildlandFires.mdb"
f =
open("C:/ArcpyBook/Ch8/WildfireData/
NorthAmericaWildfires_2007275.txt","r")
lstFires = f.readlines()
try:
  with
arcpy.da.InsertCursor("FireIncidents",
("SHAPE@XY","CONFIDENCEVALUE")) as cur:
    cntr = 1
    for fire in lstFires:
      if 'Latitude' in fire:
        continue
      vals = fire.split(",")
      latitude = float(vals[0])
      longitude = float(vals[1])
      confid = int(vals[2])
      rowValue = [(longitude,latitude),confid]
      cur.insertRow(rowValue)
      print("Record number " + str(cntr) + " written to
feature class")
      #arcpy.AddMessage("Record number" + str(cntr) + "
      written to feature class")
      cntr = cntr + 1
except Exception as e:
  print(e.message)
finally:
  f.close()
```

19. You can check your work by examining the `C:\ArcpyBook\code\Ch8\InsertWildfires.py` solution file.

20. Save and run the script. You should see messages being written to the output window as the script runs:

```
Record number: 406 written to feature class
Record number: 407 written to feature class
Record number: 408 written to feature class
Record number: 409 written to feature class
Record number: 410 written to feature class
Record number: 411 written to feature class
```

21. Open **ArcMap** and add the `FireIncidents` feature class to the table of contents. The points should be visible, as shown in the following screenshot:

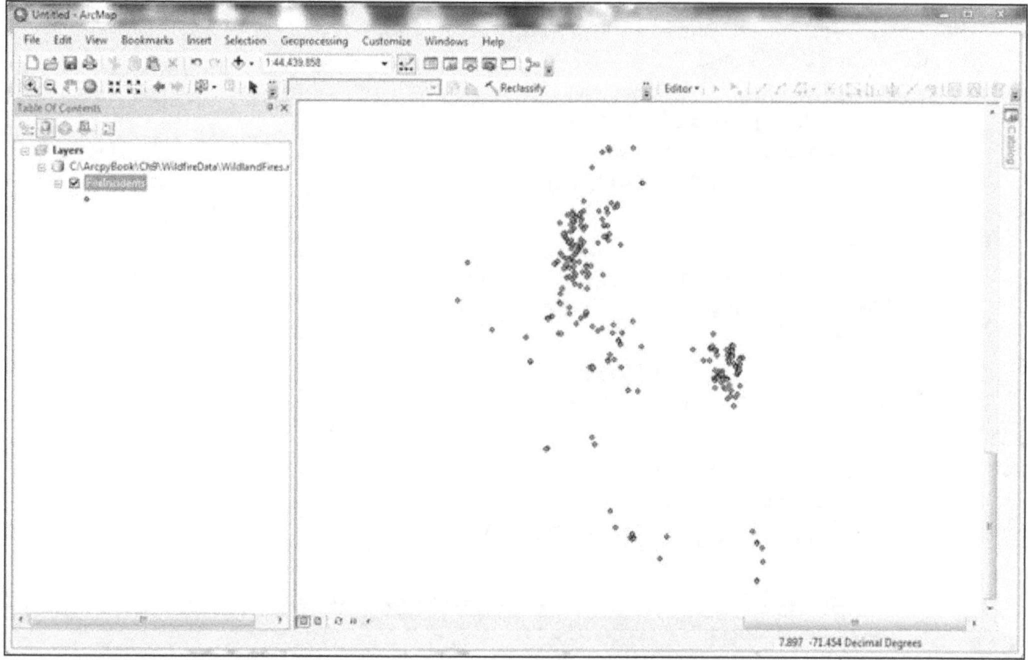

22. You may want to add a basemap to provide some reference for the data. In ArcMap, click on the **Add Basemap** button and select a basemap from the gallery.

How it works...

Some additional explanation may be needed here. The `lstFires` variable contains a list of all the wildfires that were contained in the comma-delimited text file. The `for` loop will loop through each of these records one by one, inserting each individual record into the `fire` variable. We also include an `if` statement that is used to skip the first record in the file, which serves as the header. As I explained earlier, we then pull out the individual latitude, longitude, and confidence value items from the `vals` variable, which is just a Python list object and assign them to variables called `latitude`, `longitude`, and `confid`. We then place these values into a new list variable called `rowValue` in the order that we defined when we created `InsertCursor`. Thus, the latitude and longitude pair should be placed first followed by the confidence value. Finally, we call the `insertRow()` function on the `InsertCursor` object assigned to the `cur` variable, passing in the new `rowValue` variable. We close by printing a message that indicates the progress of the script and also create the `except` and `finally` blocks to handle errors and close the text file. Placing the `file.close()` method in the `finally` block ensures that it will execute and close the file even if there is an error in the previous `try` statement.

Updating rows with UpdateCursor

If you need to edit or delete rows from a table or feature class, you can use `UpdateCursor`. As is the case with `InsertCursor`, the contents of `UpdateCursor` can be limited through the use of a `where` clause.

Getting ready

The `UpdateCursor()` function can be used to either update or delete rows in a table or feature class. The returned cursor places a lock on the data, which will automatically be released if used inside a Python `with` statement. An `UpdateCursor` object is returned from a call to this method.

The `UpdateCursor` object places a lock on the data while it's being edited or deleted. If the cursor is used inside a Python `with` statement, the lock will automatically be freed after the data has been processed. This hasn't always been the case. Previous versions of cursors were required to be manually released using the Python `del` statement. Once an instance of `UpdateCursor` has been obtained, you can then call the `updateCursor()` method to update records in tables or feature classes and the `deleteRow()` method can be used to delete a row.

In this recipe, you're going to write a script that updates each feature in the `FireIncidents` feature class by assigning a value of `poor`, `fair`, `good`, or `excellent` to a new field that is more descriptive of the confidence values using an `UpdateCursor`. Prior to updating the records, your script will add the `new` field to the `FireIncidents` feature class.

How to do it...

Follow these steps to create an `UpdateCursor` object that will be used to edit rows in a feature class:

1. Open **IDLE** and create a new script.
2. Save the script to `C:\ArcpyBook\Ch8\UpdateWildfires.py`.
3. Import the `arcpy` module:

   ```
   import arcpy
   ```

4. Set the workspace:

   ```
   arcpy.env.workspace =
   "C:/ArcpyBook/Ch8/WildfireData/WildlandFires.mdb"
   ```

5. Start a `try` block:

   ```
   try:
   ```

6. Add a new field called `CONFID_RATING` to the `FireIncidents` feature class. Make sure to indent inside the `try` statement:

```
arcpy.AddField_management("FireIncidents","CONFID_RATING",
"TEXT","10")
print("CONFID_RATING field added to FireIncidents")
```

7. Create a new instance of `UpdateCursor` inside a `with` block:

```
with
arcpy.da.UpdateCursor("FireIncidents",
("CONFIDENCEVALUE","CONFID_RATING")) as cursor:
```

8. Create a counter variable that will be used to print the progress of the script. Make sure you indent this line of code and all the lines of code that follow inside the `with` block:

```
cntr = 1
```

9. Loop through each of the rows in the `FireIncidents` fire class. Update the `CONFID_RATING` field according to the following guidelines:

   - Confidence value 0 to 40 = `POOR`
   - Confidence value 41 to 60 = `FAIR`
   - Confidence value 61 to 85 = `GOOD`
   - Confidence value 86 to 100 = `EXCELLENT`

   This can be translated in the following block of code:

```
    for row in cursor:
      # update the confid_rating field
      if row[0] <= 40:
        row[1] = 'POOR'
      elif row[0] > 40 and row[0] <= 60:
        row[1] = 'FAIR'
      elif row[0] > 60 and row[0] <= 85:
        row[1] = 'GOOD'
      else:
        row[1] = 'EXCELLENT'
      cursor.updateRow(row)
      print("Record number " + str(cntr) + " updated")
      cntr = cntr + 1
```

10. Add the `except` block to print any errors that may occur:

```
except Exception as e:
  print(e.message)
```

11. The entire script should appear as follows:

```
import arcpy

arcpy.env.workspace =
"C:/ArcpyBook/Ch8/WildfireData/WildlandFires.mdb"
try:
  #create a new field to hold the values
  arcpy.AddField_management("FireIncidents",
"CONFID_RATING","TEXT","10")
  print("CONFID_RATING field added to FireIncidents")
  with arcpy.da.UpdateCursor("FireIncidents",("CONFIDENCEVALUE",
"CONFID_RATING")) as cursor:
    cntr = 1
    for row in cursor:
      # update the confid_rating field
      if row[0] <= 40:
        row[1] = 'POOR'
      elif row[0] > 40 and row[0] <= 60:
        row[1] = 'FAIR'
      elif row[0] > 60 and row[0] <= 85:
        row[1] = 'GOOD'
      else:
        row[1] = 'EXCELLENT'
      cursor.updateRow(row)
      print("Record number " + str(cntr) + " updated")
      cntr = cntr + 1
except Exception as e:
  print(e.message)
```

12. You can check your work by examining the `C:\ArcpyBook\code\Ch8\UpdateWildfires.py` solution file.
13. Save and run the script. You should see messages being written to the output window as the script runs:

```
Record number 406 updated
Record number 407 updated
Record number 408 updated
Record number 409 updated
Record number 410 updated
```

14. Open **ArcMap** and add the `FireIncidents` feature class. Open the attribute table and you should see that a new `CONFID_RATING` field has been added and populated by `UpdateCursor`:

FireIncidents

OBJECTID *	SHAPE *	CONFIDENCEVALUE	CONFID_RATING
6577	Point	72	GOOD
6578	Point	82	GOOD
6579	Point	68	GOOD
6580	Point	53	FAIR
6581	Point	45	FAIR
6582	Point	100	EXCELLENT
6583	Point	100	EXCELLENT
6584	Point	43	FAIR
6585	Point	44	FAIR
6586	Point	59	FAIR
6587	Point	44	FAIR

When you insert, update, or delete data in cursors, the changes are permanent and can't be undone if you're working outside an edit session. However, with the new edit session functionality provided by ArcGIS 10.1, you can now make these changes inside an edit session to avoid these problems. We'll cover edit sessions soon.

How it works...

In this case, we've used `UpdateCursor` to update each of the features in a feature class. We first used the `Add Field` tool to add a new field called `CONFID_RATING`, which will hold new values that we assign based on values found in another field. The groups are poor, fair, good, and excellent and are based on numeric values found in the `CONFIDENCEVALUE` field. We then created a new instance of `UpdateCursor` based on the `FireIncidents` feature class, and returned the two fields mentioned previously. The script then loops through each of the features and assigns a value of poor, fair, good, or excellent to the `CONFID_RATING` field (`row[1]`), based on the numeric value found in `CONFIDENCEVALUE`. A Python `if/elif/else` structure is used to control the flow of the script based on the numeric value. The value for `CONFID_RATING` is then committed to the feature class by passing the row variable into the `updateRow()` method.

Deleting rows with UpdateCursor

In addition to being used to edit rows in a table or feature class, `UpdateCursor` can also be used to delete rows. Keep in mind that when rows are deleted outside an edit session, the changes are permanent.

Getting ready

In addition to updating records, `UpdateCursor` can also delete records from a table or feature class. The `UpdateCursor` object is created in the same way in either case, but instead of calling `updateRow()`, you call `deleteRow()` to delete a record. You can also apply a `where` clause to `UpdateCursor`, to limit the records returned. In this recipe, we'll use an `UpdateCursor` object that has been filtered using a `where` clause to delete records from our `FireIncidents` feature class.

How to do it...

Follow these steps to create an `UpdateCursor` object that will be used to delete rows from a feature class:

1. Open **IDLE** and create a new script.
2. Save the script to `C:\ArcpyBook\Ch8\DeleteWildfires.py`.
3. Import the `arcpy` and `os` modules:

   ```
   import arcpy
   import os
   ```

4. Set the workspace:

   ```
   arcpy.env.workspace =
   "C:/ArcpyBook/Ch8/WildfireData/WildlandFires.mdb"
   ```

5. Start a `try` block:

   ```
   try:
   ```

6. Create a new instance of `UpdateCursor` inside a `with` block. Make sure you indent inside the `try` statement:

   ```
   with
   arcpy.da.UpdateCursor("FireIncidents",("CONFID_RATING"),
   '[CONFID_RATING] = \'POOR\'') as cursor:
   ```

7. Create a counter variable that will be used to print the progress of the script. Make sure you indent this line of code and all the lines of code that follow inside the `with` block:

   ```
   cntr = 1
   ```

8. Delete the returned rows by calling the `deleteRow()` method. This is done by looping through the returned cursor and deleting the rows one at a time:

    ```
    for row in cursor:
      cursor.deleteRow()
      print("Record number " + str(cntr) + " deleted")
      cntr = cntr + 1
    ```

9. Add the `except` block to print any errors that may occur:

    ```
    except Exception as e:
      print(e.message)
    ```

10. The entire script should appear as follows:

    ```
    import arcpy
    import os

    arcpy.env.workspace =
    "C:/ArcpyBook/Ch8/WildfireData/WildlandFires.mdb"
    try:
      with arcpy.da.UpdateCursor("FireIncidents",("CONFID_RATING"),
    '[CONFID_RATING] = \'POOR\'') as cursor:
        cntr = 1
        for row in cursor:
          cursor.deleteRow()
          print("Record number " + str(cntr) + " deleted")
          cntr = cntr + 1
    except Exception as e:
      print(e.message)
    ```

11. You can check your work by examining the `C:\ArcpyBook\code\Ch8\DeleteWildfires.py` solution file.

12. Save and run the script. You should see messages being written to the output window as the script runs. 37 records should be deleted from the `FireIncidents` feature class:

    ```
    Record number 1 deleted
    Record number 2 deleted
    Record number 3 deleted
    Record number 4 deleted
    Record number 5 deleted
    ```

How it works...

Rows from feature classes and tables can be deleted using the `deleteRow()` method in `UpdateCursor`. In this recipe, we used a `where` clause in the constructor of `UpdateCursor` to limit the records returned to only features that included `CONFID_RATING` of `POOR`. We then looped through the features returned in the cursor and called the `deleteRow()` method to delete the row from the feature class.

Inserting and updating rows inside an edit session

As I've mentioned throughout the chapter, inserts, updates, or deletes made to a table or feature class done outside an edit session are permanent. They can't be undone. Edit sessions give you much more flexibility to roll back any unwanted changes.

Getting ready

Up until now, we've used insert and update cursors to add, edit, and delete data from feature classes and tables. These changes are permanent as soon as the script is executed and can't be undone. The new `Editor` class in the data access module supports the ability to create edit sessions and operations. With edit sessions, changes applied to feature classes or tables are temporary until permanently applied with a specific method call. This is the same functionality provided by the `Edit` toolbar in ArcGIS for Desktop.

Edit sessions begin with a call to `Editor.startEditing()`, which initiates the session. Inside the session, you then start an operation with the `Editor.startOperation()` method. Within this operation, you then perform various operations that perform edits on your data. These edits can also be subject to undo, redo, and abort operations to roll back, roll forward, and abort your editing operations. After the operations have been completed, you then call the `Editor.stopOperation()` method followed by `Editor.stopEditing()`. Sessions can be ended without saving changes. In this event, changes are not permanently applied. An overview of this process is provided in the following screenshot:

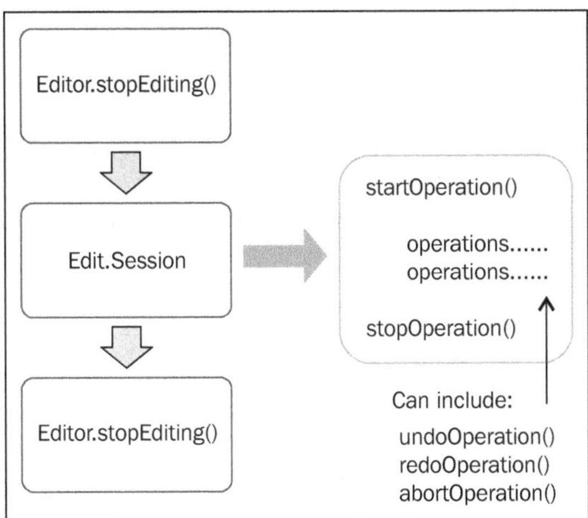

Edit sessions can also be ended without saving changes. In this event, changes are not permanently applied. Edit sessions also allow for operations to be applied inside the session and then either applied permanently to the database or rolled back. Additionally, the `Editor` class also supports undo and redo operations.

The following code example shows the full edit session stack, including the creation of the `Editor` object, the beginning of an edit session and an operation, edits to the data (an insert operation in this case), stopping the operation, and finally, the end of the edit session by saving the data:

```
edit = arcpy.da.Editor('Database Connections/Portland.sde')
edit.startEditing(False)
edit.startOperation()
with arcpy.da.InsertCursor("Portland.jgp.schools",("SHAPE","Name")) as
cursor:
  cursor.insertRow([(7642471.100, 686465.725), 'New School'])
edit.stopOperation()
edit.stopEditing(True)
```

The `Editor` class can be used with personal, file, and ArcSDE geodatabases. Also, sessions can also be started and stopped on versioned databases. You are limited to editing only a single workspace at a time, and this workspace is specified in the constructor of the `Editor` object simply by passing in a string that references the workspace. Once created, this `Editor` object then has access to all the methods to start, stop, and abort operations as well as perform undo and redo operations.

How to do it...

Follow these steps to wrap `UpdateCursor` inside an edit session:

1. Open **IDLE**.
2. Open the `C:\ArcpyBook\Ch8\UpdateWildfires.py` script and save it to a new script called `C:\ArcpyBook\Ch8\EditSessionUpdateWildfires.py`.
3. We're going to make several alterations to this existing script that updates values in the `CONFID_RATING` field.
4. Remove the following lines of code:

```
arcpy.AddField_management("FireIncidents","CONFID_RATING",
"TEXT","10")
print("CONFID_RATING field added to FireIncidents")
```

5. Create an instance of the `Editor` class and start an edit session. These lines of code should be placed inside the `try` block:

```
edit =
arcpy.da.Editor(r'C:\ArcpyBook\Ch8\WildfireData\
WildlandFires.mdb')
edit.startEditing(True)
```

6. Alter the `if` statement so that it appears as follows:

```
if row[0] > 40 and row[0] <= 60:
  row[1] = 'GOOD'
elif row[0] > 60 and row[0] <= 85:
  row[1] = 'BETTER'
else:
  row[1] = 'BEST'
```

7. End the edit session and save the edits. Place this line of code just below the counter increment:

```
edit.stopEditing(True)
```

8. The entire script should appear as follows:

```
import arcpy
import os

arcpy.env.workspace =
"C:/ArcpyBook/Ch8/WildfireData/WildlandFires.mdb"
try:
  edit = arcpy.da.Editor(r'C:\ArcpyBook\Ch8\WildfireData\
WildlandFires.mdb')
  edit.startEditing(True)
  with arcpy.da.UpdateCursor("FireIncidents",("CONFIDENCEVALUE",
"CONFID_RATING")) as cursor:
    cntr = 1
    for row in cursor:
      # update the confid_rating field
      if row[0] > 40 and row[0] <= 60:
        row[1] = 'GOOD'
      elif row[0] > 60 and row[0] <= 85:
        row[1] = 'BETTER'
      else:
        row[1] = 'BEST'
      cursor.updateRow(row)
      print("Record number " + str(cntr) + " updated")
      cntr = cntr + 1
  edit.stopEditing(True)
except Exception as e:
  print(e.message)
```

9. You can check your work by examining the `C:\ArcpyBook\code\Ch8\EditSessionUpdateWildfires.py` solution file.
10. Save and run the script to update 374 records.

How it works...

Edit operations should take place inside an edit session, which can be initiated with the `Editor.startEditing()` method. The `startEditing()` method takes two optional parameters including `with_undo` and `multiuser_mode`. The `with_undo` parameter accepts a Boolean value of `true` or `false`, with a default of `true`. This creates an undo/redo stack when set to `true`. The `multiuser_mode` parameter defaults to `true`. When it's `false`, you have full control of editing a nonversioned or versioned dataset. If your dataset is nonversioned and you use `stopEditing(False)`, your edit will not be committed. Otherwise, if set to `true`, your edits will be committed. The `Editor.stopEditing()` method takes a single Boolean value of `true` or `false`, indicating whether changes should be saved or not. This defaults to `true`.

The `Editor` class supports undo and redo operations. We'll first look at undo operations. During an edit session, various edit operations can be applied. In the event that you need to undo a previous operation, a call to `Editor.undoOperation()` will remove the most recent edit operation in the stack. This is illustrated as follows:

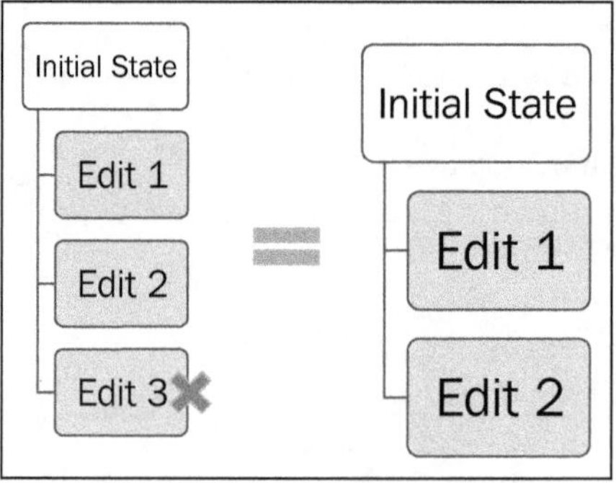

Redo operations, initiated by the `Editor.redoOperation()` method, will redo an operation that was previously undone. This is illustrated as follows:

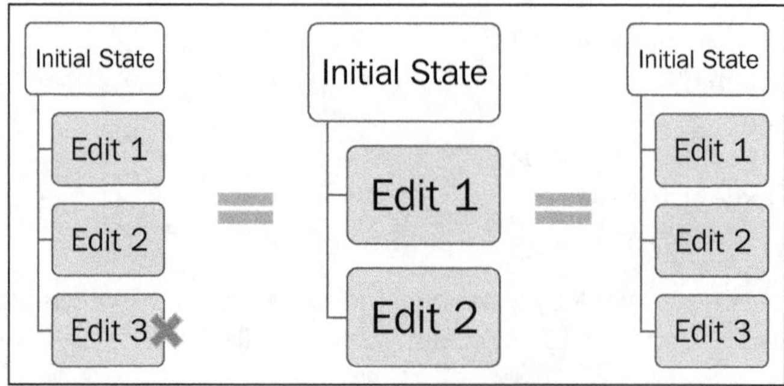

Reading geometry from a feature class

There may be times when you need to retrieve the geometric definition of features in a feature class. ArcPy provides the ability to read this information through various objects.

Getting ready

In ArcPy, feature classes have associated geometry objects, including `Polygon`, `Polyline`, `PointGeometry`, or `MultiPoint` that you can access from your cursors. These objects refer to the `shape` field in the `table` attribute of a feature class. You can read the geometries of each feature in a feature class through these objects.

Polyline and polygon feature classes are composed of features containing multiple parts. You can use the `partCount` property to return the number of parts per feature and then use `getPart()` for each part in the feature to loop through each of the points and pull out the coordinate information. Point feature classes are composed of one `PointGeometry` object per feature that contains the coordinate information for each point.

In this recipe, you will use the `SearchCursor` and `Polygon` objects to read the geometry of a polygon feature class.

How to do it...

Follow these steps to learn how to read the geometric information from each feature in a feature class:

1. Open **IDLE** and create a new script.
2. Save the script to `C:\ArcpyBook\Ch8\ReadGeometry.py`.
3. Import the `arcpy` module:

   ```
   import arcpy
   ```

4. Set the input feature class to the `SchoolDistricts` polygon feature class:

   ```
   infc =
   "c:/ArcpyBook/data/CityOfSanAntonio.gdb/SchoolDistricts"
   ```

5. Create a `SearchCursor` object with the input feature class, and return the `ObjectID` and `Shape` fields. The `Shape` field contains the geometry for each feature. The cursor will be created inside a `for` loop that we'll use to iterate all the features in the feature class:

   ```
   for row in arcpy.da.SearchCursor(infc, ["OID@", "SHAPE@"]):
   #Print the object id of each feature.
   # Print the current ID
     print("Feature {0}:".format(row[0]))
     partnum = 0
   ```

6. Use a `for` loop to loop through each part of the feature:

```
# Step through each part of the feature
for part in row[1]:
  # Print the part number
  print("Part {0}:".format(partnum))
```

7. Use a `for` loop to loop through each vertex in each part and print the `X` and `Y` coordinates:

```
  # Step through each vertex in the feature
  #
  for pnt in part:
    if pnt:
      # Print x,y coordinates of current point
      #
      print("{0}, {1}".format(pnt.X, pnt.Y))
    else:
      # If pnt is None, this represents an interior ring
      #
      print("Interior Ring:")
  partnum += 1
```

8. You can check your work by examining the `C:\ArcpyBook\code\Ch8\ReadGeometry.py` solution file.

9. Save and run the script. You should see the following output as the script writes the information for each feature, each part of the feature, and the `X` and `Y` coordinates that define each part:

```
Feature 1:
Part 0:
-98.492224986, 29.380866971
-98.489300049, 29.379610054
-98.486967023, 29.378995028
-98.48503096, 29.376808947
-98.481447988, 29.375624018
-98.478799041, 29.374304981
```

How it works...

We initially created a `SearchCursor` object to hold the contents of our feature class. After this, we looped through each row in the cursor by using a `for` loop. For each row, we looped through all the parts of the geometry. Remember that polyline and polygon features are composed of two or more parts. For each part, we also return the points associated with each part and we print the `X` and `Y` coordinates of each point.

Using Walk() to navigate directories

In this recipe, you will learn how to generate data names in a catalog tree using the `Arcpy Walk()` function. Though similar to the Python `os.walk()` function, the `da.Walk()` function provides some important enhancements related to geodatabases.

Getting ready

The `Walk()` function, which is part of `arcpy.da`, generates data names in a catalog tree by walking the tree top-down or bottom-up. Each directory or workspace yields a tuple containing the directory path, directory names, and filenames. This function is similar to the Python `os.walk()` function but it has the added advantage of being able to recognize geodatabase structures. The `os.walk()` function is file-based so it isn't able to tell you information about geodatabase structures while `arcpy.da.walk()` can do so.

How to do it...

Follow these steps to learn how to use the `da.Walk()` function to navigate directories and workspaces to reveal the structure of a geodatabase:

1. In **IDLE**, create a new Python script called `DAWalk.py` and save it to the `C:\ArcpyBook\data` folder.
2. Import the `arcpy`, `arcpy.da`, and `os` modules:

   ```
   import arcpy.da as da
   import os
   ```

3. First, we'll use `os.walk()` to obtain a list of filenames in the current directory. Add this code:

   ```
   print("os walk")
   for dirpath, dirnames, filenames in os.walk(os.getcwd()):
     for filename in filenames:
       print(filename)
   ```

4. Save the file and run it to see output similar to what you see here:

   ```
   a00000001.gdbindexes
   a00000001.gdbtable
   a00000001.gdbtablx
   a00000002.gdbtable
   a00000002.gdbtablx
   a00000003.gdbindexes
   a00000003.gdbtable
   ```

```
a00000003.gdbtablx
a00000004.CatItemsByPhysicalName.atx
a00000004.CatItemsByType.atx
a00000004.FDO_UUID.atx
a00000004.freelist
a00000004.gdbindexes
a00000004.gdbtable
a00000004.gdbtablx
```

5. Although `os.walk()` can be used to print all filenames within a directory, you'll notice that it doesn't have an understanding of the structure of Esri GIS format datasets, such as file geodatabases. Files, such as `a000000001.gdbindexes`, are physical files that make up a feature class but `os.walk()` can't tell you the logical structure of a feature class. In the next step, we'll use `da.walk()` to resolve this problem.
6. Comment out the code you just added.
7. Add the following code block:

```
print("arcpy da walk")
for dirpath, dirnames, filenames in da.Walk(os.getcwd(),datatype="
FeatureClass"):
  for filename in filenames:
    print(os.path.join(dirpath, filename)
```

8. The entire script should appear as follows:

```
import arcpy.da as da
import os

print("os walk")

for dirpath, dirnames, filenames in os.walk(os.getcwd()):
    for filename in filenames:
        print(filename)

print("arcpy da walk")

for dirpath, dirnames, filenames in
da.Walk(os.getcwd(),datatype="FeatureClass"):
    for filename in filenames:
        print(os.path.join(dirpath, filename))
```

9. You can check your work by examining the `C:\ArcpyBook\code\Ch8\Walk.py` solution file.

10. Save and execute the script to see the following output. Notice how much cleaner the output is and that the actual feature class names contained within the geodatabase are printed out instead of the physical filenames:

```
C:\ArcpyBook\data\Building_Permits.shp
C:\ArcpyBook\data\Burglaries_2009.shp
C:\ArcpyBook\data\Streams.shp
C:\ArcpyBook\data\CityOfSanAntonio.gdb\Crimes2009
C:\ArcpyBook\data\CityOfSanAntonio.gdb\CityBoundaries
C:\ArcpyBook\data\CityOfSanAntonio.gdb\CrimesBySchoolDistrict
C:\ArcpyBook\data\CityOfSanAntonio.gdb\SchoolDistricts
C:\ArcpyBook\data\CityOfSanAntonio.gdb\BexarCountyBoundaries
C:\ArcpyBook\data\CityOfSanAntonio.gdb\Texas_Counties_LowRes
C:\ArcpyBook\data\CityOfSanAntonio.gdb\Burglary
C:\ArcpyBook\data\TravisCounty\BuildingPermits.shp
C:\ArcpyBook\data\TravisCounty\CensusTracts.shp
C:\ArcpyBook\data\TravisCounty\CityLimits.shp
C:\ArcpyBook\data\TravisCounty\Floodplains.shp
C:\ArcpyBook\data\TravisCounty\Hospitals.shp
C:\ArcpyBook\data\TravisCounty\Schools.shp
C:\ArcpyBook\data\TravisCounty\Streams.shp
C:\ArcpyBook\data\TravisCounty\Streets.shp
C:\ArcpyBook\data\TravisCounty\TravisCounty.shp
C:\ArcpyBook\data\Wildfires\WildlandFires.mdb\FireIncidents
```

How it works...

The `da.Walk()` function accepts two parameters including the top-level workspace that will be retrieved (the current working directory), as well as the data type that will be used to filter the returned list. In this case, we retrieved only feature class-related files. The `Walk()` function returns a tuple containing the directory path, directory names, and filenames.

9

Listing and Describing GIS Data

In this chapter, we will cover the following recipes:

- Working with the ArcPy list functions
- Getting a list of fields in a feature class or table
- Using the Describe() function to return descriptive information about a feature class
- Using the Describe() function to return descriptive information about a raster image

Introduction

Python provides you with the ability to batch process data through scripting. This helps you automate workflows and to increase the efficiency of your data processing. For example, you may need to iterate through all datasets on disk and perform a specific action for each dataset. The first step is often to perform an initial gathering of data before proceeding to the main body of the geoprocessing task. This initial data gathering is often accomplished through the use of one or more list methods found in ArcPy. These lists are returned as true Python list objects. These list objects can then be iterated for further processing. ArcPy provides a number of functions that can be used to generate lists of data. These methods work on many different types of GIS data. In this chapter, we will examine the many functions provided by ArcPy to create lists of data. In *Chapter 2, Managing Map Documents and Layers*, we also covered a number of list functions. However, these functions were related to working with the `arcpy.mapping` module, and specifically, for working with map documents and layers. The list functions we cover in this chapter reside directly in ArcPy and are more generic in nature.

We will also cover the `Describe()` function to return a dynamic object that will contain property groups. These dynamically generated `Describe` objects contain property groups that are dependent on the type of data that has been described. For instance, when the `Describe()` function is run against a feature class, properties specific to a feature class will be returned. In addition to this, all data, regardless of the data type, acquires a set of generic properties, which we'll discuss shortly.

Working with the ArcPy list functions

Getting a list of data is often the first step in a multistep geoprocessing operation. ArcPy provides many list functions that you can use to gather lists of information, whether they are feature classes, tables, workspaces, and so on. After gathering a list of data, you will often perform geoprocessing operations against the items in the list. For example, you might want to add a new field to all the feature classes in a file geodatabase. To do this, you'd first need to get a list of all the feature classes in the workspace. In this recipe, you'll learn how to use the list functions in ArcPy by working with the `ListFeatureClasses()` function. All the ArcPy list functions work in the same fashion.

Getting ready

ArcPy provides functions to get lists of fields, indexes, datasets, feature classes, files, rasters, tables, and more. All the list functions perform the same type of basic operations. The `ListFeatureClasses()` function can be used to generate a list of all feature classes in a workspace. The `ListFeatureClasses()` function has three optional arguments that can be passed into the function that will serve to limit the returned list. The first optional argument is a wildcard that can be used to limit the feature classes that are returned based on a name, and the second optional argument can be used to limit the feature classes that are returned based on a data type (such as point, line, polygon, and so on). The third optional parameter limits the returned feature classes by a feature dataset. In this recipe, you will learn how to use the `ListFeatureClasses()` function to return a list of feature classes. You'll also learn how to restrict the list that is returned.

How to do it...

Follow these steps to learn how to use the `ListFeatureClasses()` function to retrieve a list of the feature classes in a workspace:

1. Open **IDLE** and create a new script window.
2. Save the script as `C:\ArcpyBook\Ch9\ListFeatureClasses.py`.
3. Import the `arcpy` module:

   ```
   import arcpy
   ```

4. Set the workspace:

```
arcpy.env.workspace =
"C:/ArcpyBook/data/CityOfSanAntonio.gdb"
```

[You should always remember to set the workspace using the environment settings before calling any list function in a script developed with IDLE or any other Python development environment. If this isn't done, the list function would not know which dataset the list should be pulled from. If the script is run inside ArcMap, it returns the feature classes from the default geodatabase if you don't set the workspace.]

5. Call the `ListFeatureClasses()` function and assign the results to a variable called `fcList`:

```
fcList = arcpy.ListFeatureClasses()
```

6. Loop through each of the feature classes in `fcList` and print them to the screen:

```
for fc in fcList:
    print(fc)
```

7. You can check your work by examining the `C:\ArcpyBook\code\Ch9\ListFeatureClasses_Step1.py` solution file.
8. Save and run the script. You should see this output.

```
Crimes2009
CityBoundaries
CrimesBySchoolDistrict
SchoolDistricts
BexarCountyBoundaries
Texas_Counties_LowRes
```

9. The list of feature classes returned by the `ListFeatureClasses()` function can be restricted through the use of a wildcard passed as the first parameter. The wildcard is used to restrict the contents of your list based on a name. For example, you may want to return only a list of feature classes that start with `C`. To accomplish this, you can use an asterisk along with a combination of characters. Update the `ListFeatureClasses()` function to include a wildcard that will find all feature classes that begin with an uppercase `C` and also have any number of characters:

```
fcList = arcpy.ListFeatureClasses("C*")
```

10. You can check your work by examining the `C:\ArcpyBook\code\Ch9\ListFeatureClasses_Step2.py` solution file.

11. Save and run the script to see this output:

    Crimes2009

    CityBoundaries

    CrimesBySchoolDistrict

12. In addition to using a wildcard to restrict the list returned by the `ListFeatureClasses()` function, a type restriction can also be applied, either in conjunction with the wildcard or by itself. For example, you could restrict the list of feature classes that are returned to contain only feature classes that begin with `C` and have a `polygon` data type. Update the `ListFeatureClasses()` function to include a wildcard that will find all feature classes that begin with an uppercase `C` and have a polygon data type:

    ```
    fcs = arcpy.ListFeatureClasses("C*", "Polygon")
    ```

13. You can check your work by examining the `C:\ArcpyBook\code\Ch9\ListFeatureClasses_Step3.py` solution file.
14. Save and run the script. You will see the following output:

    CityBoundaries

    CrimesBySchoolDistrict

How it works...

Before calling any list functions, you will need to set the workspace environment setting that sets the current workspace from which you will generate the list. The `ListFeatureClasses()` function can accept three optional parameters, which will limit the feature classes that are returned. The three optional parameters include a wild card, feature type, and feature dataset. In this recipe, we've applied two of the optional parameters including a wildcard and a feature type. Most of the other list functions work the same way. The parameter types will vary, but how you call the functions will essentially be the same.

There's more...

Instead of returning a list of feature classes in a workspace, you may need to get a list of tables. The `ListTables()` function returns a list of standalone tables in a workspace. This list can be filtered by name or table type. Table types can include dBase, INFO, and ALL. All values in the list are of the `string` data type and contain table names. Other list functions include `ListFields()`, `ListRasters()`, `ListWorkspaces()`, `ListIndexes()`, `ListDatasets()`, `ListFiles()`, and `ListVersions()`.

Getting a list of fields in a feature class or table

Feature classes and tables contain one or more columns of attribute information. You can get a list of the fields in a feature class through the `ListFields()` function.

Getting ready

The `ListFields()` function returns a list containing individual `Field` objects for each field in a feature class or table. Some functions, such as `ListFields()` and `ListIndexes()`, require an input dataset to operate on. You can use a wildcard or field type to constrain the list that is returned. Each `Field` object contains various read-only properties including `Name`, `AliasName`, `Type`, `Length`, and others.

How to do it...

Follow these steps to learn how to return a list of fields in a feature class.

1. Open **IDLE** and create a new script window.
2. Save the script as `C:\ArcpyBook\Ch9\ListOfFields.py`.
3. Import the `arcpy` module:

   ```
   import arcpy
   ```

4. Set the workspace:

   ```
   arcpy.env.workspace =
   "C:/ArcpyBook/data/CityOfSanAntonio.gdb"
   ```

5. Call the `ListFields()` method on the `Burglary` feature class inside a try block:

   ```
   try:
       fieldList = arcpy.ListFields("Burglary")
   ```

6. Loop through each of the fields in the list of fields and print out the name, type, and length. Make sure you indent as needed:

   ```
     for fld in fieldList:
       print("%s is a type of %s with a length of %i" %
       (fld.name, fld.type, fld.length))
   ```

7. Add the `Exception` block:

   ```
   except Exception as e:
       print(e.message)
   ```

8. The entire script should appear as follows:

```
import arcpy

arcpy.env.workspace = "C:/ArcpyBook/data/CityOfSanAntonio.gdb"
try:
   fieldList = arcpy.ListFields("Burglary")
   for fld in fieldList:
   print("%s is a type of %s with a length of %i" % (fld.name,
   fld.type, fld.length))
except Exception as e:
    print(e.message)
```

9. You can check your work by examining the `C:\ArcpyBook\code\Ch9\ListOfFields.py` solution file.
10. Save and run the script. You should see the following output:

```
OBJECTID is a type of OID with a length of 4
Shape is a type of Geometry with a length of 0
CASE is a type of String with a length of 11
LOCATION is a type of String with a length of 40
DIST is a type of String with a length of 6
SVCAREA is a type of String with a length of 7
SPLITDT is a type of Date with a length of 8
SPLITTM is a type of Date with a length of 8
HR is a type of String with a length of 3
DOW is a type of String with a length of 3
SHIFT is a type of String with a length of 1
OFFCODE is a type of String with a length of 10
OFFDESC is a type of String with a length of 50
ARCCODE is a type of String with a length of 10
ARCCODE2 is a type of String with a length of 10
ARCTYPE is a type of String with a length of 10
XNAD83 is a type of Double with a length of 8
YNAD83 is a type of Double with a length of 8
```

How it works...

The `ListFields()` function returns a list of fields from a feature class or a table. This function accepts one required parameter, which is a reference to the feature class or table the function should be executed against. You can limit the fields returned by using a wildcard or a field type. In this recipe, we only specified a feature class that indicates that all the fields will be returned. For each field returned, we printed the name, field type, and field length. As I mentioned earlier when discussing the `ListFeatureClasses()` function, `ListFields()` and all the other list functions are often called as the first step in a multistep process within a script. For example, you might want to update the population statistics contained within a `population` field for a census tract feature class. To do this, you could get a list of all the fields within a feature class, loop through this list by looking for a specific field name that contains information on the population, and then update the population information for each row. Alternatively, the `ListFields()` function accepts a wildcard as one of its parameters, so if you already know the name of the `population` field, you would pass this as the wildcard and only a single field will be returned.

Using the Describe() function to return descriptive information about a feature class

All datasets contain information that is descriptive in nature. For example, a feature class has a name, shape type, spatial reference, and so on. This information can be valuable to your scripts when you are seeking specific information before continuing with further processing in the script. For example, you might want to perform a buffer only on `polyline` feature classes instead of points or polygons. Using the `Describe()` function, you can obtain basic descriptive information about any dataset. You can think of this information as metadata.

Getting ready

The `Describe()` function provides you with the ability to get basic information about datasets. These datasets could include feature classes, tables, ArcInfo coverages, layer files, workspaces, rasters, and so on. A `Describe` object is returned and contains specific properties, based on the data type being described. Properties on the `Describe` object are organized into property groups and all datasets fall into at least one property group. For example, performing `Describe()` against a geodatabase would return the `GDB FeatureClass`, `FeatureClass`, `Table`, and `Dataset` property groups. Each of these property groups contains specific properties that can be examined.

ne Describe() function accepts a string parameter, which is a pointer to a datasource. n the following code example, we pass a feature class that is contained within a file geodatabase. The function returns a Describe object that contains a set of dynamic properties called **property groups**. We can then access these various properties as we have done in this case by simply printing out the properties using the print function:

```
arcpy.env.workspace = "c:/ArcpyBook/Ch9/CityOfSanAntonio.gdb"
desc = arcpy.Describe("Schools")
print("The feature type is: " + desc.featureType)
The feature type is: Simple
print("The shape type is: " + desc.shapeType)
The shape type is: Polygon
print("The name is: " + desc.name)
The name is: Schools
print("The path to the data is: " + desc.path)
The path to the data is: c:/ArcpyBook/Ch9/CityOfSanAntonio.gdb
```

All datasets, regardless of their type, contain a default set of properties located on the Describe object. These are read-only properties. Some of the more commonly used properties include dataType, catalogPath, name, path, and file.

In this recipe, you will write a script that obtains descriptive information about a feature class using the Describe() function.

How to do it...

Follow these steps to learn how to obtain descriptive information about a feature class:

1. Open **IDLE** and create a new script window.
2. Save the script as C:\ArcpyBook\Ch9\DescribeFeatureClass.py.
3. Import the arcpy module:

   ```
   import arcpy
   ```

4. Set the workspace:

   ```
   arcpy.env.workspace =
   "C:/ArcpyBook/data/CityOfSanAntonio.gdb"
   ```

5. Start a try block:

   ```
   try:
   ```

6. Call the Describe() function on the Burglary feature class and print out the shape type:

   ```
   descFC = arcpy.Describe("Burglary")
   print("The shape type is: " + descFC.ShapeType)
   ```

7. Get a list of fields in the feature class and print out the name, type, and length of each:

```
flds = descFC.fields
for fld in flds:
    print("Field: " + fld.name)
    print("Type: " + fld.type
    print("Length: " + str(fld.length))
```

8. Get the geographic extent of the feature class and print out the coordinates that define the extent:

```
ext = descFC.extent
print("XMin: %f" % (ext.XMin))
print("YMin: %f" % (ext.YMin))
print("XMax: %f" % (ext.XMax))
print("YMax: %f" % (ext.YMax))
```

9. Add the `Exception` block:

```
except Exception as e:
    print(e.message)
```

10. The entire script should appear as follows:

```
import arcpy
arcpy.env.workspace =
"c:/ArcpyBook/data/CityOfSanAntonio.gdb"
try:
    descFC = arcpy.Describe("Burglary")
    print("The shape type is: " + descFC.ShapeType)
    flds = descFC.fields
    for fld in flds:
        print("Field: " + fld.name)
        print("Type: " + fld.type)
        print("Length: " + str(fld.length))
    ext = descFC.extent
    print("XMin: %f" % (ext.XMin))
    print("YMin: %f" % (ext.YMin))
    print("XMax: %f" % (ext.XMax))
    print("YMax: %f" % (ext.YMax))
except:
    print(arcpy.GetMessages())
```

11. You can check your work by examining the `C:\ArcpyBook\code\Ch9\DescribeFeatureClass.py` solution file.

12. Save and run the script. You should see the following output:

```
The shape type is: Point
Field: OBJECTID
Type: OID
Length: 4
Field: Shape
Type: Geometry
Length: 0
Field: CASE
Type: String
Length: 11
Field: LOCATION
Type: String
Length: 40
.....
.....
XMin: -103.518030
YMin: -6.145758
XMax: -98.243208
YMax: 29.676404
```

How it works...

Performing a `Describe()` against a feature class, which we have done in this script, returns a `FeatureClass` property group along with access to the `Table` and `Dataset` property groups, respectively. In addition to returning a `FeatureClass` property group, you also have access to a `Table` properties group.

The `Table` property group is important primarily because it gives you access to the fields in a standalone table or feature class. You can also access any indexes on the table or feature class through this property group. The `Fields` property in `Table` Properties returns a Python list containing one `Field` object for each field in the feature class. Each field has a number of read-only properties including the `name`, `alias`, `length`, `type`, `scale`, `precision`, and so on. The most obviously useful properties are name and type. In this script, we printed out the field name, type, and length. Note the use of a Python `for` loop to process each `field` in the Python list.

Finally, we printed out the geographic extent of the layer through the use of the `Extent` object, returned by the extent property in the `Dataset` property group. The `Dataset` property group contains a number of useful properties. Perhaps, the most used properties include `extent` and `spatialReference`, as many geoprocessing tools and scripts require this information at some point during execution. You can also obtain the `datasetType` and versioning information along with several other properties.

Using the Describe() function to return descriptive information about a raster image

Raster files also contain descriptive information that can be returned by the `Describe()` function.

Getting ready

A raster dataset can also be described through the use of the `Describe()` function. In this recipe, you will describe a raster dataset by returning its extent and spatial reference. The `Describe()` function contains a reference to the general purpose `Dataset` properties group and also contains a reference to the `SpatialReference` object for the dataset. The `SpatialReference` object can then be used to get detailed spatial reference information for the dataset.

How to do it...

Follow these steps to learn how to obtain descriptive information about a raster image file.

1. Open **IDLE** and create a new script window.
2. Save the script as `C:\ArcpyBook\Ch9\DescribeRaster.py`.
3. Import the `arcpy` module:

   ```
   import arcpy
   ```

4. Set the workspace:

   ```
   arcpy.env.workspace = "C:/ArcpyBook/data "
   ```

5. Start a `try` block:

   ```
   try:
   ```

6. Call the `Describe()` function on a raster dataset:

   ```
   descRaster = arcpy.Describe("AUSTIN_EAST_NW.sid")
   ```

7. Get the extent of the raster dataset and print it out:

   ```
   ext = descRaster.extent
   print("XMin: %f" % (ext.XMin))
   print("YMin: %f" % (ext.YMin))
   print("XMax: %f" % (ext.XMax))
   print("YMax: %f" % (ext.YMax))
   ```

8. Get a reference to the `SpatialReference` object and print it out:

```
sr = descRaster.SpatialReference
print(sr.name)
print(sr.type)
```

9. Add the `Exception` block:

```
except Exception as e:
    print(e.message)
```

10. The entire script should appear as follows:

```
import arcpy
arcpy.env.workspace = "c:/ArcpyBook/data"
try:
    descRaster = arcpy.Describe("AUSTIN_EAST_NW.sid")
    ext = descRaster.extent
    print("XMin: %f" % (ext.XMin))
    print("YMin: %f" % (ext.YMin))
    print("XMax: %f" % (ext.XMax))
    print("YMax: %f" % (ext.YMax))

    sr = descRaster.SpatialReference
    print(sr.name)
    print(sr.type)
except Exception as e:
    print(e.message)
```

11. You can check your work by examining the `C:\ArcpyBook\code\Ch9\DescribeRaster.py` solution file.

12. Save and run the script. You should see the following output:

```
XMin: 3111134.862457
YMin: 10086853.262238
XMax: 3131385.723907
YMax: 10110047.019228
NAD83_Texas_Central
Projected
```

How it works...

This recipe is very similar to previous recipes. The difference is that we're using the `Describe()` function against a raster dataset instead of a `vector` feature class. In both cases, we've returned the geographic extent of the datasets using the extent object. However, in the script, we've also obtained the `SpatialReference` object for the raster dataset and printed out information about this object including its name and type.

10

Customizing the ArcGIS Interface with Add-ins

In this chapter, we will cover the following recipes:

- Downloading and installing the Python Add-in Wizard
- Creating a button add-in and using the Python add-ins module
- Installing and testing an add-in
- Creating a tool add-in

Introduction

In this chapter, we're going to cover the creation, testing, editing, and sharing of add-ins created with Python. **Add-ins** provide a way of adding user interface items to ArcGIS for Desktop through a modular code base designed to perform specific actions. Interface components can include buttons, tools, toolbars, menus, combo boxes, tool palettes, and application extensions. The add-in concept was first introduced in ArcGIS for Desktop 10.0 and could be created with .NET or Java. However, starting with the release of ArcGIS 10.1, add-ins can now be created with Python. Add-ins are created using Python scripts and an XML file that defines how a user interface should appear.

Add-ins provide an easy way to distribute user interface customizations to end users. No installation programs are necessary. A single compressed file with a file extension of `.esriaddin` is copied to a well-known folder, and ArcGIS for Desktop handles the rest. To simplify the development even further, a Python Add-In Wizard has been provided by Esri. You can download the wizard from the Esri website. We'll do this in the first recipe of this chapter.

There are a number of add-in types that can be created. Buttons and tools are the simplest types of add-ins that you can create. Buttons simply execute business logic when clicked. Tools are similar to buttons but require interaction with the map before the business logic is executed. Combo boxes provide a list of choices for the user to select from.

There are also a number of container objects, including menus, toolbars, tool palettes, and application extensions. Menus act as a container for buttons or other menus. Toolbars are a container for buttons, tools, combo boxes, tool palettes, and menus. They are the most versatile type of container for add-ins. Tool palettes also act as a container for tools, and need to be added to a toolbar before the tools are exposed. Finally, application extensions are the most complex add-in type. This type of add-in coordinates activities between other components and is responsible for listening and responding to various events, such as the addition or removal of a layer from a data frame.

Downloading and installing the Python Add-in Wizard

Esri provides a tool that you can use to make the development of add-ins easier. The Python Add-In Wizard can be downloaded from the Esri website and is a great resource to create add-ins.

Getting ready

The Python Add-In Wizard is a great resource to create the necessary files for an add-in. It generates the required files for the add-ins from a visual interface. In this recipe, you will download and install the Python Add-In Wizard.

How to do it...

Follow these steps to learn how to download and install the Python Add-in Wizard:

1. Open a web browser and navigate to `http://www.arcgis.com/home/item.html?id=5f3aefe77f6b4f61ad3e4c62f30bff3b`.

You should see a web page similar to the following screenshot:

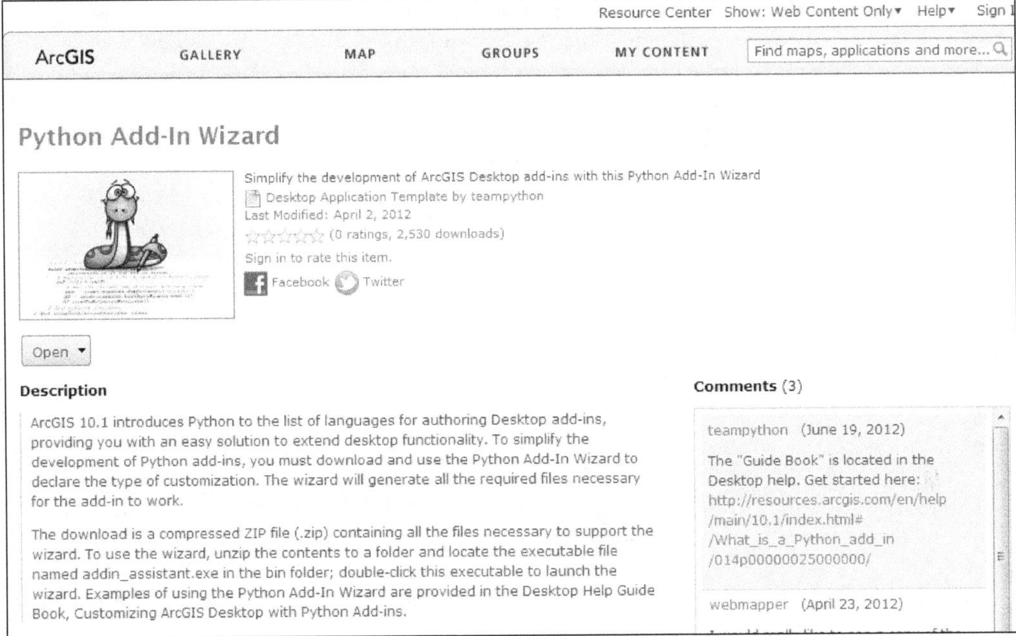

2. Click on the **Open** button to download the installer file.
3. Using Windows Explorer, create a new folder called `Python Add-In Wizard` somewhere on your computer. The name of the folder is irrelevant, but to keep things simple and easy to remember, you should go with `Python Add-In Wizard` or something similar.
4. Unzip the file to this new folder There are many utilities that can be used to unzip a file. Each will differ slightly in how they are used but with WinZip, you should be able to right-click on the file and select **Extract**.

5. Open the `bin` folder that was unzipped and double-click on `addin_assistant.exe` to run the wizard. In the following screenshot, I have created a new folder called `Python Add-In Wizard` and unzipped the downloaded file. The `bin` folder was created, and inside this folder is a file called `addin_assistant.exe`:

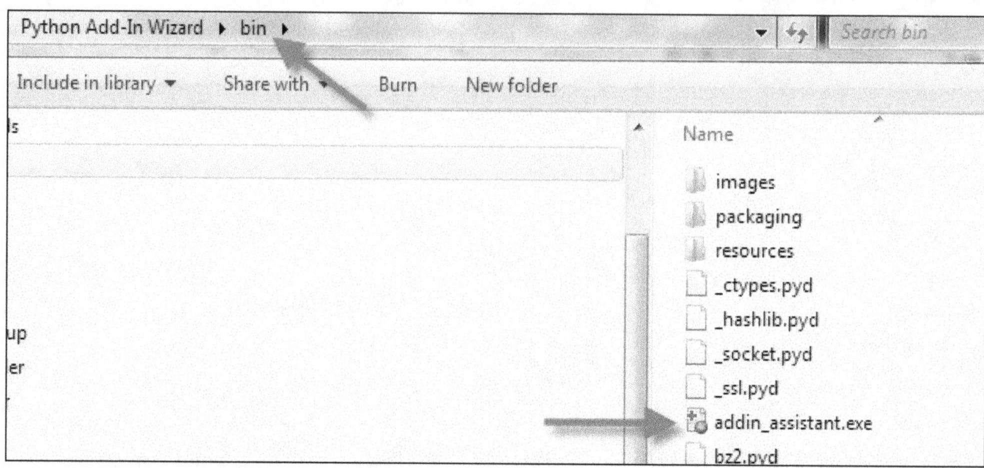

6. Double-clicking on `addin_assistant.exe` will prompt you to choose a directory to use as the add-in project root:

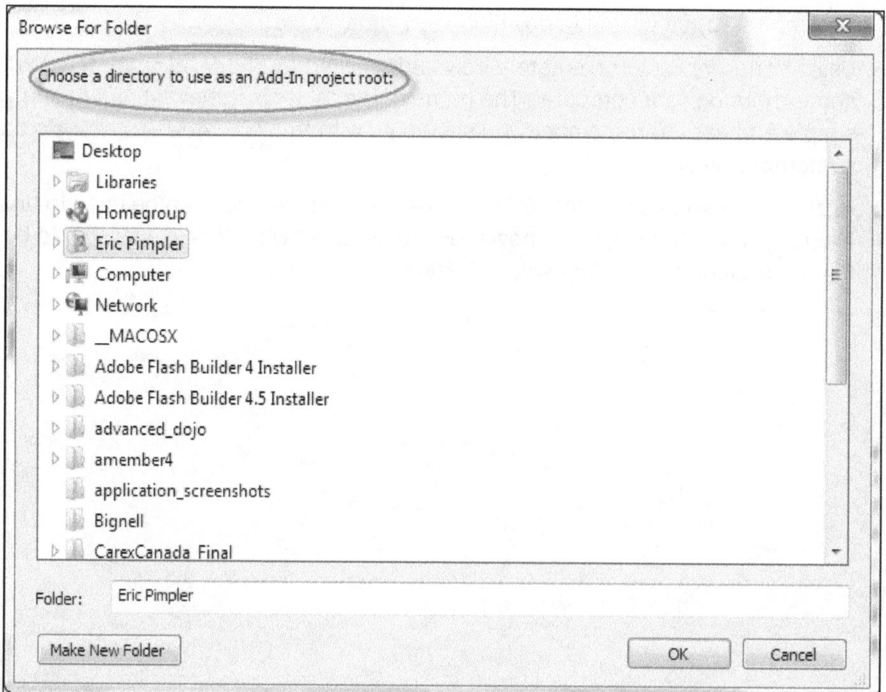

How it works...

The Python Add-In Wizard is a visual interface tool that you can use to create add-ins for ArcGIS for Desktop. It greatly simplifies the process through a point-and-click tool. In the next recipe, you'll create basic ArcGIS for Desktop add-ins using the wizard.

Creating a button add-in and using the Python add-ins module

A `Button` add-in is the simplest type of add-in and is also the most commonly used. With button add-ins, the functionality that you code in your script is executed each time the button is clicked on.

Getting ready

Creating an add-in project is the first step in the creation of a new add-in. To create a project using the Python Add-In Wizard, you select a working directory, enter various project settings, and click on the **Save** button. Creation of the add-in then follows a well-defined process, as illustrated in the following screenshot:

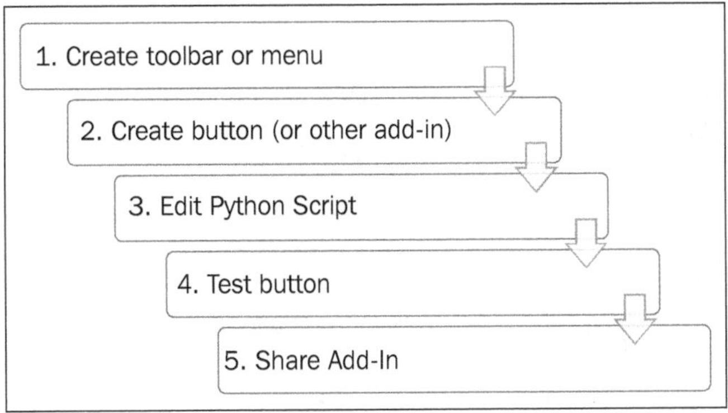

You must first create a container for the add-in and this can either be in the form of a toolbar or menu. Next, create the button, tool, or any other add-in that you want to add to the container. In this recipe, we'll create a button. Next, you need to edit the Python script that is associated with the button. You'll also want to test the button to make sure it works as expected. Finally, you can share the add-in with others. In this recipe, you'll learn how to use the Add-In Wizard to create a button add-in for ArcGIS for Desktop. The button add-in will execute code that uses the `pythonaddins` module to display a dialog that allows the user to add feature classes that have already been created for a data frame.

How to do it...

Follow these steps to learn how to create a button add-in:

1. Open the ArcGIS Python Add-In Wizard by double-clicking on the `addin_assistant.exe` file located in the `bin` folder, where you extracted the wizard.
2. Create a new project folder called `Wildfire_Addin` and select **OK**:

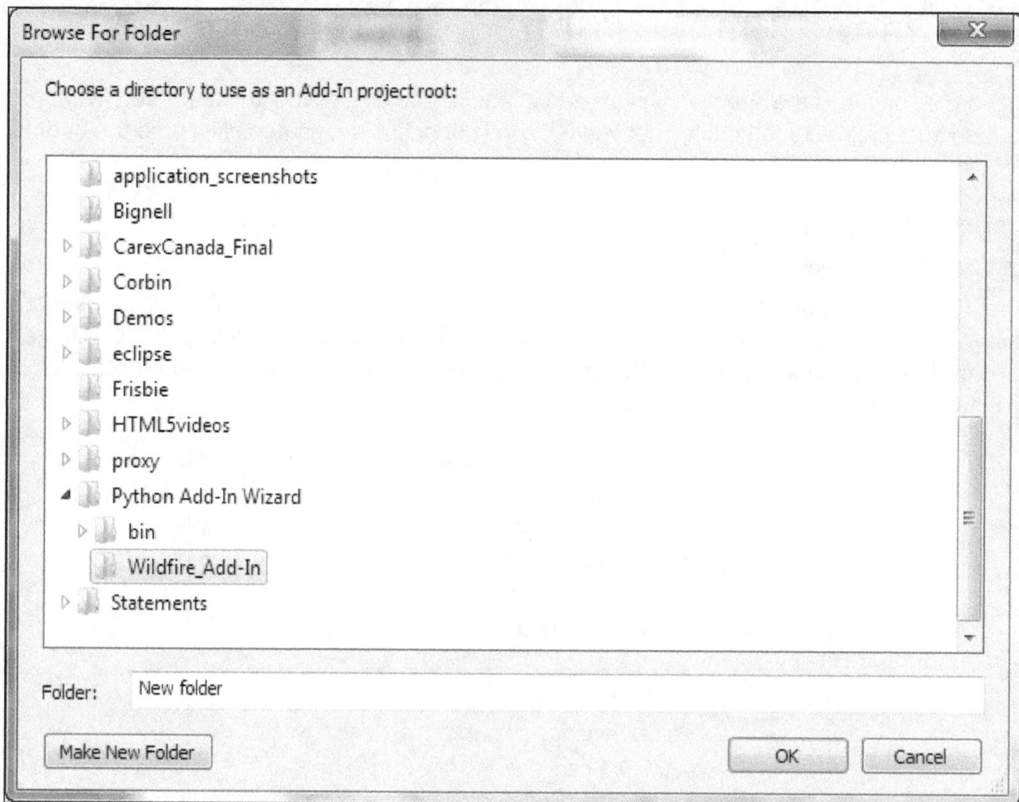

3. The **Project Settings** tab should be active initially and display the working directory that you just created. By default, **ArcMap** should be the selected product, but you should verify that this is the case:

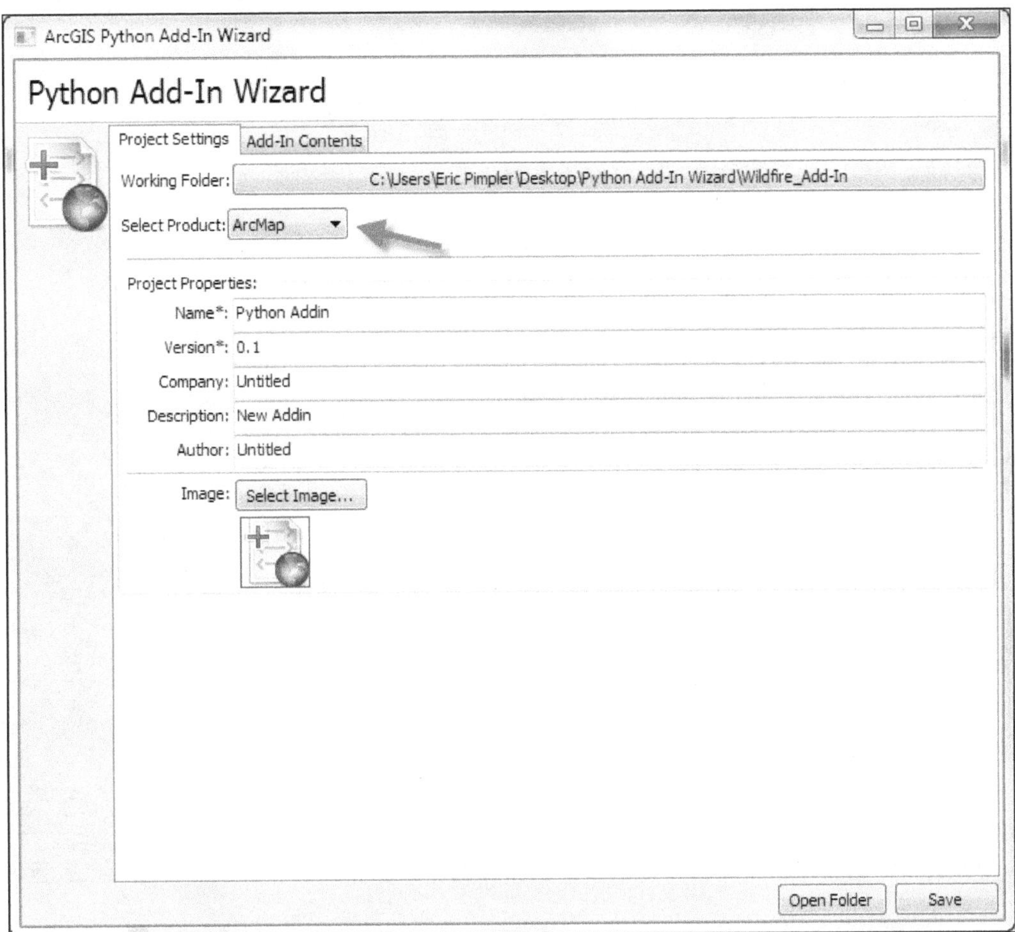

4. Give your project a name. We'll call it `Load Wildfire Data Addin`:

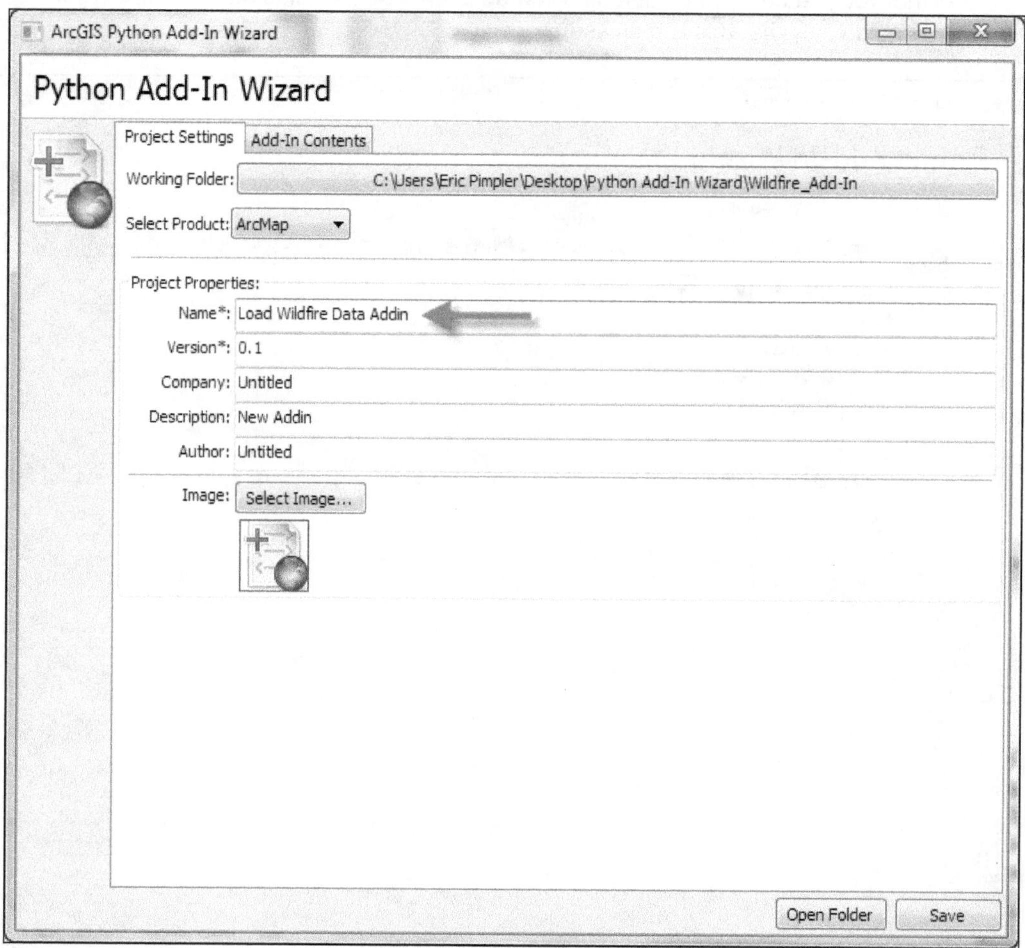

5. By default, the **Version:** is **0.1**. You can change this if you like. Version numbers should change as you update or make additions to your tool. This helps with the tracking and sharing of your add-ins:

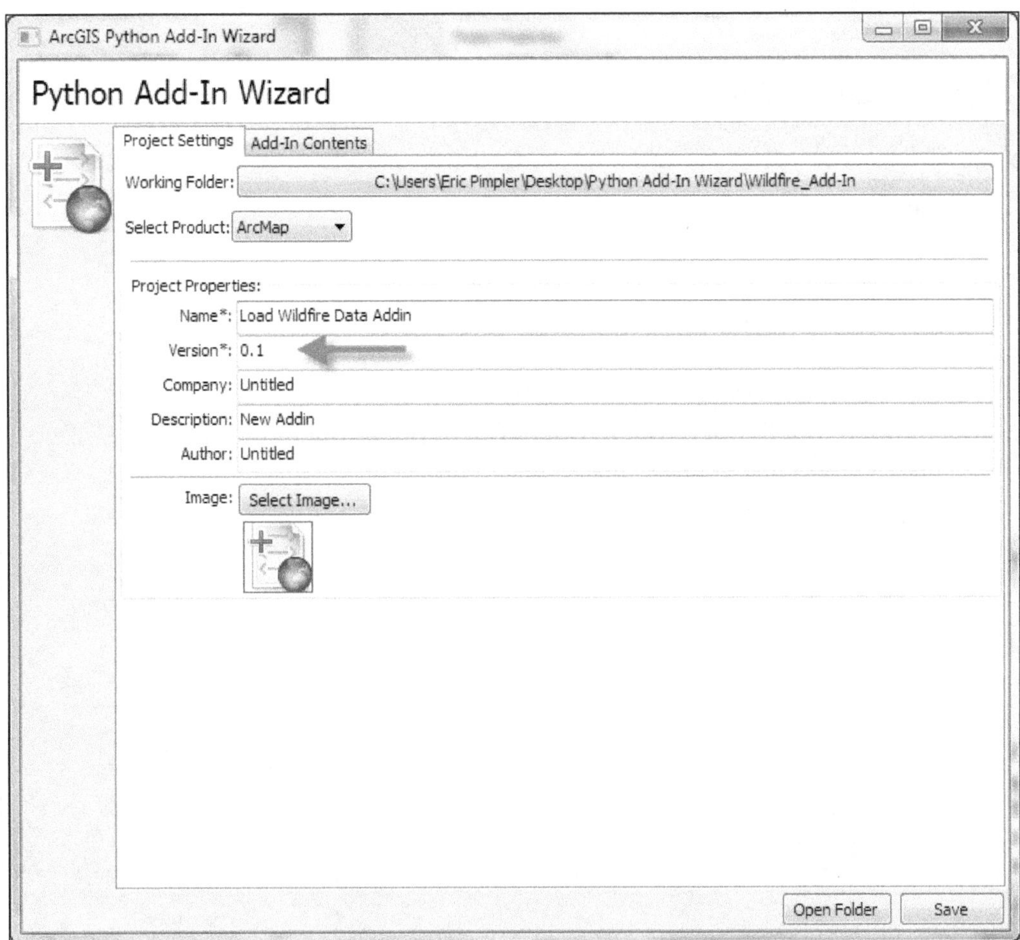

6. The **Name:** and **Version:** properties are the only two required properties. It's a good practice to go ahead and add the company, description, and author information, as shown in the following screenshot. Add your own information:

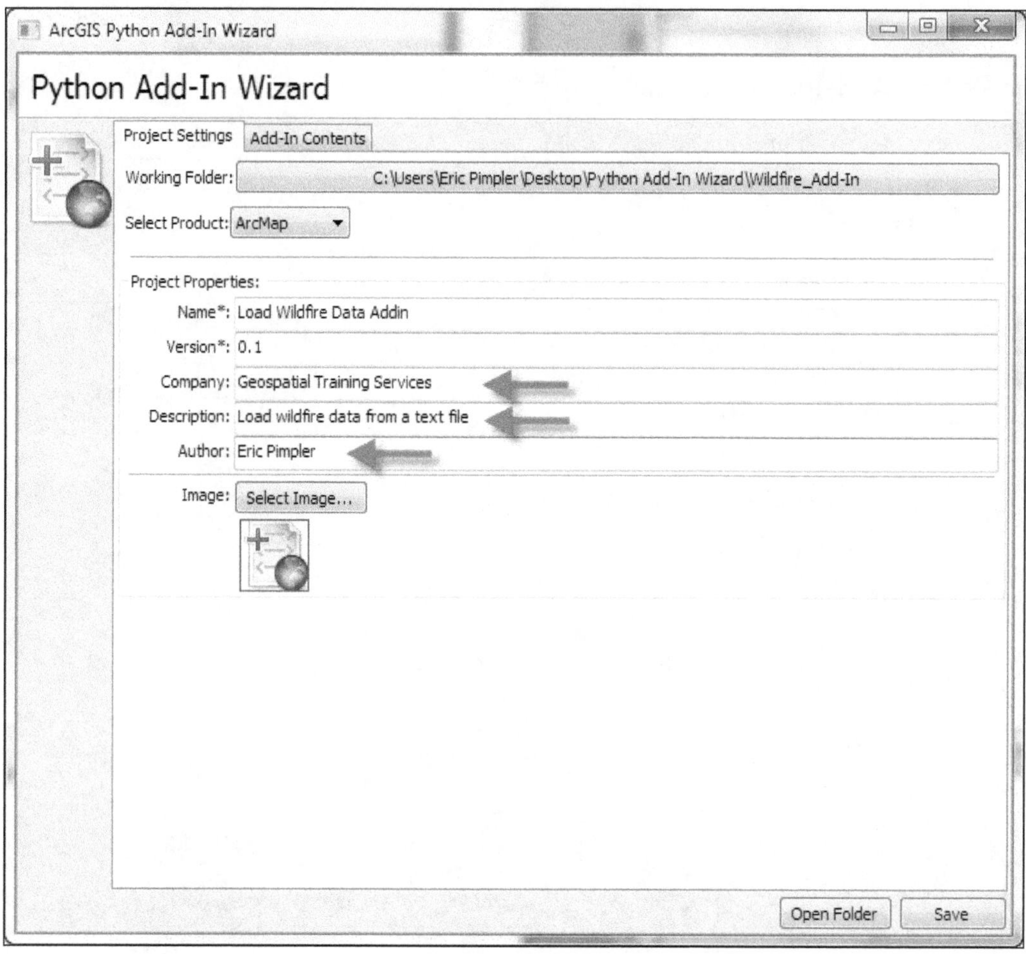

7. You may also wish to add an image for the add-in. A file called `wildfire.png` has been provided for this purpose in the `C:\ArcpyBook\Ch10` folder:

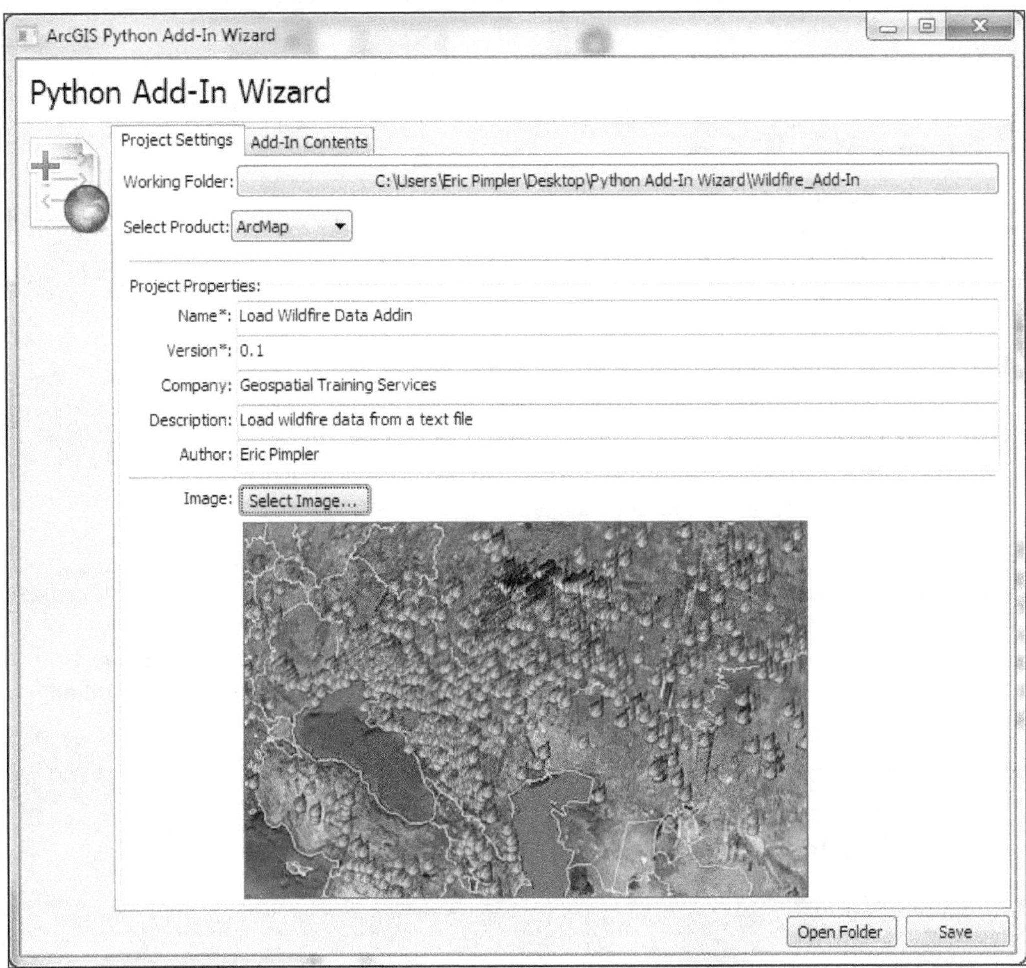

8. The **Add-In Contents** tab is used to define the various add-ins that can be created. In this step, we're going to create a toolbar to hold a single button add-in that runs a wildfire script, which imports `fires` from a text file to a feature class. Click on the **Add-In Contents** tab:

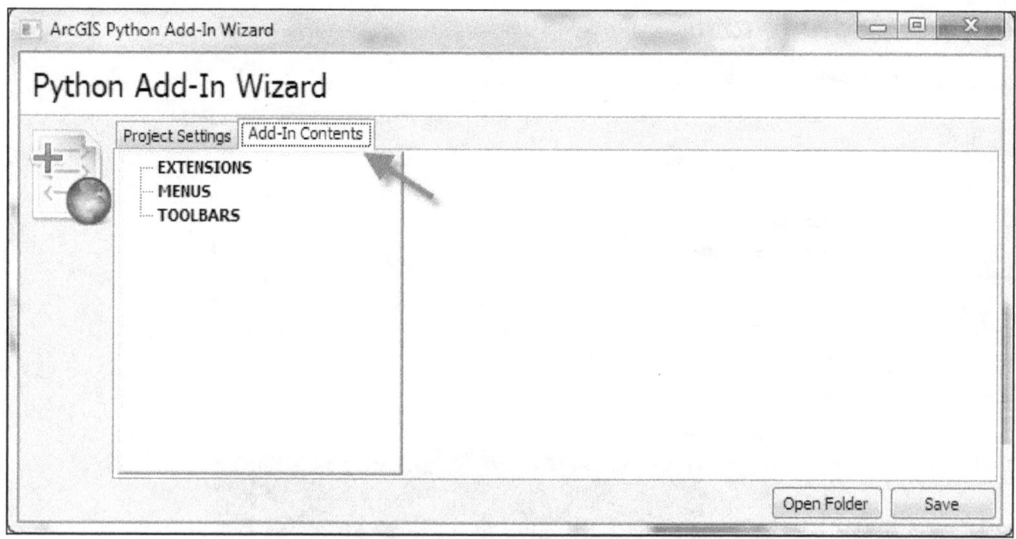

9. In the **Add-In Contents** tab, right-click on **TOOLBARS** and select **New Toolbar**. Give the toolbar a **Caption:**, accept the default name, and make sure the **Show Initially** checkbox is selected:

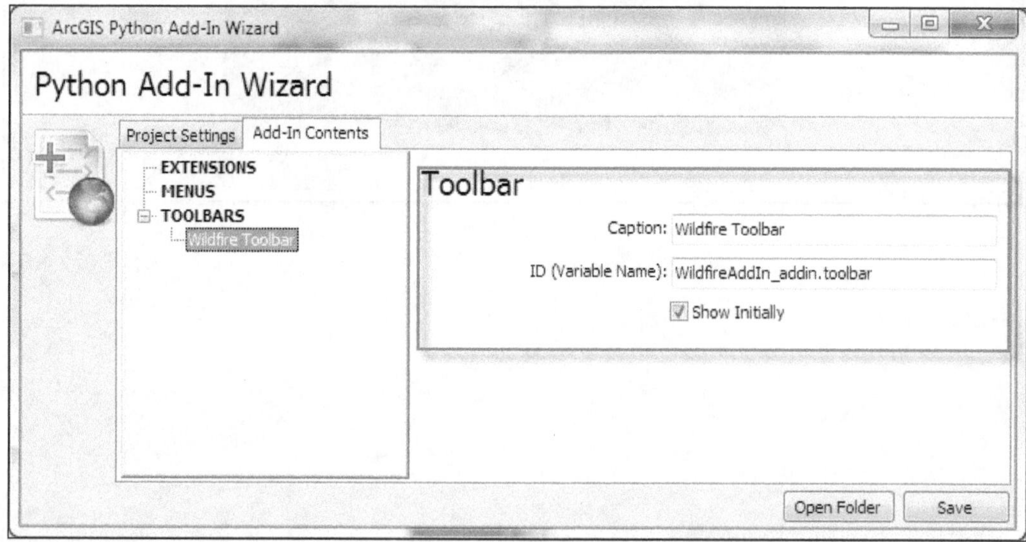

While it doesn't do a whole lot functionally, the Toolbar add-in is very important because it acts as a container for other add-ins, such as buttons, tools, combo boxes, tool palettes, and menus. Toolbars can be floating or docked. Creating a toolbar add-in is easy using the `Python Add-In Wizard`.

10. Click on the **Save** button.
11. Now, we'll add a button by right-clicking on the new **Wildfire Toolbar** option and selecting **New Button**.
12. Fill in the **Button** details, including a **Caption:**, **Class Name:**, **ID (Variable Name):**, **Tooltip:**, and so on. You can also include an **Image for control:**. I haven't done so in this case, but you may choose to do this. This information is saved to the configuration file for the add-in:

13. Click on the **Save** button. Add-ins have a Python script that they are attached to. This file, by default, will be named `AddIns_addin.py` and can be found in the `install` directory of your working project folder.

14. We've already created a custom `ArcToolbox` Python script tool that loads a comma-delimited text file from a disk containing wildfire data to a feature class. We will be using the results of this script in our add-in. In Windows Explorer, go to the `addin` directory that you created earlier. It should be called `Wildfire_Addin`. Go to the `Install` folder and you should find a file called `WildfireAddin_addin.py`. Load this file into your Python editor.

15. In this next step, we'll write code that uses the `pythonaddins` module to open a dialog that allows you to add one or more layers to a selected data frame. The `OpenDialog()` and `GetSelectedTOCLayerorDataFrame()` functions in `pythonaddins` are used to accomplish this task. Find the `onClick(self)` method, which is shown in the following code snippet. This method is triggered when the button is clicked. Remove the `pass` statement from the `onClick` event and add this code:

```
import arcpy
import pythonaddins

class ButtonClassImportWildfires(object):
    """Implementation for Wildfire_addin.button (Button)"""
    def __init__(self):
        self.enabled = True
        self.checked = False
    def onClick(self):
        layer_files = pythonaddins.OpenDialog('Select
Layers to Add', True, r'C:\ArcpyBook\data\Wildfires',
'Add')
        mxd = arcpy.mapping.MapDocument('current')
        df = pythonaddins.GetSelectedTOCLayerOrDataFrame()
        if not isinstance(df, arcpy.mapping.Layer):
            for layer_file in layer_files:
                layer = arcpy.mapping.Layer(layer_file)
                arcpy.mapping.AddLayer(df, layer)
        else:
            pythonaddins.MessageBox('Select a data frame',
'INFO', 0)
```

16. Save the file.

17. You can check your work by examining the `C:\ArcpyBook\code\Ch10\WildfireAddIn.py` solution file.

In the next recipe, you will learn how to install your new add-in.

How it works...

As you've seen in this recipe, the Python Add-In Wizard handles the creation of the add-in through a visual interface. However, behind the scenes, the wizard creates a set of folders and files for the add-in. The add-in file structure is really quite simple. Two folders and a set of files comprise the add-in structure. You can see this structure in the following screenshot:

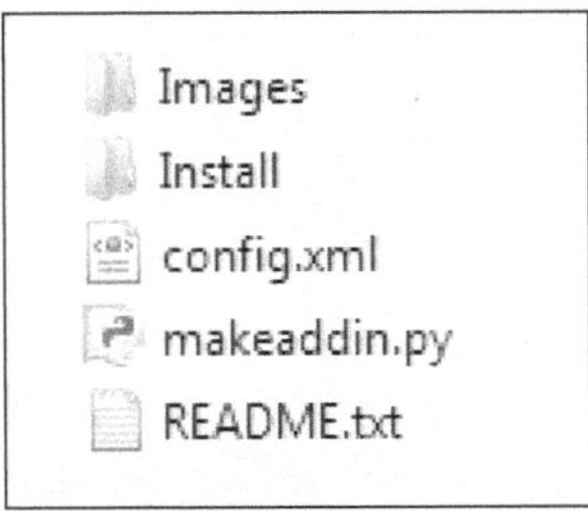

The `Images` folder contains any icons or other image files used by your add-in. In this recipe, we used the `wildfire.png` image. So, this file should now be in the `Images` folder. The `Install` folder contains the Python script that handles the business logic of the add-in. This is the file you will work with extensively to code the add-in. It performs whatever business logic needs to be performed by the buttons, tools, menu items, and so on. The `config.xml` file in the main folder of the add-in defines the user interface and static properties, such as the name, author, version, and so on. The `makeaddin.py` file can be double-clicked on to create the `.esriaddin` file, which wraps everything into a compressed file with an `.esriaddin` extension. This `.esriaddin` file is what will be distributed to end users, so that the add-in can be installed.

Installing and testing an add-in

You'll want to test add-ins before distributing them to your end users. To test these, you first need to install the add-in.

Getting ready

In the working folder of your add-in, the `makeaddin.py` script can be used to copy all files and folders to a compressed add-in folder in a working directory with the `<working folder name>.esriaddin` file format. Double-click on this `.esriaddin` file to launch the Esri ArcGIS add-in installation utility, which will install your add-in. You can then go into ArcGIS for Desktop and test the add-in. The custom toolbar or menu may already be visible and ready to test. If it is not visible, go to the **Customize** menu and click on **Add-in Manager**. The **Add-In Manager** dialog box lists the installed add-ins that target the current application. Add-in information, such as name, description, and image, which are entered as project settings, should be displayed.

How to do it...

1. Inside the main folder for your add-in, there will be a Python script file called `makeaddin.py`. This script creates the `.esriaddin` file. Double-click on the script to execute and create the `.esriaddin` file. This process is illustrated in the following screenshot:

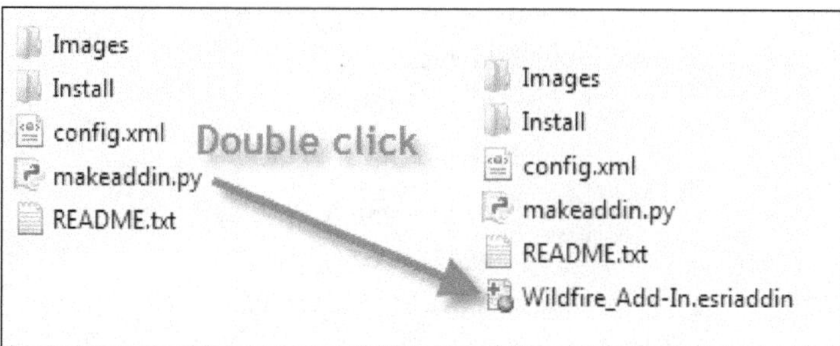

2. To install the add-in for ArcGIS for Desktop, double-click on the `Widlfire_Add-In.esriaddin` file, which will launch the **Esri ArcGIS Add-In Installation Utility** window, as shown in the following screenshot:

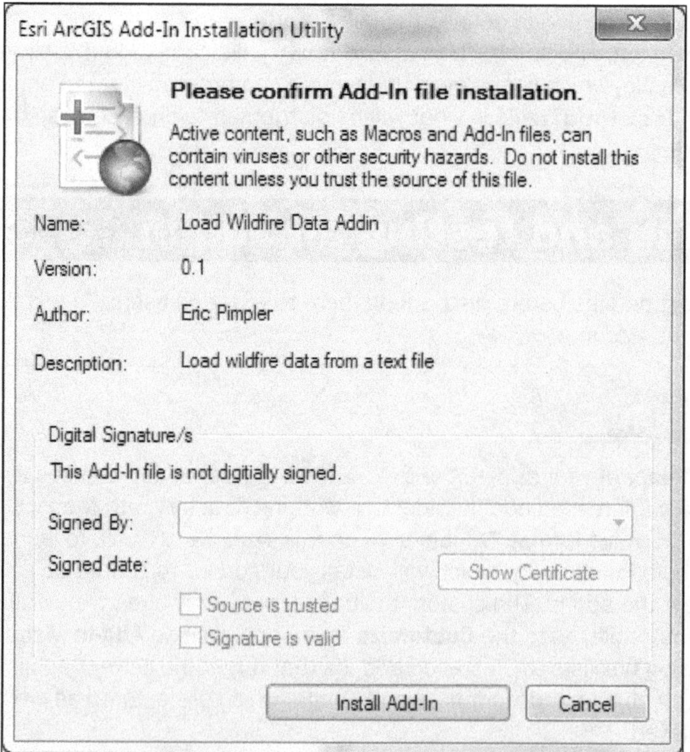

3. Click on **Install Add-In**. If everything was successful, you should see the following message:

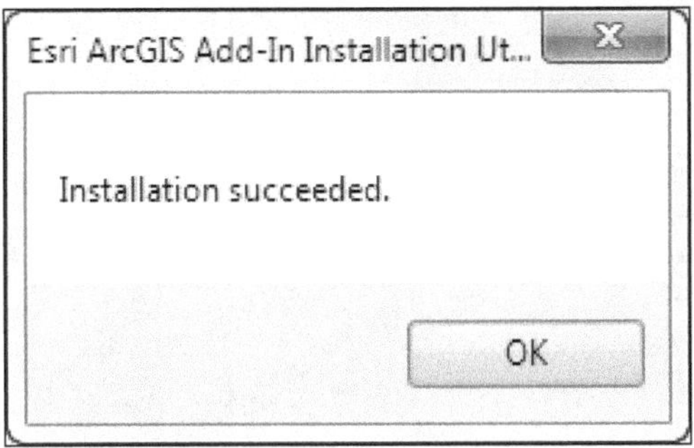

4. To test the add-in, open **ArcMap**. Your add-in may already be active. If not, navigate to **Customize** | **Add-In Manager**. This will display the **Add-In Manager** dialog box, as shown in the following screenshot. You should be able to see the add-in that you created:

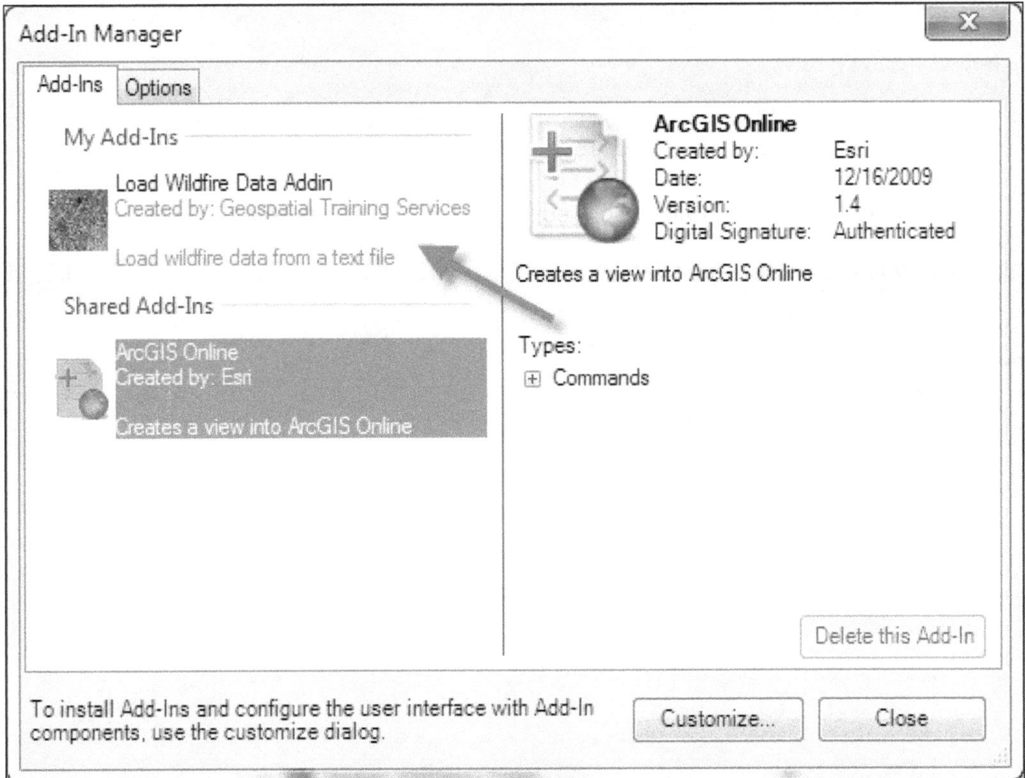

5. If needed, select the **Customize** button. To add the toolbar to the application, click on the **Toolbars** tab and choose the toolbar you created:

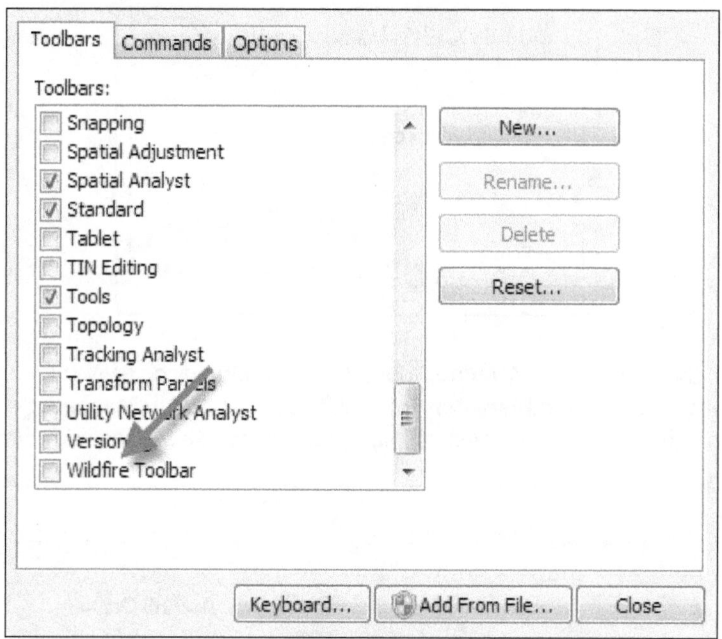

The add-in should now be displayed, as seen in this screenshot:

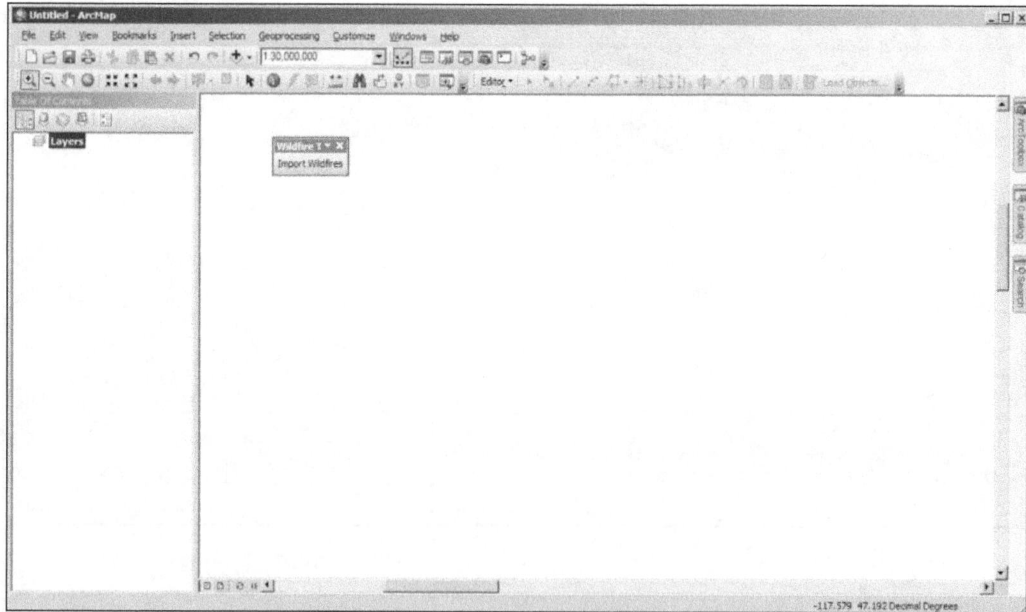

6. Click on the button and in the dialog that is displayed, navigate to the `Wildfires` layers you created earlier inside the `WildlandFires.mdb`. Select and add them to the display:

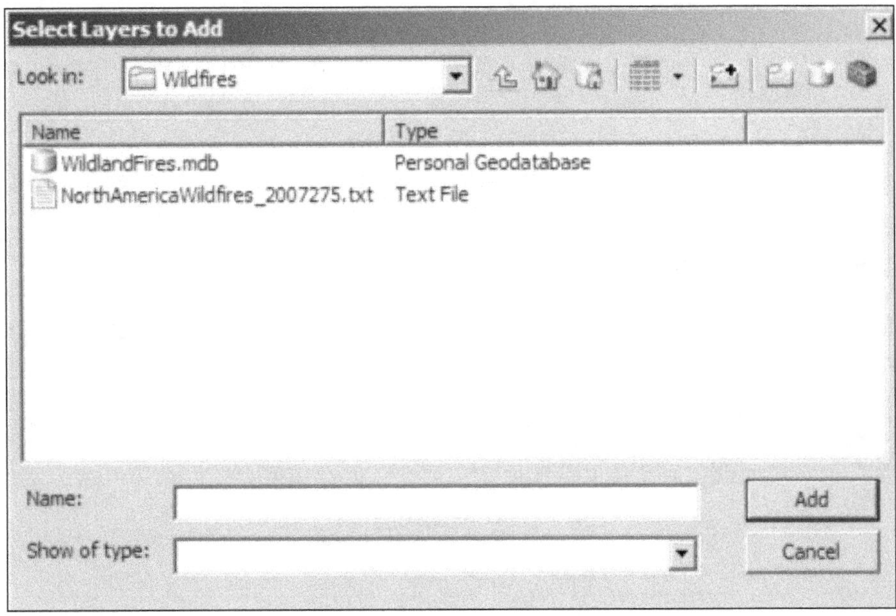

Here, you will see the output of having selected one or more layers from the dialog:

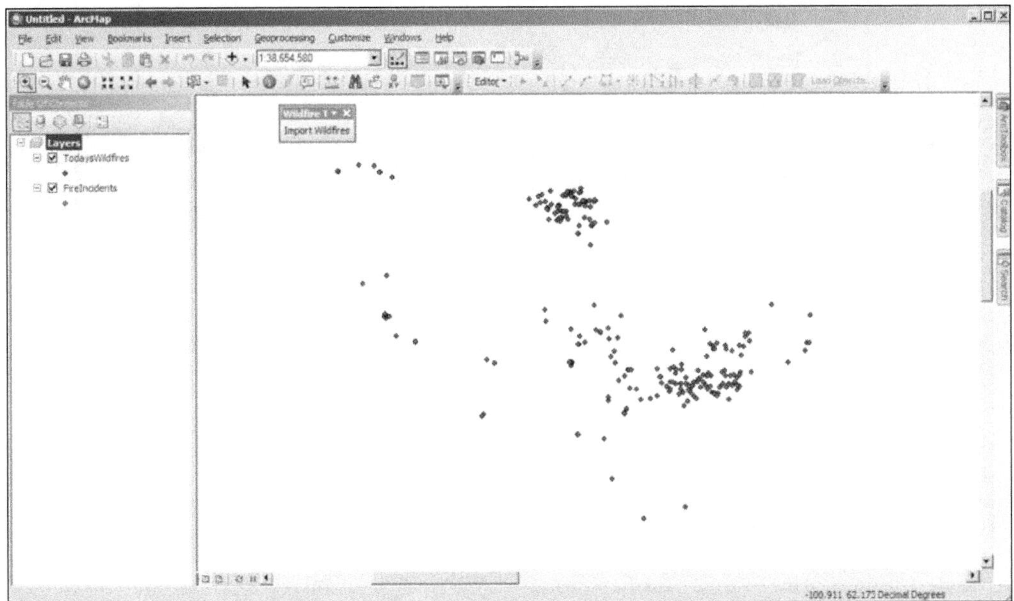

How it works...

The utility will place the add-in into a well-known folder discoverable by ArcGIS for Desktop. The locations of this folder are as follows:

- Windows 8: C:\Users\<username>\Documents\ArcGIS\AddIns\Desktop10.3
- Vista/7: C:\Users\<username>\Documents\ArcGIS\AddIns\Desktop10.3
- XP: C:\Documents and Settings\<username>\My Documents\ArcGIS\AddIns\Desktop10.3

A folder with a unique **globally unique identifier** or **GUID** name will be created inside the well-known folder. The add-in will reside inside this unique folder name. This is illustrated in the following screenshot. When ArcGIS for Desktop starts, it will search these directories and load the add-ins:

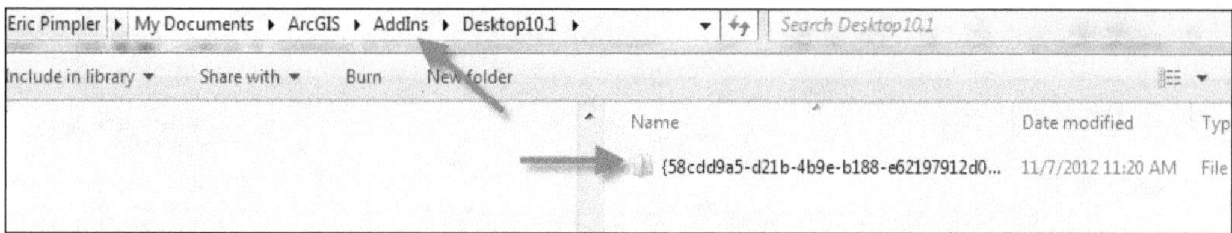

The add-in will look similar to the following:

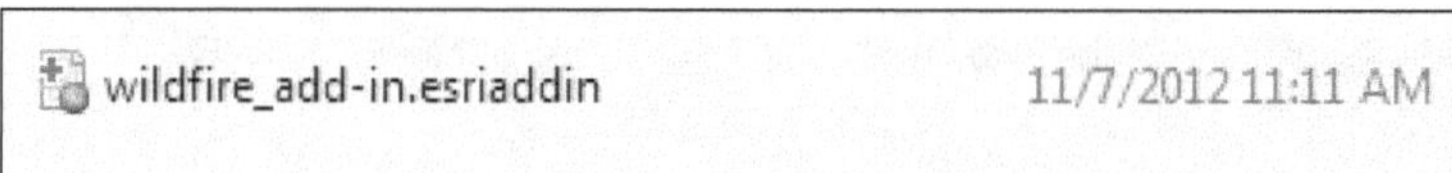

> The default add-in folder is located in the ArcGIS folder within your user account. For example, if your ArcGIS installation is version 10.1, the add-in is copied to C:\users\<username>\Documents\ArcGIS\AddIns\Desktop10.1 on a Vista or Windows 7 operating system.

You can also use a private network drive to distribute add-ins to end users. The Add-In Manager in ArcGIS for Desktop adds and maintains lists of folders that can be searched for add-ins. Select the **Options** tab and then **Add Folder** to add a network drive to the list.

Creating a tool add-in

Tool add-ins are similar to buttons with the exception that tools require some type of interaction with the map. The zoom-in tool, for example, is a type of tool. Tools should be placed inside a toolbar or tool palette. The properties similar to those of a button. You'll also need to edit the Python script.

Getting ready

The `Tool` class has a number of properties, including `cursor`, `enabled`, and `shape`. The `cursor` property sets the cursor for the tool when it is clicked on, and is defined as an integer value corresponding to the cursor types, as follows:

0	6
1	7
2	8
3	9
4	10
5	

By default, tools are enabled. This can be changed, though, by setting the `enabled` property to `false`. Finally, the `shape` property specifies the type of shape to be drawn and it can be a line, rectangle, or circle. These properties are typically set inside the constructor of the tool, which is defined by the `__init__` method, as shown in the following code example. The `self` object refers to the current object (a tool in this case) and is a variable that refers to this current object:

```
def __init__(self):
  self.enabled = True
  self.cursor = 3
  self.shape = 'Rectangle'
```

There are a number of functions associated with the `Tool` class. All classes will have a constructor, which is used to define the properties for the class. You saw an example of this `__init__` function earlier. Other important functions of the tool class include `onRectangle()`, `onCircle()`, and `onLine()`. These functions correspond to the shape that will be drawn on the map with the tool. The geometry of the drawn shape is passed into the function. There are also a number of mouse and key functions that can be used. Finally, the `deactivate()` function can be called when you want to deactivate the tool.

We've already seen the constructor for the `Tool` class in action. This function, called `__init__`, is used to set various properties for the tool when it is created. Here, we've also shown the `onRectangle()` function for the `Tool` class. This function is called when a rectangle is drawn on the map. The geometry of the rectangle is passed into the function along with a reference to the tool itself:

```
def onRectangle(self, rectangle_geometry):
```

In this recipe, you will learn how to create a tool add-in that responds to the user dragging a rectangle on the map. The tool will use the **Generate Random Points** tool to generate points within the rectangle.

How to do it...

Follow these steps to create a tool add-in with the **ArcGIS Python Add-In Wizard**:

1. Open the **ArcGIS Python Add-In Wizard** by double-clicking on the `addin_assistant.exe` file that is located in the `bin` folder, where you extracted the wizard.
2. Create a new project folder called `Generate_Random_Points` and select **OK**.
3. Enter properties, including **Name:**, **Version:**, **Company:**, **Description:**, and **Author:**, in the **Project Settings** tab:

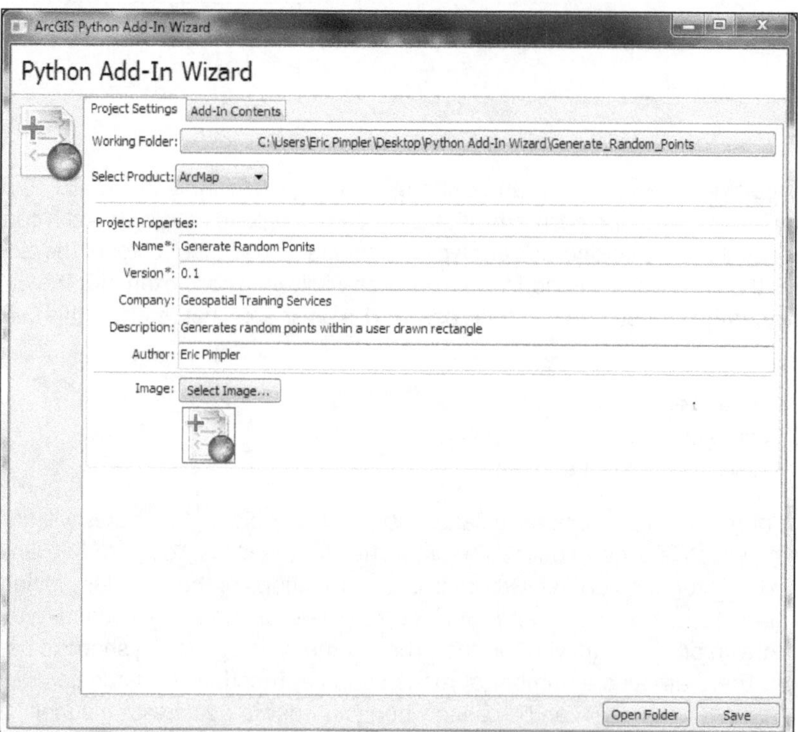

4. Click on the **Add-In Contents** tab.
5. Right-click on **TOOLBARS** and select **New Toolbar**.
6. Set the caption for the toolbar to `Random Points Toolbar`.
7. Right-click on the newly created `Random Points Toolbar` and select **New Tool**.
8. Enter items for the tool as shown in the following screenshot:

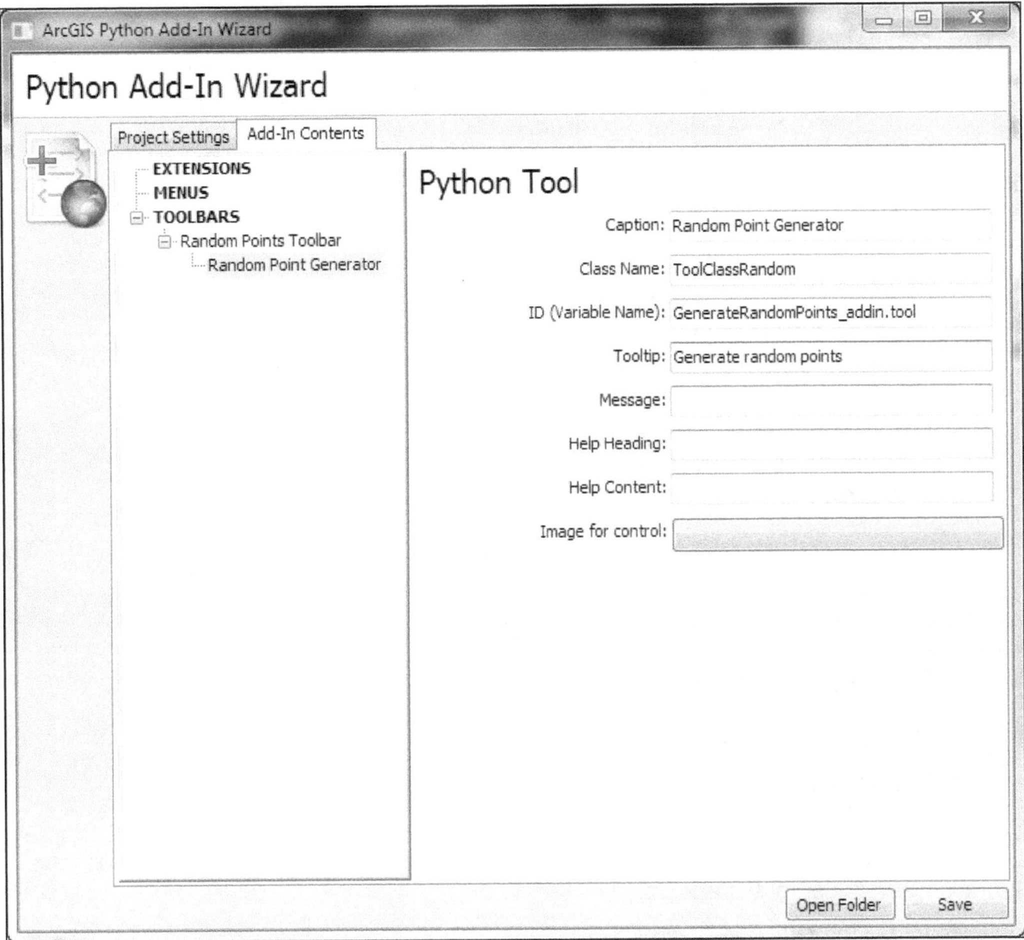

9. Click on **Save**. This will generate the folder and file structure for the add-in.
10. Go to the `Install` folder for the new add-in and open `GenerateRandomPoints_addin.py` in IDLE.
11. Add the following code to the `__init__` function, which is the constructor for the tool:

```
def __init__(self):
  self.enabled = True
  self.cursor = 3
  self.shape = 'Rectangle'
```

12. In the `onRectangle()` function, write a code to generate a set of random points within the rectangle drawn on the screen:

```
import arcpy
import pythonaddins

def __init__(self):
  self.enabled = True
  self.cursor = 3
  self.shape = 'Rectangle'

def onRectangle(self, rectangle_geometry):
    extent = rectangle_geometry
    arcpy.env.workspace = r'c:\ArcpyBook\Ch10'
    if arcpy.Exists('randompts.shp'):
        arcpy.Delete_management('randompts.shp')
        randompts = arcpy.CreateRandomPoints_management(arcpy.env.
workspace,'randompts.shp',"",rectangle_geometry)
        arcpy.RefreshActiveView()
    return randompts
```

13. Save the file.
14. You can check your work by examining the `C:\ArcpyBook\code\Ch10\GenerateRandomPoints_addin.py` solution file.
15. Generate the `.esriaddin` file by double-clicking on the `makeaddin.py` file in the `main` folder for the add-in.
16. Install the add-in by double-clicking on `GenerateRandom_Points.esriaddin`.
17. Open **ArcMap** and add the `Generate Random Points` toolbar, if necessary.
18. Add the `BexarCountyBoundaries` feature class from `C:\ArcpyBook\data\CityOfSanAntonio.gdb`.

19. Test the add-in by dragging a rectangle on the map. The output should appear similar to the following screenshot. Your map will vary because the points are generated randomly:

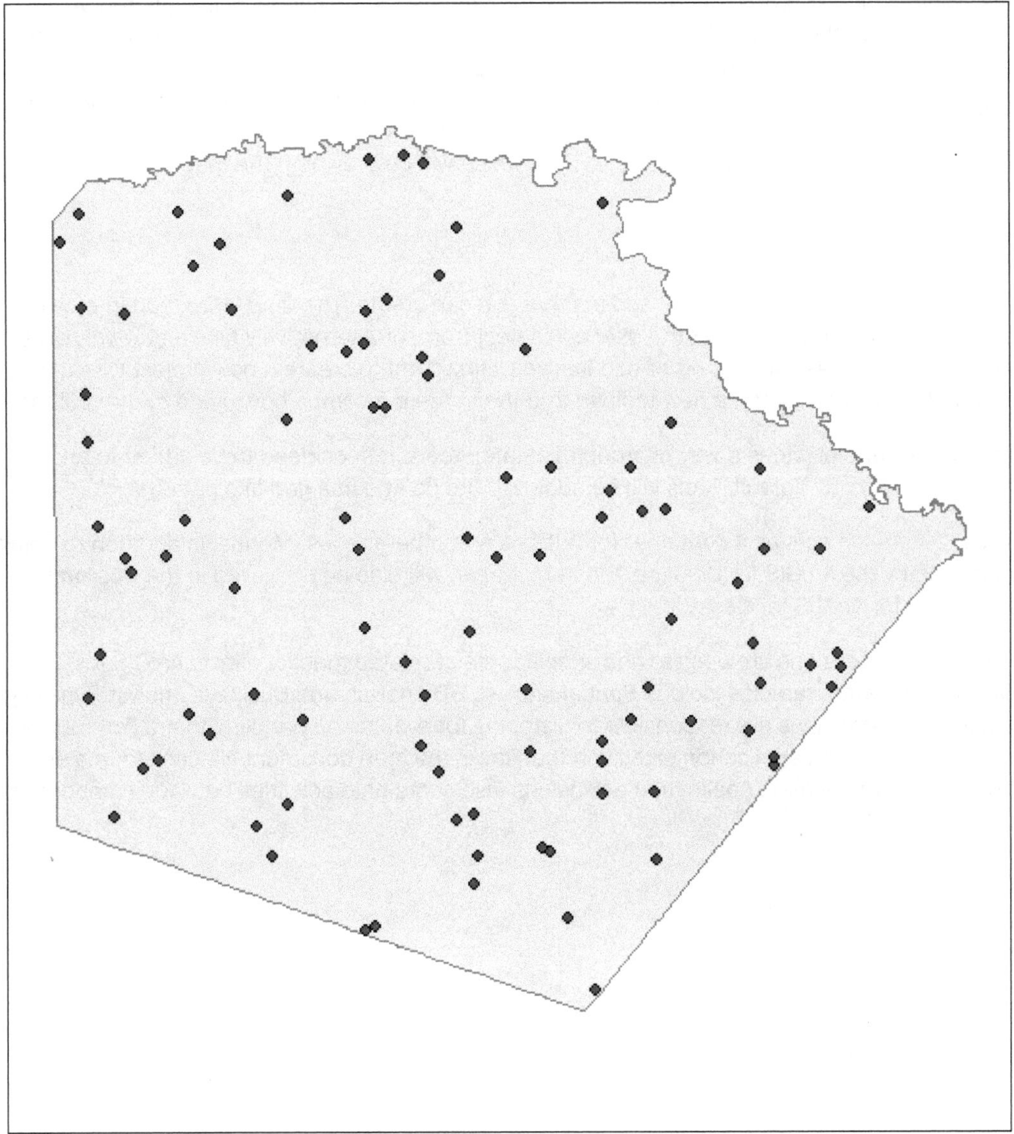

How it works...

Tool add-ins are very similar to button add-ins with the difference being that tool add-ins require some sort of interaction with the map before the functionality is triggered. An interaction with the map can include a number of things, such as clicking on the map, drawing a polygon or rectangle, or performing various mouse or key events. Python code is written to respond to one or more of these events. In this recipe, you learned how to write a code that responds to the `onRectangle()` event. You also set various properties inside the constructor for the add-in, including `cursor` and `shape`, which will be drawn on the map.

There's more...

There are a number of additional add-ins that you can create. The `ComboBox` add-in provides a drop-down list of values that the user can select from, or alternatively type a new value into an editable field. As with the other add-ins, you'll first want to create a new project with the Python Add-In Wizard, add a new toolbar, and then create a combo box to add to the toolbar.

The Tool Palette provides a way of grouping related tools. It does need to be added to an existing toolbar. By default, tools will be added to the palette in a grid-like pattern.

The `Menu` add-in acts as a container for buttons and other menus. Menus, in addition to being displayed by the ArcGIS for Desktop Add-in Manager, will also be displayed in the **Customize** dialog box for ArcGIS for Desktop.

Application extensions are used to add specific sets of related functionality to ArcGIS for Desktop. Several examples include Spatial Analyst, 3D Analyst, and Business Analyst. Typically, application extensions are responsible for listening for events and handling them. For example, you could create an application extension that saves the map document file each time a user adds a layer to the map. Application extensions also coordinate activities between components.

11

Error Handling and Troubleshooting

In this chapter, we will cover the following recipes:

- Exploring the default Python error message
- Adding Python exception handling structures (try/except/else)
- Retrieving tool messages with GetMessages()
- Filtering tool messages by the level of severity
- Testing for and responding to specific error messages

Introduction

Various messages are returned during the execution of ArcGIS geoprocessing tools and functions. These messages can be informational in nature or indicate warning or error conditions that can result in the tool not creating the expected output or result in outright failure of the tool to be executed. These messages do not appear as message boxes. Instead, you will need to retrieve them by using various ArcPy functions. Up to this point in the book, we have ignored the existence of these messages, warnings, and errors. This is mainly due to the fact that I wanted you to concentrate on learning some basic concepts, without adding the extra layer of code complexity that is necessary to create robust geoprocessing scripts that can handle error situations gracefully. This being said, it's now time that you learn how to create geoprocessing and Python exception handling structures that will enable you to create versatile geoprocessing scripts. These scripts can handle messages that indicate warnings, errors, and general information, which are generated while your script is running. These code details will help make your scripts more flexible and less error prone. You've already used the basic `try` and `except` blocks to perform some basic error handling. However, in this chapter, we'll go into more detail about why and how these structures are used.

Exploring the default Python error message

By default, Python will generate an error message whenever it encounters a problem in your script. These error messages will not always be very informative to the end user who is running the script. However, it is valuable to take a look at these raw messages. In later recipes, we'll use Python error handling structures to get a cleaner look at the errors and respond as required.

Getting ready

In this recipe, we will create and run a script that intentionally contains error conditions. We will not include any geoprocessing or Python exception handling techniques in the script. We are doing this intentionally because we want you to see the error information returned by Python.

How to do it...

Follow these steps to see a raw Python error message, which is generated when an error occurs while a tool is being executed in a script:

1. Open **IDLE** and create a new script.
2. Save the script to `C:\ArcpyBook\Ch11\ErrorHandling.py`.
3. Import the `arcpy` module:

   ```
   import arcpy
   ```

4. Set the workspace:

   ```
   arcpy.env.workspace = "c:/ArcpyBook/data"
   ```

5. Call the `Buffer` tool. The `Buffer` tool requires a buffer distance be entered as one of its parameters. In this code block, we have intentionally left out the distance parameter:

   ```
   arcpy.Buffer_analysis("Streams.shp","Streams_Buff.shp")
   ```

6. You can check your work by examining the `C:\ArcpyBook\code\Ch11\ErrorHandling1.py` solution file.
7. Run the script. You should see the following error message:

   ```
   Runtime error Traceback (most recent call last): File "<string>",
   line 1, in <module> File "c:\program files (x86)\arcgis\
   desktop10.1\arcpy\arcpy\analysis.py", line 687, in Buffer  raise e
   ExecuteError: Failed to execute. Parameters are not valid. ERROR
   000735: Distance [value or field]: Value is required Failed to
   execute (Buffer).
   ```

How it works...

This output error message isn't terribly informative. If you are a fairly experienced programmer, you'll generally be able to make out what the problem is in this case (it did not include buffer distance). However, in many cases, the returned error message will not give you much information that you can use to resolve the problem. Errors in your code are simply a fact of life in programming. However, how your code responds to these errors, also called exceptions, is very important. You should plan to handle errors gracefully through the use of Python error handling structures, which examine `arcpy` generated exceptions and act accordingly. Without these structures in place, your scripts will fail immediately, frustrating your users in the process.

Adding Python exception handling structures (try/except/else)

Python has built-in exception handling structures that allows you to capture error messages that are generated. Using this error information, you can then display a more appropriate message to the end user and respond to the situation as needed.

Getting ready

Exceptions are unusual or error conditions that occur in your code. Exception statements in Python enable you to trap and handle errors in your code, allowing you to gracefully recover from error conditions. In addition to error handling, exceptions can be used for a variety of other things, including event notification and handling of special cases.

Python exceptions occur in two ways. Exceptions in Python can either be intercepted or triggered. When an error condition occurs in your code, Python automatically triggers an exception, which may or may not be handled by your code. It is up to you as a programmer to catch an automatically triggered exception. Exceptions can also be triggered manually by your code. In this case, you would also provide an exception handling routine to catch these manually triggered exceptions. You can manually trigger an exception by using the `raise` statement.

The `try/except` statement is a complete, compound Python statement, which is used to handle exceptions. This variety of `try` statement starts with a `try` header line followed by a block of indented statements, then one or more optional `except` clauses that name exceptions to be caught, and an optional `else` clause at the end.

The `try/except/else` statement works as follows. Once inside a `try` statement, Python marks the fact that you are in a `try` block and knows that any exception condition that occurs within this block will be forwarded to the various `except` statements for handling.

Each statement inside the `try` block is executed. Assuming there aren't any conditions in which exceptions occur, the code pointer will then jump to the `else` statement and execute the code block contained within the `else` statement before moving to the next line of code below the `try` block. If an exception occurs inside the `try` block, Python searches for a matching exception code. If a matching exception is found, the code block inside the `except` block is executed. The code then reappears below the full `try` statement. The `else` statements are not executed in this case. If a matching exception header is not found, Python will propagate the exception to a `try` statement above this code block. In the event that no matching `except` header is found, the exception comes out of the top level of the process. This results in an unhandled exception and you wind up with the type of error message that we saw in our first recipe in this chapter. This is illustrated in the following figure:

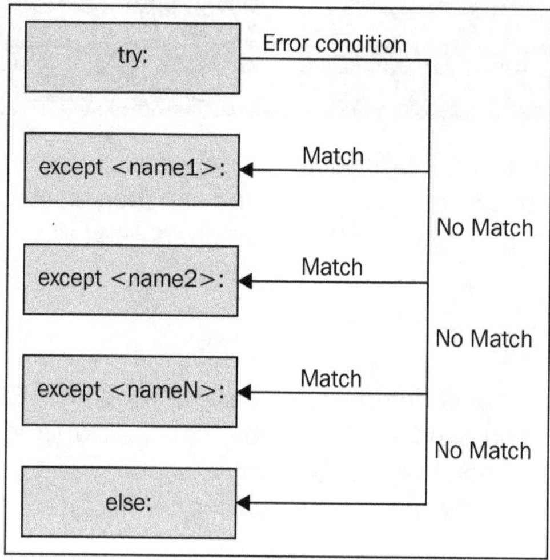

In this recipe, we're going to add in some basic Python exception handling structures. There are several variations of the `try/except/else/finally` exception handling structure. In this recipe, we'll start with a very simple `try/except` structure.

How to do it...

Follow these steps to add Python error handling structures to a script.

1. If necessary, open the `C:\ArcpyBook\Ch11\ErrorHandling.py` file in **IDLE**.
2. Alter your script to include a `try/except` block:

```
import arcpy
try:
  arcpy.env.workspace = "c:/ArcpyBook/data"
  arcpy.Buffer_analysis("Streams.shp","Streams_Buff.shp")
except:
  print("Error")
```

3. You can check your work by examining the `C:\ArcpyBook\code\Ch11\ErrorHandling2.py` solution file.
4. Save and run the script. You should see the simple `Error` message. This is no more helpful than the output we received in our first recipe. In fact, it's even less useful. However, the point of this recipe is simply to introduce you to the `try/except` error handling structure.

How it works...

This is an extremely simple structure. The `try` block indicates that everything indented under the `try` statement will be subject to exception handling. If an exception of any type is found, control of the code processing jumps to the `except` section and prints the error message(s), which in this case is simply `Error`. Now, as I mentioned, this is hardly informative to your users, but hopefully, it gives you a basic idea of how the `try/except` blocks work, and as a programmer you will better understand any errors reported by your users. In the next recipe, you'll learn how to add tool-generated messages to this structure.

There's more...

The other type of `try` statement is the `try/finally` statement, which allows for finalization actions. When a `finally` clause is used in a `try` statement, its block of statements always run at the very end, whether an error condition occurs or not. This is how the `try/finally` statement works: if an exception occurs, Python runs the `except` block, then the `finally` block. If an exception does not occur during execution, Python runs the `try` block, and then the `finally` block. This is useful when you want to make sure that an action takes place after a code block runs, regardless of whether or not an error condition occurs.

Retrieving tool messages with GetMessages()

ArcPy includes a `GetMessages()` function that you can use to retrieve messages generated when an ArcGIS tool is executing. Messages can include informational messages, such as the start and ends times of a tool execution as well as warnings and errors, which can result in something less than the desired result or complete failure of the tool to execute to completion.

Getting ready

During the execution of a tool, various messages are generated. These messages include informational messages, such as the start and end times of a tool execution, parameter values passed to the tool, and progress information. In addition to this, warnings and errors can also be generated by the tool. These messages can be read by your Python script, and your code can be designed to appropriately handle any warnings or errors that have been generated.

ArcPy stores the messages from the last tool that was executed and you can retrieve these messages using the `GetMessages()` function, which returns a single string containing all messages from the tool that was last executed. You can filter this string in terms of severity to return only certain types of messages such as warnings or errors. The first message will always include the name of the tool executed, and the last message is the start and end time.

In this recipe, you will add a line of code to the `except` statement, which will print more descriptive information about the current tool run.

How to do it...

Follow these steps to learn how to add a `GetMessages()` function to your script that generates a list of messages from the tool that was last executed:

1. If necessary, open the `C:\ArcpyBook\Ch11\ErrorHandling.py` file in IDLE.
2. Alter your script to include the `GetMessages()` function:

   ```
   import arcpy
   try:
     arcpy.env.workspace = "c:/ArcpyBook/data"
     arcpy.Buffer_analysis("Streams.shp","Streams_Buff.shp")
   except:
     print(arcpy.GetMessages())
   ```

3. You can check your work by examining the `C:\ArcpyBook\code\Ch11\ErrorHandling3.py` solution file.
4. Save and run the script. This time, the error message should be much more informative. Also notice that there are other types of messages that are generated including the start and end times of the script's execution:

   ```
   Executing: Buffer c:/ArcpyBook/data\Streams.shp c:/ArcpyBook/data\
   Streams_Buff.shp # FULL ROUND NONE #
   Start Time: Tue Nov 13 22:23:04 2012
   Failed to execute. Parameters are not valid.
   ERROR 000735: Distance [value or field]: Value is required
   Failed to execute (Buffer).
   Failed at Tue Nov 13 22:23:04 2012 (Elapsed Time: 0.00 seconds)
   ```

How it works...

The `GetMessages()` function returns all the messages generated by the last tool that was run. I want to emphasize that it only returns messages from the last tool that was run. Keep this in mind if you have a script with multiple tools that are being run. Historical tool messages are not accessible through this function. However, there is a `Result` object that you can use if you need to retrieve historical tool messages.

Filtering tool messages by the level of severity

As I mentioned in the last recipe, all tools generate a number of messages that can be classified as information, warnings, or error messages. The `GetMessages()` method accepts a parameter that allows you to filter the messages that are returned. For example, you may not be interested in the informative or warning messages in your script. However, you will certainly be interested in error messages as they indicate a fatal error that will not allow a tool to successfully execute. Using `GetMessages()`, you can filter the returned message to include only error messages.

Getting ready

Messages are classified into one of three types, which are indicated by the level of severity. **Informational messages** provide descriptive information concerning things, such as a tools progress, start and end times of the tool, output data characteristics, and much more. The severity of an informational message is indicated by a value of `0`. **Warning messages** are generated when a problem has occurred during execution that may affect the output. Warnings are indicated with a severity level of `1` and don't normally stop a tool from running. The last type of message is an **error message**, which is indicated by a numeric value of `2`. These indicate fatal events that prevent a tool from running. Multiple messages may be generated during the execution of a tool, and these are stored in a list. More information about the severity of message is provided in the following image. In this recipe, you will learn how to filter the messages generated by the `GetMessages()` function:

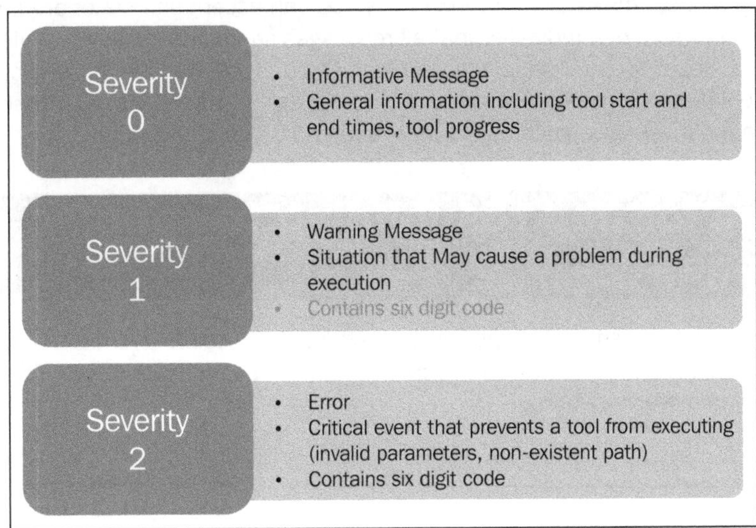

How to do it...

Filtering the messages returned by a tool is really quite simple. You simply provide the severity level you'd like to return as a parameter for the `GetMessages()` function.

1. If necessary, open the `C:\ArcpyBook\Ch11\ErrorHandling.py` file in IDLE.
2. Alter the `GetMessages()` function so that you pass in a value of `2` as the only parameter:

```
import arcpy
try:
  arcpy.env.workspace = "c:/ArcpyBook/data"
  arcpy.Buffer_analysis("Streams.shp","Streams_Buff.shp")
except:
  print(arcpy.GetMessages(2))
```

3. You can check your work by examining the `C:\ArcpyBook\code\Ch11\ErrorHandling4.py` solution file.
4. Save and run the script to see the output:

```
Failed to execute. Parameters are not valid.
ERROR 000735: Distance [value or field]: Value is required
Failed to execute (Buffer).
```

How it works...

As I mentioned earlier, the `GetMessages()` method can accept an integer argument of `0`, `1`, or `2`. Passing a value of `0` indicates that all messages should be returned, while passing a value of `1` indicates that you wish to see warnings. In our case, we have passed a value of `2`, which indicates that we only want to see error messages. Therefore, you won't see any of the other information messages, such as the start and end times of the script.

Testing for and responding to specific error messages

All errors and warnings generate a specific error code. It is possible to check for specific error codes in your scripts and perform some type of action based on these errors. This can make your scripts even more versatile.

Getting ready

All errors and warnings generated by a geoprocessing tool contain both a six-digit code and a description. Your script can test for specific error codes and respond accordingly. You can get a listing of all the available error messages and codes in the ArcGIS for Desktop help system by navigating to **Geoprocessing** | **Tool errors and warnings**. This is illustrated in the following screenshot. All errors have a unique page that briefly describes the error by the code number:

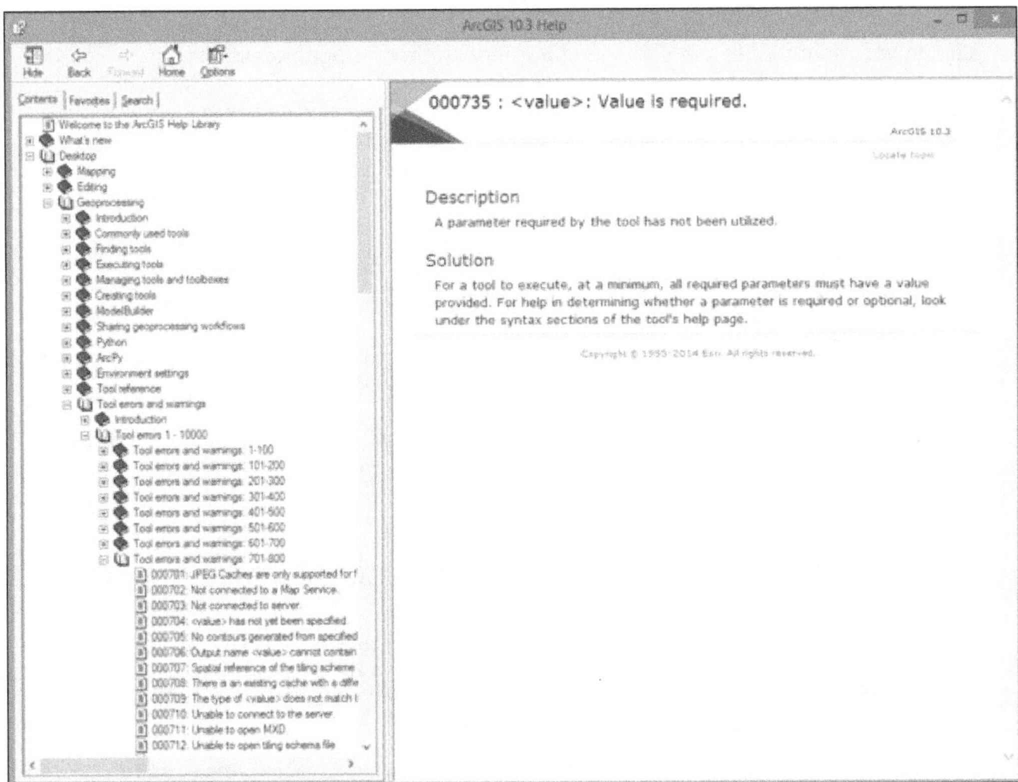

How to do it...

Follow these steps to learn how to write code that responds to specific error codes generated by the execution of a geoprocessing tools:

1. Open the ArcGIS for Desktop help system by navigating to **Start** | **All Programs** | **ArcGIS** | **ArcGIS for Desktop Help**
2. Navigate to **Geoprocessing** | **Tool errors and warnings** | **Tool errors 1-10000** | **Tool errors and warnings 701-800**.

3. Select **000735:<value>:Value is required**. This error indicates that a parameter required by the tool has not been provided. You'll recall from running this script earlier that we have not provided the buffer distance and the resulting error message generated, as a result, contains the error code that we are viewing in the help system. In the following code, you will find the full text of the error message. Notice the error code:

   ```
   ERROR000735:Distance[valueorfield]:Valueisrequired
   ```

4. If necessary, open the `C:\ArcpyBook\Ch11\ErrorHandling.py` file in IDLE.
5. In your script, alter the `except` statement so that it appears as follows:

   ```
   import arcpy
   try:
     arcpy.env.workspace = "c:/ArcpyBook/data"
     arcpy.Buffer_analysis("Streams.shp", "Streams_Buff.shp")
   except:
     print("Error found in Buffer tool \n")
     errCode = arcpy.GetReturnCode(3)
     if str(errCode) == "735":
       print("Distance value not provided \n")
       print("Running the buffer again with a default valuevalue \n")
       defaultDistance = "100 Feet"
       arcpy.Buffer_analysis("Streams.shp", "Streams_Buff",
   defaultDistance)
       print("Buffer complete")
   ```

6. You can check your work by examining the `C:\ArcpyBook\code\Ch11\ErrorHandling5.py` solution file.
7. Save and run the script. You should see various messages printed, as follows:

   ```
   Error found in Buffer tool
   Distance value not provided for buffer
   Running the buffer tool again with a default distance value
   Buffer complete
   ```

How it works...

What you've done in this code block is use the `arcpy.GetReturnCode()` function to return the error code generated by the tool. Then, an `if` statement is used to test whether the error code contains the `735` value, which is the code that indicates that a required parameter has not been provided to the tool. You then provided a default value for the buffer distance and called the `Buffer` tool again, providing the default buffer value this time.

12
Using Python for Advanced ArcGIS

In this chapter, we will cover the following recipes:

- Getting started with the ArcGIS REST API
- Making HTTP requests and parsing the response with Python
- Getting layer information with the ArcGIS REST API and Python
- Exporting a map with the ArcGIS REST API and Python
- Querying a map service with the ArcGIS REST API and Python
- Geocoding with the Esri World Geocoding Service
- Using FieldMap and FieldMappings
- Using a ValueTable to provide multivalue input to a tool

Introduction

In this chapter, we will cover some topics that are of a more advanced nature. Specifically, you will learn how to access the ArcGIS REST API using the Python `requests` module. In doing so, you will learn how to access data and services published by ArcGIS Server and ArcGIS Online. The Python `requests` module includes capabilities that allow your script to submit requests to a URL endpoint and receive responses in various formats, including the popular JSON format. Toward the end of the chapter, we will also over a couple of miscellaneous ArcPy topics, including the use of the `FieldMap` and `FieldMappings` objects to merge datasets and also working with `ValueTables` for situations where a tool has the capability of accepting multiple inputs.

Getting started with the ArcGIS REST API

Before we dive too far into the coding, you need to understand some basic concepts of the ArcGIS REST API. You need to specifically know how to construct a URL and interpret the response that is returned.

Getting ready

All the resources and operations of the ArcGIS REST API are exposed through a hierarchy of endpoints, which we'll examine as we move through the course of this book. For now, let's examine the specific steps that you need to understand to submit a request to the API through Python. In this recipe, you will learn how to use the ArcGIS Server Services directory to construct URL requests.

How to do it...

We're going to use a publicly available ArcGIS Server instance to learn how to use the tools provided by the `Services` directory to construct a URL request:

1. Open a web browser (preferably Google Chrome or Firefox).
2. Go to `http://sampleserver1.arcgisonline.com/arcgis/rest/services`:

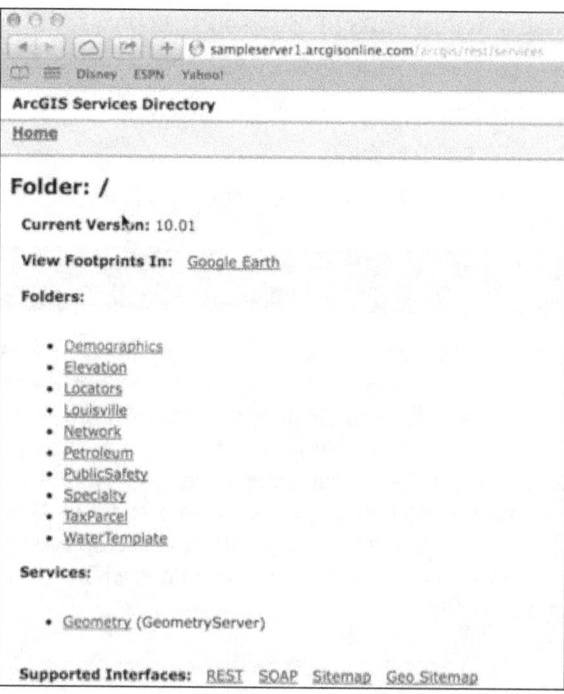

3. Next, we need to determine the well-known endpoint. This represents a server catalog that is a set of operations that ArcGIS Server can perform along with specific services. Navigate to **Demographics** | **ESRI_Census_USA**. This is a well-known endpoint. If you look at the address bar in your browser you should see this:

```
http://sampleserver1.arcgisonline.com/ArcGIS/rest/services/
Demographics/ESRI_Census_USA/MapServer.
```

   Notice that this follows the pattern seen here:

```
http://<host>/<site>/rest/services/<folder>/<serviceName>/<serv
iceType>
```

4. Spend some time clicking on the various links. As you do this, notice how the URL changes in the address bar. This URL is very important because it provides you with the content that will be submitted through a Python request:

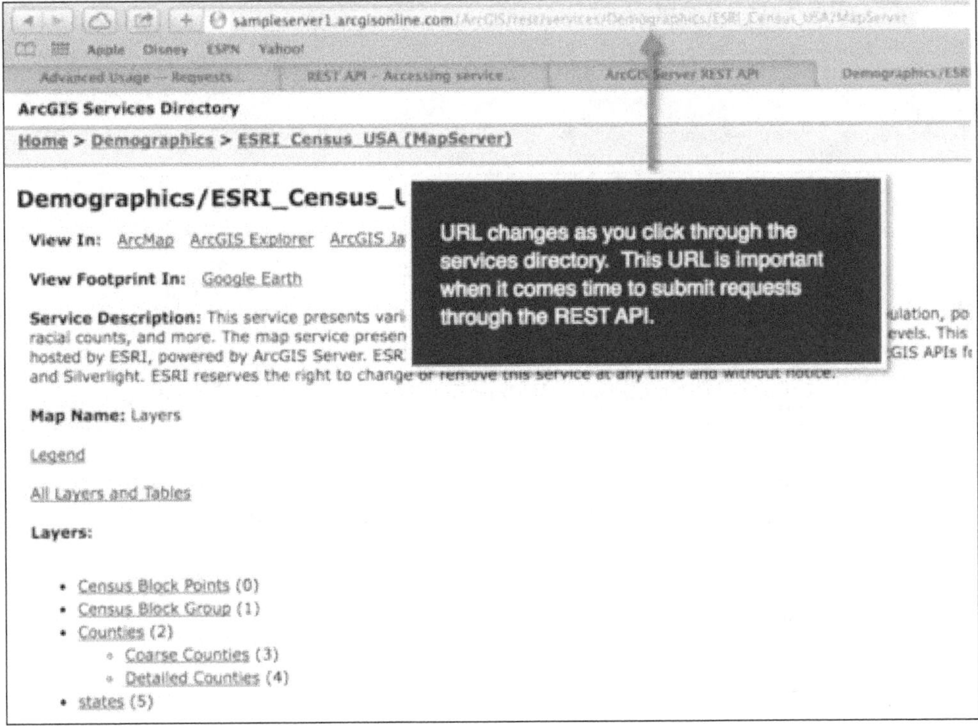

5. Next, you'll learn how to further construct URLs that can be submitted as requests to the ArcGIS REST API. This is a very important step. The syntax for the request includes the path to the resource along with an operation name followed by a list of parameters. The operation name indicates the kind of operation that will be performed against the resource. For example, you might want to export a map to an image file.

6. The question mark begins the list of parameters. Each parameter is then provided as a set of key/value pairs separated by an ampersand. All of this information is combined into a single URL string. This is illustrated in the following URL:

```
http://<resource-url>/<operation>?<parameter1=value1>&<paramete
r2=value2>
```

   For now, we're going to just enter the URL into the address bar of the browser. Copy and paste `http://sampleserver1.arcgisonline.com/ArcGIS/rest/services/Demographics/ESRI_Census_USA/MapServer/3/query?text=&geometry=&geometryType=esriGeometryPoint&inSR=&spatialRel=esriSpatialRelIntersects&relationParam=&objectIds=&where=name+%3D+%27Bexar%27&time=&returnCountOnly=false&returnIdsOnly=false&returnGeometry=true&maxAllowableOffset=&outSR=&outFields=&f=json` into the address bar in your browser. You may want to use the digital version of this book to copy and paste this URL, rather than trying to type this into the address bar. Hit return to see this output:

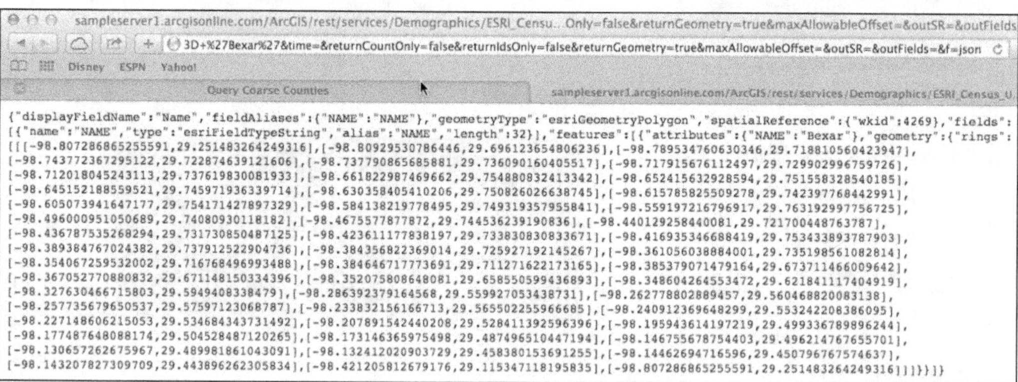

You can use the Python `requests` module to simplify this process and access the response information directly from within your geoprocessing script. The `requests` module allows you to define the list of parameters as a Python dictionary and then it handles the creation of the URL query string, including URL encoding. You'll learn how to do that at the end of this exercise.

7. The Services Directory contains dialog boxes that you can use to generate parameter values. You can find links to these dialog boxes at the bottom of the services page. In your browser, navigate to `http://sampleserver1.arcgisonline.com/ArcGIS/rest/services/Demographics/ESRI_Census_USA/MapServer/1`.
8. Go to the bottom of the page and click on the **Query** link to display the dialog box, as seen in this screenshot:

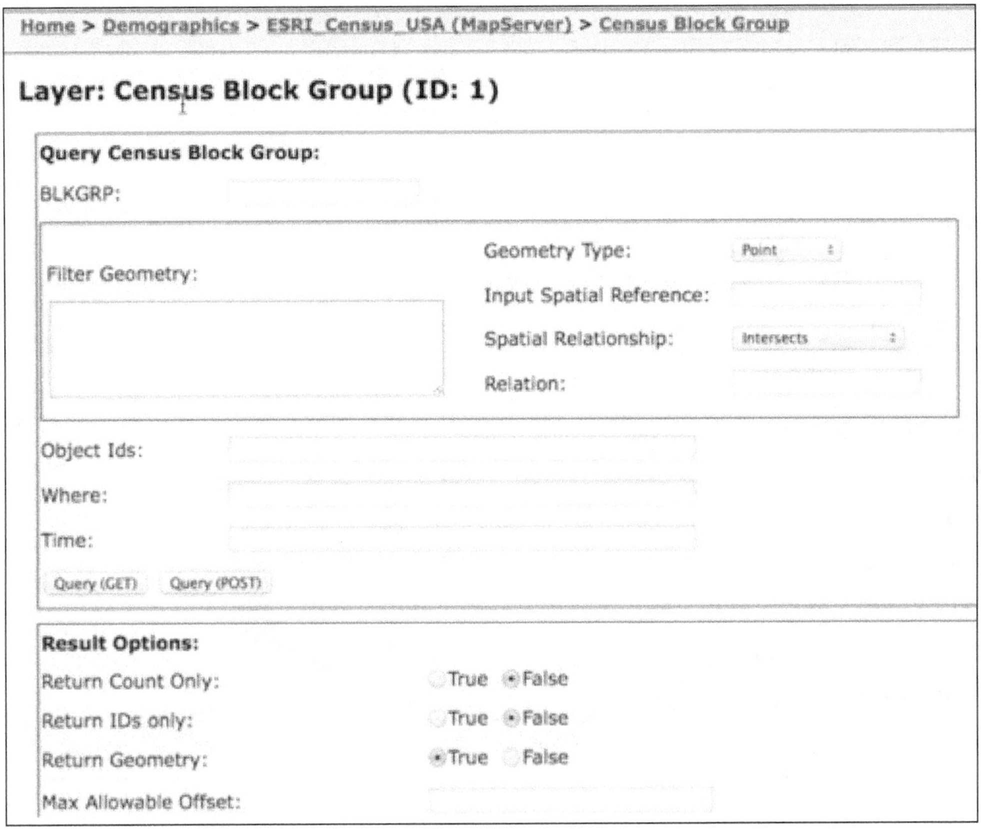

Home > Demographics > ESRI_Census_USA (MapServer) > Census Block Group

Layer: Census Block Group (ID: 1)

Query Census Block Group:

BLKGRP:

Filter Geometry:

Geometry Type: Point

Input Spatial Reference:

Spatial Relationship: Intersects

Relation:

Object Ids:

Where:

Time:

Query (GET) Query (POST)

Result Options:

Return Count Only: True False

Return IDs only: True False

Return Geometry: True False

Max Allowable Offset:

9. Add a `where` clause, as seen in the following screenshot. Set the **Return Fields (Comma Seperated)** to `POP2000, POP2007`, and `BLKGRP`. Change **Format:** to `JSON` and **Return Geometry:** to `False`. Then, click on **Query (GET)**:

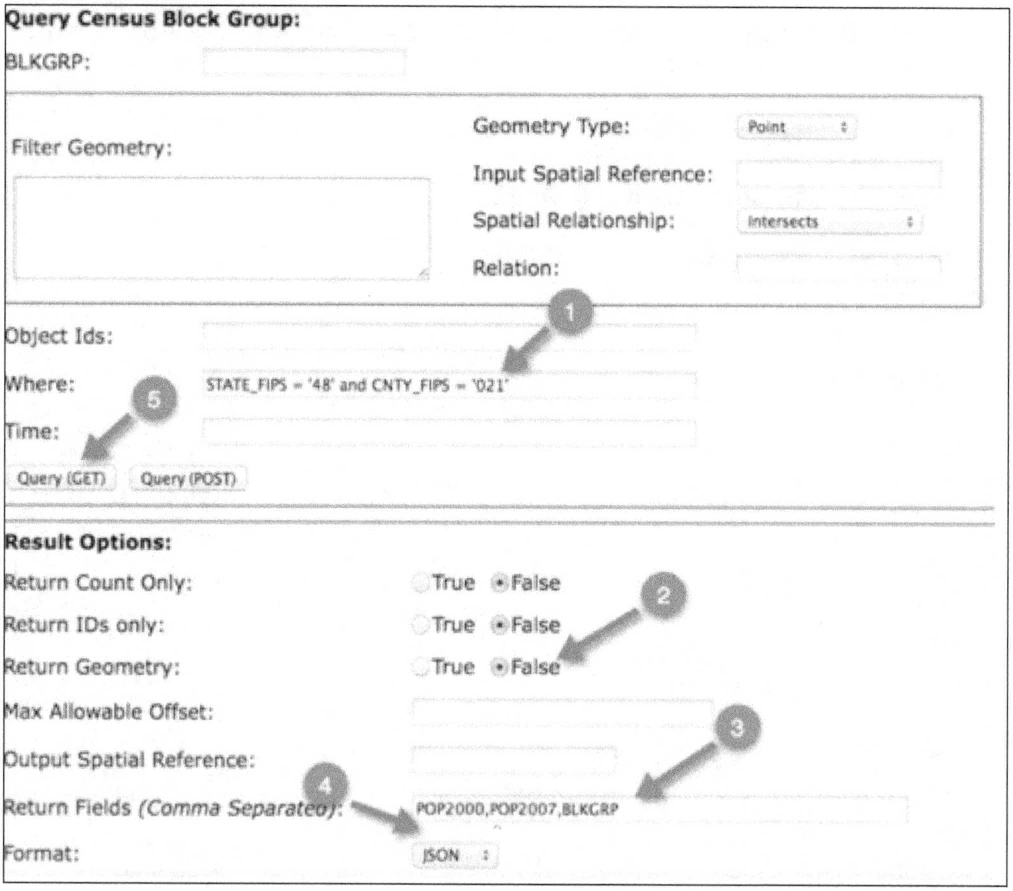

10. The query will run and these results will be returned:


```
{
  "displayFieldName" : "BLKGRP",
  "fieldAliases" : {
    "POP2000" : "POP2000",
    "POP2007" : "POP2007",
    "BLKGRP" : "BLKGRP"
  },
  "fields" : [
    {
      "name" : "POP2000",
      "type" : "esriFieldTypeInteger",
      "alias" : "POP2000"
    },
    {
      "name" : "POP2007",
      "type" : "esriFieldTypeDouble",
      "alias" : "POP2007"
    },
    {
      "name" : "BLKGRP",
      "type" : "esriFieldTypeString",
      "alias" : "BLKGRP",
      "length" : 1
    }
  ],
  "features" : [
    {
      "attributes" : {
        "POP2000" : 986,
        "POP2007" : 1285,
        "BLKGRP" : "1"
      }
    },
    {
      "attributes" : {
        "POP2000" : 1794,
        "POP2007" : 2208,
        "BLKGRP" : "2"
      }
```


11. Examine the address bar in your browser to see the URL that was generated: `http://sampleserver1.arcgisonline.com/ArcGIS/rest/services/Demographics/ESRI_Census_USA/MapServer/1/query?text=&geometry=&geometryType=esriGeometryPolygon&inSR=&spatialRel=esriSpatialRelIntersects&relationParam=&objectIds=&where=STATE_FIPS+%3D+%2748%27+and+CNTY_FIPS+%3D+%27021%27&time=&returnCountOnly=false&returnIdsOnly=false&returnGeometry=false&maxAllowableOffset=&outSR=&outFields=POP2000%2CPOP2007%2CBLKGRP&f=pjson`.

12. In an upcoming recipe, you'll take this same URL, submit the request, and process the results using Python.

How it works...

The Services Directory of an ArcGIS Server instance provides a variety of tools that you can use to generate URL requests and examine the responses those requests produce. In this recipe, you learned how to use the query task to construct an attribute query. In doing so, you learned how a URL request is constructed.

Making HTTP requests and parsing the response with Python

There are a number of Python modules that you can use to make REST requests. There are really too many! Modules include `urllib2`, `httplib2`, `pycurl`, and `requests`. `requests` is definitely the best of the bunch in my opinion. It is cleaner and easier to use for repeated interaction with RESTful APIs. Once you've made the request, you can then parse the JSON response with the Python `json` module. In this recipe, you will learn how to do this.

Getting ready

The Python `requests` module can be used to submit `requests` to an ArcGIS Server resource and process the returned response. Follow these steps to learn the basic steps involved in submitting `requests` and processing the response using the `requests` module:

How to do it...

Before we get started, make sure that you have downloaded and installed the `requests` module, using `pip`. If you haven't already done so, I have provided the following instructions to install both `pip` and the `requests` module:

> This recipe and all subsequent recipes in this chapter use the Python `requests` module. If you don't already have this module installed on your computer, you will need to do so at this time. The `requests` module is installed using `pip`, which needs to be installed on your computer before the `requests` module is installed. Later versions of Python including 2.7.9 (on the Python2 series) and Python 3.4 include `pip` by default, so you may have it already. To test to see if you already have `pip` installed, you can enter the following from a DOS prompt:
>
> **`pip install requests`**
>
> If you don't have `pip` installed, you'll get an error message and you'll need to `install pip` (`https://pip.pypa.io/en/latest/installing.html`). Once installed, you can download and install the `requests` module by using the preceding install command.

1. Open **IDLE** (or another Python development environment) and select **File** | **New Window**. Save the file under the name `C:\ArcpyBook\Ch12\ReqJSON.py`.
2. Import the `requests` and `json` modules:

```
import requests
import json
```

3. Create a new variable that contains a URL to a list of services provided by ArcGIS Online. This URL contains an output format of `pjson`, a JSON format contained in a pretty format to provide easy readability:

```
import requests
import json
agisurl =
"http://server.arcgisonline.com/arcgis/rest/
services?f=pjson"
```

4. Use the `get()` method in the `requests` module to submit an HTTP request to the ArcGIS REST API. You'll store the response in a variable called `r`:

```
import requests
import json
agisurl = "http://server.arcgisonline.com/arcgis/rest/
services?f=pjson"
r = requests.get(agisurl)
```

5. Now, let's print out the response that is returned:

```
import requests
import json
agisurl = "http://server.arcgisonline.com/arcgis/rest/
services?f=pjson"
r = requests.get(agisurl)
print(r.text)
```

6. Save your script.

7. Run your script and you will see the following output. This is the JSON response that has been returned by the ArcGIS REST API:


```
{
 "currentVersion": 10.2,
 "folders": [
  "Canvas",
  "Demographics",
  "Elevation",
  "Ocean",
  "Reference",
  "Specialty",
  "Utilities"
 ],
 "services": [
  {
   "name": "ESRI_Imagery_World_2D",
   "type": "MapServer"
  },
  {
   "name": "ESRI_StreetMap_World_2D",
   "type": "MapServer"
  },
  {
   "name": "I3_Imagery_Prime_World",
   "type": "GlobeServer"
```


8. Use the `json.loads()` method to parse the returned `json` into a Python dictionary object. Go ahead and remove the previous print statement as well:

```
import requests
import json
agisurl = "http://server.arcgisonline.com/arcgis/rest/
services?f=pjson"
r = requests.get(agisurl)
decoded = json.loads(r.text)
print(decoded)
```

9. You can check your work by examining the `C:\ArcpyBook\code\Ch12\ReqJSON.py` solution file.

10. Save and run your script to see the output. The `loads()` method has converted the `json` output into a Python dictionary:

```
{u'folders': [u'Canvas', u'Demographics', u'Elevation',
u'Ocean', u'Reference', u'Specialty', u'Utilities'],
u'services': [{u'type': u'MapServer', u'name':
u'ESRI_Imagery_World_2D'}, {u'type': u'MapServer', u'name':
u'ESRI_StreetMap_World_2D'}, {u'type': u'GlobeServer',
u'name': u'I3_Imagery_Prime_World'}, {u'type':
u'GlobeServer', u'name': u'NASA_CloudCover_World'},
{u'type': u'MapServer', u'name': u'NatGeo_World_Map'},
{u'type': u'MapServer', u'name': u'NGS_Topo_US_2D'},
{u'type': u'MapServer', u'name': u'Ocean_Basemap'},
{u'type': u'MapServer', u'name': u'USA_Topo_Maps'},
{u'type': u'MapServer', u'name': u'World_Imagery'},
{u'type': u'MapServer', u'name': u'World_Physical_Map'},
{u'type': u'MapServer', u'name': u'World_Shaded_Relief'},
{u'type': u'MapServer', u'name': u'World_Street_Map'},
{u'type': u'MapServer', u'name': u'World_Terrain_Base'},
{u'type': u'MapServer', u'name': u'World_Topo_Map'}],
u'currentVersion': 10.2}
```

How it works...

In this simple recipe, you learned how to use the Python `requests` module to submit a request to an ArcGIS Server instance by using the `requests.get()` method, and then process the response from the server. The `json.loads()` method was used to convert the response to a Python dictionary object for easier processing. The response contains basic data about the ArcGIS Server instance, including folders, services, and versions. We'll look at more complex examples in the coming recipes.

Getting layer information with the ArcGIS REST API and Python

A map service resource contains datasets that can include tables or layers. It contains basic information about a service, including feature layers, tables, and service descriptions. In this recipe, you will learn how to return layer information from a map service, using Python and the ArcGIS REST API.

Getting ready

To get information about a specific layer in a map service, you will need to reference the index number that is associated with the layer. When you examine the Services Directory page for a service, you will find a list of layers that are part of the map service along with index numbers for each layer. The index numbers are used instead of the layer name when requesting information about a layer. As we've done in the past few recipes, we'll use the Python `requests` module to make the request and process the response.

How to do it...

Follow these steps to learn how to get information about a layer from a map service:

1. In IDLE or another Python development environment, create a new Python script called `GetLayerInformation.py` and save it to the `C:\ArcpyBook\Ch12` folder.
2. Import the `requests` and `json` modules:

```
import requests
import json
```

3. Create the following `agisurl` variable. This will serve as the base URL that references a specific layer in the `ESRI_CENSUS_USA` map service. Here, we are referring to a layer with an index number of `1`. Also, include an output format of `pjson`:

```
import requests
import json
agisurl =
"http://sampleserver1.arcgisonline.com/ArcGIS/rest/
services/Demographics/ESRI_Census_USA/MapServer/1?f=pjson"
```

4. Create a `payload` variable. This variable will hold a Python dictionary object containing the parameters that will be passed as part of the request. We'll include a `where` clause and set a few other properties:

```
import requests
import json

agisurl = "http://sampleserver1.arcgisonline.com/ArcGIS/rest/
services/Demographics/ESRI_Census_USA/MapServer/1"
payload = { 'where': 'STATE_FIPS = \'48\' and CNTY_FIPS =
\'021\'','returnCountyOnly': 'false',
'returnIdsOnly': 'false', 'returnGeometry': 'false',
'f': 'pjson'}
```

5. Call the `requests.get()` method and pass the `agisurl` variable. The response will be stored in a variable called `r`:

```
import requests
import json
agisurl = http://sampleserver1.arcgisonline.com/ArcGIS/rest/
services/Demographics/ESRI_Census_USA/MapServer/1?f=pjson
payload = { 'where': 'STATE_FIPS = \'48\' and CNTY_FIPS =
\'021\'','returnCountyOnly': 'false', \
            'returnIdsOnly': 'false', 'returnGeometry': 'false', \
            'f': 'pjson'}

r = requests.get(agisurl, params=payload)
```

6. Convert the JSON to a Python dictionary:

```
r = requests.get(agisurl, params=payload)
decoded = json.loads(r.text)
```

7. Print out the name, geographic extent, and fields of the layer:

```
r = requests.get(agisurl, params=payload)

decoded = json.loads(r.text)

print("The layer name is: " + decoded['name'])
print("The xmin: " + str(decoded['extent']['xmin']))
print("The xmax: " + str(decoded['extent']['xmax']))
print("The ymin: " + str(decoded['extent']['ymin']))
print("The ymax: " + str(decoded['extent']['ymax']))
print("The fields in this layer: ")
for rslt in decoded['fields']:
    print(rslt['name'])
```

8. You can check your work by examining the `C:\ArcpyBook\code\Ch12\GetLayerInformation.py` solution file.

9. Save the script and run it to see this output:

```
The layer name is: Census Block Group
The xmin: -178.227822
The xmax: -65.2442339474
The ymin: 17.8812420006
The ymax: -65.2442339474
The fields in this layer:
ObjectID
Shape
STATE_FIPS
CNTY_FIPS
STCOFIPS
TRACT
BLKGRP
FIPS
POP2000
POP2007
POP00_SQMI
```

How it works...

In this recipe, we passed a reference to a URL that contains the path to a specific layer within a map service. The layer was specified through the use of an index number (`1`, in this case). This URL was passed to the Python `requests.get()` method. The response was returned in `json` format and we then converted this to a Python dictionary. The dictionary included key/value pairs for the name, extent, and fields of the layer. That information was printed to the console.

Exporting a map with the ArcGIS REST API and Python

The ArcGIS REST API has a large set of operations that you can use when requesting information from an ArcGIS Server instance. For example, you can export maps, query layers, geocode addresses, and much more. In this recipe, you will learn how to export a map image from a map service.

Getting ready

The `export` operation can be used to create a map image from a map service. The response to this request includes the URL of the image, width, height, extent, and scale. In this recipe, you'll use the export operation to export a map as an image file.

How to do it...

1. In your Python development environment, create a new script, save it as `C:\ArcpyBook\Ch12\ExportMapToImage.py`.
2. Import the `requests` and `json` modules:

```
import requests
import json
```

3. Create a new variable called `agisurl`, assign the URL, and export the operation, as seen here:

```
import requests
import json
agisurl = "http://sampleserver1.arcgisonline.com/ArcGIS/rest/
services/Specialty/ESRI_StateCityHighway_USA/MapServer/export"
```

4. Create a new dictionary object that will hold the key/value pairs that help define the query string. These are the parameters that will be passed to the export operation:

```
import requests
import json
agisurl = "http://sampleserver1.arcgisonline.com/ArcGIS/rest/
services/Specialty/ESRI_StateCityHighway_USA/MapServer/export"
payload = { 'bbox':'-115.8,30.4, 85.5,50.5',
            'size':'800,600',
            'imageSR': '102004',
            'format':'gif',
            'transparent':'false',
            'f': 'pjson'}
```

5. Call the `requests.get()` method, passing the URL and the Python dictionary of parameters. The response will be stored in a variable called `r`:

```
import requests
import json
agisurl =
"http://sampleserver1.arcgisonline.com/ArcGIS/rest/services/
Specialty/ESRI_StateCityHighway_USA/MapServer/export"
payload = { 'bbox':'-115.8,30.4, 85.5,50.5',
            'size':'800,600',
            'imageSR': '102004',
            'format':'gif',
            'transparent':'false',
            'f': 'pjson'}
r = requests.get(agisurl, params=payload)
```

6. Print out the contents of the `response` object:

```
import requests
import json
agisurl = "http://sampleserver1.arcgisonline.com/ArcGIS/rest/
services/Specialty/ESRI_StateCityHighway_USA/MapServer/export"
payload = { 'bbox':'-115.8,30.4, 85.5,50.5',
            'size':'800,600',
            'imageSR': '102004',
            'format':'gif',
            'transparent':'false',
                  'f': 'pjson'}
r = requests.get(agisurl, params=payload)
print(r.text)
```

7. You can check your work by examining the `C:\ArcpyBook\code\Ch12\ExportMapToImage.py` solution file.
8. Save and run the script to see an output similar to this:


```
{
  "href" : "http://sampleserver1b.arcgisonline.com/arcgisoutput/_ags_map0cd30b23f8ae4228a12a1380ff2afd4d.gif",
  "width" : 800,
  "height" : 600,
  "extent" : {
    "xmin" : -2034271.95615396,
    "ymin" : -952407.265726716,
    "xmax" : 1148422.50936727,
    "ymax" : 1434613.5834142,
    "spatialReference" : {
      "wkid" : 102004
    }
  },
  "scale" : 15036321.7329085
}
```

9. Copy and paste the URL for the `.gif` file that was generated into your browser address bar, and click on return on your keyboard to see the file:

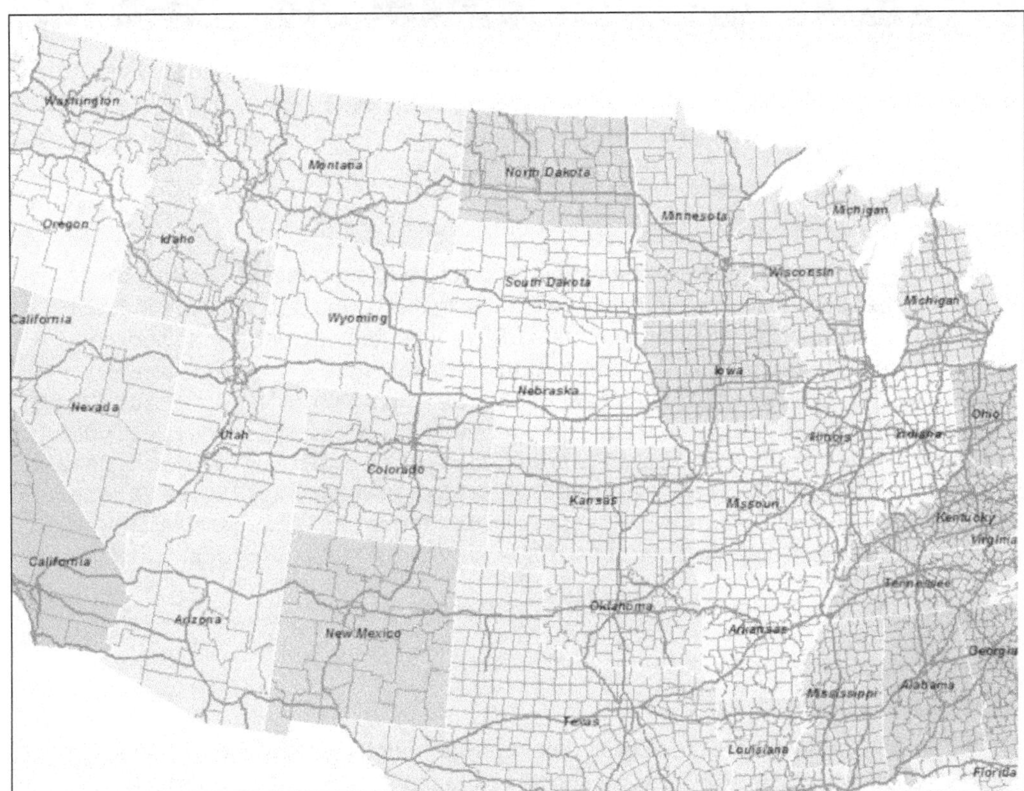

How it works...

The export operation in the ArcGIS REST API can be used to export an image file from a map service. If you examine `http://sampleserver1.arcgisonline.com/ArcGIS/rest/services/Specialty/ESRI_StateCityHighway_USA/MapServer/export`, which we used to generate the map image in this recipe, you'll see the term `export` at the end of the URL. This is what triggers the execution of the `export` operation. In addition to this, we also appended a bounding box (map extent), size, spatial reference for the image, and format through the payload variable. The request is sent to the server through the `requests.get()` method which accepts both the URL and payload variable.

Querying a map service with the ArcGIS REST API and Python

The query operation in the ArcGIS REST API performs a query against a map service and returns a feature set. The feature set includes values for fields requested by the user and can also return geometry, if requested.

Getting ready

In this recipe, you will build on the first recipe, in which you generated a URL using the ArcGIS Services page dialog box to generate results. In this recipe, you will use the ArcGIS Server Services page dialog box to generate a URL request that queried a map service layer and returned results. You may recall that the URL was http://sampleserver1.arcgisonline.com/ArcGIS/rest/services/Demographics/ESRI_Census_USA/MapServer/1/query?text=&geometry=&geometryType=esriGeometryPolygon&inSR=&spatialRel=esriSpatialRelIntersects&relationParam=&objectIds=&where=STATE_FIPS+%3D+%2748%27+and+CNTY_FIPS+%3D+%27021%27&time=&returnCountOnly=false&returnIdsOnly=false&returnGeometry=false&maxAllowableOffset=&outSR=&outFields=POP2000%2CPOP2007%2CBLKGRP&f=pjson.

Now, let's learn how to submit this request using Python.

How to do it...

1. In IDLE or another Python development environment, create a new Python script called QueryMapService.py and save it to the C:\ArcpyBook\Ch12 folder.
2. In your browser, navigate to: http://resources.arcgis.com/en/help/arcgis-rest-api/index.html#//02r3000000p1000000. This is the REST API page for the query operation against a layer in a map service. As you scroll down the help page, you should see the same parameters as were generated using the dialog box, such as geometry, geometryType, inSR, spatialRel, where, and others.
3. In your script, import the requests and json modules:

```
import requests
import json
```

4. Create the following agisurl variable. This will serve as the base URL that references the query operation on the census block group layer (identified by an identifier of 1 in the URL) in the ESRI_Census_USA map service:

```
import requests
import json
agisurl =
"http://sampleserver1.arcgisonline.com/ArcGIS/rest/services
/Demographics/ESRI_Census_USA/MapServer/1/query"
```

5. Now, create a Python dictionary object, as shown in the following code. We're going to leave out some of the parameters that were not defined or used in the dialog box. We're just creating an attribute query in this instance so that all the geometry parameters can be removed:

```
import requests
import json
agisurl = "http://sampleserver1.arcgisonline.com/ArcGIS/rest/
services/Demographics/ESRI_Census_USA/MapServer/1/query"
payload = { 'where':'STATE_FIPS = \'48\' and CNTY_FIPS =
\'021\'','returnCountOnly':'false',
'returnIdsOnly': 'false', 'returnGeometry':'false',
'outFields':'POP2000,POP2007,BLKGRP',
'f': 'pjson'}
```

6. The `requests.get()` method can accept a Python dictionary object as the second parameter. This dictionary defines the set of key/value pairs that help define the query string. Add the `requests.get()` method:

```
import requests
import json
agisurl = "http://sampleserver1.arcgisonline.com/ArcGIS/rest/
services/Demographics/ESRI_Census_USA/MapServer/1/query"
payload = { 'where':'STATE_FIPS = \'48\' and CNTY_FIPS =
\'021\'','returnCountOnly':'false', \
'returnIdsOnly': 'false', 'returnGeometry':'false', \
'outFields':'POP2000,POP2007,BLKGRP', \
'f': 'pjson'}
r = requests.get(agisurl, params=payload)
```

7. Include a `print` statement in order to print the response that is returned.

```
import requests, json
agisurl = "http://sampleserver1.arcgisonline.com/ArcGIS/rest/
services/Demographics/ESRI_Census_USA/MapServer/1/query"
payload = { 'where':'STATE_FIPS = \'48\' and CNTY_FIPS =
\'021\'','returnCountOnly':'false', \
'returnIdsOnly': 'false', 'returnGeometry':'false', \
'outFields':'POP2000,POP2007,BLKGRP', \
'f': 'pjson'}
r = requests.get(agisurl, params=payload)
print(r.text)
```

8. Save the script and run it to see this output:

```
{
  "displayFieldName" : "BLKGRP",
  "fieldAliases" : {
    "POP2000" : "POP2000",
    "POP2007" : "POP2007",
    "BLKGRP" : "BLKGRP"
  },
  "fields" : [
    {
      "name" : "POP2000",
      "type" : "esriFieldTypeInteger",
      "alias" : "POP2000"
    },
    {
      "name" : "POP2007",
      "type" : "esriFieldTypeDouble",
      "alias" : "POP2007"
    },
    {
      "name" : "BLKGRP",
      "type" : "esriFieldTypeString",
      "alias" : "BLKGRP",
      "length" : 1
    }
  ],
  "features" : [
    {
      "attributes" : {
        "POP2000" : 986,
        "POP2007" : 1285,
        "BLKGRP" : "1"
      }
    },
```

9. Now, convert this JSON object to a Python dictionary. Also, comment out the `print` statement that you added in the last step:

```
r = requests.get(agisurl, params=payload)
#print(r.text)
decoded = json.loads(r.text)
```

10. The Python dictionary object returned by the `json.loads()` method will contain the contents of the JSON object. You can then pull the individual data elements out of the dictionary. In this case, we want to pull out the attributes of each of the feature returned (`BLKGRP`, `POP2007`, and `POP2000`). We can do so by using the following code, which you'll need to add to your script:

```
r = requests.get(agisurl, params=payload)
#print(r.text)
decoded = json.loads(r.text)
for rslt in decoded['features']:
    print("Block Group: " +
str(rslt['attributes']['BLKGRP']))
    print("Population 2000: " +
str(rslt['attributes']['POP2000']))
    print("Population 2007: " +
str(rslt['attributes']['POP2007']))
```

11. You can check your work by examining the `C:\ArcpyBook\code\Ch12\QueryMapService.py` solution file.
12. Save and execute your script to see these results:

```
Block Group: 1
Population 2000: 986
Population 2007: 1285
Block Group: 2
Population 2000: 1794
Population 2007: 2208
Block Group: 3
Population 2000: 3064
Population 2007: 4279
Block Group: 4
Population 2000: 1442
Population 2007: 1802
Block Group: 1
Population 2000: 1409
Population 2007: 1531
Block Group: 2
Population 2000: 762
Population 2007: 917
```

How it works...

The `query` operation in the ArcGIS REST API can be used to perform spatial and attribute queries against a layer in an ArcGIS Server map service. We used the `requests.get()` method to perform an attribute query against the `census block groups` layer. We included various parameters, including a where clause that will only return records where the `ST_FIPS` code is `48` and the `CNTY_FIPS` code is `021` (Bexar County, Texas). The `response` object was then converted to a Python dictionary and we included a `for` loop to iterate through each of the returned records and print out the block group name, and the population for the years 2000 and 2007.

Geocoding with the Esri World Geocoding Service

The Esri World Geocoding Service can be used to find addresses and places in supported countries. This service contains both free and paid operations. The `find` operation, which finds one address per request, is always a free service. The `geocodeAddresses` operation accepts a list of addresses for geocoding and is a paid service only. The other operations can be free or paid. If you are using the operations in a temporary capacity, they are free. Temporary simply means that you aren't storing the results for later use. If this is the case, then it is a paid service. In this recipe, you will use the Esri World Geocoding service to geocode an address.

Getting ready

The ArcGIS REST API `find` operation can be used to find the geographic coordinates of a single address. As we've done in the past few recipes, we'll use the Python `requests` module to make the request and process the response.

How to do it...

1. In IDLE or another Python development environment, create a new Python script called `GeocodeAddress.py` and save it to the `C:\ArcpyBook\Ch12` folder.
2. Import the `requests` and `json` modules:

   ```
   import requests
   import json
   ```

3. Create the following `agisurl` variable. This will point to the Esri World Geocoding Service and the `find` operation for a particular service. Also, define a Python dictionary that will hold the address to be submitted and the output format. You can change the address, if you wish:

   ```
   import requests
   import json
   ```

```
agisurl = "http://geocode.arcgis.com/arcgis/rest/services/World/
GeocodeServer/find"
payload = { 'text': '1202 Sand Wedge, San Antonio, TX,
78258','f':'pjson'}
```

4. Call the `requests.get()` method and pass the URL and parameters. The response will be stored in a variable called `r`. Then, convert the returned JSON object to a Python dictionary:

```
import requests
import json
agisurl = "http://geocode.arcgis.com/arcgis/rest/services/World/
GeocodeServer/find"
payload = { 'text': '1202 Sand Wedge, San Antonio, TX,
78258','f':'pjson'}

r = requests.get(agisurl, params=payload)

decoded = json.loads(r.text)
```

5. Print out some of the results:

```
import requests
import json
agisurl = "http://geocode.arcgis.com/arcgis/rest/services/World/
GeocodeServer/find"
payload = { 'text': '1202 Sand Wedge, San Antonio, TX,
78258','f':'pjson'}

r = requests.get(agisurl, params=payload)

decoded = json.loads(r.text)

print("The geocoded address: " +
decoded['locations'][0]['name'])
print("The longitude: " + str(decoded['locations'][0]['feature']
['geometry']['x']))
print("The lattitude: " + str(decoded['locations'][0]['feature']
['geometry']['y']))
print("The geocode score: " +
str(decoded['locations'][0]['feature']['attributes']
['Score']))
print("The address type: " +
str(decoded['locations'][0]['feature']['attributes']
['Addr_Type']))
```

6. You can check your work by examining the `C:\ArcpyBook\code\Ch12\GeocodeAddress.py` solution file.

7. Save the script and run it to see the following output:

```
The geocoded address: 1202 Sand Wedge, San Antonio, Texas,
78258
The longitude: -98.4744442811
The lattitude: 29.6618639681
The geocode score: 100
The address type: PointAddress
```

How it works...

The `find` operation in the ArcGIS REST API can be used to perform geocoding operations for a single address. As we've done in the past few recipes, we used the Python `requests.get()` method to submit an operation request (find, in this case) along parameters that include the address to be geocoded. The response that was returned included the latitude and longitude of the address, geocoded score, and the address type.

Using FieldMap and FieldMappings

Up until this point in the chapter, we've covered how to use Python with the ArcGIS REST API to access ArcGIS Server services. Now, we're going to switch gears and go back into the ArcPy module and discuss the `FieldMap` and `FieldMappings` classes.

Getting ready

A common GIS operation is to merge several disparate datasets into a single dataset of a larger area. Often, the fields in the datasets to be merged will be the same and there won't be any problems. However, there will be times when the fields of the various datasets do not match. In this case, you will need to map the relationship between fields in one dataset to fields in another dataset.

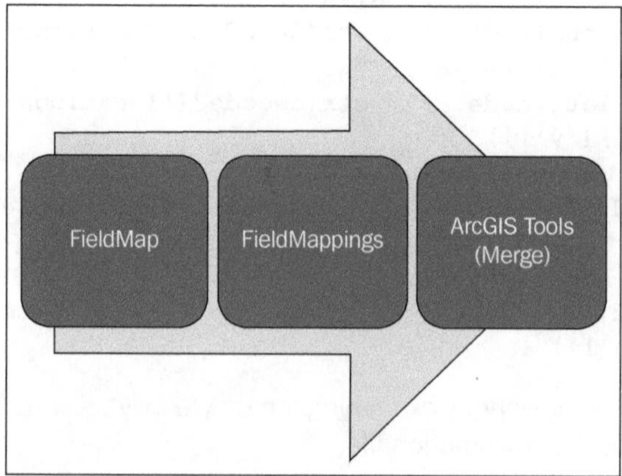

The preceding diagram displays the relationship between the various ArcPy classes that are used to define field mapping. A `FieldMap` object contains a field definition and a list of input fields from one or more tables, or feature classes that provide the values for the field. Each `FieldMap` object that you create is then added to a `FieldMappings` object, which serves as a container for these objects. Finally, the `FieldMappings` object can then be sent as input to various geoprocessing tools, such as the `Merge` tool.

How to do it...

In this exercise, you'll learn how to use the FieldMap and FieldMappings objects:

1. In IDLE or another Python development environment, create a new Python script called `UsingFieldMap.py` and save it to your `C:\ArcpyBook\Ch12` folder.
2. Import `arcpy`:

   ```
   import arcpy
   ```

3. Set the workspace environment variable and a variable that will point to the output feature class:

   ```
   import arcpy

   arcpy.env.workspace = r"c:\ArcpyBook\data"
   outFeatureClass = r"c:\ArcpyBook\data\AllTracts.shp"
   ```

4. Create a `FieldMappings` object and three `FieldMap` objects. The `FieldMap` objects will hold references to fields for a state **Federal Information Processing Standard** (**FIPS**) code, county FIPS code, and a tract:

   ```
   arcpy.env.workspace = r"c:\ArcyBook\data"
   outFeatureClass = r"c:\ArcpyBook\data\AllTracts.shp"

   fieldmappings = arcpy.FieldMappings()
   fldmap_STFIPS = arcpy.FieldMap()
   fldmap_COFIPS = arcpy.FieldMap()
   fldmap_TRACT = arcpy.FieldMap()
   ```

5. Get a list of all the County polygon feature classes in the current workspace. Each County feature class has a field called `STFID`, which contains the state FIPS code, county FIPS code, and a tract for each feature. This information is stored as one long string (`48491020301`, for example), where the first two characters are the state code, the third through fifth characters are the county code, and the remaining characters are the tract. As part of the merge operation, we're going to pull each of the individual elements out and store them in separate fields:

   ```
   fieldmappings = arcpy.FieldMappings()
   fieldmap_STFIPS = arcpy.FieldMap()
   fieldmap_COFIPS = arcpy.FieldMap()
   ```

```
fieldmap_TRACT = arcpy.FieldMap()

#List all feature classes that start with 'County' and type
Polygon
fclss = arcpy.ListFeatureClasses("County*", "Polygon")
```

6. Create a `ValueTable` object to hold the feature classes that are to be merged. `ValueTable` functions as a container object. It will hold the mapping information for each of the feature classes in the workspace. All the information is pulled from a single field (`STFID`), but we need to create separate `FieldMap` input fields for `STFIPS`, `COFIPS`, and `TRACT`:

```
fclss = arcpy.ListFeatureClasses("County*", "Polygon")

vTab = arcpy.ValueTable()
for fc in fclss:
  fieldmappings.addTable(fc)
  fldmap_STFIPS.addInputField(fc, "STFID")
  fldmap_COFIPS.addInputField(fc, "STFID")
  fldmap_TRACT.addInputField(fc, "STFID")
  vTab.addRow(fc)
```

7. Add the content for the `STFIPS` field. We use the `startTextPosition()` function to pull out the first two characters from the `STFID` column. The first position is `0`, so we need to use `setStartTextPosition(x,0)`. In this step, we also define the output field for the `STFIPS FieldMap` object, name the field, and define the output field name:

```
vTab = arcpy.ValueTable()
for fc in fclss:
  fieldmappings.addTable(fc)
  fldmap_STFIPS.addInputField(fc, "STFID")
  fldmap_COFIPS.addInputField(fc, "STFID")
  fldmap_TRACT.addInputField(fc, "STFID")
  vTab.addRow(fc)

# STFIPS field
for x in range(0, fldmap_STFIPS.inputFieldCount):
  fldmap_STFIPS.setStartTextPosition(x, 0)
  fldmap_STFIPS.setEndTextPosition(x, 1)

fld_STFIPS = fldmap_STFIPS.outputField
fld_STFIPS.name = "STFIPS"
fldmap_STFIPS.outputField = fld_STFIPS
```

8. Add content for the `COFIPS` field. The position of these three characters is `2-4` from the string pulled out of the `STFID` column:

```
# STFIPS field
for x in range(0, fldmap_STFIPS.inputFieldCount):
  fldmap_STFIPS.setStartTextPosition(x, 0)
  fldmap_STFIPS.setEndTextPosition(x, 1)

fld_STFIPS = fldmap_STFIPS.outputField
fld_STFIPS.name = "STFIPS"
fldmap_STFIPS.outputField = fld_STFIPS

# COFIPS field
for x in range(0, fldmap_COFIPS.inputFieldCount):
  fldmap_COFIPS.setStartTextPosition(x, 2)
  fldmap_COFIPS.setEndTextPosition(x, 4)

fld_COFIPS = fldmap_COFIPS.outputField
fld_COFIPS.name = "COFIPS"
fldmap_COFIPS.outputField = fld_COFIPS
```

9. Add content for the **TRACT** field:

```
# COFIPS field
for x in range(0, fldmap_COFIPS.inputFieldCount):
        fldmap_COFIPS.setStartTextPosition(x, 2)
        fldmap_COFIPS.setEndTextPosition(x, 4)

fld_COFIPS = fldmap_COFIPS.outputField
fld_STFIPS.name = "COFIPS"
fldmap_COFIPS.outputField = fld_COFIPS

# TRACT field
for x in range(0, fldmap_TRACT.inputFieldCount):
  fldmap_TRACT.setStartTextPosition(x, 5)
  fldmap_TRACT.setEndTextPosition(x, 12)

fld_TRACT = fldmap_TRACT.outputField
fld_TRACT.name = "TRACT"
fldmap_TRACT.outputField = fld_TRACT
```

10. Add the `FieldMap` objects to the `FieldMappings` object:

```
# TRACT field
for x in range(0, fldmap_TRACT.inputFieldCount):
      fldmap_TRACT.setStartTextPosition(x, 5)
      fldmap_TRACT.setEndTextPosition(x, 12)

fld_TRACT = fldmap_TRACT.outputField
fld_TRACT.name = "TRACT"
fldmap_TRACT.outputField = fld_TRACT

#Add fieldmaps into the fieldmappings objec
fieldmappings.addFieldMap(fldmap_STFIPS)
fieldmappings.addFieldMap(fldmap_COFIPS)
fieldmappings.addFieldMap(fldmap_TRACT)
```

11. Run the `Merge` tool, passing in the `vTab`, output feature class, and `fieldmappings` object:

```
#Add fieldmaps into the fieldmappings objec
fieldmappings.addFieldMap(fldmap_STFIPS)
fieldmappings.addFieldMap(fldmap_COFIPS)
fieldmappings.addFieldMap(fldmap_TRACT)

arcpy.Merge_management(vTab, outFeatureClass,fieldmappings)
print("Merge completed")
```

12. The entire script should appear as follows:

```
import arcpy

Arcpy.env.workspace = r"c:\ArcyBook\data"
outFeatureClass = r"c:\ArcpyBook\data\AllTracts.shp"

fieldmappings = arcpy.FieldMappings()
fldmap_STFIPS = arcpy.FieldMap()
fldmap_COFIPS = arcpy.FieldMap()
fldmap_TRACT = arcpy.FieldMap()

#List all feature classes that start with 'County' and type
Polygon
fclss = arcpy.ListFeatureClasses("County*", "Polygon")

vTab = arcpy.ValueTable()
for fc in fclss:
  fieldmappings.addTable(fc)
  fldmap_STFIPS.addInputField(fc, "STFID")
```

```
      fldmap_COFIPS.addInputField(fc, "STFID")
      fldmap_TRACT.addInputField(fc, "STFID")
      vTab.addRow(fc)

    # STFIPS field
    for x in range(0, fldmap_STFIPS.inputFieldCount):
      fldmap_STFIPS.setStartTextPosition(x, 0)
      fldmap_STFIPS.setEndTextPosition(x, 1)

    fld_STFIPS = fldmap_STFIPS.outputField
    fld_STFIPS.name = "STFIPS"
    fldmap_STFIPS.outputField = fld_STFIPS

    # COFIPS field
    for x in range(0, fldmap_COFIPS.inputFieldCount):
      fldmap_COFIPS.setStartTextPosition(x, 2)
      fldmap_COFIPS.setEndTextPosition(x, 4)

    fld_COFIPS = fldmap_COFIPS.outputField
    fld_COFIPS.name = "COFIPS"
    fldmap_COFIPS.outputField = fld_COFIPS

    # TRACT field
    for x in range(0, fldmap_TRACT.inputFieldCount):
            fldmap_TRACT.setStartTextPosition(x, 5)
            fldmap_TRACT.setEndTextPosition(x, 12)

    fld_TRACT = fldmap_TRACT.outputField
    fld_TRACT.name = "TRACT"
    fldmap_TRACT.outputField = fld_TRACT

    #Add fieldmaps into the fieldmappings objec
    fieldmappings.addFieldMap(fldmap_STFIPS)
    fieldmappings.addFieldMap(fldmap_COFIPS)
    fieldmappings.addFieldMap(fldmap_TRACT)

    arcpy.Merge_management(vTab, outFeatureClass,fieldmappings)
    print("Merge completed")
```

13. You can check your work by examining the `C:\ArcpyBook\code\Ch12\UsingFieldMap.py` solution file.
14. Save the script and run it.

15. In ArcMap, add the `All_Tracts.shp` file that was created as a result of the script. You should see a merged set of counties and if you open the attribute table, you'll see the new fields that were created as well as the original fields:

AllTracts

FID	Shape	GIST_ID	FIPSSTCO	TRT2000	STFID	TRACTID	EditedBy	STFIPS	COFIPS	TRACT
0	Polygon	6	48491	020301	48491020301	203.01		48	491	020301
1	Polygon	8	48491	020303	48491020303	203.03		48	491	020303
2	Polygon	9	48491	020305	48491020305	203.05		48	491	020305
3	Polygon	10	48491	020306	48491020306	203.06		48	491	020306
4	Polygon	11	48491	020307	48491020307	203.07		48	491	020307
5	Polygon	12	48491	020308	48491020308	203.08		48	491	020308
6	Polygon	17	48491	020404	48491020404	204.04		48	491	020404
7	Polygon	18	48491	020405	48491020405	204.05		48	491	020405
8	Polygon	20	48491	020407	48491020407	204.07		48	491	020407
9	Polygon	23	48491	020503	48491020503	205.03		48	491	020503
10	Polygon	24	48491	020504	48491020504	205.04		48	491	020504
11	Polygon	28	48491	020703	48491020703	207.03		48	491	020703
12	Polygon	31	48491	020801	48491020801	208.01		48	491	020801
13	Polygon	32	48491	020802	48491020802	208.02		48	491	020802
14	Polygon	33	48491	020900	48491020900	209		48	491	020900
15	Polygon	1	48453	000101	48453000101	1.01		48	453	000101
16	Polygon	2	48453	000102	48453000102	1.02		48	453	000102
17	Polygon	3	48453	000201	48453000201	2.01		48	453	000201

16. In the data view for the `All_Tracts.shp` file, you should now see a single merged polygon layer, as seen in the screenshot below.

How it works...

The FieldMap and FieldMappings objects in the ArcPy module along with the Merge tool, can be used for GIS operations that need to merge datasets that have fields that do not match. The FieldMap object can also be used when you need to pull out a contiguous sequence of string values from a longer set of string values. In this recipe, you learned how to use the FieldMap object to pull state, county, and census information from a single field. We created individual FieldMap objects to hold this information and then added them to a FieldMappings object that was then passed into the Merge tool to create a new layer, which contains three distinct fields that hold this information.

Using a ValueTable to provide multivalue input to a tool

Many geoprocessing tools have input parameters that accept more than one value. For example, the multiring buffer tool accepts multiple buffer distances, the delete field tool accepts multiple fields that can be deleted, and there are many other examples. In this recipe, you will learn how to create a ValueTable object that serves as multivalue input to a tool.

Getting ready

There are three ways to specify a multivalue parameter: as a Python list, a string with each value separated by semicolons, or an ArcPy ValueTable object. In this recipe, we're going to take a look at how to specify mutlivalue input parameters by using ValueTable.

How to do it...

Follow these steps to learn how to use a ValueTable to submit multiple values to a tool:

1. Open **IDLE** (or your favorite Python development environment) and create a new script called ValueTable.py.
2. Import arcpy and set the workspace:

```
import arcpy

arcpy.env.workspace = r"c:\ArcyBook\data"
```

3. Create a new ValueTable object:

```
import arcpy

arcpy.env.workspace = r"c:\ArcyBook\data"
vTab = arcpy.ValueTable()
```

4. Create three rows for the table and assign them distances of `5`, `10`, and `20`:

```
vTab = arcpy.ValueTable()
vTab.setRow(0, "5")
vTab.setRow(1, "10")
vTab.setRow(2, "20")
```

5. Define variables for the input feature class, output feature class, distance, and buffer units. The distance variable (`dist`) is created as a reference to the `ValueTable`, which you have already created:

```
vTab = arcpy.ValueTable()
vTab.setRow(0, "5")
vTab.setRow(1, "10")
vTab.setRow(2, "20")

inFeature = 'Hospitals.shp'
outFeature = 'HospitalMBuff.shp'
dist = vTab
bufferUnit = "meters"
```

6. Call the `MultipleRingBuffer` tool and pass the variables as parameters:

```
inFeature = 'Hospitals.shp'
outFeature = 'HospitalMBuff.shp'
dist = vTab
bufferUnit = "meters"

arcpy.MultipleRingBuffer_analysis(inFeature, outFeature, dist,
bufferUnit, '', 'ALL')
print("Multi-Ring Buffer Complete")
```

7. You can check your work by examining the `C:\ArcpyBook\code\Ch12\ValueTable.py` solution file.

8. Save and run the script. Examine the output to see the multiple buffer rings.

How it works...

`ValueTable` is a simple virtual table that you can use as input to tools that accept multiple values. In this recipe, we created a `ValueTable` object, added three values, and then passed this object into the `MultipleRingBuffer` tool. The `MultipleRingBuffer` tool used this information to create new polygon layers based on the buffer distances provided in the `ValueTable` object.

13
Using Python with ArcGIS Pro

In this chapter, we will cover the following topics:

- Using the new Python window in ArcGIS Pro
- Coding differences between ArcGIS for Desktop and ArcGIS Pro
- Installing Python for standalone ArcGIS Pro scripts
- Converting ArcGIS for Desktop Python code to ArcGIS Pro

Introduction

In this chapter, we will briefly cover several concepts related to using Python in ArcGIS Pro. There are many similarities between using Python in ArcGIS for Desktop and ArcGIS Pro, so what you've learned up to this point will almost certainly translate to the new ArcGIS Pro environment. However, there are some differences in ArcGIS for Desktop and ArcGIS Pro, also there is a new Python Window that you can use.

There are some differences between using Python in ArcGIS for Desktop and ArcGIS Pro. In general, you can break down the differences as follows:

- Functionality differences
- Python version 3 instead of version 2
- Unsupported data formats

Changes to functionality in ArcPy for ArcGIS Pro includes the removal of some geoprocessing tools, including the Coverage, Data Interoperability, Parcel Fabric, Schematics, and Tracking Analyst toolboxes. There are some additional tools in other toolboxes that are not available as well. The full list of geoprocessing tools that are not included can be found at `http://pro.arcgis.com/en/pro-app/tool-reference/appendices/unavailable-tools.htm`.

ArcGIS Pro uses version 3.4 of Python, while ArcGIS for Desktop 10.3 uses version 2.7. There are some significant differences between the two releases and they are incompatible. A lot of the language is the same, but there are some significant differences related to strings, dictionaries, and other objects.

A number of data formats will not be supported in the new ArcGIS Pro environment, including personal geodatabases, raster catalogs, geometric networks, topologies, layer and map packages, and others. If you have been using one of these data formats in ArcGIS for Desktop, please keep in mind that they are not supported, so any scripts that you have written that use these formats will not be able to execute.

Using the new Python window in ArcGIS Pro

If you've been using the Python window in ArcGIS for Desktop, you'll already be pretty familiar with the Python window in ArcGIS Pro. However, there are some differences between the two and some improvements as well. In this recipe, you'll learn how to use the ArcGIS Pro Python window.

The Python window in ArcGIS Pro functions in much the same way as the window in ArcGIS for Desktop. It serves as an integrated tool used to execute Python code for geoprocessing operations. Using the Python Window, you can execute Python functionalities, including ArcPy, core Python functionalities, and third-party libraries. Python code that you write in the window can be saved or loaded from an existing script source. The inclusion of autocompletion functionality makes it easier to complete coding operations, including calling tools and passing parameters. In this recipe, you'll learn how to use the ArcGIS Pro Python window.

Follow these steps to learn how to use the ArcGIS Pro Python window:

1. Open **ArcGIS Pro** and select a project or create a new project.

2. Click on the **ANALYSIS** menu item in ArcGIS Pro and then the **Python** tool, as shown in the following screenshot:

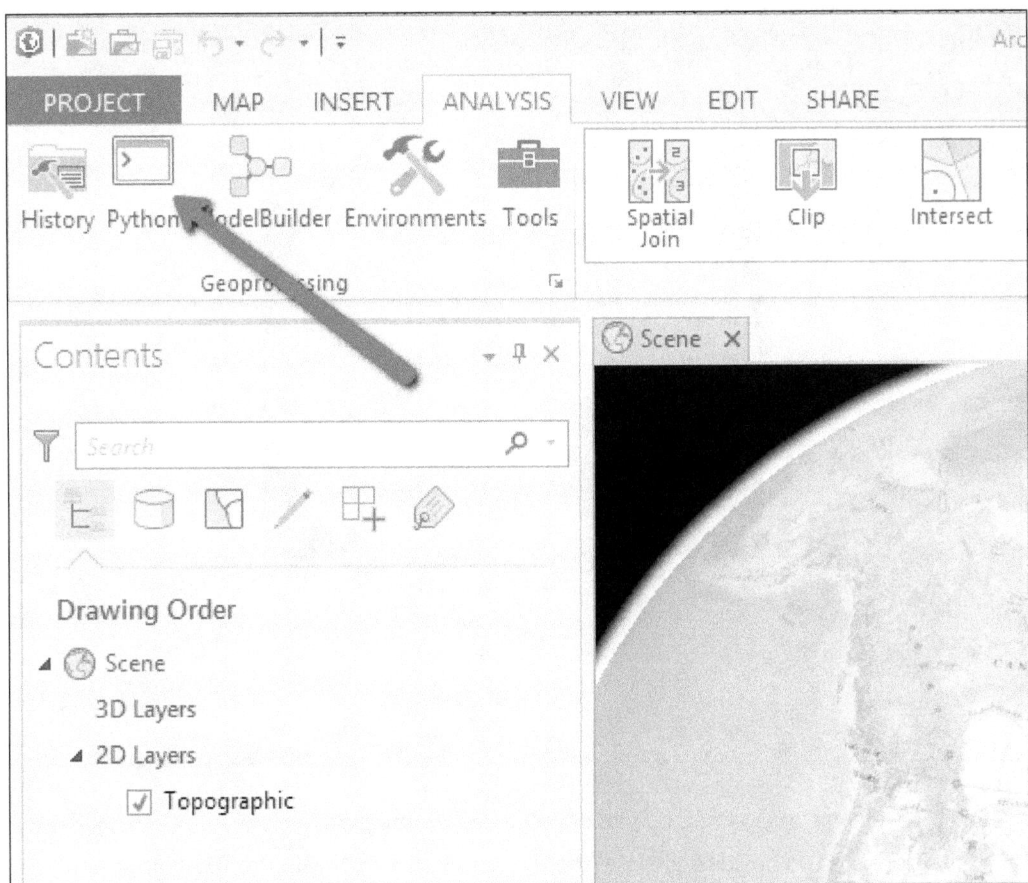

3. This will display the **Python** window at the bottom of the ArcGIS Pro window, as seen in the following screenshot:

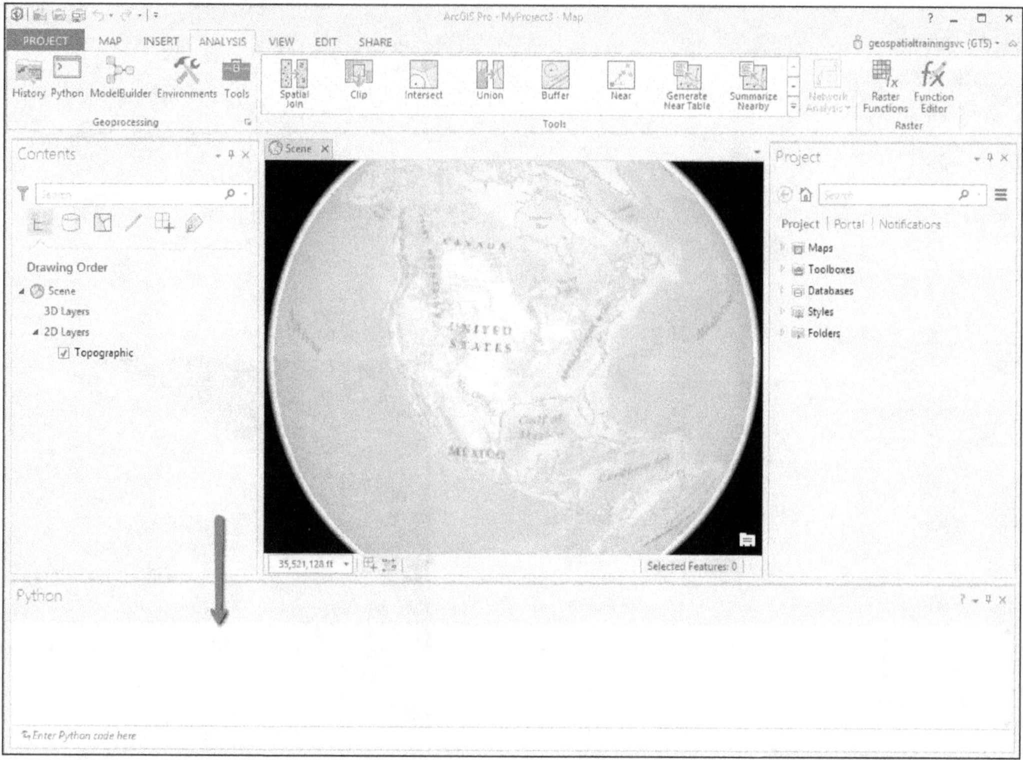

4. The Python window can be pinned, unpinned, and resized.
5. There are two basic sections of the Python window in ArcGIS Pro: **Transcript** and **Python prompt**. Both are shown in the following screenshot. You will write code in the Python prompt section one line at a time. The transcript section provides a record of Python code that has already been executed.

6. After typing in a line of code, you press the *Enter* key on your keyboard and the code is executed and moved to the transcript section. Print messages are written to the transcript window as errors. Type the following line of code to import the ArcPy mapping module:

```
import arcpy.mp as MAP
```

7. The ArcGIS Pro Python window has a code completion functionality so that as you begin typing, various matching options will be presented that provide a current match to what you have typed. You can select one of the items from the presented list to complete the typing. You can see an illustration of this by typing `arc` in the Python prompt. The code completion functionality will present two options: `arcgis` and `arcpy`.
8. You can access the built-in help system by using the `help()` method. Type `help(arcpy.ListFeatureClasses())` in order to see an illustration of the help documentation that is provided:

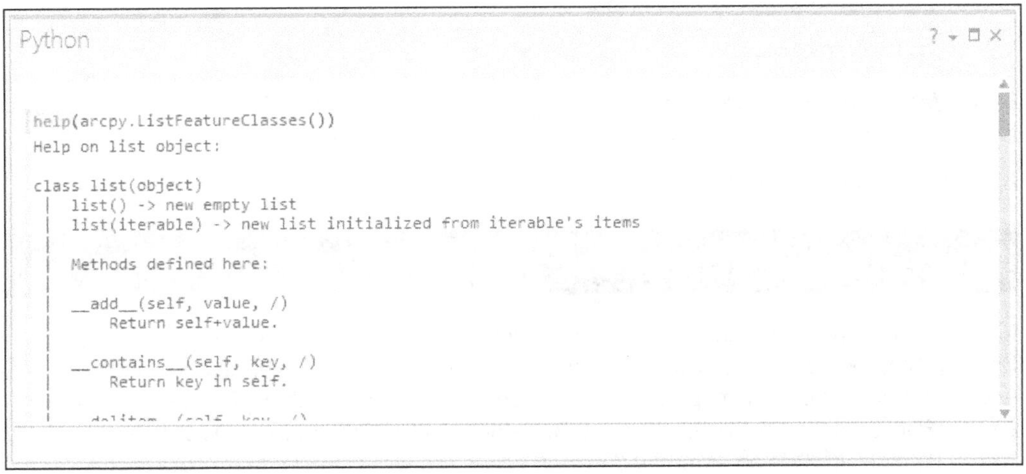

```
Python

help(arcpy.ListFeatureClasses())
Help on list object:

class list(object)
 |  list() -> new empty list
 |  list(iterable) -> new list initialized from iterable's items
 |
 |  Methods defined here:
 |
 |  __add__(self, value, /)
 |      Return self+value.
 |
 |  __contains__(self, key, /)
 |      Return key in self.
 |
```

9. You can save any Python code that you have written by right-clicking inside the transcript section and selecting **Save Transcript**. In addition to this, you can load an existing Python script into the window by right-clicking in the prompt section and selecting **Load Code**.

The ArcGIS Pro Python window can be used to write basic Python geoprocessing scripts, execute tools, access ArcPy and its associated modules, Python core modules and third-party modules, load and execute existing Python scripts, save Python scripts for later use, and obtain help for ArcPy classes and functions. However, there are coding differences between ArcGIS for Desktop and ArcGIS Pro.

Coding differences between ArcGIS for Desktop and ArcGIS Pro

In this section, we'll discuss some of the differences between Python code written in ArcGIS for Desktop and ArcGIS Pro. Fortunately, there aren't many differences.

ArcPy supports a variety of modules, including the data access, mapping, spatial analyst, network analyst, and time modules. As you have already learned, to use these modules, you must first import them into your script. For most of these modules, the way that you import them will be the same regardless of whether you're using ArcGIS for Desktop or ArcGIS Pro. However, there are some differences when importing the ArcPy mapping module.

In the ArcGIS Pro Python environment, you'll need to use the following syntax to import the mapping module. The use of a two-character reference to the mapping module is in line with how all the other modules are imported:

```
import arcpy.mp
```

This differs from how you reference the ArcPy mapping module in ArcGIS for Desktop, as seen in this code example:

```
import arcpy.mapping
```

Installing Python for ArcGIS Pro

Many of you will probably have become quite familiar with executing your Python ArcGIS for Desktop geoprocessing scripts in standalone environments. Examples of this would include executing a script from an integrated development environment, such as IDLE as a scheduled task, or from an operating system prompt. By default, ArcGIS Pro does not include this capability. ArcGIS Pro does include an embedded Python editor that will allow you to execute your code in the Python window as a script tool or a geoprocessing tool. However, if you need to be able to access ArcGIS Pro functionalities from a standalone environment, you will need to download and install a Python setup file from **My Esri** (`https://my.esri.com/#/downloads`). This installer file will install Python 3.4.1 and other requirements needed by ArcGIS Pro.

Converting ArcGIS for Desktop Python code to ArcGIS Pro

As I mentioned earlier in this chapter, there aren't many differences between the Python code you would write for ArcGIS for Desktop and ArcGIS Pro. We've already discussed the primary differences between the two. The versions of Python used are quite different with ArcGIS for Desktop 10.3, which runs Python 2.7 and ArcGIS Pro 1.0, which runs Python 3.4. These two versions of Python are incompatible and there are some tools that you can use when migrating your existing code to ArcGIS Pro.

The first tool that we'll examine is the `AnalyzeToolsForPro`. This geoprocessing tool can be found in the `Management` toolbox. This tool analyzes Python scripts and custom geoprocessing tools, and toolboxes for functionalities that are not supported by ArcGIS Pro. This tool will identify any geoprocessing tools and environment settings that are not supported by ArcGIS Pro, the replacement of `arcpy.mapping` with `arcpy.mp`, and any unsupported data formats, such as personal geodatabases that are not supported by ArcGIS Pro. For issues related to Python 2 and Python 3, the tool also uses the `2to3` utility to identify any Python-specific issues.

The following is the syntax for this tool:

```
AnalyzeToolsForPro_management(input, {report})
```

The input for this tool can be a geoprocessing toolbox, Python file, or tool name, and the optional report parameter is a output text file that includes any issues that were identified.

You can also use the standalone `2to3` Python tool that will identify any Python-specific coding issues related to the differences between the two versions of the language. This is a command-line utility provided with Python 2 and 3 installations. The utility can be found in a path similar to `C:\Python34\Tools\Scripts\2to3.py` or `C:\Python27\Tools\Scripts\2to3.py`. This is not a perfect tool, but has been estimated to identify approximately 95 percent of the differences.

A

Automating Python Scripts

In this chapter, we will cover the following topics:

- Running Python scripts from the command line
- Using sys.argv[ ] to capture command-line input
- Adding Python scripts to batch files
- Scheduling batch files to run at prescribed times

Introduction

Python geoprocessing scripts can be executed either outside ArcGIS as standalone scripts or inside ArcGIS as script tools. Both methods have their advantages and disadvantages. Up to this point in the book, all our scripts have been run either inside ArcGIS as a script tool, from a Python development environment such as IDLE, or the Python window in ArcGIS. However, Python scripts can also be executed from the Windows operating system command line. The command line is a window that you can use to type in commands, rather than the usual point-and-click approach provided by Windows. This method of running Python scripts is useful for scheduling the execution of a script. There are a number of reasons why you might want to schedule your scripts. Many geoprocessing scripts take a long time to fully execute and need to be scheduled to run during nonworking hours on a regular basis. Additionally, some scripts need to be executed on a routine basis (every day, week, month, and so on), and should be scheduled for efficiency. In this chapter, you will learn how to execute scripts from the command line, place scripts inside a batch file, and schedule the execution of scripts at prescribed times. Keep in mind that any scripts run from the command line will still need access to an ArcGIS for Desktop license in order to use the `arcpy` module.

Running Python scripts from the command line

Up to this point in the book, all your Python scripts have been run as either script tools in ArcGIS or from a Python development environment. The Windows command prompt provides yet another way of executing your Python scripts. The command prompt is used primarily to execute scripts that will be run as a part of a batch file and/or as scheduled tasks.

Getting ready

There are a couple advantages of running Python geoprocessing scripts from the command prompt. These scripts can be scheduled to batch process your data during off hours for more efficient processing, and they are easier to debug due to the built-in Python error handling and debugging capabilities.

In this recipe, you will learn how to use the Windows command prompt to execute a Python script. You will need administrative rights to complete this recipe, so you may need to contact your information technology support group to make this change.

How to do it...

Follow these steps to learn how to run a script from the Windows command prompt:

1. In Windows, navigate to **Start** | **All Programs** | **Accessories** | **Command Prompt** which will display a window similar to the following screenshot:

The window will display the current directory. Your directory will differ to some degree. Let's change to the directory for this appendix.

2. Type `cd c:\ArcpyBook\Appendix1`.
3. Type `dir` to see a listing of the files and subdirectories. You should see only a single Python file called `ListFields.py`:

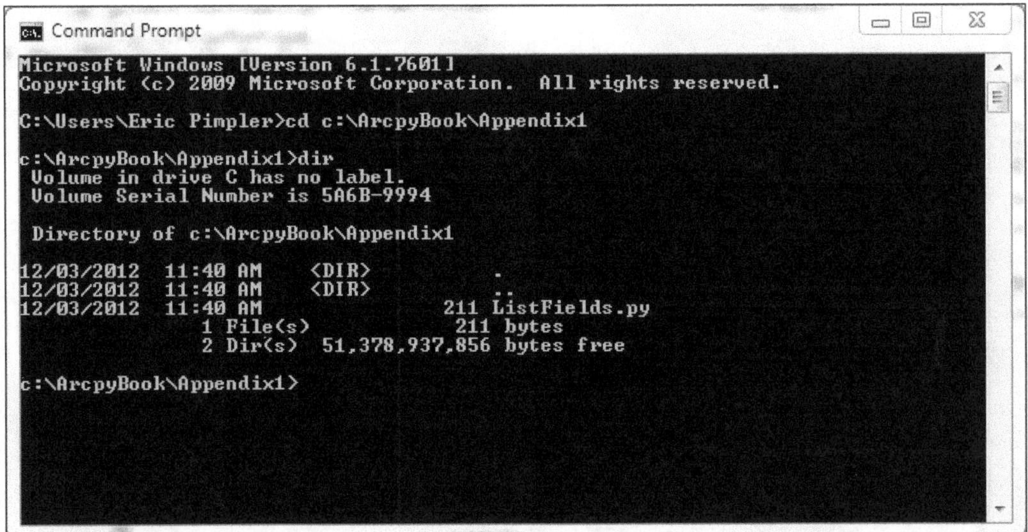

4. You will need to make sure that the Python interpreter can be run from anywhere in your directory structure. Navigate to **Start** | **All Programs** | **Accessories** | **System Tools** | **Control Panel** as shown in the following screenshot:

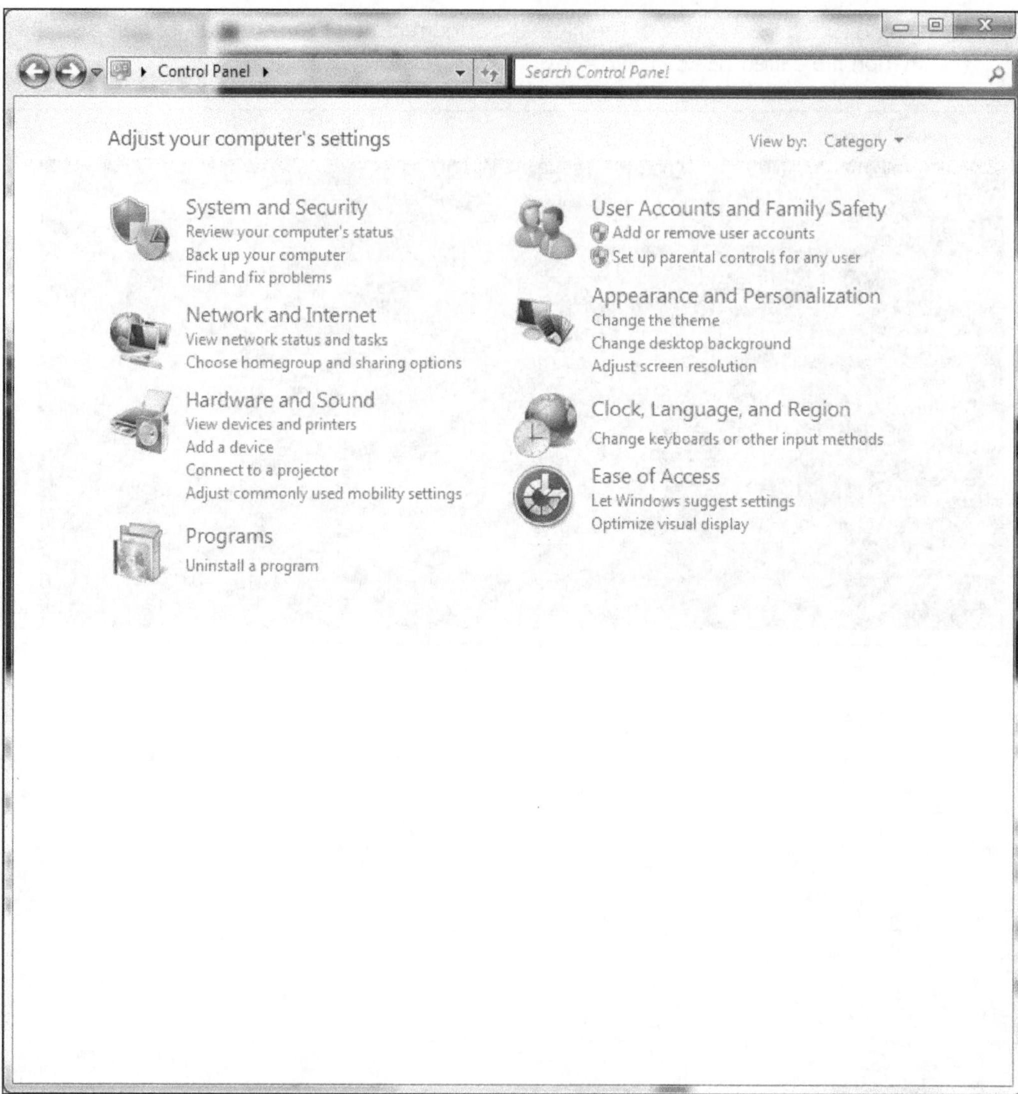

5. Click on **System and Security**.
6. Click on **System**.
7. Click on **Advanced system settings**.

8. In the **System Properties** dialog box, select the **Advanced** tab and then the **Environment Variables** button, as shown in the following screenshot:

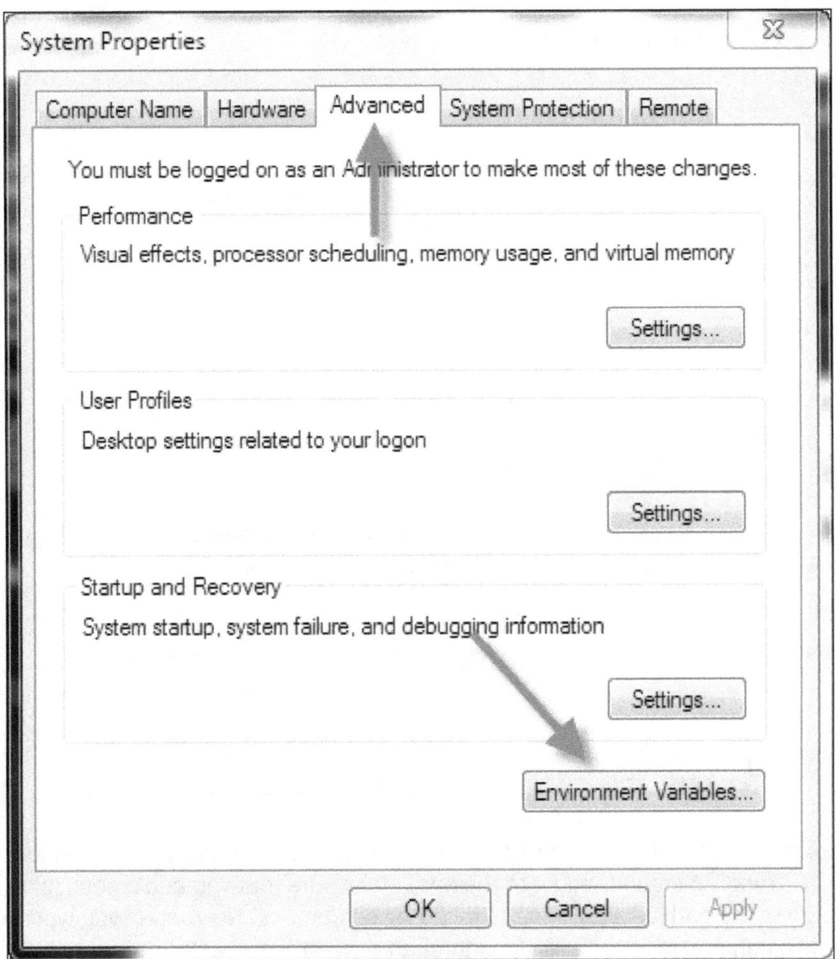

9. Find the **Path** system variable, as can be seen in the following screenshot, and click on **Edit...**:

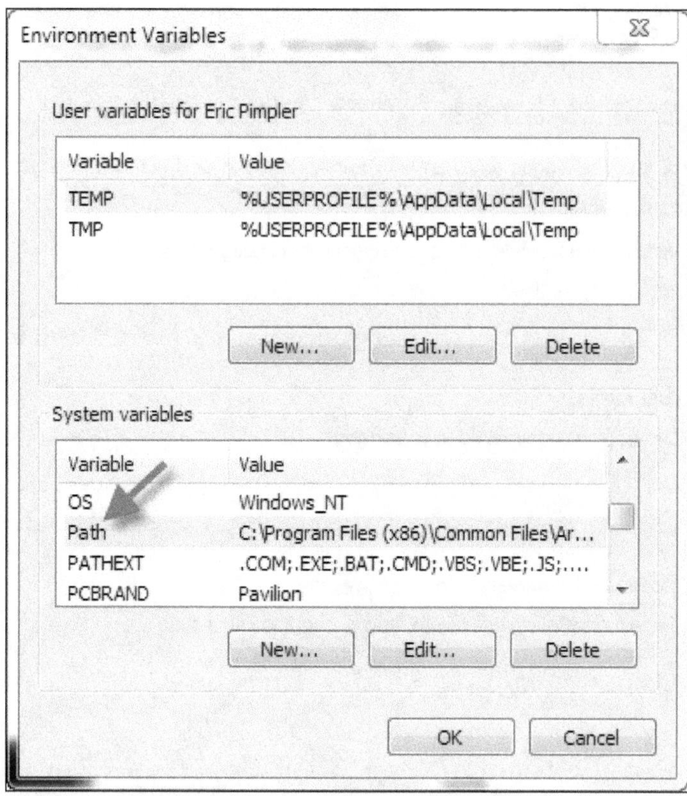

10. Examine the entire text string for the `C:\Python27\ArcGIS10.3` directory. If the text string isn't found, add it to the end. Make sure that you add a semicolon before adding the path as shown in the following screenshot. Now, when you type `python` in the command prompt, it will look through each of the directories in the **Path** system variable, checking for an executable called `python.exe`.

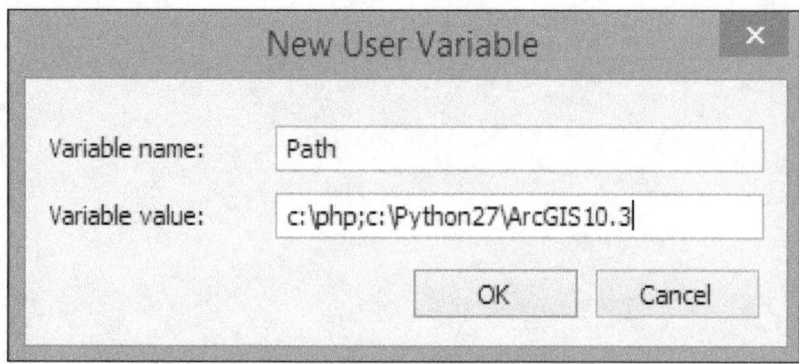

11. Click on **OK** to dismiss the **Edit System Variable** dialog box.
12. Click on **OK** to dismiss the **Environment Variables** dialog box.
13. Click on **OK** to dismiss the **System Properties** dialog box.
14. Return to the command prompt.
15. Type `python ListFields.py`. This will run the `ListFields.py` script. After a brief delay, you should see the following output:

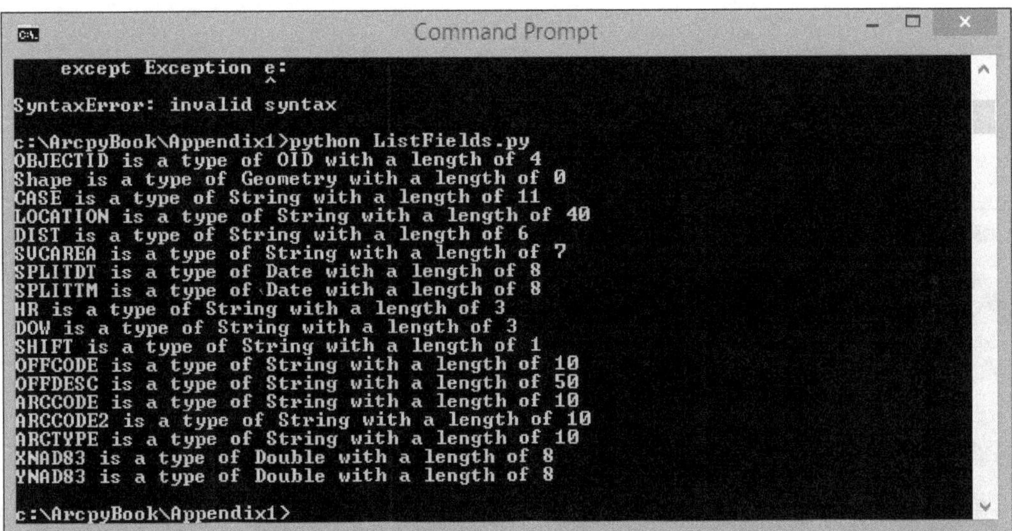

The delay is caused by the first line of code that imports the `arcpy` module.

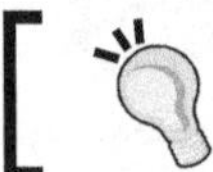

Consider adding a `print` statement before `import` to inform users of the delay.

How it works...

The `ListFields.py` script provided for you in this recipe is a simple script that lists the attribute fields for `Burglary feature class`. The workspace and feature class name are hardcoded in the script. Typing `python` followed by the name of the script, which is `ListFields.py` in this case, triggered the execution of a script using the Python interpreter. As I mentioned earlier, the workspace and feature class names were hardcoded in this script. In the next recipe, you will learn how to pass in arguments to the script so that you can remove the hardcoding and make your script more flexible.

Using sys.argv[ ] to capture command-line input

Instead of hardcoding your scripts with paths to specific datasets, you can make your scripts more flexible by allowing them to accept input in the form of parameters from the command prompt. These input parameters can be captured using Python's `sys.argv[]` object.

Getting ready

Python's `sys.argv[]` object allows you to capture input parameters from the command line when a script is executed. We will use an example to illustrate how this works. Take a look at the following screenshot:

Each word must be separated by a space. These words are stored in a zero-based list object called `sys.argv[]`. In the `sys.argv[]` object, the first item in the list referenced by the `0` index, stores the name of the script. In this case, it would be `ListFields.py`. Each successive word is referenced by the next integer. Therefore, the first parameter (`c:\ArcpyBook\data`) will be stored in `sys.argv[1]`, and the second parameter (`Burglaries.shp`) will be stored in `sys.argv[2]`. Each of the arguments in the `sys.argv[]` object can be accessed and used inside your geoprocessing script. In this recipe, you're going to update the `ListFields.py` script so that it accepts input parameters from the command line.

How to do it...

Follow these steps to create a Python script that can accept input parameters from the command prompt, using `sys.argv[]`:

1. Open `C:\ArcpyBook\Appendix1\ListFields.py` in IDLE.
2. Import the `sys` module:

   ```
   import arcpy
   import sys
   ```

3. Create a variable to hold the workspace that will be passed into the script:

   ```
   wkspace = sys.argv[1]
   ```

4. Create a variable to hold the feature class that will be passed into the script:

   ```
   fc = sys.argv[2]
   ```

5. Update the lines of code that set the workspace and call the `ListFields()` function:

   ```
   arcpy.env.workspace = wkspace
   fields = arcpy.ListFields(fc)
   ```

   Your completed script should appear as follows:

   ```
   import arcpy
   import sys
   wkspace = sys.argv[1]
   fc = sys.argv[2]
   try:
     arcpy.env.workspace = wkspace
     fields = arcpy.ListFields(fc)
     for fld in fields:
       print(fld.name)
   except Exception as e:
     print(e.message)
   ```

6. You can check your work by examining the `C:\ArcpyBook\code\Appendix1\ListFields_Step2.py` solution file.
7. Save the script.
8. If necessary, open the command prompt and navigate to `C:\ArcpyBook\Appendix1`.
9. On the command line, type the following and press the *Enter* key:

   ```
   python ListFields.py c:\ArcpyBook\data Burglaries_2009.shp
   ```

10. Once again, you should see the output detailing the attribute fields for the `Burglaries_2009.shp` file. The difference is that your script no longer has a hardcoded workspace and feature class name. You now have a more flexible script, which is capable of listing the attribute fields for any feature class.

How it works...

The `sys` module contains a list object called `argv[]`, which is used to store the input parameters for the command-line execution of a Python script. The first item stored in the list is always the name of the script. So, in this case, `sys.argv[0]` contains `ListFields.py`. Two parameters are passed into the script, including the workspace and a feature class. These are stored in `sys.argv[1]` and `sys.argv[2]`, respectively. These values are then assigned to variables and used in the script.

Adding Python scripts to batch files

Scheduling your Python scripts to run at prescribed times will require that you create a batch file containing one or more scripts and or operating system commands. These batch files can then be added to the Windows scheduler to run at a specific time interval.

Getting ready

Batch files are text files containing command-line sequences to run Python scripts or perform operating system commands. They have a file extension of `.bat`, which Windows recognizes as an executable file. Since batch files simply contain command-line sequences, they can be written with any text editor, though it is recommended that you use a basic text editor, such as Notepad. This is done so that you can avoid the inclusion of invisible special characters, which are sometimes inserted by programs, such as Microsoft Word. In this recipe, you will create a simple batch file that navigates to the directory containing your `ListFields.py` script and executes it.

How to do it...

Follow these steps to create a batch file:

1. Open a Notepad.
2. Add the following lines of text to the file:

```
cd c:\ArcpyBook\Appendix1
python ListFields.py c:\ArcpyBook\data Burglaries_2009.shp
```

3. Save the file to your desktop as `ListFields.bat`. Make sure you change the **Save as Type** drop-down list to **All Files**, otherwise you'll wind up with a file called `ListFields.bat.txt`.

4. In Windows, navigate to your desktop and double-click on `ListFields.bat` to execute the sequence of commands.
5. A command prompt will be displayed during execution. After the commands have been executed, the command prompt will automatically close.

How it works...

Windows treats a batch file as an executable, so double-clicking on the file will automatically execute the sequence of commands contained within the file in a new command prompt window. All the `print` statements will be written to the window. After the commands have been executed, the command prompt will automatically close. In the event that you need to keep a track of the output, you can write the statements to an output log file.

There's more...

Batch files can contain variables, loops, comments, and conditional logic. These functionalities are beyond the scope of this recipe. However, if you're writing and running a number of scripts for your organization, it's worthwhile spending some time learning more about batch files. Batch files have been around for a long time, so there is no shortage of information about these files on the Web. For more information about batch files, please consult the Wikipedia page for this topic.

Scheduling batch files to run at prescribed times

Once created, your batch files can then be scheduled to run at prescribed times using the Windows scheduler.

Getting ready

Many geoprocessing scripts are time-intensive and best run after hours when they can take full advantage of system resources and free up your time to concentrate on other tasks. In this recipe, you will learn how to use the Windows scheduler to schedule the execution of your batch file.

How to do it...

Follow these steps to schedule a batch file with the Windows scheduler:

1. Open the Windows scheduler by navigating to **Start** | **All Programs** | **Accessories** | **System Tools** | **Control Panel** | **Administrative Tools**. Select **Task Scheduler**. The scheduler should appear, as shown in the following screenshot:

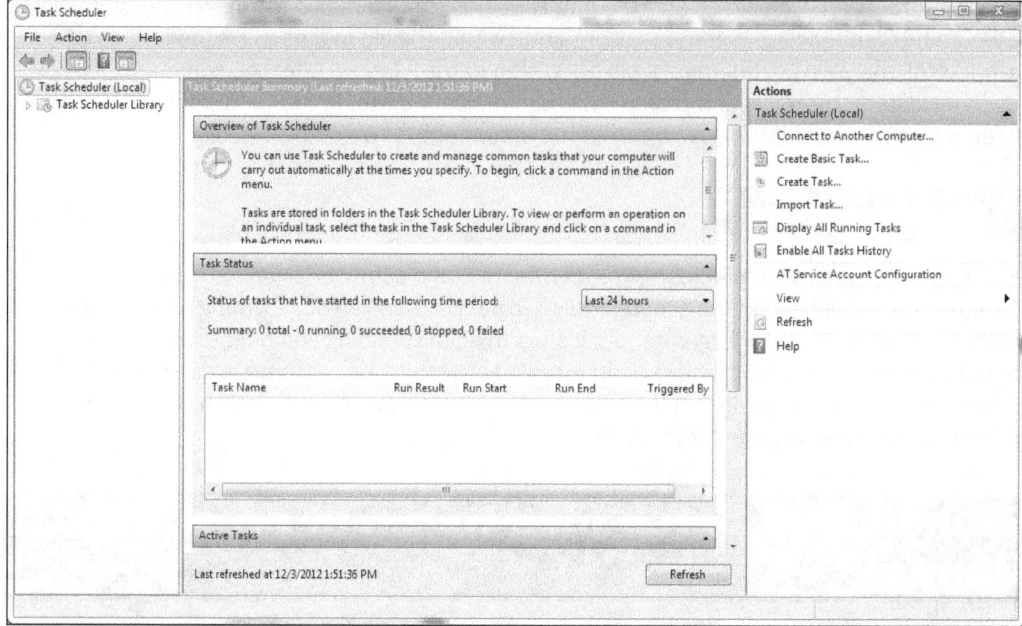

2. Select the **Action** menu item and then **Create Basic Task** to display the **Create Basic Task Wizard** dialog box, as shown in the next screenshot.
3. Give your task a name. In this case, we will call it `List Fields from a Feature Class`. Click on **Next**:

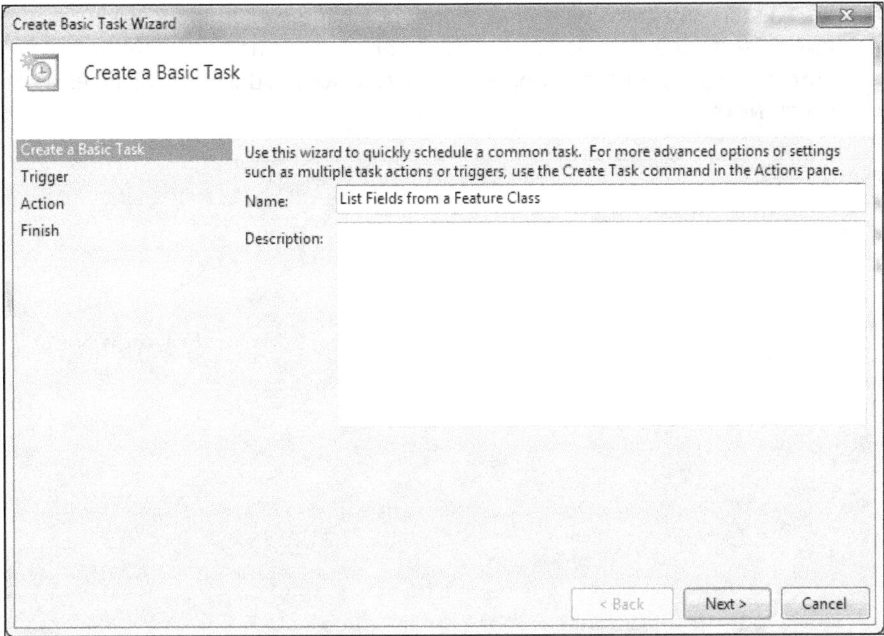

4. Select a trigger for when the task should be executed. This can, and often will be a time-based trigger, but there can also be other types of triggers, such as a user login or computer start. In this case, let's just select **Daily**. Click on **Next**:

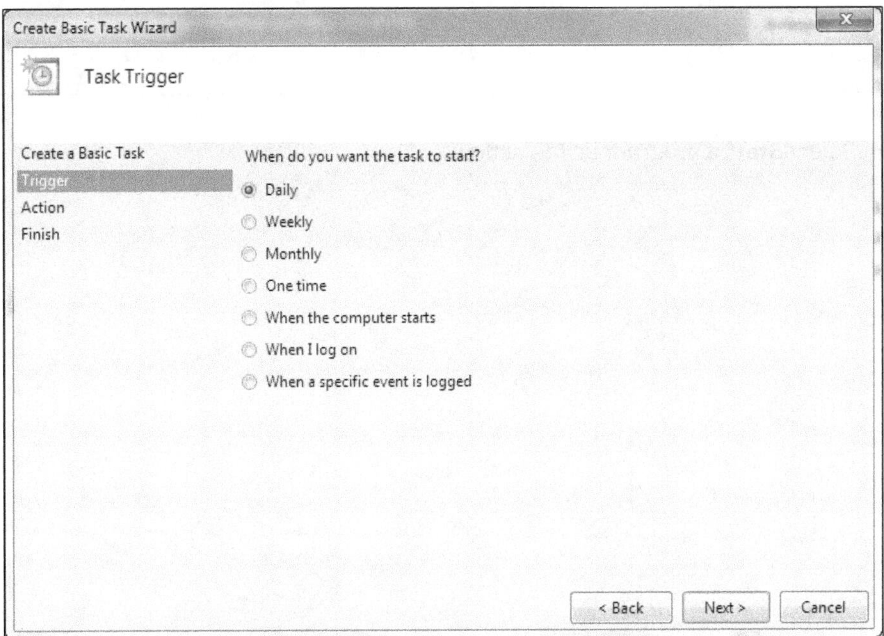

5. Select a start date/time as well as a recurrence interval. In the following screenshot, I have selected the date as `12/3/2012`, with the time as `1:00:00 AM`, and a recurrence interval of `1` day. So, every day at 1:00 AM, this task will be executed. Click on **Next**:

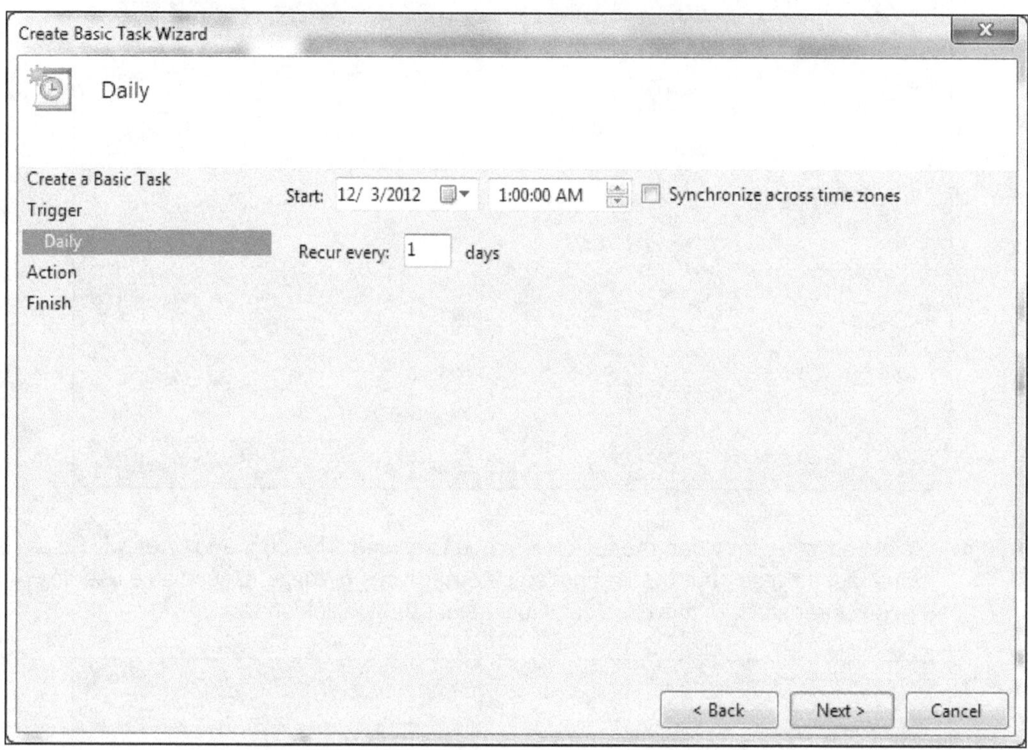

6. Select **Start a program** as the action:

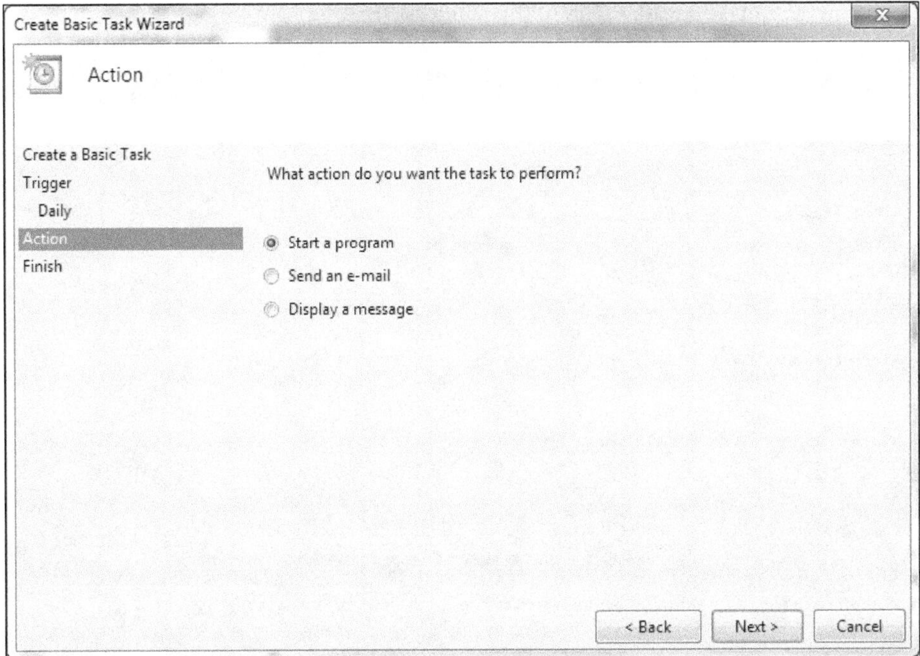

7. Browse to your script and add the parameters. Click on **Next**:

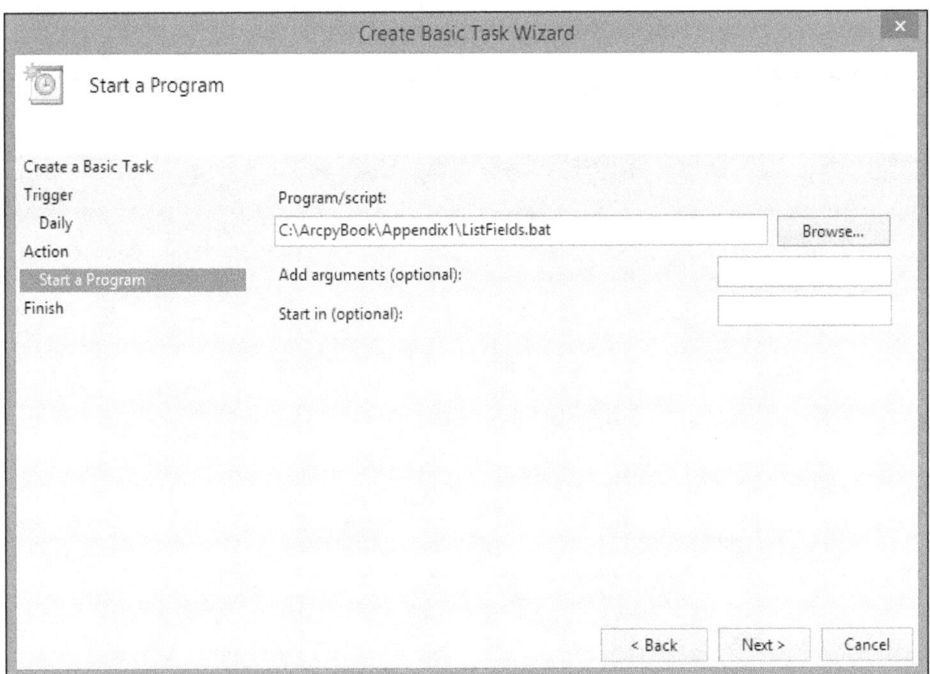

8. Click on **Finish** to add a task to the scheduler:

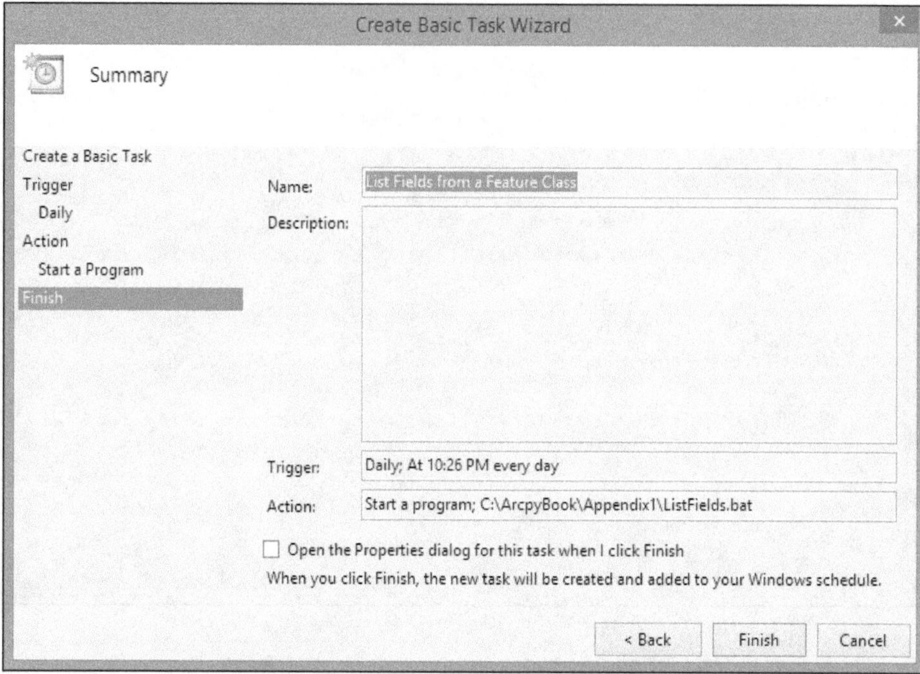

9. The tasks should now be displayed in the list of active tasks:

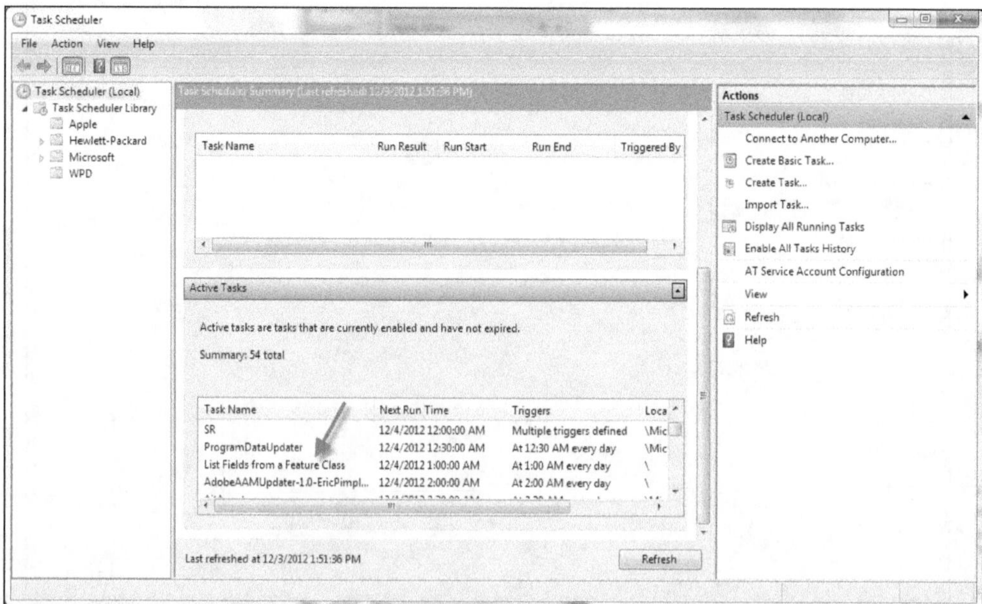

How it works...

The Windows task scheduler keeps track of all the active tasks and handles the execution of these tasks when the prescribed trigger is fired. In this recipe, we have scheduled our task to execute each day at 1:00 AM. At this time, the batch file we created will be triggered and the arguments we specified when creating the task will be passed into the script. Using the scheduler to automatically execute geoprocessing tasks after hours, without the need for GIS staff to interact with the scripts gives you more flexibility and increases your efficiency. You might also want to consider logging the errors in your Python scripts to a log file for more information about specific problems.

B
Five Python Recipes Every GIS Programmer Should Know

In this chapter, we will cover the following topics:

- Reading data from a delimited text file
- Sending e-mails
- Retrieving files from an FTP server
- Creating ZIP files
- Reading XML files

Introduction

In this chapter, you will learn how to write scripts that perform general purpose tasks with Python. Tasks, such as reading and writing delimited text files, sending e-mails, interacting with FTP servers, creating `.zip` files, and reading and writing JSON and XML files, are common. Every GIS programmer should know how to write Python scripts that incorporate these functionalities.

Reading data from a delimited text file

File handling with Python is a very important topic for GIS programmers. Text files have been used as an interchange format to exchange data between systems. They are simple, cross-platform, and easy to process. Comma and tab-delimited text files are among the most commonly used formats for text files, so we'll take an extensive look at the Python tools available to process these files. A common task for GIS programmers is to read comma-delimited text files containing *x* and *y* coordinates, along with other attribute information. This information is then converted into GIS data formats, such as shapefiles or geodatabases.

Getting ready

To use Python's built-in file processing functionality, you must first open the file. Once open, data within the file is processed using functions provided by Python, and finally, the file is closed.

Always remember to close the file when you're done. Python does not necessarily close the files for you, so it is possible that you could run out of resources or overwrite something. Also, some operating system platforms won't let the same file be simultaneously open for read-only and writing purposes.

In this recipe, you will learn how to open, read, and process a comma-delimited text file.

How to do it...

Follow these steps to create a Python script that reads a comma-delimited text file:

1. In your `C:\ArcpyBook\data` folder, you will find a file called `N_America.A2007275.txt`. Open this file in a text editor. It should appear as follows:

```
18.102,-94.353,310.7,1.3,1.1,10/02/2007,0420,T,72
19.300,-89.925,313.6,1.1,1.0,10/02/2007,0420,T,82
19.310,-89.927,309.9,1.1,1.0,10/02/2007,0420,T,68
26.888,-101.421,307.3,2.7,1.6,10/02/2007,0425,T,53
26.879,-101.425,306.4,2.7,1.6,10/02/2007,0425,T,45
36.915,-97.132,342.4,1.0,1.0,10/02/2007,0425,T,100
```

> This file contains data related to wildfire incidents that was derived from a satellite sensor from a single day in 2007. Each row contains latitude and longitude information for the fire along with additional information, including the date and time, satellite type, confidence value, and other details. In this recipe, you are going to pull out only the latitude, longitude, and confidence value. The first item contains the latitude, the second contains longitude, and the final value contains the confidence value.

2. Open **IDLE** and create a file called `C:\ArcpyBook\Appendix2\ReadDelimitedTextFile.py`.
3. Use the Python `open()` function to open the file in order to read it:

```
f = open("c:/ArcpyBook/data/N_America.A2007275.txt','r')
```

4. Add a `for` loop to iterate all the rows:

```
for fire in f:
```

5. Use the `split()` function to split the values into a list, using a comma as the delimiter. The list will be assigned to a variable called `lstValues`. Make sure that you indent this line of code inside the for loop you just created:

```
lstValues = fire.split(",")
```

6. Using the index values that reference latitude, longitude, and confidence values, create new variables:

```
latitude = float(lstValues[0])
longitude = float(lstValues[1])
confid = int(lstValues[8])
```

7. Print the values of each with the `print` statement:

```
print("The latitude is: " + str(latitude) + " The longitude
is: " + str(longitude) + " The confidence value is: " +
str(confid))
```

8. Close the file:

```
f.close()
```

9. The entire script should appear as follows:

```
f = open('c:/ArcpyBook/data/N_America.A2007275.txt','r')
for fire in f.readlines():
  lstValues = fire.split(',')
  latitude = float(lstValues[0])
  longitude = float(lstValues[1])
  confid = int(lstValues[8])
```

```
  print("The latitude is: " + str(latitude) + " The
longitude is: " + str(longitude) + " The confidence value
is: " + str(confid))
f.close()
```

10. You can check your work by examining the `C:\ArcpyBook\code\Appendix2\ReadDelimitedTextFile.py` solution file.
11. Save and run the script. You should see the following output:

```
The latitude is: 18.102 The longitude is: -94.353 The confidence
value is: 72
The latitude is: 19.3 The longitude is: -89.925 The confidence
value is: 82
The latitude is: 19.31 The longitude is: -89.927 The confidence
value is: 68
The latitude is: 26.888 The longitude is: -101.421 The confidence
value is: 53
The latitude is: 26.879 The longitude is: -101.425 The confidence
value is: 45
The latitude is: 36.915 The longitude is: -97.132 The confidence
value is: 100
```

How it works...

Python's `open()` function creates a file object, which serves as a link to a file residing on your computer. You must call the `open()` function on a file before reading or writing data in a file. The first parameter for the `open()` function is a path to the file you'd like to open. The second parameter of the `open()` function corresponds to a mode, which is typically read (`r`), write (`w`), or append (`a`). A value of `r` indicates that you'd like to open the file for read-only operations, while a value of `w` indicates that you'd like to open the file for write operations. If the file you open in write mode already exists, it will overwrite any existing data in the file, so be careful when using this mode. Append (`a`) mode will open a file for write operations, but instead of overwriting any existing data, it will append data to the end of the file. So, in this recipe, we have opened the `N_America.A2007275.txt` file in read-only mode.

Inside the `for` loop, which is used to loop through each of the values in the text file one line at a time, the `split()` function is used to create a list object from a line of text that is delimited in some way. Our file is comma-delimited, so we can use `split(",")`. You can also split based on other delimiters, such as tabs, spaces, or any other delimiter. This new list object created by `split()` is stored in a variable called `lstValues`. This variable contains each of the wildfire values. This is illustrated in the following screenshot. You'll notice that latitude is located in the first position, longitude is located in the second position, and so on. Lists are zero-based:

```
   0      1      2   3   4      5        6   7  8
36.913,-97.143,320.1,1.0,1.0,10/02/2007,0425,T,100
```

Using the index values (which references latitude, longitude, and confidence values), we create new variables called `latitude`, `longitude`, and `confid`. Finally, we print each of the values. A more robust geoprocessing script might write this information into a feature class using an `InsertCursor` object. We actually did this in a previous recipe in *Chapter 8, Using the ArcPy Data Access Module with Feature Classes and Tables*.

It would be possible to use the `readlines()` function to read the entire contents of the file into a Python list, which could then be iterated. Each row in the text file will be a unique value in the list. Since this function reads the entire file into a list, you need to use this method with caution, as large files can cause significant performance problems.

There's more...

Similar to instances of reading files, there are a number of methods that you can use to write data to a file. The `write()` function is probably the easiest to use. It takes a single string argument and writes it to a file. The `writelines()` function can be used to write the contents of a list structure to a file. Before writing data to a text file, you will need to open the file in either a write or append mode.

Sending e-mails

There will be occasions when you may need to send an e-mail from a Python script. An example of this might be an alert for the successful completion or errors incurred in a long-running geoprocessing operation. On these and other occasions, sending an e-mail can be helpful.

Getting ready

Sending an e-mail through a Python script will require you to have access to a mail server. This can be a public e-mail service, such as Yahoo, Gmail, or others. It can also use outgoing mail servers that is configured with applications, such as Microsoft Outlook. In either case, you'll need to know the host name and port of the e-mail server. The Python `smtplib` module is used to create connections to the mail server and to send e-mails.

The Python `email` module contains a `Message` class that represents e-mail messages. Each message contains both headers and a body. This class can't be used to send e-mails, it just handles its object representation. In this recipe, you'll learn how to use the `smtp` class to send e-mails containing an attachment through your script. The `Message` class can parse a stream of characters or a file containing an e-mail by using either the `message_from_file()` or `message_from_string()` functions. Both will create a new `Message` object. The body of the mail can be obtained by calling `Message.getpayload()`.

We are using the Google Mail service for this exercise. If you already have a Gmail account, then simply provide your username and password as the values for these variables. If you don't have a Gmail account, you'll need to create one or use a different mail service to complete this exercise. Gmail accounts are free. Google may block attempts to send an e-mail through scripts, so be aware that this may not work as expected if you're using Gmail.

How to do it...

Follow these steps to create a script that can send e-mails:

1. Open **IDLE** and create a file called `C:\ArcpyBook\Appendix2\SendEmail.py`.
2. In order to send e-mails with attachments, you're going to need to import the `smtplib` module along with the `os` module, and several classes from the e-mail module. Add the following import statements to your script:

```
import smtplib
from email.MIMEMultipart import MIMEMultipart
from email.MIMEBase import MIMEBase
from email.MIMEText import MIMEText
from email import Encoders
import os
```

3. Create the following variables and assign your Gmail username and password as the values. Keep in mind that this method of e-mailing from your Python script can invite problems, as it requires that you include your username and password:

```
gmail_user = "<username>"
gmail_pwd = "<password>"
```

Note that including an e-mail `username` and `password` in a script is not secure so you wouldn't want to include these in a production script. There are ways of encrypting these values but that is beyond the scope of this recipe.

4. Create a new Python function called `mail()`. This function will accept four parameters: `to`, `subject`, `text`, and `attach`. Each of these parameters should be self-explanatory. Create a new `MIMEMultipart` object and assign the `from`, `to`, and `subject` keys. You can also attach the text of the e-mail to this new `msg` object using `MIMEMultipart.attach()`:

```
def mail(to, subject, text, attach):
  msg = MIMEMultipart()
  msg['From'] = gmail_user
```

```
msg['To'] = to
msg['Subject'] = subject

msg.attach(MIMEText(text))
```

5. Attach the file to the e-mail:

```
part = MIMEBase('application', 'octet-stream')
part.set_payload(open(attach, 'rb').read())
Encoders.encode_base64(part)
part.add_header('Content-Disposition',
  'attachment; filename="%s"' %
  os.path.basename(attach))
msg.attach(part)
```

6. Create a new SMTP object that references the Google Mail service, passes in the username and password to connect to the mail services, sends the e-mail, and closes the connection:

```
mailServer = smtplib.SMTP("smtp.gmail.com", 587)
mailServer.ehlo()
mailServer.starttls()
mailServer.ehlo()
mailServer.login(gmail_user, gmail_pwd)
mailServer.sendmail(gmail_user, to, msg.as_string())
mailServer.close()
```

7. Call the `mail()` function, passing in the recipient of the e-mail, a subject for the e-mail, the text of the e-mail, and the attachment:

```
mail("<email to send to>",
"Hello from python!",
"This is an email sent with python",
"c:/ArcpyBook/data/bc_pop1996.csv")
```

8. The entire script should appear as follows:

```
import smtplib
from email.MIMEMultipart import MIMEMultipart
from email.MIMEBase import MIMEBase
from email.MIMEText import MIMEText
from email import Encoders
import os

gmail_user = "<username>"
gmail_pwd = "<password>"

def mail(to, subject, text, attach):
 msg = MIMEMultipart()

 msg['From'] = gmail_user
```

```
    msg['To'] = to
    msg['Subject'] = subject

    msg.attach(MIMEText(text))

    part = MIMEBase('application', 'octet-stream')
    part.set_payload(open(attach, 'rb').read())
    Encoders.encode_base64(part)
    part.add_header('Content-Disposition',
        'attachment; filename="%s"' % os.path.basename(attach))
    msg.attach(part)

    mailServer = smtplib.SMTP("smtp.gmail.com", 587)
    mailServer.ehlo()
    mailServer.starttls()
    mailServer.ehlo()
    mailServer.login(gmail_user, gmail_pwd)
    mailServer.sendmail(gmail_user, to, msg.as_string())
    mailServer.close()

mail("<email to send to>", "Hello from python!", "This is
an email sent with python", "bc_pop1996.csv")
```

9. You can check your work by examining the `C:\ArcpyBook\code\Appendix2\SendEmail`.py solution file.
10. Save and run the script. For testing, I used my personal Yahoo account as the recipient. You'll notice that my inbox has a new message from my Gmail account; also, notice the attachment:

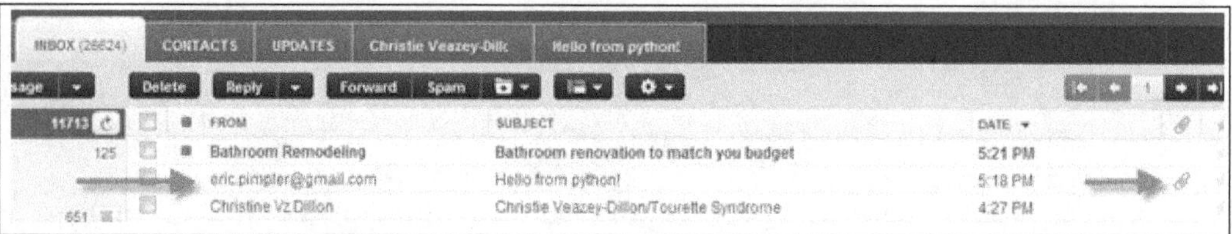

How it works...

The first parameter passed into the `mail()` function is the e-mail address that will receive the e-mail. This can be any valid e-mail address, but you'll want to supply a mail account that you can actually check, so that you can make sure your script runs correctly. The second parameter is just the subject line of the e-mail. The third parameter is the text. The final parameter is the name of a file that will be attached to the e-mail. Here, I've simply defined that the `bc_pop1996.csv` file should be attached. You can use any file you have access to, but you may want to just use this file for testing.

We then create a new `MIMEMultipart` object inside the `mail()` function, and assign the `from`, `to`, and `subject` keys. You can also attach the text of the e-mail to this new `msg` object using `MIMEMultipart.attach()`. The `bc_pop1996.csv` file is then attached to the e-mail using a `MIMEBase` object and attached to the e-mail using `msg.attach(part)`.

At this point, we've examined how a basic text e-mail can be sent. However, we want to send a more complex e-mail message that contains text and an attachment. This requires the use of MIME messages, which provide the functionality to handle multipart e-mails. MIME messages need boundaries between multiple parts of an e-mail along with extra headers to specify the content being sent. The `MIMEBase` class is an abstract subclass of `Message` and enables this type of an e-mail to be sent. Since it is an abstract class, you can't create actual instances of this class. Instead, you use one of the subclasses, such as `MIMEText`. The last step of the `mail()` function is to create a new SMTP object that references the Google Mail service, passes in the username and password in order to connect to the mail services, sends the e-mail, and then closes the connection.

Retrieving files from an FTP server

Retrieving files from an FTP server for processing is a very common operation for GIS programmers and can be automated with a Python script.

Getting ready

Connecting to an FTP server and downloading a file is accomplished through the `ftplib` module. A connection to an FTP server is created through the FTP object, which accepts a host, username, and password to create the connection. Once a connection has been opened, you can then search for and download files.

In this recipe, you will connect to the **National Interagency Fire Center Incident** FTP site and download a PDF file for a wildfire in Colorado. Before you run the following script, you will need to create a username/password through `http://gis.nwcg.gov/data_nifcftp.html`.

How to do it...

Follow these steps to create a script that connects to an FTP server and downloads a file:

1. Open **IDLE** and create a file called `C:\ArcpyBook\Appendix2\ftp.py`.
2. We'll be connecting to an FTP server at the NIFC. Visit their website at `http://gis.nwcg.gov/data_nifcftp.html` for more information.
3. Import the `ftplib`, `os`, and `socket` modules:

```
import ftplib
import os
import socket
```

4. Add the following variables that define the URL, directory, and filename:

```
HOST = 'ftp.nifc.gov'
USER = '<your username here>'
PASSW = '<your password here>'
DIRN = '/Incident_Specific_Data/2012
HISTORIC/ROCKY_MTN/Arapaho/GIS/20120629'
FILE = '20120629_0600_Arapaho_PIO_0629_8x11_land.pdf'
```

5. Add the following code block to create a connection. If there is a connection error, a message will be generated. If the connection was successful, a success message will be printed:

```
try:

  f = ftplib.FTP(HOST,USER,PASS)
except (socket.error, socket.gaierror), e:
  print('ERROR: cannot reach "%s"' % HOST)
print('*** Connected to host "%s"' % HOST)
```

6. Add the following code block to anonymously log in to the server:

```
try:
  f.login()
except ftplib.error_perm:
  print('ERROR: cannot login')
  f.quit()
print('*** Logged in ')
```

7. Add the following code block to change to the directory specified in our `DIRN` variable:

```
try:
  f.cwd(DIRN)
except ftplib.error_perm:
  print('ERROR: cannot CD to "%s"' % DIRN)
  f.quit()
print('*** Changed to "%s" folder' % DIRN)
```

8. Use the `FTP.retrbinary()` function to retrieve the PDF file:

```
try:
  f.retrbinary('RETR %s' % FILE,
     open(FILE, 'wb').write)
except ftplib.error_perm:
  print('ERROR: cannot read file "%s"' % FILE)
  os.unlink(FILE)
else:
  print('*** Downloaded "%s" to CWD' % FILE)
```

9. Make sure you disconnect from the server:

```
f.quit()
```

10. The entire script should appear as follows:

```
import ftplib
import os
import socket

HOST = 'ftp.nifc.gov'
USER = '<your username here>'
PASSW = '<your password here>'
DIRN = '/Incident_Specific_Data/2012
HISTORIC/ROCKY_MTN/Arapaho/GIS/20120629'
FILE = '20120629_0600_Arapaho_PIO_0629_8x11_land.pdf'

try:
  f = ftplib.FTP(HOST,USER,PASSW)
except (socket.error, socket.gaierror), e:
  print('ERROR: cannot reach "%s"' % HOST)
print('*** Connected to host "%s"' % HOST)

try:
  f.login()
except ftplib.error_perm:
  print('ERROR: cannot login')
  f.quit()
print('*** Logged in ')

try:
  f.cwd(DIRN)
except ftplib.error_perm:
  print('ERROR: cannot CD to "%s"' % DIRN)
  f.quit()
print('*** Changed to "%s" folder' % DIRN)

try:
  f.retrbinary('RETR %s' % FILE,
     open(FILE, 'wb').write)
except ftplib.error_perm:
  print('ERROR: cannot read file "%s"' % FILE)
  os.unlink(FILE)
else:
  print('*** Downloaded "%s" to CWD' % FILE)
f.quit()
```

11. You can check your work by examining the `C:\ArcpyBook\code\Appendix2\ftp.py` solution file.
12. Save and run the script. If everything is successful, you should see the following output:

```
*** Connected to host "ftp.nifc.gov"
*** Logged in as "anonymous"
*** Changed to "'/Incident_Specific_Data/2012
HISTORIC/ROCKY_MTN/Arapaho/GIS/20120629'" folder
*** Downloaded "'20120629_0600_Arapaho_PIO_0629_8x11_land.pdf
" to CWD
```

13. Check your `C:\ArcpyBook\Appendix2` directory for the file. By default, FTP will download files to the current working directory.

How it works...

To connect to an FTP server, you need to know the URL. You also need to know the directory and filename for the file that will be downloaded. In this script, we have hardcoded this information, so that you can focus on implementing the FTP-specific functionality. Using this information, we then created a connection to the NIFC FTP server. This is done through the `ftplib.FTP()` function, which accepts a URL to the host.

Keep in mind that you'll need to obtain a username/password to log in and download the data. Once logged in, the script then changes directories from the root of the FTP server to the path defined in the `DIRN` variable. This was accomplished with the `cwd(<path>)` function. The PDF file was retrieved by using the `retrbinary()` function. Finally, you will want to close your connection to the FTP server when you're done. This is done with the `quit()` method.

There's more...

There are a number of additional FTP-related methods that you can use to perform various actions. Generally, these can be divided into directory-level operations and file-level operations. Directory level methods include the `dir()` method to obtain a list of files in a directory, `mkd()` to create a new directory, `pwd()` to get the current working directory, and `cwd()` to change the current directory. Keep in mind that the actions you attempt to perform through your script will be governed by the privileges assigned to your account, so you may not be able to successfully execute every method that I mention.

The `ftplib` module also includes various methods to work with files. You can upload and download files in a binary or plain text format. The `retrbinary()` and `storbinary()` methods are used to retrieve and store binary files, respectively. Plain text files can be retrieved and stored using `retrlines()` and `storlines()`.

There are several others methods on the FTP class that you should be aware of. Deleting a file can be done with the `delete()` method, while renaming a file can be accomplished with `rename()`. You can also send commands to the FTP server through the `sendcmd()` method.

Creating ZIP files

GIS often requires the use of large files that will be compressed into a `.zip` format for ease of sharing. Python includes a module that you can use to decompress and compress files in this format.

Getting ready

ZIP is a common compression and archive format and is implemented in Python through the `zipfile` module. The `ZipFile` class can be used to create, read, and write `.zip` files. To create a new `.zip` file, simply provide the filename along with a mode as `w`, which indicates that you want to write data to the file. In the following code example, we are creating a `.zip` file called `datafile.zip`. The second parameter, `w`, indicates that a new file will be created. A new file will be created or an existing file with the same name will be truncated in the write mode. An optional compression parameter can also be used when creating the file. This value can be set to either `ZIP_STORED` or `ZIP_DEFLATED`:

```
zipfile.ZipFile('dataFile.zip', 'w',zipfile.ZIP_STORED)
```

In this exercise, you will use Python to create file, add files, and apply compression to a `.zip` file. You'll be archiving all the shapefiles located in the `C:\ArcpyBook\data` directory.

How to do it...

Follow these steps to learn how to create a script that builds a `.zip` file:

1. Open **IDLE** and create a script called `C:\ArcpyBook\Appendix2\CreateZipfile.py`.
2. Import the `zipfile` and `os` modules:

   ```
   import os
   import zipfile
   ```

3. Create a new `.zip` file called `shapefiles.zip` in write mode and add a compression parameter:

   ```
   zfile = zipfile.ZipFile("shapefiles.zip", "w",
   zipfile.ZIP_STORED)
   ```

4. Next, we'll use the `os.listdir()` function to create a list of files in the data directory:

   ```
   files = os.listdir("c:/ArcpyBook/data")
   ```

5. Loop through a list of all the files and write to the `.zip` file if the file ends with `shp`, `dbf`, or `shx`:

```
for f in files:
  if f.endswith("shp") or f.endswith("dbf") or
f.endswith("shx"):
    zfile.write("C:/ArcpyBook/data/" + f)
```

6. Print out a list of all the files that were added to the ZIP archive. You can use the `ZipFile.namelist()` function to create a list of files in the archive.

```
for f in zfile.namelist():
    print "Added %s" % f
```

7. Close the `.zip` archive:

```
zfile.close()
```

8. The entire script should appear as follows:

```
import os
import zipfile

#create the zip file
zfile = zipfile.ZipFile("shapefiles.zip", "w",
zipfile.ZIP_STORED)
files = os.listdir("c:/ArcpyBook/data")

for f in files:
  if f.endswith("shp") or f.endswith("dbf") or
f.endswith("shx"):
    zfile.write("C:/ArcpyBook/data/" + f)

#list files in the archive
for f in zfile.namelist():
    print("Added %s" % f)

zfile.close()
```

9. You can check your work by examining the `C:\ArcpyBook\code\Appendix2\CreateZipfile_Step1`.py solution file.

10. Save and run the script. You should see the following output:

```
Added ArcpyBook/data/Burglaries_2009.dbf
Added ArcpyBook/data/Burglaries_2009.shp
Added ArcpyBook/data/Burglaries_2009.shx
Added ArcpyBook/data/Streams.dbf
Added ArcpyBook/data/Streams.shp
Added ArcpyBook/data/Streams.shx
```

11. In Windows Explorer, you should be able to see the output `.zip` file, as shown in the following screenshot. Note the size of archive. This file was created without compression:

12. Now, we're going to create a compressed version of the `.zip` file to see the difference. Make the following changes to the line of code that creates the `.zip` file:

```
zfile = zipfile.ZipFile("shapefiles2.zip", "w",
zipfile.ZIP_DEFLATED)
```

13. You can check your work by examining the `C:\ArcpyBook\code\Appendix2\CreateZipfile_Step2.py` solution file.
14. Save and rerun the script.
15. Take a look at the size of the new `shapefiles2.zip` file that you just created. Note the decreased size of the file due to compression:

How it works...

In this recipe, you created a new `.zip` file called `shapefiles.zip` in write mode. In the first iteration of this script, you didn't compress the contents of the file. However, in the second iteration, you did it by using the `DEFLATED` parameter that was passed into the constructor for the `ZipFile` object. The script then obtained a list of files in the data directory and looped through each of the files. Each file that has an extension of `.shp`, `.dbf`, or `.shx` is then written to the archive file, using the `write()` function. Finally, the names of each of the files written to the archive are printed to the screen.

There's more...

The contents of an existing file stored in a ZIP archive can be read by using the `read()` method. The file should first be opened in a read mode, and then you can call the `read()` method passing a parameter that represents the filename that should be read. The contents of the file can then be printed to the screen, written to another file, or stored as a list or dictionary variable.

Reading XML files

XML files were designed as a way to transport and store data. They are platform-independent since the data is stored in a plain text file. Although similar to HTML, XML differs from HTML since the former is designed for display purposes, whereas XML data is designed for data. XML files are sometimes used as an interchange format for GIS data that is going between various software systems.

Getting ready

XML documents have a tree-like structure that is composed of a `root` element, `child` elements, and element attributes. Elements are also called **nodes**. All XML files contain a `root` element. This `root` element is the parent to all other elements or child nodes. The following code example illustrates the structure of an XML document. Unlike HTML files, XML files are case sensitive:

```
<root>
 <child att="value">
 <subchild>.....</subchild>
 </child>
</root>
```

Python provides several programming modules that you can use to process XML files. The module that you use should be determined by the module that is right for the job. Don't try to force a single module to do everything. Each module has specific functions that they are good at performing.

In this recipe, you will learn how to read data from an XML file using the `nodes` and `element` attributes that are a part of the document.

There are a number of ways that you can access nodes within an XML document. Perhaps, the easiest way to do so is to find nodes by tag name and then through walk the tree containing a list of the child nodes. Before doing so, you'll want to parse the XML document with the `minidom.parse()` method. Once parsed, you can then use the `childNodes` attribute to obtain a list of all the `child` nodes starting at root of the tree. Finally, you can search the nodes by tag names with the `getElementsByTagName(tag)` function, which accepts a tag name as an argument. This will return a list of all `child` nodes that are associated with the tag.

You can also determine if a node contains an attribute by calling `hasAttribute(name)`, which will return a `true/false` value. Once you've determined that an attribute exists, a call to `getAttribute(name)` will obtain the value for the attribute.

In this exercise, you will parse an XML file and pull out values associated with a particular element (node) and attribute. We'll load an XML file containing wildfire data. In this file, we'll look for the `<fire>` node and the `address` attribute for each of these nodes. The addresses will be printed out.

How to do it...

1. Open **IDLE** and create a script called `C:\ArcpyBook\Appendix2\XMLAccessElementAttribute.py`.
2. The `WitchFireResidenceDestroyed.xml` file will be used. The file is located in your `C:\ArcpyBook\Appendix2` folder. You can see a sample of its contents, as follows:

```
<fires>
  <fire address="11389 Pajaro Way" city="San Diego"
state="CA" zip="92127" country="USA" latitude="33.037187"
longitude="-117.082299" />
  <fire address="18157 Valladares Dr" city="San Diego"
state="CA" zip="92127" country="USA" latitude="33.039406"
longitude="-117.076344" />
  <fire address="11691 Agreste Pl" city="San Diego"
state="CA" zip="92127" country="USA" latitude="33.036575"
longitude="-117.077702" />
  <fire address="18055 Polvera Way" city="San Diego"
state="CA" zip="92128" country="USA" latitude="33.044726"
longitude="-117.057649" />
</fires>
```

3. Import `minidom` from `xml.dom`:

```
from xml.dom import minidom
```

4. Parse the XML file:

```
xmldoc = minidom.parse("WitchFireResidenceDestroyed.xml")
```

5. Generate a list of nodes from the XML file:

```
childNodes = xmldoc.childNodes
```

6. Generate a list of all the `<fire>` nodes:

```
eList = childNodes[0].getElementsByTagName("fire")
```

7. Loop through the list of elements, test for the existence of the `address` attribute and print the value of the attribute, if it exists:

```
for e in eList:
  if e.hasAttribute("address"):
    print(e.getAttribute("address"))
```

8. You can check your work by examining the `C:\ArcpyBook\code\Appendix2\XMLAccessElementAttribute.py` solution file.
9. Save and run the script. You should see the following output:

```
11389 Pajaro Way
18157 Valladares Dr
11691 Agreste Pl
18055 Polvera Way
18829 Bernardo Trails Dr
18189 Chretien Ct
17837 Corazon Pl
18187 Valladares Dr
18658 Locksley St
18560 Lancashire Way
```

How it works...

Loading an XML document into your script is probably the most basic thing you can do with XML files. You can use the `xml.dom` module to do this through the use of the `minidom` object. The `minidom` object has a method called `parse()`, which accepts a path to an XML document and creates a **document object model** (**DOM**) tree object from the `WitchFireResidenceDestroyed.xml` file.

The `childNodes` property of the DOM tree generates a list of all the nodes in the XML file. You can then access each of the nodes using the `getElementsByTagName()` method. The final step is to loop through each of the `<fire>` nodes contained within the `eList` variable. For each node, we then check for the `address` attribute with the `hasAttribute()` method, and if it exists, we call the `getAttribute()` function and print the address to the screen.

There's more...

There will be times when you will need to search an XML document for a specific text string. This requires the use of the `xml.parsers.expat` module. You'll need to define a search class derived from the basic `expat` class and then create an object from this class. Once created, you can call the `parse()` method on the `search` object to search for data. Finally, you can then search the nodes by tag names with the `getElementsByTagName(tag)` function, which accepts a tag name as an argument. This will return a list of all child nodes that are associated with the tag.

Index

A

B

C

D

E

F

G

N

O

P

R

S

T

U

V

W

Thank you for buying
Programming ArcGIS with Python Cookbook
Second Edition

About Packt Publishing

Packt, pronounced 'packed', published its first book, *Mastering phpMyAdmin for Effective MySQL Management*, in April 2004, and subsequently continued to specialize in publishing highly focused books on specific technologies and solutions.

Our books and publications share the experiences of your fellow IT professionals in adapting and customizing today's systems, applications, and frameworks. Our solution-based books give you the knowledge and power to customize the software and technologies you're using to get the job done. Packt books are more specific and less general than the IT books you have seen in the past. Our unique business model allows us to bring you more focused information, giving you more of what you need to know, and less of what you don't.

Packt is a modern yet unique publishing company that focuses on producing quality, cutting-edge books for communities of developers, administrators, and newbies alike. For more information, please visit our website at `www.packtpub.com`.

About Packt Open Source

In 2010, Packt launched two new brands, Packt Open Source and Packt Enterprise, in order to continue its focus on specialization. This book is part of the Packt open source brand, home to books published on software built around open source licenses, and offering information to anybody from advanced developers to budding web designers. The Open Source brand also runs Packt's open source Royalty Scheme, by which Packt gives a royalty to each open source project about whose software a book is sold.

Writing for Packt

We welcome all inquiries from people who are interested in authoring. Book proposals should be sent to `author@packtpub.com`. If your book idea is still at an early stage and you would like to discuss it first before writing a formal book proposal, then please contact us; one of our commissioning editors will get in touch with you.

We're not just looking for published authors; if you have strong technical skills but no writing experience, our experienced editors can help you develop a writing career, or simply get some additional reward for your expertise.

[PACKT] open source
community experience distilled
PUBLISHING

Building Web and Mobile ArcGIS Server Applications with JavaScript
Master the ArcGIS API for JavaScript, and build exciting, custom web and mobile GIS applications with the ArcGIS Server
Eric Pimpler
PACKT

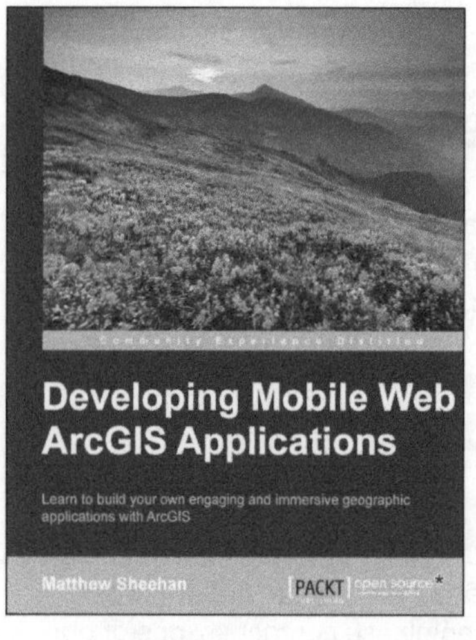
Developing Mobile Web ArcGIS Applications
Learn to build your own engaging and immersive geographic applications with ArcGIS
Matthew Sheehan
PACKT open source

ArcPy and ArcGIS – Geospatial Analysis with Python

ISBN: 978-1-78398-866-2 Paperback: 224 pages

Use the ArcPy module to automate the analysis and mapping of geospatial data in ArcGIS

1. Perform GIS analysis faster by automating tasks, such as selecting data or buffering data, by accessing GIS tools using scripting.

2. Access the spatial data contained within shapefiles and geodatabases, for updates, analysis and even transformation between spatial reference systems.

3. Produce map books and automate the mapping of geospatial analyses, reducing the time needed to produce and display the results.

ArcGIS for Desktop Cookbook

ISBN: 978-1-78355-950-3 Paperback: 372 pages

Over 60 hands-on recipes to help you become a more productive ArcGIS Desktop user

1. Learn how to use ArcGIS Desktop to create, edit, manage, display, analyze, and share geographic data.

2. Use common geo-processing tools to select and extract features.

3. A guide with example-based recipes to help you get a better and clearer understanding of ArcGIS Desktop.

Please check **www.PacktPub.com** for information on our titles

CPSIA information can be obtained
at www.ICGtesting.com
Printed in the USA
LVHW101419041218
599224LV00010B/278/P

9 781785 282898

Programming ArcGIS with Python Cookbook

Second Edition

The book kicks off with the fundamentals of starting to use Python with ArcGIS, followed by recipes on managing map documents and layers, including how to find and fix broken data links in these files.

In the second part of the book, you will learn to create custom geoprocessing tools and how to use the Attribute and Location tools to select specific features.

The third part of the book covers topics for advanced users including the REST API, and also teaches you how to use Python with ArcGIS Pro. The book finishes with appendices covering how to automate Python scripts, and the five things that should be at the back of every GIS programmer's mind.

What this book will do for you...

- **Manage your map document files, layer files, feature classes, and tables**
- **Programmatically update layer properties and symbology**
- **Find and fix broken data links in your map document files**
- **Automate map production, printing, and the creation of PDF map books**
- **Develop custom geoprocessing tools that can be shared with others**
- **Query and select data from feature classes and tables**
- **Create new feature classes or tables and add, update, and delete records**
- **Customize the ArcGIS for Desktop interface with Python add-ins**

Inside the Cookbook...

- A straightforward and easy-to-follow format
- A selection of the most important tasks and problems
- Carefully organized instructions to solve problems efficiently
- Clear explanations of what you did
- Apply solutions to other real-world situations

$ 44.99 US
£ 28.99 UK

Prices do not include local sales tax or VAT where applicable

ISBN 978-1-78528-289-8

54499

9 781785 282898

[PACKT] PUBLISHING open source* community experience distilled

Visit **www.PacktPub.com** for books, eBooks, code, downloads, and PacktLib.